Australian History

2nd Edition

by Alex McDermott

for
dummies®
A Wiley Brand

Australian History For Dummies®, 2nd Edition

Published by

John Wiley & Sons Australia, Ltd

42 McDougall Street

Milton, Qld 4064

www.dummies.com

A catalogue record for this book is available from the National Library of Australia

ISBN: 978-0-730-39545-4

Cover image: © omersukrugoksu/Getty Images

Typeset by SPi

READERS OF THIS BOOK SHOULD BE AWARE THAT, IN SOME ABORIGINAL AND TORRES STRAIT ISLANDER COMMUNITIES, SEEING IMAGES OF DECEASED PERSONS IN PHOTOGRAPHS MAY CAUSE SADNESS OR DISTRESS AND, IN SOME CASES, OFFEND AGAINST STRONGLY HELD CULTURAL PROHIBITIONS. THIS BOOK CONTAINS IMAGES OF PEOPLE WHO ARE DECEASED.

Contents at a Glance

Table of Contents

Introduction

O ver the past 20 years, I've taught history, studied history, written history, talked and listened about it with all sorts of different people, learning all the time. What's struck, and stayed with me through this whole time, is just how big the for good history is. And good history, in my own frankly biased opinion, generally involves helping people answer some of the really compelling questions. Questions like, who are we, really? (And, sure, are we even a 'we'?) And how did we come to be as we are now, today? History can be as small as what's happened over a few decades on one neighbourhood street, but no matter how small its immediate subject matter, if it's good history, it can't help but relate back some sort of answer for the big questions too. The reason there's a history profession at all is because there's enough folks who want to know the answers to these questions, and want their kids to know, and their friends, relations and various others to think and ask these questions too.

Now, obviously there is no one final, finished ultimate set of answers to these questions. That's the beauty of history for me — with every year and decade that passes, from one generation to the next, our view of the past changes. In this sense I like to think of history as one great big ongoing conversation between the past and the present. And the conversation keeps changing and evolving and shifting as the society it's in keeps changing with it. At the heart of this changing, ever-shifting conversation though, is the need in us to tell each other the basic story, as clearly and as well as possible. And providing that story is what this book is all about.

About This Book

At first glance, Australian history appears to be nice and neat and compartmentalised, doesn't it? There it is, most of it fitting into the last 230+ years (aside, of course, from the 50,000 years or more of Indigenous Australian history that preceded it, but we'll get to that). So it can be positively weird just how often bits of it get sliced, diced and served up as completely different dishes. 'First contact' history gets separated out from Gallipoli, say; the conscription controversy of World War I and the Vietnam War might get placed in separate boxes; convicts are set aside from the rise of colonial towns and cities; and it's all completely separate from the Great Depression. From the Tent Embassy and Gough Whitlam's 'It's Time!' election win in 1972, to John Howard, Julia Gillard, Asylum seekers, Carbon tax and Same Sex Marriage since the 2000s.

Okay, this separation isn't always a bad thing — they're all good topics worthy of being teased apart in isolation. But it can be useful — not to mention interesting! — to also have them available to a reader in one easily accessible, easily readable volume, and this is where the *For Dummies* books shine.

You might want to read the whole of Australian history from go to whoa — from first Indigenous arrivals to practically just last week. With this book, you can do that. Or, this month, you might want to find out what caused separate, self-sufficient colonies to federate into a nation but, next month, be wondering exactly how a supposed convict hellhole managed to create a 'workingman's paradise' within 70 years of first settlement. You can dip, you can skip, you can cross-reference — jump from one item to another as you see fit. The book is designed to work the way you want it to.

Foolish Assumptions

In writing the book, I've been making some assumptions about what you as a reader might be bringing to the book. I've been assuming that you want to know more about Australian history, and that some or all of the following might apply to you:

>> You might have done some Australian history at school, but in a hodgepodge sort of way. At different points of your schooling, you might have bumped into convicts, bushrangers, Gallipoli and other different topics. These interested you at the time but you weren't quite sure how they all fitted together, and what else there was to know about.

>> Alternatively, you might have *hated* history at school and tried to ignore it as much as possible. But you've always suspected that the actual history of the place might be a darn sight more interesting than what school history did to it, and wondered what that history might look like.

>> You might be entirely new to Australia and keen to get inside the head of the country, and understand what makes the place tick, and how it came to be this way.

I've also used a few conventions in this book to make the information easy to get to and understand:

>> *Italics* for terms or words that might not be immediately understandable (and I follow the italics up with an explanation in brackets like this one).

>> Sidebars for things that are interesting in their own right but are a little removed from the main point.

>> The spelling of 'Labor' for the Australian Labor Party. Officially, the spelling was standardised by the party in 1912 to be Labor rather than Labour (although plenty of newspapers ignored this and kept spelling it the old way until after World War II ended in 1945). To make it simpler, I've spelt it the same way — 'Labor' — all the way through.

>> The description of the main non-Labor political party as 'Liberal' for pretty much all of the 20th century. Even though the final reorganisation of the party into the Liberal Party we know today only happened in 1944, a non-Labor party acted like the Liberal Party, and really was the Liberal party, and sometimes even called itself the Liberal Party, ever since Alfred Deakin got the various liberal forces together under the one banner in 1909. Rather than change the name to reflect the various name-changes they went through over the next 30-odd years (which they did with irritating frequency), I've just chosen to call the lot of them Liberals and be done with it.

Icons Used in This Book

Along with the parts, the chapters and the sections in this book, something else should make your navigating through it a whole lot easier: Different icons placed at different points in the margin of the text to highlight some key things. I've used the following icons:

HISTORICAL ROOTS

The main events, decisions and actions in a country's history don't usually just happen — you can often dig up their causes and influences from the past. When I've done this for events in this book, I've labelled the information with a 'Historical Roots' icon.

IN THEIR WORDS

This icon, I confess, is a special favourite of mine. These are the moments in the book where I get to hand over the metaphorical microphone to the people who made Australia's history and give them the chance to explain what they thought they were doing — or to contemporary commentators, to explain what Australia was thinking when these events happened. For all the explaining that an historian does (and I promise you I've tried to make it as clear and to the point as I possibly can) sometimes there's just no substitute for getting the actual protagonists or observers to have their say on what was going on. When they do, it carries this icon next to it.

LIFE DOWN UNDER

This flags things in Australian history that go directly to explaining the distinctive society that we can recognise today as tellingly Australian.

REMEMBER

These are the bits that, if books came with batteries, would flash and buzz 'Important!' when you got near them. These are the things that give an essential understanding of exactly how or why Australia has developed the way it did, and by keeping them in mind, you'll never lose your historical bearings.

TECHNICAL STUFF

This icon highlights further information, such as statistics, that can deepen your understanding of the topic, but aren't essential reading. Read the information so you have some extra facts to impress your mates with, or feel free to skip it.

Where to Go from Here

The short answer to this, of course, is the beauty of a Dummies book — anywhere! Anywhere at all you darn well please. You can start at the start and motor along right through the various parts until you get down to the contemporary scene, or you can just jump to a point that explains what you really want to know about right now. If you want to see exactly what Australia did with its new federated nation powers after 1901, then Chapter 12 at the start of Part 3 is your next stop. If you want to see the colonial world that emerged in the wake of the massive gold finds of the 1850s, then Chapter 8 is a good place to start. If the very first years of convict settlement make you curious, head for Chapter 3, with the following decades of settling in and teething troubles also worth checking out in Chapters 4 and 5.

Remember that aside from the table of contents, you've also got an index that alphabetically lists the main events and subject areas. Using all this, you can go pretty much anywhere in Australian history without having to wait around to be told which parts should be considered before first, second and 23rd. It's there for you to read and use when you need it, as you see fit.

1

Let's Get This Country Started

Find out more about Australia's unlikely set of origins and why the highly problematic mix of Indigenous Australians and newly arriving British settlers was not one that spelt much in the way of recognition, respect or rights for the Indigenous peoples.

Discover why the new colony of Australia unexpectedly became a place to start again for the convicted criminals, soldiers and officials who arrived here.

Understand why by the time British authorities got around to noticing the widespread laxness in their convict colony, it was too late — the ex-cons had already established themselves as major players in Australian life.

IN THIS CHAPTER

» Considering the realities of Australia's Indigenous and convict origins

» Seeing the transformation created by the discovery of gold

» Creating an 'ideal' society after Federation

» Getting knocked around by two world wars and a Great Depression

» Growing up and making changes with the baby boomers

» Opening up Australia's economy and its borders

» Seeing in the new millennium

Chapter **1**

Aussie, Aussie, Aussie

The first thing about Australian history that probably strikes you — aside from the very obvious exception of millennia of successful Indigenous adaptation — is that practically all of it is modern history. Getting your head around Australian history — what the big events were, and what the major forces shaping people's actions, reactions and various ideas were — means you also get your head around the major shifts and changes of the modern era. Australian history provides an invaluable window onto the flow of the modern era, while also being a pretty interesting story of the emergence of a distinctive nation in its own right.

The contrast between Australia being home to one of the longest continuing societies and most people thinking of Australian history in terms of only recent events is one thing. But another striking thing about Australia is that it is a land

and society of many more contrasts. The country was colonised as a place to punish people, yet being sent here often turned out to be the convicts' greatest opportunity. Australia was a place where British convicts were sent to be deprived of their rights, yet was one of the first places to bestow on men an almost universal right to vote (and, a few decades later, to almost all women). And, after Federation, Australia was set up as something of a 'new society,' yet was one that refused entry to non-Brits for most of the 20th century. The playing out of these contrasts adds to the depth and colour of the Australian story.

When Oldest Meets Newest

Australian modern history largely begins with the strange encounter between the oldest continuing culture in the world and the most rapidly changing one. The first Australians were Indigenous Aboriginals (see Chapter 2 for more on their way of life pre-European settlement). They were brought into contact with an invading group of settlers from an island on the other side of the world and off the west coast of Europe — Great Britain.

IN THEIR WORDS

Explorer James Cook had been given a secret set of instructions to open only after he'd done his scientific work in Tahiti: Search for the elusive *Terra Australis Incognita*. If he found it, according to the instructions, he was then to 'with the consent of the natives take possession of convenient situations in the name of the King . . . or if you find the land uninhabited, take possession for His Majesty'.

Cook found the land inhabited — he even observed that, despite their apparent material lack, Aboriginals may be the happiest people on earth — but he then went ahead and claimed possession of the whole east coast of Australia anyway. As far as intercultural harmony went, this set an ominous tone for how Australia's first inhabitants would be viewed by the colonisers. Britain established the convict colony of New South Wales (NSW) shortly after. (See Chapter 3 for more on Cook and the decision to settle NSW.)

Getting ahead in the convict world

If I say to you the words 'convict colony', certain mental images probably automatically flash up. Chances are, they'd be pretty grim 'hellhole'-type images: A basic slave society with clanking chains and floggings.

Setting up a penal colony on the other side of the known world, with minimal chance of convicts returning to Britain once they'd served their time, certainly sounds like a recipe for disaster. But this is where the story of Australia gets interesting.

According to English law, criminals usually lost most of their legal rights after being convicted for a crime — and they lost them permanently. They couldn't own property. They couldn't give evidence in court. If the original colony planners or early governors had really been set on making life in NSW as miserable as possible for transported convicts, the scope was there. But that's not what happened at all. In the new settlement, convicts not only kept their rights — they could own property, and could sue and give evidence in court — but they also became major economic players.

Convicts were allowed to retain legal rights and were given plenty of opportunities partly out of necessity: They were the vast majority of the population. How do you run a society where some 80 to 90 per cent of people can't hold property or talk in court? Convicts were the labour force (and the police force!), and they were the tradesmen and a large chunk of the entrepreneurial class. If you wanted to get anything done in this strange new colony, you had to see a convict about it. Indeed, if you wanted a *date*, you needed a convict. Most of the soldiers and officials had come out without womenfolk. While the soldiers and convict women entered into common-law partnerships (or de facto marriages), plenty of officers had relationships where convict women were their lovers and mistresses, sometimes even setting them up in businesses, having families and children with them, and occasionally even marrying them.

Economically, the new colony offered plenty of opportunities to make money, especially in importing and exporting — and, most notably, trading in alcohol for a very thirsty populace. Military officers, convicts and ex-convicts were all quick to get in on the act. None of them was super-scrupulous about how they did it, either.

By a weird quirk of fate, which neither transportation's administrators nor its detractors wanted publicised too much, getting caught, convicted and transported for crimes committed in Britain in the late 18th or early 19th centuries was frequently the luckiest break a criminal ever scored. (See Chapters 4 and 5 for more on the opportunities and second chances offered to new arrivals in NSW.)

Eventually, Britain got around to designing and building proper convict hellholes — at Port Arthur, Norfolk Island, Moreton Bay and Macquarie Harbour (see Chapter 6). But that took decades, and life in these places was never the reality for the majority of convicts.

The myth of NSW as a convict hellhole was at least in part a creation of free settlers. In the 1840s, plenty of now successful free settlers wanted to separate their new home from the stigma of convict association, so they dwelt on the horror of the exceptional places and practices — the chain-gangs, the isolated outposts designed for severe punishments — as if they were the usual thing. They weren't. But they created a myth that still shapes our thoughts about convict life.

Leaping into the big time with wool

At first, NSW was a trading and maritime colony. In 1808, 20 years after first settlement (and about the same time Governor Bligh was arrested by an extremely irritated populace — see Chapter 4) the population of the main port town, Sydney, was about half that of the entire colony. In the 1820s and 1830s, a real foothold finally started to be put down on the broader continent because of one main factor — the take-off of wool.

Australia's south-eastern grasslands, the end product of millennia of firestick farming burn-offs by Aboriginals (performed to attract kangaroos and other game to the new-growth grassland), were discovered to be perfect for grazing sheep on. And sheep grew wool. And wool was just what the new textile industries of Britain's industrial revolution wanted a lot of. (See Chapter 6 for more on the prosperity brought about by sheep farming and the land grab that followed.)

LIFE DOWN UNDER

Not for the last time, Australia's jump into big-time prosperity had everything to do with high demand for raw materials from a nation flexing its muscles as a newly arrived industrial giant. (America, Japan and China would all play similar roles at different times in the 20th century.) Not for the last time, either, would a massive inward surge of investment capital make for a leveraging up of debt levels that meant when crunch time came, as crunch time tends to do, bankruptcies started popping up like toadstools everywhere (see Chapter 7).

Gold, Gold, Gold for Australia

At the end of the 1840s, Australia and the world were emerging from economic depression. Then along came the discovery of gold to dazzle everyone. The idea of getting your very own hands on a jackpot of wealth was what brought men and women to Australia in their hundreds and thousands in the 1850s, making for a transformation of colonial society.

Gold, an insanely profitable export, started being shipped out of the country, filling the treasuries of newly self-governing colonies as it did so. (This was in the days before Federation, when the states that now make up Australia acted as independent colonies.) And those who were lucky enough to have found gold and were newly cashed up had no shortage of things to spend their money on, as imports started flooding in. (See Chapter 8 for more on the gold rush and its effects.)

A building boom also followed. While the massive surge of new arrivals was happy enough to live in tents and canvas towns for the first few months, and makeshift shelters, shanties and lean-tos for another few years after that, ultimately they wanted to live in proper houses — which all had to be built. As did roads. And schools for all the children being born. Then railways, telegraphs — why not?! 'If the world has it, we shouldn't lack for it' was the generally agreed sentiment (see Chapter 9). Limitless progress, development and prosperity were there to be enjoyed. The newest inventions and technology were certain requirements as the 'steam train of progress' of the 19th century took off with rattling speed, with the colonies demanding to be in the front carriage.

Welcoming in male suffrage

Democracy was another accidental by-product of the gold rushes — although, at this stage, for 'democracy' read 'votes for most men'. The Australian colonies were some of the very first places anywhere in the world to grant practically universal male *suffrage* (voting rights). (And, 40 to 50 years later, Australia would be one of the very first places to give votes to almost all women.)

HISTORICAL ROOTS

The granting of the right to vote to most men in the 1850s was one of those sublimely unexpected twists in Australian history. In Britain at the time, constraints were placed on who qualified for the *franchise* (that is, who was allowed to vote). Traditionally, those who owned large amounts of property or paid big amounts of rental qualified to vote. When Australian colonies were granted elected Legislative Councils, constraints similar to those operating in Britain were put in place. But what members of the British parliament didn't know was that rents were much, much higher in Australian cities. Thanks to gold, everything had shot up — prices, wages, rents, the lot. Without realising it, the British parliament had set constraints that allowed a much higher proportion of men to vote than in Britain. So, without great agitation or publicity campaigns or fanfare, practically all men got the right to vote in elections that formed the colonial governments. Politicians changed their pitch and their promises accordingly. (See Chapter 8 for some of the initial political effects of the more universal male suffrage.)

LIFE DOWN UNDER

Even after winning the vote, it seemed that many people in the colonies didn't really *care* about politics. They hadn't come here to vote, after all. They'd come here to get rich. And the 'native-born' white settler Australians were notoriously unconcerned about political life. Many newly arrived British immigrants were veterans of the great political struggles of 1840s Britain. They complained that all the locals seemed to care about (and here you'd better brace yourself for a bit of a shock) was making money, getting drunk, racing horses and playing sport. How un-Australian can you get?! Wait, better not answer that . . . (See Chapters 8 and 10 for more on how new immigrants in the 1840s and 1850s influenced colonial politics.)

So it turns out plenty of defining Australian characteristics were embedded in the culture of the place from very early on. What many people in the colonies wanted most tended to be plenty of leisure time to do with as they saw fit (see the sidebar 'The great Australian leisure time experiment').

THE GREAT AUSTRALIAN LEISURE TIME EXPERIMENT

In the period of the long boom that followed the gold rushes in Australia, one of the things that people began pushing for was more leisure time. The eight-hour working day movement was very successful (see Chapter 8), and workers often showed that if they had to choose between more pay (and more working hours) and less pay (and fewer working hours), they would choose the latter.

With this leisure time, many Australians started passionately playing sport and games. In 1858, what became known as Australian Rules, a uniquely colonial code of football, was developed. (In all likelihood, this code drew on an Indigenous game, perhaps Gaelic football and definitely the still-developing British codes of rugby and soccer). In 1861, the Melbourne Cup, the renowned 'race that stops the nation', started stopping the nation, with the race results being telegraphed to the rest of the colonies. By 1879, Melbourne Cup Day was a public holiday in Melbourne (as it still is today). From 1865, rugby was being played regularly in Sydney. (See Chapter 10 for more on the use of leisure time during the long boom and the development of different football codes in different colonies.)

Cricket was played everywhere, including by Indigenous Australians — with the first Australian cricket team to tour England being made up of 13 Aboriginal men. The (white) colonials proved so adept at picking up the game that they were able to defeat English teams first in 1877 in Melbourne then in 1880 in London. This provoked shock and consternation among the English, and some wag placed an obituary in the papers for English cricket, which, the obituary mockingly declared, had died at the Oval — its body was to be cremated and the ashes sent to Australia. These mythical 'ashes' of English cricket have been at stake in The Ashes series of test cricket matches between England and Australia ever since.

The crowds that came to watch these burgeoning spectator sports — particularly Australian Rules and the Melbourne Cup — showed a distinctively colonial disregard for old world rigid class distinctions. Workers, business owners, bankers and farmers, men and women — all mingled freely and barracked loudly.

Striving for the 'workingman's paradise'

From the early 1850s through to the late 1880s, Australia went through a long boom, and it was during this period that the phrase 'workingman's paradise' first began to be regularly applied. Obviously, a fair bit of grandiose hyperbole is associated with the phrase (hello — *paradise*?!) but it also contained an important element of truth.

LIFE DOWN UNDER

Life for workers in Australia was dramatically better than what they were used to in Britain and other parts of the world. With all the demand for building, construction and the rest, unemployment was largely non-existent, the eight-hour day became almost the norm and pay rates were generally good. In Australia, an ordinary white male worker could work and put enough away in savings to eventually buy his own house — an impossible dream for most workers in Britain.

During the long boom, schooling began to be supplied by the state. It was compulsory (which had the effect of eliminating child labour) and *secular* (non-religious) to avoid playing favourites with the different religious denominations of different immigrants from Britain. Most remarkably of all, the schooling was free. Parents from all different classes started sending their children to the same schools, which had been precisely the legislators' intent. (See Chapter 10 for more on the politics and social reforms made during the 19th century long boom.)

For as long as the boom period sustained itself, the occasionally mentioned desire for *federation* — uniting the various self-governing colonies into one nation — struggled to gain much traction. Different citizens in different colonies would at times talk about intercolonial union, and politicians held tentative conferences. However, for as long as the passionate central beliefs of colonial Australia — progress, ever-increasing material wealth and chasing after the various luxury consumer goods that go with it — were able to be maintained, it was hard to stir up sufficient enthusiasm.

LIFE DOWN UNDER

WAIT A SECOND! WHERE ARE THE EXPLORERS AND THE BUSHRANGERS?

Most people come to Australian history with a few embedded expectations. They expect convict life to be one of unremitting hell. (Refer to the section 'Getting ahead in the convict world', earlier in this chapter, for how that one works out.) They also tend to think of colonial Australians as, if not explorers, gold diggers or bushrangers, at least living out on the backblocks of a ruggedly frontier life, struggling as *selectors* (farmers of small parcels of land) to eke out a barren existence on bad soil, or wrestling rams and clipping ewes as shearers. And, certainly, some people did things exactly like that, but most colonial Australians didn't. The most remarkable thing about colonial Australia, really, was not the exotic figures — the bushrangers, the explorers and so on — but how extraordinarily similar most people's lives were to what we're familiar with today.

Now, if you really like the explorers and bushrangers, don't worry! They're here in *Australian History For Dummies* also. Anyone who wants the lowdown on Burke and Wills, Ben Hall or Ned Kelly will be kept happy (see Chapter 9). But there's also the other question — what were most colonial Australians doing? The big unexpected answer is that by the 1860s, most Australians were living in the colonies' urban centres.

Luckily (for the future prospects of Australian federation), a devastating economic crash hit the colonies hard in the 1890s. The idea of inevitable progress, increased prosperity and constant social harmony was set firmly back on its heels, and a federated nation became much more attractive (see Chapter 11).

Solving the Problems of the World (By Keeping Out the World)

When depression hit in 1891, the sustaining ideas of the long boom — of ever-increasing abundance, technological advancement and continued riches — came undone. The assumption that old-world problems such as class antagonism had been solved turned out to be untrue, as seen in a series of savage strikes that broke out in the early 1890s — on the docks, in the shearing sheds and in the mines of Broken Hill. The various progressive colonial governments came down on the side of the bosses, sending in troops to maintain order and protect the rights and property of bosses and owners. 'So much for the workingman's paradise', said the workers. 'So much for social harmony and real progress', said the middle class.

LIFE DOWN UNDER

In the end, the middle classes had supported the decision of governments to send in troops against strikers to keep order and maintain public safety. However, they were furious about having to make such a choice at all. Colonial Australia wasn't meant to be like that: Most people in Australia had spent 30 or so years proudly boasting that Australia was far too progressive to let things like that happen.

From the widespread disillusionment felt by many during the 1890s depression, a series of new factors emerged:

>> The union movement, which had seen its power largely broken in the strikes, decided it was time to form a political party, get voted into government and change the laws themselves to make them friendlier to workers. From this ideal, the Australian Labor Party was born (see Chapter 11) and, by the end of the first decade of the 1900s, had established itself as the dominant force in Australian politics.

>> Federation, the idea of forming a new country out of the old self-governing colonies, took on a new momentum after being kickstarted at the 'people's convention' at Corowa on the Murray River in 1893. Federation succeeded largely as a powerful symbol of new unity — 'a nation for a continent and a continent for a nation' — which would help colonial Australians move beyond the divisions and struggles that had so divided sections of the community in the 1890s (see Chapter 11).

> **»** The idea of a newly federated nation became not simply an end in itself but a means to establish a 'social laboratory'. Federation would allow Australia to insulate itself from the rest of the world and implement solutions to problems, such as worker–employer conflict and poverty. These problems were apparent in other modern nations (for example, in Britain, the US and France) and had recently become apparent in the colonies. Heavily restricting immigration (with the now-notorious White Australia Policy) and bringing in heavy *tariffs* (taxes, or customs duties) on overseas imports to protect local jobs and industries were both brought in during the first decade after Federation to achieve this insulation, as were many social reforms (see Chapter 12).

Now for War, Division, Depression and More War

At the start of the 20th century things looked good, really good, for the social laboratory of Federation, social harmony and Australian Labor. Then World War I hit. While the war provided a new national hero — the 'digger' soldier — and stories of national bravery, it proved to be a big disaster for Labor and the harmony of Australian society. This was followed, in seemingly quick succession, by the Great Depression and more war, with a brief period of big dreams during the 1920s.

Joining the Empire in the war

When World War I started, few Australians doubted that Australia would be in the war and on the side of Britain. But the war dragged on and on, with horrific casualty lists and a constantly rising number of deaths. Labor was in government, and had promised to fight 'to the last man and the last shilling' — before it became apparent that it actually might come to that. Unionists, who made up the bulk of Labor's support, started to mutter loudly that fighting foreign wars on behalf of foreign capitalists wasn't such a bright idea. Then, to make things worse, Ireland staged a rebellion in 1916.

HISTORICAL ROOTS

One of the biggest challenges in the Australian colonies had always been that its three main ethnic groups — English, Scottish and Irish, who had very long traditions of hating each other's guts — were forced to live cheek by jowl with each other, something they had very little experience with elsewhere. But this integration had been the young nation's greatest achievement.

But Ireland, and Britain's rule of it, had always been a touchy subject in Australia. Now, in the middle of world war, a rebellion broke out in Ireland and in Australia, support for Britain (read England) in the world war ceased to be unquestioned for many.

In the turmoil, the Labor Party split and lost government and spent most of the next 20 years as a political irrelevance, their one triumph the successful campaign against compulsory military service overseas. The ex–Labor prime minister, Billy Hughes, got huge support from the public for doing everything to win the war, and the Liberals, which he now led, claimed centrestage as the 'natural' choice for patriotic Australians.

Australia ended the war a far more divided and fractured place than it had been when the war began. The animosity felt between Irish Catholic Australians and the Anglo-Protestant majority would eat away at Australian unity for some 40 years. (See Chapter 13 for more on Australia's role during World War I and the tensions that emerged at home.)

Dreaming of 'Australia Unlimited'

By the end of World War I, Australia was profoundly divided and strangely schizoid. Everything was jagged and everyone was on edge — the number of strikes and working days lost peaked just after the war. 'Patriotism' was a far more loaded term, with many ex-soldiers resenting 'disloyals', who were deemed to have not done everything to support Australia's involvement in the war. Because these animosities often divided Australian society along religious, ethnic and class lines, the sense of rancour and of a nation divided was acute as the 1920s began.

Yet, the 1920s were also — in classic Charles Dickens 'best of times, worst of times' style — a period when Australia emerged as newly cocky about its prowess and capabilities on the world stage. Australia had 'proved itself' during World War I, and by the end of the conflict in 1918 had emerged as one of the elite fighting forces on the Western Front. A new expansive optimism began to prevail, which rekindled old dreams of exponential development and progress — and the ideal of 'Australia Unlimited' was born (see Chapter 14).

LIFE DOWN UNDER

During the 1920s, Australia was frequently compared to the US, a country which appears about the same size as Australia on the map, but which had begun its history some 200 years earlier. Many argued America had blazed a trail that Australia could be expected to follow and emulate, and big plans began to be hatched. Enormous migration schemes were implemented (bringing in British migrants) and rural development projects begun. All this was largely funded by masses of government overseas borrowing, mostly from Britain.

Getting hit by the Great Depression . . .

After the dreams and excess of the 1920s came a doozie of a global economic depression, which began on the Wall Street stock market in New York and spread rapidly to take in most of the world. Australia, up to its eyeballs in debt at the same time as prices for its major export commodities such as wool and wheat were crashing through the floor, was acutely vulnerable.

When the economic crisis hit, the politicians and bankers proved themselves unable to agree on what measures should be followed. The Labor Party, which had the misfortune of regaining government for the first time since the end of World War I at about the exact same moment as Wall Street crashed, split for a second time within 20 years over the disagreement.

Unemployment trended upward to a peak of around 30 per cent. After the frenetic expansion years of the 1920s, and the pursuit of new enjoyments with new inventions such as automobiles, cinema and radio (see Chapter 14), ordinary people found themselves thrown back upon their own resources. Luxury items that had been considered essentials a few years previously were now eschewed, garden lawns were converted back to vegetable plots and broken items now found themselves being fixed rather than replaced. (See Chapter 15 for more on life in Australia during the Great Depression.)

. . . And another war

In 1939, Australians faced up to another world war, but this time one fought not only on faraway battlefields (as World War I had been) but also much closer to home. Japan's downward thrust meant that, for the first time in its history, Australia felt itself to be directly menaced with possible invasion. Darwin and other northern towns were repeatedly bombed but Britain, its hands full defeating Nazi Germany, was unable to send much in the way of help.

Luckily, America's interests and Australia's coincided: America needed a geographic base from which to launch a counteroffensive against Japan, and Australia needed the reassuring presence of a great and powerful ally. Australia geared its economy up to full capacity, converting all possible industries to war production. (See Chapter 16 for more on Australia's involvement in World War II and events back home.)

As the tide of the war turned, the Curtin Government began preparing postwar reconstruction plans. Along with implementing a bold new immigration scheme (for the first time taking in large numbers of European immigrants as well as those from Britain), considerable economic and social progress was made (see Chapter 17). This laid the groundwork that helped sustain an economic boom that proved second only to the long boom of the 19th century for duration (see Chapter 18).

The Postwar Boom Broom

Prosperity unleashed a new generation — the postwar baby boomers — onto the world, coinciding with a social revolution in the 1960s. This younger generation had grown up in an era of prosperity and increasing material affluence — an experience quite unlike the Depression and war years in which their parents had reached maturity. The Beatles, miniskirts and tie-dye psychedelia — you have the 1960s to thank for them. The 1960s also spawned a series of social movements, including:

>> **Vietnam War protests:** Many in the baby-boomer generation refused point-blank to serve as conscripts or soldiers in the Vietnam War, which Australia had entered in 1962.

>> **Calls for the end of the White Australia Policy:** This policy was aimed at excluding non-whites from immigration into Australia (under the old social homogeneity argument or, as Labor minister Arthur Calwell unfortunately joked, the argument that 'Two Wongs don't make a White'.) By the 1960s, the policy was becoming increasingly odious to newly independent non-white nations. The policy was progressively dismantled from 1966.

>> **Campaigns for civil rights for Aboriginals:** Inspired by the civil rights movement for African Americans in the US, Indigenous Australians began agitating to have all constitutional bars against their full recognition as Australian citizens removed.

>> **Women's rights campaigns:** Liberated by access to a recently developed contraceptive ('the pill') and 'no-fault' divorce, Australian women began calling for equal rights, including equal payment for work done, the right to work after getting married or having children, and the removal of old segregation rules (such as those that fined pub owners for serving women in the front bar of pubs) that were starting to appear, quite frankly, a little archaic.

See Chapter 19 for more on the changes wreaked during the 1960s and 1970s in Australia.

Breaking Down the Fortress Australia Mentality

The ambition for pushing through and instituting great waves of social change came to a head under the government of Labor leader Gough Whitlam in 1972 to 1975 (see Chapter 19). Unfortunately for Gough, however, the economic good times of the postwar boom that had been sustaining the plans for social change came to an end during his prime ministership. The recession destroyed his government, as it did his successor, Liberal Malcolm Fraser.

The challenge of fixing the economic problems — including the special guest stars of high inflation, rising unemployment and declining industries — was so great that it took a concerted revision and ultimate termination of the original Fortress Australia economic policies first implemented early in the 1900s. This was a long period of sustained and largely unquestioned economic orthodoxy to up-end, but up-ended it was.

At the same time, another revolution was taking place — this one with a more multicultural flavour.

Opening up the economy

By the end of the 1980s, Australia had begun winding back tariffs used to protect uncompetitive industries. It had also opened up the financial market, and allowed the Australian dollar to 'float' and find its own level of value on international exchange markets rather than being kept fixed at an artificial and government-maintained level.

HISTORICAL ROOTS

The 'closed shop' era was over, and in the early 1990s, Australia experienced acute economic trauma during what economists glibly labelled the 'structural readjustment phase', a phase that included the worst recession of the postwar era. But Australia emerged from the recession ready to take advantage of a new period of economic expansion, prosperity and growth. Thanks to the various economic reforms introduced through the 1980s and 1990s, Australia surprised many by weathering the Asian financial crisis of the late 1990s the best of any country in the region. It was also well placed to take advantage of the China boom of the 2000s, and sail serenely through the global financial crisis of 2008. (See Chapter 20 for more on the changes introduced through the 1980s, and their short-term effects.)

Opening up the borders (mostly)

At the same time as the economic revolution, a sustained and at times ferocious debate was taking place over Australia's cultural direction. When the White Australia Policy had been dismantled in the 1960s, it was done with loud public reassurances that 'social homogeneity' continued to be the key ambition informing immigration policy. Australia was welcoming immigrants from many diverse and new parts of the world, but the job of the immigrants was to adjust and assimilate. The thought that Australia could be genuinely enriched by these diverse new arrivals was slow to dawn in policy circles.

The big turnaround took place in the late 1970s, when Malcolm Fraser launched a policy of multiculturalism and also began accepting large numbers of predominantly Asian migrants — refugees from the Vietnam War (see Chapter 20). The idea behind multiculturalism — that it was okay for immigrants to want to retain their own culture while living in Australia, and that Australia might actually benefit from these cultures — was a shift in Australia's approach to the world and its attitude to itself so profound as to be seismic.

By the late 1980s, the policy of multiculturalism was provoking murmurs of discontent. A report to the Hawke Labor Government concluded that the pendulum had now swung too far in the other direction — that many people were worried that embracing multiculturalism and diversity meant valuing and esteeming all other cultures and heritages but downgrading and devaluing Australia's own, the core British–Australian culture that had provided all the building blocks for modern Australia.

LIFE DOWN UNDER

The tensions came to flashpoint in the late 1990s, when resentment against the economic changes of the 1980s, the recession of the late 1980s and early 1990s, and suspicion about the influx of new immigrants coalesced into support for Pauline Hanson's 'One Nation' political movement. This movement combined nostalgia for the certainties of old Australia with the rejection of economic and social revolutions refashioning Australia. In the short-term it was a short-lived phenomenon, dissipating as economic circumstances improved and something resembling boom conditions returned to Australian life for the first time in 30 years. But it was also a harbinger of some of the debates and divisions which would challenge Australia in the 21st century as well.

Entering the New Millennium

The 21st century began just as Australia was emerging from hard times and into a new era of prosperity and widespread wealth. Thanks to the hard yards of economic reforms in the 1980s and 90s, from 2004 Australia was in a great position to benefit by the China boom, China's dramatic economic development after joining the World Trade Organisation in 2001. This created huge demand for Australia's natural resources, as well as creating huge new markets for Australian education and tourism sectors. In significant part because of this Australia was able to avoid many of the disastrous problems that beset the north Atlantic countries in Europe and the US in the wake of the 2008 global financial crisis. In the 2010s though, China's geostrategic expansion began to create a host of new problems for its regional neighbours to wrestle with, and Australia has had to navigate these changing realities.

Aside from 'the China Question', other global challenges haven't been shy about imposing themselves. How best to deal with climate change continues to vex us, and has triggered the fall of Prime Ministers, Opposition leaders and whole governments. The Islamist attacks of September the 11th, 2001, (aka '9/11') was followed by another terror attack on Australian and other western tourists at Bali in October 2002. The 'War on Terror', and protracted conflicts in Iraq and Afghanistan was another by-product of the 2001 terror attacks, and have ensured argument amongst Australians on the rights and wrongs of this practically ever since. Whilst all this was happening other issues also demanded attention: Indigenous reconciliation, Same Sex Marriage, Asylum Seekers, sexual harassment of women, free speech and the freedom of religion have all elicited debate, much of which continues ongoing. And then there was that COVID thing . . .

As the third decade of the new millennium gets under way, the ongoing story of Australia is showing no signs of slowing up any time soon.

Chapter **2**

First Australians: Making a Home, Receiving Visitors

I n this chapter, you get to stand back and take the long, long view. While most of the rest of the book is chiefly concerned with the events that took place after British settlers started arriving in the late 18th century, this chapter looks at the almost unthinkably long period of human occupation of the Australian continent before that.

Indigenous Australians arrived multiple millennia ago. They developed a uniquely successful system of living that stood the test of time. Then, in the last few hundred years before British settlement, other visitors started turning up too. In this chapter, I provide some sense of the world Indigenous Australians developed and maintained, and a feel for what was going on with the Macassans, Spanish, Portuguese and Dutch later on.

Indigenous Australians

Australia is the driest, flattest inhabited continent in the world. The country is a vast span of stony deserts with only a fringe of arable land clinging to the edges where the weather is milder and rain more reliable. But during the last Ice Age (around 40,000 years Before Present), the situation was much, much worse. Almost all the world's fresh water was locked up in the enormous glaciers that covered the north of Europe, leaving scarcely any to spare for the Great Southern Land. The continent of Australia was a landscape desolate beyond anything we can picture now.

And yet — people lived here. These people had a complex culture, they traded, and they told stories and sang songs in hundreds of languages (see Figure 2-1). The people who sang those songs were masters of survival in the harshest landscape on Earth.

Settling in early

During the Ice Age, sea levels were much lower than today (all that ice had to come from somewhere, after all). One advantage of this was that it was a lot easier to walk to new places, as distinct from swimming or sailing. Australia and New Guinea were connected by a giant land bridge, which explains why these now-distant countries have so many plant and animal species in common. Nevertheless, it was still a long way over open water for prehistoric humans to get to Australia, so whatever else we may conjecture about the first settlers, we're certain they knew their way around a boat.

No-one knows exactly when the First Australians arrived. The evidence is scanty and, at times, contradictory. Even genetic research is unable to resolve whether Aboriginal people came in one big push or many successive waves. Like all humans, they originated in ancient Africa, but after that, their lineage is still quite murky.

Recent genome sequencing, for example, seems to indicate the one big push theory is correct. However, DNA testing of Aboriginal remains (estimated to be around 40,000 years old) found at Lake Mungo revealed they didn't share ancestry with modern human beings. Some scientists have speculated that this means migration to Australia didn't occur in one wave.

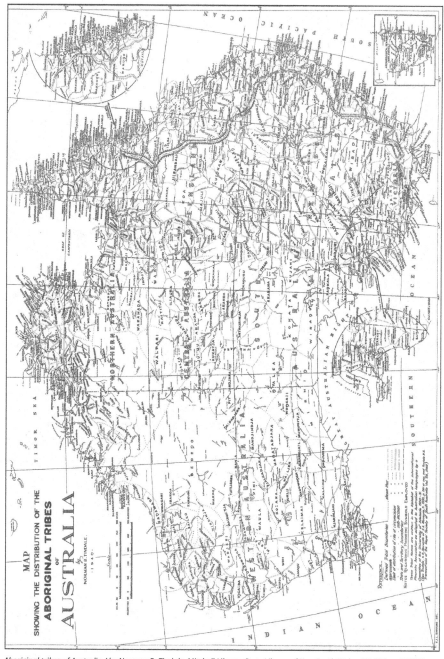

FIGURE 2-1:
Aboriginal
Australia
pre–European
settlement.

Aboriginal tribes of Australia / by Norman B. Tindale, Mitchell Library, State Library of New South Wales, M3 804eca/1788/1.

According to the genome research from 2016, Papuan and Aboriginal ancestors reached the supercontinent that included what would become Australia around 50,000 years ago, picking up the DNA of Neanderthals, Denisovans and another extinct hominin along the way. The same study indicated Papuans and Aboriginals then split around 37,000 years ago, long before the continents were finally cut off from each other around 8,000 years ago. Although they must have passed through South-East Asia on their way to Australia, they aren't related to any known Asian population. Today, linguistic similarities exist between some Aboriginal people and the indigenous peoples of New Guinea, but this is likely to be the result of (relatively) recent trade and intermarriage.

REMEMBER

Who these first settlers were, where they came from, and why they came to Australia may always remain a mystery. All we know is, when the glaciers melted and the sea levels rose again, Aboriginal people abandoned boating and stayed where they were.

LIFE DOWN UNDER

In Tasmania, the people became further isolated when the land bridge to the mainland vanished under the rising water. It's a vivid image: Picture a populated fertile promontory with a thriving trade across a slowly eroding isthmus. One day, it's a short swim to the local hunting ground, then a few years down the track it's crossable by canoe . . . until, finally, the mainland recedes from sight, memories fade, and the Tasmanians are on their own for the next 12,000 years.

Exactly how long it took for Aboriginals to spread out over the continent is disputed (as is just about everything in this very remote period). Anywhere from a few thousand to over 10,000 years has been suggested. What isn't disputed is that, despite the immense diversity of the continent (desert in the centre, tropical rainforest on the Cape, glaciers on the mountains of Tasmania), Aboriginal peoples found ways to thrive in every ecological niche available.

Life in Aboriginal Australia

Find a carpenter's tape measure. Pretend each centimetre equals ten years. Unreel the tape measure and look at the very first 22 centimetres — that's the entire history of European settlement in Australia. Now (in a good long room and if your tape is long enough) unreel the tape measure to 50 metres — that's a conservative estimate of the length of Aboriginal history (or 5,000 years). Some scientists argue that, based on archaeological evidence, Aboriginal people arrived in Australia at least 65,000 years ago.

LIFE DOWN UNDER

The Europeans who first encountered the Australian Aboriginals observed that they had no agriculture, no domestic livestock and didn't appear to wash. To the European way of thinking, this made them a primitive people, unchanged since the Stone Age. Those same Europeans might have asked themselves, when the wind killed their crops and their wells ran dry, how these 'primitive' people had managed to survive for so long in such a harsh landscape — without the aid of tinned food and sacks of British grain.

Evidence exists of trade and cultural exchange between Aboriginal peoples and South-East Asians dating back thousands of years, so it can hardly be likely that Aboriginals were unaware of agriculture. They simply had little use for it in the dry, unfertile soils of their home. Agriculture was unsuited to Australia's grasslands and deserts (some argue agriculture still is, despite all the water and modern fertilisers we can throw at it), so Aboriginal communities predominately survived by hunting and gathering, managing resources extremely prudently — and maintaining their population at a sustainable level. While they did grow crops of tubers such as yams, grain such as native millet, macadamia nuts, fruits and berries, their farming has been described as an activity rather than a lifestyle.

LIFE DOWN UNDER

Although Aboriginal Australians didn't undertake large-scale agriculture, they did develop techniques that helped control their environment. One of these techniques is now known as *firestick farming*. Aboriginal people used fire in a deliberate and systematic way to clear undergrowth and encourage regrowth to attract fauna, as well as to flush out game. (For more on their lifeways, and how this affected the modern Australian landscape, see the sidebar 'Shaping Australia with nomadic lifeways'.)

The Aboriginals were careful not to damage the fragile web of ecological relationships that sustains life on this dry island, because they depended on the web for survival. (And, incidentally, they didn't wash much because they were well aware that water was too valuable to waste — something all Australians have been learning recently.) When the Europeans landed, Aboriginal peoples actually had a better life expectancy than the colonists, as well as almost no instances of the 'modern' diseases — tooth decay, heart disease, tuberculosis and cancer. The effectiveness of their resource management (such as the controlled burns to increase hunting pasture) gave them far more leisure time than the arriving agriculturalists, which equalled time to play, talk and dream. That's right — the original affluent society.

This isn't to make the mistake of romanticising the tougher elements of Aboriginal life. Records suggest that even *infanticide* (killing newborn babies) was carried out in some cultural or tribal groups to ensure sustainable population levels. Deaths from tribal warfare and feuds were relatively commonplace. Life was no picnic. Aboriginals needed to make hard choices and ruthless decisions simply to survive, as well as develop infinite resourcefulness and adaptability. But no-one can deny that, survival-wise, the Aboriginal way of life was a tremendous success. Aboriginals have managed to maintain a continuous culture through millennia, which is something no other people — anywhere — has achieved.

SHAPING AUSTRALIA WITH NOMADIC LIFEWAYS

Indigenous Australians didn't engage in intensive, settled agriculture. Their lifeways were nomadic rather than sedentary — which is another way of saying they didn't structure their whole way of life around living in settled villages, nearby fenced-in paddocks and fields. Instead, they moved about relatively frequently, even as they harvested native grasses, constructed elaborate dams and, in some places, stone houses.

As they moved about their country they also practised firestick farming, using fire to manage different environments. This helped create and sustain the enormous grasslands across the plains of south-eastern Australia — and so helped shape and curate the landscape we recognise today as Australian.

In two very direct ways, the lifeways of Aboriginal peoples created the conditions that subsequent Australian society would build with:

- The British–European settler society that established itself after 1788 did so in a physical environment that had been crafted, curated and maintained by Indigenous Australians over many millennia. Those who came after benefitted from the tens of thousands years of sustained occupation by this original nomadic society — and they especially benefitted from the fertile grasslands just perfect for sheep and cattle (see Chapter 7).

- When the British first came to Australia, they found a low-population density compared to sedentary agricultural societies in other nearby places. In Polynesia and Maori New Zealand, for instance, fortified villages and more intensive cultivation occurred, which meant that when Europeans arrived any violent resistance could draw on more numbers. Australian nomadic society flourished as a small-scale proliferation of small bands, which left them vulnerable to the really huge numbers and resources settler societies could call upon when they arrived in the 18th and 19th centuries.

Violent resistance to European invasion in Australia still occurred, of course. Everywhere the frontier extended, violent conflict took place. But in terms of sheer numbers and scale of response, the dice were stacked against the original possessors of the continent.

History without books

Above all, the prehistoric Aboriginals were masters of language. Historians estimate that up to 750 distinct languages existed on the Australian continent when the European settlers arrived (refer to Figure 2-1), which implies that the average person would probably have had to be fluent in quite a few different languages just to get along with his or her neighbours.

In Aboriginal society, age meant authority — in large part because of the copious survival knowledge acquired with the years. A culture with no written records had to preserve and pass on all ideas, arguments, technology and traditions from one generation to the next through the spoken word. It's therefore no surprise that Aboriginal society was heavy on song, gesture, story and elaborate ceremony. Learning responsibility and the rules that govern stable society went hand in hand with acquiring the skills of food gathering and resource management.

Trading with the neighbours

Pre-European Australia was a very social place — it took teamwork to survive in such a challenging land! Tribes had complex kinship and trading connections over vast distances, and even overseas. (Many are surprised to learn that the Aboriginals were not 'pre-contact' at all when the First Fleet arrived — they'd been trading, intermarrying and presumably speaking with the Macassans of Indonesia for decades, and quite possibly centuries). As in much of the world at the time, the barter economy was a part of life.

Key items for trading included:

>> Pituri, a mildly narcotic plant, which the Aboriginals exchanged for Indonesian tobacco

>> Pearls and pearl shells, farmed by northern tribes and useful as ornamentation and for magic rituals

>> Stone suitable for tools

>> Ochre, used heavily in ritual and ceremony

No books, maps or made roads existed in Aboriginal Australia, and so these overland trading routes — sometimes hundreds of kilometres long — had to be memorised. Being able to navigate your way across a desert continent without cars, trains or even pack animals is no mean feat.

For more on Aboriginal people pre–European settlement, see *Indigenous Australia For Dummies*, 2e, by Larissa Behrendt, Wiley Australia Publishing.

Visitors from Overseas

Although the British explorers such as Cook and Flinders often get the credit for 'discovering' Aboriginal Australia, they were by no means the first. The Spanish, the Portuguese, the Dutch and (much earlier) the Indonesians all beat Britain to the flag. The waters around Australia were, from the 1600s on, a hotbed of navigators, explorers, traders — and sailors who were just plain lost.

Macassan fishermen

Macassar was a port on the island of Sulawesi, part of what is today Indonesia, and the centre of a thriving trade in sea cucumbers (also known as *trepang*, or *beche-de-mer*). These were considered a pretty wild delicacy in China as an aphrodisiac — think an early version of modern-day Viagra (or perhaps don't) — and they were plentiful in the shallow seas along the coast of northern Australia between Arnhem Land in the Northern Territory and the Kimberleys in Western Australia.

Because plenty of profit could be had from feeding heavy Chinese demand, every year from at least the 1720s on (but probably earlier) Macassan fishermen would sail their boats with the monsoon winds down to Australia. Here they'd stay for about half a year, catching, gutting, boiling, drying and smoking trepang before sailing back to Macassar with a full cargo.

The Macassans camped onshore each summer, and built big fireplaces for large iron pots and cauldrons to boil the trepang. Afterwards, the trepang would be buried in sand to help them dry. (If you've ever been in Australia's top end during the sultry monsoonal summer months, you'll understand why they had to be buried to get properly dried!). They'd then be smoked in bamboo sheds the Macassans had built for the purpose.

LIFE DOWN UNDER

Throughout their visits to Australia, Macassans interacted constantly with the local Aboriginals, who began to paint distinctive Macassan images — of the boats or of steel knives — in their rock art. Relations weren't always rosy — outbursts of violence and retaliation occurred periodically — but, for the most part, the interactions were punctuated by exchange. Tobacco, pipes, the new technique of dugout canoe-making, new words, steel knives and axes were all things Indigenous Australian tribes acquired from the Macassans (as well as smallpox, unfortunately). In turn, Macassans were given access to the trepang resource, and were allowed to take some Aboriginal women as wives.

Portuguese and Spanish navigators

In the 1400s and 1500s, Portuguese and Spanish ships established a trading supremacy throughout the world, with colonies and ports established in Asia, India, China, Africa and both North and South America. It was only a matter of time before they started looking around in the part of the world where Australia was, too. Spanish and Portuguese navigators went looking — and almost discovered Australia.

The Spanish were already prominent around the rim of the Pacific Ocean — in the Philippines, Chile, Peru, Mexico and California — while the Portuguese were in and around the Indian Ocean with stations at East Timor, Aceh, Goa and east Africa.

A Portuguese fellow by the name of Pedro Fernandez de Quiros led an expedition to find the 'unknown southern land' in 1605, and in 1606 he thought he'd found it — but it turned out to be the Pacific island of Vanuatu. Heading back, disappointed, the fleet got separated in a storm and de Quiros's second in command, a Spaniard, Fernando Torres, led the bulk of the fleet to the Philippines.

En route, Torres was the first to find a passage between Papua New Guinea and Australia (the strait is now called Torres Strait). Torres and his fleet saw the northern part of what is now Queensland (Cape York) but he didn't realise it. Assuming it was just another island, Torres sailed on.

Lost Dutch traders and wandering explorers

Most of the trade, loot and riches that came from the New World of North and South America in the 1400s and 1500s were divided up between Portugal and Spain. However, in the 1600s a new heavyweight started muscling itself in on the global scene. This was Holland, which had managed to fight a successful war of independence against the Spanish.

In the 1600s, the Dutch began running successful trade operations of their own, setting up new trading stations and pioneering new navigation courses. One of the new routes ran right past the western coast of Australia — sometimes too close. The history of Dutch encounters with Australia can be summed up with a loud 'bump' noise, followed by a surprised 'What was that?!' and ending with 'Oh — Australia' (or rather, 'New Holland').

The Dutch dominated much of the shipping trade in and around Europe, distributing the spices and goods that Portugal was bringing in to their ports. The Spanish, well and truly miffed at the Dutch not wanting to be governed by Spain anymore, decided to cut them out of this trade at the start of the 1600s. The Dutch retaliated by smuggling in some secret Portuguese maps of the known world and setting off to establish a little trading supremacy of their own. At this they were spectacularly successful. They moved especially into the East Indies (modern-day Indonesia), setting up a trading company with an administrative centre in Batavia (modern-day Jakarta). The Dutch soon established a monopoly in the European trade of cloves, nutmegs, cinnamon and pepper, from which they made bucket-loads of money.

Setting up an administrative centre in modern-day Jakarta created one problem for the Dutch: The time it took to sail from Europe to the East Indies was incredibly long. If you think 24 hours is a long time to put up with flying in a plane from Amsterdam to Jakarta, imagine multiplying it by 364. A round-trip in a 17th-century sailing ship took a year. Then, by accident, the Dutch discovered the *roaring forties*. This was a powerful circuit of winds that blew all the way round the world but further south than just about anyone had been. The Dutch found that after rounding the Cape of Africa they could continue south and then get a nice little ripping wind to blow them all the way along to Indonesia.

The only snag with this was that the Dutch had to know when to turn north again and sail up to the East Indies islands. Before a method of measuring longitude had been developed, knowing exactly how far along one had been blown was difficult. A lot of guesswork was involved. Mistakes were made. If the Dutch ships went too far they ended up running into the west coast of Australia before they made the port of Batavia. Sometimes, the Dutch ships ran aground and were even shipwrecked. Other times, they just ran alongside the Australian coastline, mapping it and looking out for signs of commodities for which to barter or that would make the place worthy of further investigation. Here, they drew a blank.

The comment of Dutch explorer Jan Carstensz sums up a whole series of disappointed Dutch traders and navigators with regards to what they thought of New Holland (modern-day Western Australia): It was 'the most arid and barren region that could be found anywhere on the earth; the inhabitants too are the most wretched and poorest creatures that I have ever seen'. For traders wanting fancy things to take back to Europe, the 'walking lightly on the earth' style of Aboriginals appeared wretched and poor.

When he made his way up the east coast of Australia, British explorer James Cook had a different impression of Aboriginal life. He saw past the lack of tradeable material abundance in Aboriginal cultures and actually declared them the most contented — because most self-sufficient — of all peoples he'd encountered anywhere, including Europeans and Brits. But when Britain came calling in the late 18th century, Australia appealed to it for reasons other than trade (see Chapter 3).

IN THIS CHAPTER

» Surveying the east coast of 'New Holland' with Cook

» Choosing New South Wales to start a convict settlement

» Getting there with Phillip

» Staying alive once there — just

» Encountering hardship in the new land

Chapter **3**

Second Arrivals and First Colonials

I f you take a casual glance at a map of the world, you'd be pretty hard pressed to find two regions that are further away from each other, and less directly related, than Britain and Australia. One's southern hemisphere, the other's northern. One is a continent, the other an island. One has crummy weather, the other has Bondi (you get the drift). And yet, after the Indigenous Australians (who arrived millennia previously), it was the British who were the first people to take enough of an interest in Australia to decide to establish a colony here late in the 18th century.

Britain established maritime dominance in most of the seas of the world in the second half of the 18th century, with the Pacific being the 'last frontier' to explore for new trade and supplies. The British also had a couple of men who proved to be outstandingly good at not only exploring the region but also, in the case of one of them at least, pushing for a colony to be established there. Captain James Cook was the explorer, while Sir Joseph Banks, his botanist on the first exploring voyage, pulled strings with powerful men once back in Britain to help convince people to plant a colony on the coast of New South Wales.

The British, when they did establish a colony in Australia, decided to begin the settlement with convicted criminals as first settlers. In the first years of the colony, the new settlers encountered all kinds of problems, made worse by global events.

In this chapter, I cover Britain's 'discovery' of Australia, the reasons behind their eventual decision to establish a settlement here, and what happened in the initial years of the colony.

'Discovering' the Great Southern Land

By 1763 the British had gained supremacy of the world's oceans, except for one final frontier (bom, bom, boom): The Pacific Ocean.

HISTORICAL ROOTS

Ideas about a great southern land mass in the Pacific Ocean had been circulating for millennia. In ancient times, Ptolemy had surmised that *some* big land mass had to be down there to counterbalance Europe and Asia, and stop the planet going all topsy-turvy and flipping over. Throughout the 17th century, more solid evidence started emerging, largely thanks to reports from the mostly Dutch explorers in the region. (Refer to Chapter 2 for more on these explorers and traders.) It was time for Britain to make its mark.

For this daring task, two men were chosen: James Cook and Joseph Banks. Between them, they managed to chart the east coast of Australia, and have some lovely fun documenting all the weird and wonderful new flora and fauna they encountered along the way.

Finding the right men for the job

Two men from each side of the tracks. This part of the story belongs to Englishmen James Cook and Joseph Banks: One born in rural obscurity as a son of a labourer in Yorkshire; the other born the son of a gentleman and parliamentarian of significant wealth. One would end his life being clubbed to death on a beach in Hawaii (this would be Cook); the other as a Privy Council member and Royal Society President, dividing his time between Bath and Soho Square (big hello to Banks). (See the sidebar 'The original odd couple: Cook and Banks' for more on this unlikely duo.)

Between them, Cook and Banks not only managed to put Australia on the map in the most literal sense (even if it was still being called New Holland; see Chapter 5 for more on how the continent's name was changed to Australia), but also helped ensure that the first European settlement of the Australian continent was begun. The founding of the modern nation of Australia begins with these two men — and the British Royal Society.

THE ORIGINAL ODD COUPLE:
COOK AND BANKS

James Cook and Joseph Banks were integral to the charting and settlement of Australia by Britain, but two more different men could not have been picked for the job.

James Cook was born in 1728. He grew up on a farm in rural Yorkshire and began his working life apprenticed to a grocer. Not finding that to be quite the adventure best suited to his mental horizons, however, Cook managed to get himself apprenticed instead to a coal-shipper who operated in the North Sea. From this, he graduated to the Royal Navy, picking up expertise in mathematics and navigation somewhere along the way.

By 30 he was serving in Canada during the Seven Years War with France. Thanks to his precision surveying in the St Lawrence River, the French city of Quebec was captured. After this he was given a bigger job — surveying Newfoundland, something he clearly enjoyed so much that getting married in 1762 delayed him only temporarily. He was soon back in the harness finishing the job (perhaps aligning wife Elizabeth with the Quebecois on the list of people he was rubbing the wrong way). His work in Newfoundland, however, was what got him noticed and meant he was selected as commander for the1768 scientific expedition to the South Seas.

Cook, it seems, was meticulous with everything he did, whether surveying and charting inlets and rivers, or ensuring his crew stuck rigorously to a new diet to avoid scurvy. He was a stickler with those beneath him — he flogged often (especially in his third and last expedition to the South Pacific) — but was trusted too.

Joseph Banks was born in 1743. His father a member of parliament, and young Joseph himself enjoyed Harrow, Eton and Oxford. The wildflowers at Eton (he later said) sparked an interest in botany — this interest certainly helps explain why such a bright lad did so lamentably badly at his study of Greek and Latin. On getting to Oxford, he was horrified to find that the university had no botanist on hand to tutor him, so he was allowed to bag one from Cambridge.

At 21, Joseph came into his inheritance (his father having died when Joseph was 18). Leaving Oxford without bothering to finish his degree, Banks didn't do the usual thing expected at the time of a young gentlemen of large fortune (go on the 'Grand Tour' of Europe) but instead went off on a naturalist tour of Newfoundland and Labrador in North America. By curious coincidence, around the same time Cook was charting the coast of Newfoundland, Banks was amassing a huge collection of the island's natural specimens.

Banks was knighted in 1781.

In 1768, the Royal Society (a learned society originally set up by Royal Charter a century before for the advancement of scientific knowledge, and of which Banks was a member) managed to persuade the British Admiralty to send an expedition to observe the transit of Venus on the Pacific Island of Tahiti (the weather forecast for England that year being overcast with rain).

By this time, Cook was a lieutenant in the Royal Navy and he was selected to command the expedition. The Royal Society suggested Banks, 'Gentleman of large fortune . . . well versed in natural history', along with his 'suite', could accompany Lieutenant Cook on the voyage. Banks's suite was a cast of eight — naturalists, artists and servants — there to help him pick, pluck, catch and collect as many new zoological and botanical specimens as possible, and draw, describe and preserve them as well.

As well as observing the transit of Venus, however, the British Admiralty also gave Cook a set of secret instructions to follow: To establish once and for all if the 'Unknown Southern Land', or 'Terra Australis Incognita' was anything more than a pipe dream. If it was there, and Cook found it, he was told claiming it for Britain mightn't be a bad idea.

Setting (British) eyes on New South Wales

After observing the transit of Venus in Tahiti, Cook sailed south and then west expectantly, but what he found was just more Pacific Ocean. Charting New Zealand, he sailed further again, finding nothing until encountering the bottom south-east corner of what was known as New Holland — where Victoria and New South Wales meet each other today. This was disappointing, all things considered, but at least there was a nice lot of charting to do. Just as he'd done in New Zealand, Tahiti, Newfoundland and Nova Scotia, Cook set about surveying the coastline he was passing. Banks, meanwhile, gathered new and previously unknown zoological specimens everywhere they stopped, surely feeling a lot like a kid who'd just been let loose in a completely untouched (to European eyes, at least) lolly shop.

IN THEIR WORDS

Banks didn't think much of the land, though. He'd later change his tune significantly, but at the time he said it was without doubt 'in every respect the most barren country I have seen'. The soil was sandy, the grass thin and the water scarce. Although he'd had the time of his life catching and picking specimens, he didn't think the place was particularly good to settle in or trade with. The most he could allow was that, *perhaps*, if they were lucky, a group of people 'who should have the misfortune of being shipwreckd [sic]' might be able to support themselves.

Cook, having sailed up the Pacific coast of Australia in the *Endeavour*, reached the top of the east coast in August 1770. He claimed possession of the entire coast and planted the flag on the rather unimaginatively titled Possession Island (at the top of modern-day Cape York in far-north Queensland). Later on, noting it down in his journal, he racked his brain for a good name for the coast he'd just claimed (without asking any of the Indigenous Australians he'd encountered along the way what they thought of the idea, obviously). He first tried New Wales and then must have said to himself at last, 'Here's just the thing', and wrote down New South Wales.

On Cook's return to Britain from this first great voyage (he would go on two more before his voyaging ended abruptly in Hawaii) he was promoted to captain.

The Brits are Coming!

New South Wales (NSW), which had been charted and claimed by Cook, turned out to be the right place at the right time. By the time Banks returned from the voyage of discovery, Britain was facing a few international and logistical issues that made founding a new colony a much more attractive proposition. A few years after his return, Banks (along with a few others) piped up with the novel idea of making NSW a new British settlement and, after a few Parliamentary Committees debated the issue, it was indeed chosen.

Quick! New settlement required

Britain didn't decide to settle in a region as far-flung as NSW just because Cook had claimed possession of it. Those pesky commoners, those pesky Americans, and those pesky French, Spanish and Dutch all factored into the thinking.

Turing to crime in the 18th century

Along with a population boom, Britain in the 18th century experienced a period of rapid transformation — one that would produce a great deal more prosperity for more people but which also uprooted a lot of people from their traditional lives and livelihoods.

HISTORICAL
ROOTS

A series of Enclosure Acts shifted people off the land, which led to the breakdown of traditional rural order in the 18th century. Before this, agriculture in Britain was mostly communal — each farmer would use a strip in three different fields to grow crops and would graze cattle on the common. This communal style was good for everybody but inefficient. No big improvements in agricultural production could be made until the communal fields were amalgamated into one big plot, which is what the Enclosure Acts did in the 17th and 18th centuries. While enclosure created lots more work (all the enclosing for starters — with fences and hedges — and the intense cultivation that followed), it drove out the smallholders from their traditional claims and people began moving from the country to the cities.

Many people moved into cities such as Birmingham, Liverpool, Manchester and London, which offered plenty of job opportunities and, with no police force, plenty of crime opportunities too. As the town populations burgeoned, so too did the criminal underworld.

CONNECTING A FEAR OF POWERFUL KINGS TO BOTANY BAY

It's a slightly roundabout way to get to Botany Bay, but real connections can be drawn between the political revolutions against the central state and the powerful kings of the 16th century in England, and the institution of transportation. And these connections produce a lot of the momentum to start a colony on the other side of the world in a just-discovered-by-us-practically-yesterday continent.

In what sort of country does shipping your convicted criminals off to the other side of a huge ocean seem like a good idea? In 18th-century Britain is the answer, and here's why.

Britain was unique in 18th century Europe because it was a country governed essentially without police, and without a large army constantly ready to put down rebellions and keep order. One quirk of this system (or lack of system) was the form of punishment developed to deal with all the crime — transportation.

In the 17th and 18th centuries, most countries in Europe had established strong central states with plenty of power. (We could call these states 'draconian' if we were feeling impolite.) Kings, princes and assorted monarchs had established their right to rule as something absolute, ordained by God. In Europe, before the French Revolution, the 'Divine Right of Kings', or of 'Absolute Monarchs', was still a definite thing.

Figuring this sounded like a pretty good way of running things (and, if you're a king, I can definitely see the appeal), English kings had tried this out themselves in the 17th century, only to run into troubles with a deeply annoyed populace and a stroppy institution called 'parliament'. Two civil wars aimed to settle the point, and the English king in question lost both times. In 1648 he lost his head as well, and in 1688 one of his sons to exile.

One effect of this was that the victors in this tug of war became seriously paranoid about giving the central state (and the monarch who happened to be attached to it at the time) extensive powers. The rich and powerful feared the prospect of a king with a powerful army or an effective police force that could be used against them, so they severely constrained the reach of the central state, bound the monarch in 'constitutional limits', and pretty much did away with any police force.

What happens when you do away with a police force?

Well, in this particular time and place, the answer is you get a truckload of crime. No police or military force could be called out for assistance. The rich continued to hold the reins of power, but it wasn't easy to keep order. Pretty much the only option they had to hand was making the punishment for crimes committed by any criminals they did manage to catch completely over the top ('draconian' again comes to mind).

From the early 18th century, a whole new series of laws were passed by the wealthy Members of parliament, which punished lots of ordinary crimes with either the death penalty or, you guessed it, transportation.

Losing America and a terrible outbreak of peace

Britain had sent convicts to American colonies during the 18th century. When the American War of Independence (1775–1783) deprived Britain of its American colonies, one of the things that was lost was a handy place to send convicted criminals. Felons had been sent from Britain as bonded labour for decades, at a time of rapid demographic increase. Now convicts continued to be sentenced to 'transportation across the seas', but with nowhere to transport them to. A stopgap measure was housing them in *prison hulks* (old ships refitted for the purpose of holding prisoners) moored on the River Thames, and putting them to public work in chain gangs.

A few problems arose with this system. Firstly, the authorities had always thought that transportation should send convicts far away to some largely unknown place overseas, and now this option was gone. Secondly, in the course of the 18th century the British people had become used to getting rid of felons in such a fashion, and had a real problem with the sight of men chained up in gangs in public. Other countries in Europe had followed this route, and it was seen as a sort of continental 'despotism'. Thirdly, pretty soon they were running out of hulks!

But the twist here is that the system coped all right with losing the American colonies, just so long as a nice couple of wars were bubbling along to keep would-be crims pleasantly occupied fighting in the British army or navy. If it wasn't the Americans, there was always the French, and if no-one else was around then you could always pick on the Dutch. But in 1782 a terrible spectre arose: Peace. By 1784 and 1785, returned soldiers and seamen were being *demobbed* (stood down from the armed services) and coming back into the country via the southern ports of England. As they did so, an explosion in crime occurred.

Getting access to vital resources

In the second half of the 18th century, Britain managed to get herself tangled up in conflicts with all the other major global powers — France, Spain and Holland. These protracted conflicts made Britain vulnerable as it ran short of vital commodities controlled by enemy nations. Without flax plants and pine trees, Britain was going to have difficulty getting new masts, spars, canvas and cordage, and without these, its navy would have great difficulty maintaining the powerbase it had fought so hard to win.

Pushing for a settlement in NSW

After leading the voyage that charted the east coast of Australia in 1770, Cook led two more exploratory voyages around the world. His journeying came to an abrupt end in Hawaii in 1779 when some seriously irritated natives clubbed him to death.

Banks, meanwhile, settled back into a comfortable and sedentary existence in Soho, London — perhaps getting a little *too* comfortable, as gout would plague his later years. On good terms with everyone from the King downwards, he became a prime mover, shaker and patron behind establishing a settlement in NSW some years after he'd been there himself.

IN THEIR WORDS

Completely reversing his earlier negative opinion (refer to the section 'Setting (British) eyes on New South Wales' earlier in this chapter), Banks confidently predicted to the Beauchamp Committee in 1779 that nothing could be easier than establishing a colony near Botany Bay in NSW. This area had enough rich soil 'to support a very large Number of People', the grass long and luxuriant, and the country well supplied with water. Equip two or three hundred people with 'all kinds of tools for labouring the Earth, and building Houses', then a year on, 'with a moderate Portion of Industry, they might, undoubtedly, maintain themselves without any Assistance from England'.

In 1785 Banks repeated this advice to another committee, strongly recommending Botany Bay for penal settlement and saying NSW was 'in every way adapted to the purpose'. 'But what about the natives?' someone wondered. Wouldn't they be difficult? Not at all, assured Banks jovially. They were 'extremely cowardly', and would 'soon abandon the country to the new comers'.

Sounds so wonderfully simple, doesn't it? Take livestock and tools, add crop seeds, mix well with humans, stir for 12 months, and voila — instant colony. Reality would prove to be very far removed from such rosy predictions.

CLAIMING THE 'TERRA NULLIUS'

HISTORICAL ROOTS

While the British were happy enough to strike treaties with Native Americans and New Zealand Maori, they didn't even accept that Indigenous Australians owned the land they lived on. This was because Indigenous Australians were nomadic. The British logic was that if they didn't build and live in houses, didn't fence land and grow crops, Aboriginal people didn't own the land, they only lived on top of it. Indigenous Australians were pretty clear in their minds that they *did* own the land they lived on, and that it was incredibly precious to them. But the British saw differently (this was a debate that wouldn't be fully resolved until the Mabo and Wik cases in the 1990s — see Chapter 21).

Picking a winner: NSW it is!

After the crime explosion in Britain in 1784 and 1785 (refer to the section 'Losing America and a terrible outbreak of peace', earlier in this chapter), and the resulting urgent need to get rid of convicts, Banks was pushing for NSW to be established as the settlement to send them to.

However, many other possibilities existed — the Falkland Islands, Newfoundland, Nova Scotia, the West Indies, the East Indies, the Malay Archipelago and South Africa were all mentioned in public debate and were taken more or less seriously. Britain ended up choosing the NSW coast, which these days we tend to assume was natural, even inevitable, but at the time it was an odd choice. Certainly, it was satisfyingly remote — not many escapees paddling their way back to Britain in a hurry — but there was such a thing as *too* remote for a penal settlement. Ideally, you wanted a port of call on an already existing major trade route. Extremely isolated exile wasn't preferred from the start — the presumption being that after convicts had served their time, they should be able to catch a ship home.

The proposed Botany Bay colony was outside any established shipping routes, and not a region with great existing trade, meaning that transportation costs would be very high. Although the influence of Banks can't be denied, what other factors led the British Government to choose NSW? Here the plot thickens. This is an area that sustains a healthy amount of strong disagreement among historians, but some clear factors emerge:

>> **NSW was near vital raw materials for maintaining a global navy:** Britain had found out the hard way in recent wars that if shut off from crucial supplies from Europe, their vaunted navy ran the risk of disintegration. Flax plants were needed to make sails, ropes and cords, while long straight timber, preferably pine, was needed to replace masts. Cook had reported spruce

pines of 'vast size' on Norfolk Island, not far from the NSW coast: 'Here . . . masts for the largest ships may be had'. Flax plants were also seen growing in abundance.

>> **Access to all the tea in China could be made less volatile:** In the 1780s, trade with the Chinese port of Canton increased dramatically, with the importation of tea tripling in two years alone. But getting there was tricky. The French had established themselves in Indochina (modern-day Vietnam and surrounding areas), and the Dutch held the East Indies (modern-day Indonesia). While the British had signed a treaty that gave them a right to sail through Dutch waters, they worried that in the event of war both regions would become highly dangerous to move through. So an alternative route, one that went from India southwards, below Australia and then up the east coast, sailing between the New South Wales coastline and Norfolk Island, could be a handy Plan B.

>> **The British East India Company's monopoly was looking likely to end:** For most of the 18th century, this company had enjoyed a monopoly over all trade that went back to Britain from India and the entire region that lay beyond, as they came to exercise an often regal-type power in that part of the world. For trading companies and shipping agencies not directly aligned with the company, this monopoly was a profound disincentive for moving operations into the Pacific. The monopoly was widely expected to be terminated in the early 1790s, however, allowing a rush of new trading shipping interest into the area.

>> **The French were still an enemy to be feared:** The French and British had an animosity that went back centuries (Joan of Arc, anyone?) but in the second half of the 18th century, Britain and France were locked in an intense battle for global supremacy that often sparked wars. The British Ambassador in Paris in the summer of 1785 reported worrying rumours that the French scientific expedition about to set off under comte de La Pérouse was going to be instructed to establish a convict settlement in New Zealand to take advantage of the pines reputed to be there. Interest in the Pacific and New Holland as a strategic resource was on the rise in the other major player in world affairs.

HISTORICAL ROOTS

So why not kill a multiple number of birds with one big convict stone? Convicts were intended as a stop-gap measure to help establish a key British strategic post in the Pacific. Plenty of other reasons could be put forward to establish settlement in NSW, but plenty of good reasons also to keep quiet about it. The British had no wish, after all, to needlessly provoke or alarm the Dutch and French, or to offend British East India Company sensitivities. (The company had been largely shut out of the decision-making for the new settlement, and was already viewing it suspiciously.) Much easier, then, to talk only of offloading unwanted convicts on a coastline that was declared to be land belonging to no-one (see the sidebar 'Claiming the "terra nullius"').

In 1786, George III declared to the House of Commons that his government and prime minister would soon transport 'a number of convicts' to Botany Bay in order to relieve 'the crowded state of the gaols'.

SHAPING AUSTRALIA WITH TWO BIG DECISIONS

In 1780s London, two decisions would have gob-smackingly enormous consequences for the sort of country Australia would become.

The first big decision is fairly obvious — deciding to establish a colony for trading, and for strategic and convict transportation purposes on the Australian continent. When you consider levels of subsequent impact from particular decisions, that's about as big as it gets, really.

The second big decision, though, was also far-reaching, even if at first glance it seems more subtle. It was a decision made by the minister in charge of the arrangements for what sort of settlement this would be.

The government minister was Thomas Townsend — 'Tommy' to his mates, but known to history as 'Lord Sydney'. He raised eyebrows when he decided, quite late in the day as it happened, that the penal colony in NSW would be run according to ordinary civil law rather than as a military society. What this meant was that the law that would operate here would recognise all the usual rights and liberties outlined in English law at home. In comparison to most places in the world at the time, an Englishman's rights and liberties were something to brag about (and they did). This decision meant that NSW would be established as a free society, even if most of the new population arriving were convicts! (Ah, the irony.)

The first ever civil trial to take place after the arrival of the First Fleet, run according to the rules of an ordinary English court, was brought by a young convict couple, who sued one of the ship captains for losing their valuable luggage on the journey out. This couple was Henry and Susannah Kable.

They won, too. (See Chapter 4 for more on this couple's continuing successes in the new colony.)

Sailing for Botany Bay

After the selecting of the site came the settling. Organising and equipping a party to settle a colony in a part of the world that had been seen once some 15 years previously meant a lot of planning and preparation had to be done. Aside from getting there, the British had the question of exactly who they would take as first settlers. One suggestion was to send American colonists who had stayed loyal to Britain in the American War of Independence. In the end, they went with convicted criminals (for reasons explained in the preceding section). Exactly what sort of people these convicted criminals were, however, is another matter.

Getting there with the First Fleet

The actual getting to NSW and the initial settling in was remarkably trouble-free, thanks in large part to the expedition's leader, Captain Arthur Phillip, carefully overseeing preparations. The government responded seriously to his demands that this long voyage, bigger than any large-scale journey and relocation ever before attempted, should be fitted out properly. When the ships of what we now call the 'First Fleet' finally got underway in May 1787, no-one could say it was a slap-dash affair.

The ships were of good quality and sturdy. Fresh provisions were laid in during the weeks prior to the fleet's departure. No callous disregard for convicts' welfare was shown, with one observer going so far as to complain that the weekly rations were superior to what ordinary sailors would generally receive. The convicts themselves were selected on the basis of good health (and possibly youth). As many mechanics and farm hands as could be found were strategically selected by the government.

TECHNICAL STUFF

Largely due to these meticulous preparations, out of the 1,403 people who left Portsmouth, only 69 died (or deserted) in the course of the long voyage. Given that ships on long voyages at this time could often lose up to a quarter or even half of their crew, this was no mean feat. In January 1788, some 1,023 settlers disembarked, including 751 convicts and their children and 252 marines and their families.

Botany Bay, contrary to Banks's suavely confident predictions (refer to the 'Pushing for a settlement in NSW' section, earlier in this chapter), was not suitable for settlement — the bay was too open and the land without good fresh water — and they soon relocated to Sydney Cove, in Port Jackson, where modern-day Sydney now stands.

The human material: Who were these people?

The First Fleet had arrived in NSW. So far so good. But now the hard work began. What sort of material did Captain Phillip have to work with here? Well. The human material wasn't great, actually. While convicts arriving in early NSW were a mixed bag — including first-time offenders, 'fall guys', people in regular work, and those from the country and from Ireland (who were often transported for nothing much at all) — the main core of the convicts were career crims.

Most of the convicts under Phillip's charge, and the bulk of convicts for the subsequent decades, were predominantly from urban areas, and many were from the criminal subculture. Through the 18th century, people had moved (or been moved) off the land and away from the traditional rural order, and many had drifted into the major cities. As the town populations burgeoned, so too did the criminal underworld, and among Phillip's founding settlers were card-carrying members of it. More than half the criminals transported for the next 80 years came from cities, with nearly a third before 1819 coming from London.

HISTORICAL ROOTS

Many of the convicts were literate criminals, such as forgers and embezzlers. Others were petty thieves (more than 80 per cent of convicts overall were transported for some kind of theft), burglars, horse-, cattle- and sheep-stealers (many were members of professional gangs), shoplifters, pickpockets and (the real convict royals) the occasional highwayman. Largely, the convicts were either professional thieves, living off their wits and enjoying their gains while they could, or itinerant tramps and wanderers, notoriously 'improvident', pugnacious, restless, big fans of egalitarianism (no differences between thieves) and with a love of independence (no bosses thanks).

In summer, these career criminals tramped around the countryside, haunting fairs, market days and race meetings, stealing chickens from gardens and sleeping under hedges. They were often drunk, and would have been prime candidates for any Gamblers Anonymous meeting. Although the line 'honour among thieves' was regularly trotted out, they tended to show little mutual trust, thieving from each other, dobbing each other in with the authorities after a fight or an argument, and frequently turning witness for the Crown in a trial and giving evidence against associates. If you think they probably weren't ideal material to start a colony with, after the first couple of months Phillip would have emphatically agreed.

REMEMBER

A negative character reference didn't particularly distinguish the convicts from most of the other people who had accompanied them out to NSW — namely, the marines and soldiers. People sometimes make the mistake of thinking of these two groups as occupying rigidly differentiated categories. The opposite was usually the case. Today's soldier was tomorrow's crim: Today, you're a soldier defending His Majesty's best interests in a pitched battle on Bunker Hill in Boston as part of the American War of Independence; tomorrow, you're demobbed in Portsmouth with little money and no livelihood, and happen to walk past a shop stocked with expensive linen and calicos and spy that the wares are invitingly unattended and unsupervised. Before you know it, you're bound for Botany Bay, old son.

Holding Out at Sydney

Once the First Fleet had arrived in what would become Sydney, Captain Phillip tried to get the convicts to work, which didn't go too well. Taken out of 18th-century London criminal subculture, dumped down in an alien wilderness, and expected to toil each day to establish crops and a settlement wasn't their idea of smart living. They wandered off whenever they could, threw away tools into the bush, and generally behaved like grumpy contestants on an episode of *Big Brother*.

The assumption on the part of Lord Sydney in the Colonial Office in London had been that the convicts' main punishment was exile — that once they'd been transported and had arrived in NSW, they'd be 'free on the ground'. 'Not on your life!' said Arthur Phillip (or something similar). 'You can see how little they do as servants of the Crown. Can you imagine what a disaster it would be if they were left to their own devices?' So he insisted that the convicts should work on public farms under guard, and he continued to coerce, cajole and browbeat them. Neither of these two moves met with much success.

Using convicts as guards

Phillip had his problems getting convicts to work in the new settlement at Sydney, but the convicts weren't the only troublesome bunch. Phillip's other big problem was the officers and soldier marines.

LIFE DOWN UNDER

The soldiers refused to guard the convicts, insisting it wasn't their job because they weren't prison wardens. The ensuing discussion must have been something like the following: 'You're kidding?'(from Arthur Phillip). 'Can't you at least keep an eye on them? Encourage them to till the soil a little more enthusiastically?' 'Nope' (delivered flatly, from the soldiers). 'We're officers and soldiers. We're here to protect you from foreign attack, or put down uprisings. Anything else is most definitively Not Our Problem.'

So Phillip was forced to appoint convicts as overseers, which made for a strange situation (prisoners guarding prisoners), but was nothing compared to when Phillip was forced by necessity to make convicts nightwatchmen and constables. This meant, of course, that soon enough you had convict constables arresting marines doing wrong. The officers flipped, but Phillip's sympathy was, shall I say, not greatly discernible.

LIFE DOWN UNDER

Phillip wrote to Britain with complaints — the convicts wouldn't farm and the soldiers wouldn't guard — and asked that Britain start sending out free settlers, arguing he could provide each settler with convicts as labourers. From his comfortable digs in Soho Square, Sir Joseph Banks (the botanist who had sailed with Cook and had pushed for the settlement of NSW in the first place) thought this was a terrific thing to do. He urged the government to send out free families, and to give them land grants, ten convicts and four years' support. Both Phillip and Banks were ignored, however, and the plan went nowhere. As time went on, it became more and more clear that the people sent out on the First Fleet would be the kind of material the new colony had to work with. The colony would sink or swim with these most dubious elements of Georgian Britain.

Issuing ultimatums (and being ignored)

With no free settlers forthcoming from Britain, Phillip had to try to make the most of the convicts and marines he was stuck with in NSW. To do this, he tried threats, issuing the convicts with an ultimatum: No work, no eat. Rations would be given only to those who put in. The convicts called his bluff. 'What?' they said (or something similar). 'You're going to just let us all starve, are you? The government is just going to send us out here, to the other side of the world, and leave us to die?'

REMEMBER

The convicts who arrived on the First Fleet weren't left to die — the Governor couldn't let that happen to convict settlers he'd been charged with looking after (and the convicts knew it) — but starvation did become a real threat. In 1789, a British ship en route to the colony with supplies struck an iceberg and sank. The great risks involved with establishing a settlement in a remote part of the world with no pre-existing shipping or trade routes became more and more apparent with each passing day as famine loomed. By early 1790, the colony's supplies had dwindled alarmingly.

Soldiering on regardless

In addition to the difficulties with the criminals and the marines, the ground Phillip was trying to grow crops on proved to be largely barren and infertile. But Phillip showed his mettle, and his genius for combining real fairness with great toughness. A man who'd been living on and commanding ships for much of his life, he was used to the world of rough equality that prevailed on ships. This world was often brutal, but on the ship everyone knew they had no-one else to rely on outside their fellow crew, whatever their rank may be. This same logic applied now and Phillip followed it ruthlessly.

Phillip declared that all rations would be divided equally, no matter if you were free or felon. The officers, again, were outraged, but Phillip, again, ignored them. Then he showed the same impartiality with executions. Stealing provisions was made a capital offence. In the year of their arrival, he'd shown this by hanging convicts who stole supplies. He then followed it up in 1789 by hanging soldiers who were caught running a scam of pilfering the main store. No-one could be under any illusions now as to how things stood.

New Colony Blues

The first two years of settlement were no picnic, and 1790 wasn't much better. The Second Fleet, which arrived in June 1790, wasn't able to do much to help NSW out of near-starvation, because many of the new arrivals were on death's door by the time they arrived. Meanwhile the Indigenous Australians had to deal with an invasion of overwhelming numbers into their country.

Second Fleet horrors

By the time the Second Fleet arrived in June 1790, a quarter of the settlement had died. But the fleet itself, while carrying supplies, brought with them a human disaster. While the First Fleet had been well planned and supervised, the second was a story of neglect, brutality and deliberate starvation. The job of transporting the convicts had been given to private contractors, whose usual cargo was African slaves. Slaves fared slightly better, however, because with slaves came the incentive for those in charge to keep as many as possible alive to sell at the other end of the journey. Here, however, no such rule applied and the more who died, the easier the contractors' job got.

Of the 750 convicts who actually made it to NSW, 500 were hospital cases, and the half-starved colony set to work putting up emergency hospital tents. When news got back to London, a scandal erupted, and a trial of the contractors was held. (The contractors got off.) The outcry meant that even though convicts were being transported out of sight, they weren't completely out of mind. In future, more rigorous regulations and official supervision would ensure the vast majority transported arrived alive and in reasonable health.

HORROR SCENES ON THE BOATS

The colony's parson, Reverend Johnson, described the apocalyptic scene when the Second Fleet pulled into what would become Sydney Harbour, with people throwing the bodies of those who'd just died overboard. The bodies floated in on the tide in front of the ships, and came to rest on the rocks. On shore many of the convicts being unloaded were so weak they couldn't walk: 'Some creeped upon their hands and knees, and some were carried upon the backs of others'.

Going on board one of the ships, Reverend Johnson found 'a sight truly shocking to the feelings of humanity, a great number of them lying, some half and others nearly quite naked, without either bed or bedding, unable to turn or help themselves'.

Courting disaster with the interlopers

The local Eora and Darug people had pragmatically tried to adjust to the invasion, as fear and curiosity mingled on either side of the massive cultural divide. To begin with at least, relations were more cordial than hostile. Many of the marine officers were fascinated with these people from a completely 'new' and previously unknown culture. The Indigenous Australians mostly got along with the officers — the young warrior men especially.

With convicts, however, relations between black and white quickly soured. Quite early on — in May 1788 — two young convicts, William Okey and Samuel Davis, were killed while cutting grass at a place now known as Rushcutters Bay to make a thatch roof for the Store House. The killings were gruesome — the bodies described as 'jellied' — and while their clothes and provisions were untouched, their rush-cutting tools were taken. The exact cause of the death of these two was difficult to establish, but the settlement's surgeon, John White, suspected that 'from the civility shown on all occasions to the officers by the natives, whenever any of them were met, I am strongly inclined to think that they must have been provoked and injured by the convicts'. Phillip thought likewise.

Indigenous–convict relations continued to degenerate. Aboriginal Australians, prizing warrior prowess and with a keen eye for status and prestige, largely enjoyed the company of First Fleet officers, who were for their part more curious and respectful than hostile. Convicts and Aboriginals, however, despised each other. Mutual distrust reigned, and thefts, rape and payback killings began to increase.

But the convicts themselves weren't the great fracturing event. A year after the killings at Rushcutters Bay, a smallpox epidemic struck the settlement. Most of the white settlers had already established immunity to the disease, but the effect on Indigenous Australians was devastating. Some 50 per cent of Aboriginal people in the Sydney region died as a consequence.

LIFE DOWN UNDER

This, as much as the Rushcutters Bay deaths, was to be the tragic signature tune for the encounter between British and Indigenous societies as settlement spread outward. However many Aboriginal people died as a result of direct conflict with the white invaders and targeted killings — and plenty did — the impact of epidemic diseases, to which they had no established immunity, was far more devastating. Combined with the effect of a brand new intoxicant — alcohol — the consequences of white settlement were profound.

Bennelong and Phillip

One of the Eora leaders, a man named Bennelong, developed a unique relationship with Governor Phillip — which is pretty amazing, because he started out by being kidnapped, on Governor Phillip's direct orders, in November 1789.

Phillip really wanted to learn the local Aboriginal languages and get a better sense of the local customs. Essentially, he wanted to find out how he could discuss and negotiate, and, well, let's just say that that moment in the meeting where someone points out, 'Kidnapping people to initiate good relations with the neighbours is actually a really, incredibly stupid idea, sir' just didn't happen that day. The instructions from the British Government were to live harmoniously with the local tribes, and to get to know them as well. And abduction . . . just seemed to be the way to go about realising those aims.

Bennelong clearly wasn't too thrilled at the prospect of becoming the Governor's captive ambassador. He engaged, he picked up the newcomers' language, and he filled them in on local names and peoples — and he then took off pretty much as soon as he got the chance, shortly after the leg irons had been removed and he'd gained his captors' trust.

LIFE DOWN UNDER

Bennelong wasn't against continued relations with Phillip and the whitefellas, and was willing to engage in ongoing cultural broking between the two groups. As much as we can tell from this distance, he and Phillip seemed to actually like and respect each other. And it absolutely made good cultural sense for Bennelong to establish close relations with the leader of the white folk, for himself, his clan, and the wider Eora nation.

First, though, some sort of payback was required.

Phillip was speared at Manly Cove near Sydney, after he'd been invited there by Bennelong as he and his clan feasted on a stranded whale there. Manly was the place Bennelong had been originally abducted from, and this hardly seems a coincidence. The spear wound wasn't fatal, but then it wasn't meant to be. Soon after this, Bennelong re-established relations with the Governor, this time not as captive but on some sort of equality, or mutual recognition.

For the rest of the time Phillip was governor of NSW, Bennelong was invited to Government House regularly. He was welcome company at the Governor's dinner table, where lively conversation dominated proceedings. Phillip had a hut built for Bennelong to live in at the settlement. (This hut was built on the point where the Sydney Opera House stands today.)

When Phillip left Sydney to return to London in 1792, Bennelong went with him. He wasn't the first Indigenous Australian to be abducted by the Governor (another man, Arabanoo, preceded him), but along with a young kinsman, Yemmerrawanne, Bennelong was the first Indigenous Australian to voyage out from their home country to make their own journey of discovery, to the alien country of Britain, at the other corner of the world. Here he lodged in Mayfair, was measured for and wore Georgian frock coat and breeches, went to the theatre, watched Opera from a private box, caused a minor sensation when he visited the Houses of Parliament at Westminster, pined badly when Yemmerrawanne died of a lung complaint, and sailed back to Australia on the HMS *Reliance*.

He returned to life as clan leader, described by one settler as 'the chief, or king of his tribe'.

While Bennelong adopted some of the habits and customs of the British, dressing in their clothes and learning their language, Barangaroo, Bennelong's wife, wasn't as impressed. She opposed what she saw as her husband's conciliatory relationship with the people who were establishing themselves on Aboriginal land. She refused to adopt the European customs or clothing, angering her husband. All she ever wore was a slim bone through her nose, even when dining with the Governor.

For more on relationships between local Aboriginal people and the new arrivals, see *Indigenous Australia For Dummies*, 2e, by Larissa Behrendt, Wiley Australia Publishing.

Then the rest of the world goes bung

While things had been going badly at Sydney, in the rest of the world the situation was changing rapidly and not for the better, especially for the new colony. In particular, the following events affected them:

>> The great hope of Norfolk Island — that it would provide vital supplies for Britain's navy and maritime trade — fell through. The great tall pines that

Cook had originally admired proved to be no good as masts. And the flax plant proved to be the wrong type for making cords and sails.

>> War broke out in Europe in the aftermath of the 1789 French Revolution. The Revolutionary and Napoleonic Wars lasted from the early 1790s until Napoleon's final defeat at Waterloo in 1815. Britain's energies and attention began to be drawn inexorably into this great conflict, with action seen across the most of the northern hemisphere. Exactly how a bunch of convicts on the other side of the planet were faring started slipping down the list of Things to Be Worried About. But things would change once that war was over — see Chapter 5 to read about what happened when the British started paying attention again (which wasn't necessarily a good thing, either).

>> A new decision was finally made in 1793 on the trade monopoly of the British East India Company: Instead of being terminated, the monopoly was renewed for another 20 years, lasting until 1813. The hope of Sydney being parked on the side of a burgeoning new trade region seemed to be dashed.

Instead of being a source of vital strategic supplies, and on a new shipping route where trade was burgeoning, the colony was now marooned on the other side of the world, unable to grow its own food, in the middle of a no-go trade zone, and Britain was preoccupied. And Phillip was going home.

The convicts, intended to be a stopgap measure to be used to establish a key British strategic post, were now the whole purpose of the colony. Interesting times promised to ensue.

Chapter **4**

Colony Going Places (With Some Teething Troubles)

A ustralia, originally planned to serve multiple purposes, ended up being solely a prison dump for convicts (refer to Chapter 3). At the same time as the new colony was settled, Britain became seriously distracted by the French Revolutionary and Napoleonic Wars. Britain, fighting off invasion threats and struggling for world domination, wasn't massively concerned with what the penal dump on the other side of the world was doing.

Facing failing crops and a huge wait between resupply ships, life for arrivals on the First and Second Fleets — convict and soldier alike — was pretty grim. Yet, within 20 years of settlement, many of those who'd been sent out here in exile were making fortunes, and were making a life much freer and in most ways better than they could ever have hoped of getting in Britain.

In this chapter, I cover the way officers of the NSW Corps stepped into the vacuum left by Britain's lack of real planning or ongoing involvement in the development of the economic life of NSW. From 1792, resourceful officers from this permanent regiment of soldiers started using government money — and rum, that other great motivator — to expand cultivation and settlement. They also established a cartel on incoming trade, and made themselves seriously wealthy in the process. I also look at how their monopoly was short-lived — convict men and women who the officers originally set up to handle the retail side of things pretty quickly cut in on their turf.

And I cover the governors sent to wrest power out of the hands of the NSW Corps and various ex-convict traders — governors Hunter, King and Bligh.

Rising to the Task: The NSW Corps Steps Up

Under Captain Phillip's rule, little land was cleared and few crops grown. The convicts were practically impossible to extract labour from, and remained listless and idle on the government farms (refer to Chapter 3). After Phillip left the colony at the end of 1792 due to ill health, for the next three years the colony was administered by the head of the NSW Corps: Major Francis Grose and then Major William Paterson.

The NSW Corps was a permanent regiment of the British army and had been sent out to relieve the Marines sent with the First Fleet. The officers of this Corps, which became known as the Rum Corps, set up trading monopolies, increasing (at hugely inflated prices) the amount of goods available in the settlement. They also found a way to convince the convicts to do some work — through paying them in rum.

Under the administration of the Corps, Sydney thrived. The settlement became a shanty metropolis doing a roaring trade in imported goods, expanding trade in the Pacific — sandalwood and pork from Tahiti found a particularly ready market — and exploring newly opened sealing and whaling grounds. And convicts and ex-convicts by and large thrived too.

LIFE DOWN UNDER

One of the great surprises of this period of Australia's history is what happened to the convicts themselves — transportation, before it became greatly systematised, gave them a chance to step out of the vicious poverty cycle that many of the urbanised lower orders were doomed to in Britain. In the early years of the new colony, the emphasis was never on punishment or misery. Men and women were frequently given freedom before their terms expired, chiefly as a money-saving measure — if they had the talent or skill to earn their own living, then make them free as soon as possible and get them off the government store and ration books.

LIFE ON THE FRONTIER: A LAND OF BRUTALITY AND OPPORTUNITY

LIFE DOWN UNDER

In the first few years of settlement in Australia, convicts had about half of their working hours free to themselves. If a convict was assigned to daily task work, that meant no work after lunchtime, even if it spent the whole morning raining. If it was weekly task work, then a convict was generally free by about Thursday. A far cry from work conditions at this time in Britain (minors being sent to work, long working hours, poor conditions, exploitation, and so on).

Convicts were clothed, fed and housed at the expense of the government. Their masters tended to be people exactly like them — ex-convicts who had been granted land along with their freedom and had now been given convict labourers as well. The convicts would often live in the same hut as the family. These masters weren't just owners of convict labour, weren't only employers of convicts in their free time, but could be business partners as well: They would frequently offer profit-sharing schemes with the convicts they had living and working for them.

If you are looking for scenes of absolute squalor in this early period, you have to look quite selectively. Yes, plenty of floggings were dished out — for drunkenness, desertion of labour and being generally at large, and stealing — and hangings (like in Britain) remained frequent. But this doesn't make NSW a place of misery. This makes it normal in the context of the period. Flogging took place everywhere — on ships, in schoolrooms and yards, with apprentices and servants in workplaces — with the Georgian age's attitude towards corporal punishment being vastly different to most attitudes today.

For those trying to carve out a life on a farm, the conditions were no joke: Small land grants covered in bush and scrub had to be cleared; the soil was often of low fertility, and subject to the vagaries of a new climate — not to mention the often extortionate prices being charged for supplies by various traders and retailers. All of this added to the hardship of living in a frontier environment. Many preferred to sell up and move back into Sydney town (where demand for labour was high and the pay good) and get work there. But some stuck with their land grants, picked up more land, and used their allocated convict labour to run livestock and grow cash crops. Slowly the criminal class that had arrived en masse from Britain were becoming settlers in a new country.

NSW in the early years, then, was a place of casual brutality, squalor and frontier hardship, yet simultaneously a place of remarkable and unprecedented opportunity for the outcasts and criminal 'refuse' who were sent here. The colony turned out to be an unexpected jackpot for many convicts, far better than anything they could have reasonably expected if they'd remained in the Britain they knew — either locked in a rural yet landless poverty or the London underclass.

Setting up trading monopolies

When planning the new colony in NSW, the British Government had completely failed to provide it with any coinage or currency, expecting (vaguely) that after a year everyone would be self-sufficient, with the convicts growing enough to meet everyone's needs.

When this failed to happen, ship captains realised that they had a wonderful captive market in NSW — an isolated outpost dependent on imports to survive. They started arriving with much needed goods but charging prohibitively extortionate prices. While convicts and soldiers could scrape together some money, the officers in the NSW Corps, paid in British pounds sterling, were the only ones who could bargain the ships' captains down, purchasing an entire ship's consignment at reduced prices. So they did, but then started charging their own extortionate prices through their convict and common soldier middlemen.

What had originally begun as a meeting of opportunity and necessity, quickly turned into a trade monopoly.

REMEMBER

Taking an overseas posting, going overseas and doing everything you could to get rich was widely accepted as common military officer practice at the time. However, officers of the NSW Corps still couldn't be seen directly involving themselves in trade. So they set up their convict servants (or convict mistresses) as retail frontmen (or women) for their retail operations.

The ascendancy of the 'Rum Corps'

As head of the NSW Corps, Major Grose started giving land grants to officers, and to emancipists (the ex-convicts) and the few free settlers who were turning up here and there. Suddenly, the gears of the colony shifted. Not only did the new farmers start clearing and growing and reaping and rearing with new energy, but the convict labourers who were assigned to them were also launching themselves into the task with gusto.

HISTORICAL ROOTS

In the first few years of settlement, the convict settlers weren't remotely interested in being settlers or farmers. However, the NSW Corps (who, as new landholders, now had a vested interest in getting the convicts to work the land) found a way to unlock an incredible capacity for productivity. It turned out all they needed was the right incentive. The convicts were already being fed and provisioned with clothes and basic necessities. What more could they want for? The answer, of course, was alcohol. And for the more sophisticated, gambling and alcohol. The NSW Corps (which, for obvious reasons, quickly became known as the Rum Corps) provided these and the colony started to thrive.

Suddenly convicts were working incredibly hard, often putting in overtime to get tasks done. Not having had much chance to get alcohol since they'd left London, now they went after it with a zest that was almost awe-inspiring. One observer who saw it (David Collins, the future founding governor of Van Diemen's Land) said that 'the passion for liquor was so predominant among the people that it operated like a mania'.

IN THEIR WORDS

Major Grose reported back to London, professing great wonderment: 'Whether their efforts result from the novelty of the business, or the advantages they promise themselves, I cannot say, but their exertions are really astonishing'. What Grose neglected to mention, of course, was the crucial and illicit trigger for this explosion of activity.

The convicts kept coming from Britain, so the NSW Corps officers also had a great number of convicts to use. Grose and the Inspector of Public Works, John Macarthur, ensured that the officers were given about ten convicts each. The Home Office wrote to Grose, specifically instructing him that the government would pay for only two convicts per officer for a period of two years, adding that spirits not be sold to convicts (word had started getting back). But the convicts *would* drink, and alcohol was one of the biggest motivators that had been found to get them to work. So Grose completely ignored these instructions. And a certain degree of chaotic and riotous abandonment ensured.

With proper order and proper morality largely ignored in favour of what you could call a culture of highly productive alcoholism, the colony was no longer an economic basket case, limping along at or below subsistence level. The colony had taken off like a rocket, and was starting to make a lot of people a lot of money very quickly — but not everyone was happy with the trajectory of the rocket.

Upsetting the reverends

Word was beginning to get back to London: NSW was no place of punishment, and was out of control, said the alarmed reports. Many of the reports were written by furious Evangelicals — religious Anglican ministers (such as Reverend Johnson and Reverend Samuel Marsden) who had arrived in the colony expecting to be respected as pillars of the establishment order, only to find themselves largely ignored by the convicts, and by the common soldiers and the officer Corps as well.

LIFE DOWN UNDER

Early NSW was anything but pious. Neither the convicts, nor the common soldiery, nor many of the officers, military or civil, set any real store on forswearing their preferred pursuits — swearing, gambling, drinking and fornicating. In this they were broadly reflective of the habits and pursuits of the bulk of Georgian England, but in NSW the established authorities and arbiters of proper morality held far less sway.

HISTORICAL ROOTS

The Evangelicals were just launching their great moral revival at this time in late Georgian Britain; its chief exponent, William Wilberforce, experienced his 'conversion' at about the same time as the First Fleet was sailing. The Evangelists' deep sense was that England had 'fallen' from the state of religious zeal of the previous century, and been seduced and corrupted by the luxuries and excesses that modern life offered. They wanted to 'reclaim' modern Britain from the various excesses and debaucheries that the 18th century had become famous for. The Evangelicals had some really positive social reform to their credit — most notably, the abolition of slavery in Britain — but they had their work cut out for them in the new colony of NSW.

Under the tutelage, direct and indirect, of Wilberforce, who was a friend of Prime Minister William Pitt and Sir Joseph Banks (a lot more about Banks in Chapter 3), clergymen of Evangelical bent were sent out to the new settlement.

Once in NSW, Reverend Johnson railed against the laxness of the Corps when it came to enforcing piety, and for allowing convicts to throw 'aside all regard or reverence for the Sabbath Day, and to render all public solemn worship utterly contemptible'. Convicts were paid to work on Sundays. Other convicts were left to pretty much do whatever they wanted.

IN THEIR WORDS

While Johnson was conducting services, he claimed the bulk of convicts 'were either asleep in their hammocks or sitting in their huts, or otherwise gone out to work for officers or other individuals'. Just as bad, 'spiritous liquor was the most general article and mode of payment for such extra labour, and hence in the evening the whole camp has been nothing else, often, but a scene of intoxication, riots, disturbances, etc'. Evangelical missionaries escaping from threatened violence in Tahiti in 1799, according to Johnson, found in the colony of NSW 'Adultery, Fornication, Theft, Drunkenness, Extortion, Violence and Uncleanness of every kind'.

REMEMBER

These expressions of horror and outrage were generally applied by Evangelicals to the various 'unclaimed' parts of England itself — whether it was the 'debased' aristocrats or the 'lower orders' then chiefly congregating in London. Yes, the people in NSW liked to whore, gamble, swear and drink, often to excess — but that didn't mark them out as particularly different from a lot of people in the Georgian era.

Ruling with Goodhearted Incompetence: Governor Hunter

The Evangelical reverends in NSW were aghast at the lack of morality in the new colony, and all this righteous anger was reported back to William Wilberforce, who was the chief exponent of the Evangelical movement. The reports soon spread, with the Duke of Portland in Whitehall claiming, 'Great evils have arisen from the unrestrained importation of spiritous liquors into our said settlement . . . whereby both the settlers and convicts have been induced to barter and exchange their live stock and other necessary articles for the said spirits to their particular loss and detriment'. In response, the next governor, John Hunter, arrived in NSW in 1795 with clear instructions from the Duke: Clean the place up.

Yet on his arrival in the settlement, Hunter — himself a deeply religious Christian and sympathetic to the Evangelicals — raved about the place. Having been in NSW with Governor Phillip at the beginning of white settlement, he was staggered that so much progress had been made in so little time.

IN THEIR WORDS

Hunter wrote to the Duke of Portland in London describing the 'very great success' that individual farmers had had in growing grain and breeding livestock. True, Hunter conceded a little reluctantly, it was self-interest rather than the public good that motivated everyone. Yet 'it certainly succeeds better with them than in the hands of Government'. And he also approved of the rum incentive payments — initially, at least. 'Much work will be done by labourers, artificers and others for a small reward in this article, and (without any injury to health) which money could not purchase.'

But Hunter was pretty lazy when it came to governing this newly productive colony. During his time as governor, Hunter failed to

>> Manage the emerging trade and import market in the new colony

>> Ensure the newly established government store was restocked after initial supplies sold out

>> Control the distribution of land according to a well thought out plan — or any plan

However, Hunter's lack of attention to detail actually had some positive effects for the colony.

Ending the trading monopoly game

When the administration of the new colony was in the hands of the NSW Corps, the officers in the Corps set up trading monopolies over all imported goods. On his arrival, Hunter made no attempt to control or manage the emerging trade, and issued no rulings on whether the monopolies should be broken or maintained.

However, failing to control trade actually had the positive effect of allowing the market to open up. The monopoly was broken not by a governor, nor an order issued from London, but by convicts and common soldiers made good — convicts and soldiers put in place, moreover, by the officers themselves.

Because the officers prized so highly their status as 'gentlemen', they couldn't be seen to be involved in trade, so they put their underlings and go-betweens in the cockpit. Convict servants and soldier privates didn't take long to corner the market for themselves, quickly proving they were more than savvy enough to strike their own deals with ships' captains once they'd built up enough capital to do so. They and newly arrived entrepreneurs from British India undercut the officers — who were furious, but couldn't do much about it. (They'd started falling out among themselves by this stage, anyway.) The NSW Corps officers started getting out of the trading game, including the grog trade, and concentrated instead on developing their landed holdings.

The rum monopoly was over. Yet no-one had told the powerful men in England that.

A government store with empty shelves

Skyrocketing inflation caused by the officers' monopoly on imported goods (refer to preceding section) could have been mediated when Hunter established a government store, which provided farmers and others with reasonable prices for essential items ordered in from Britain, such as clothes, spirits, tea, tobacco and sugar.

But once the store ran out of its initial supplies, Hunter neglected to re-stock. Being unable to foresee that you'd need to order regular consignments of merchandise that were being widely used by the mass of the rural population is a telling failure.

Handing out land higgledy-piggledy

Phillip, who didn't think much of convicts as settlers, had fairly strictly separated the areas where convicts, ex-convicts and free settlers would be given land to settle, and Grose and Paterson (as heads of the NSW Corps) had largely followed this process. Yet Hunter, through his negligence, shook up the established pattern of giving out land grants. Hunter didn't follow any fixed rule when distributing grants — he just assigned grants higgledy-piggledy.

This alteration had profound consequences. NSW society became increasingly homogenous (if not harmonious); the free and unfree and ex-unfree-but-now-free all mixed together to a remarkable degree. Completely by laxness and accident, the NSW populace became tightly knit. The colony seethed with the feuds, fights and factions common to all small outposts, but avoided any type of segregation or caste alignment, which turned out to be a very good thing indeed and became a defining feature of Australian society.

CRIMINALS OF GREAT ENTERPRISE

Young convicts coming to the new settlement in NSW found plenty of opportunities to make good. Often illiterate, without any great training or skills — beyond a sharp eye for the main chance, which had got them into trouble in the first place — individual convicts with enough luck, initiative and sheer hustling ambition began making their way up the colonial ladder, setting up lucrative businesses even as they were still serving their sentences. Here are two good examples.

Aged 19, Simeon Lord had been sentenced to seven years transportation for theft in Manchester in 1790. He'd been lucky not to be hanged, because the jury had deliberately underestimated the worth of the goods — 100 hundred yards (91 metres) of muslin and the same amount of calico was worth far more than the 10 pence it was valued at, but juries preferred to have a person transported rather than executed for such crimes. Getting to Sydney on the Third Fleet, he was assigned as servant to Officer Thomas Rowley, who obviously spotted a lad with sharpness about him and set him up as his retail frontman. Lord proved so valuable that when he was emancipated — sooner rather than later — Rowley set him up as a licensed victualler (supplier of goods) and baker. Officers purchased large amounts of cargos of merchandise and put it all in Lord's hands to sell on commission, both wholesale and retail. Ship captains also found him useful, especially when they found out how much profit the officers were making off the imported goods. They started to bypass the officers and sell their goods by auction. Lord was the auctioneer, took 5 per cent for selling the cargo and collecting the bills, and built a huge warehouse on the site of Macquarie Place — and began making a killing selling from there. By 1806, Lord had a house bigger and more luxurious than the Governor's residence, had bought ships and was trading with India, China, England, New Zealand and the Cape of South Africa.

Henry Kable was an illiterate man who arrived, aged 25, with his soon-to-be wife, Susannah Holmes, on the First Fleet. Phillip made him one of the constables of the early settlement. Soon he was running the gaol and selling liquor at steep prices to the drunks and malefactors that he locked up. In 1794 he was granted 30 acres at Petersham, and in 1799 he was appointed chief constable of the colony. Demoted for illegally importing pigs in 1802, his trading went on from strength to strength. In the early 1800s he became heavily involved in the new sealing industry, turning the sealskins into leather boots and shoes in a Sydney manufactory, and exporting sealskins to first Canton and Calcutta, and then London. By 1806 he employed five convicts, held 215 acres, and owned 10 horses and numerous cattle and sheep.

Hunter's wheels fall off

John Hunter, originally so enthused, found his inspiration waning as he became embroiled in a power struggle with the hustler-in-chief of the officers of the NSW Corps, John Macarthur.

HISTORICAL ROOTS

Having arrived in 1790 with a young family as part of the main body of the NSW Corps on the notorious Second Fleet, and highly ambitious with it, John Macarthur did much of the work under Grose, and later Paterson, to expand cultivation and make things highly lucrative for the officer cartel. Stationed at Parramatta in the rural hinterland, he had repeated run-ins with Reverend Marsden on policing convicts' morality and other matters of order, decorum and discipline, and they cordially despised each other.

When Hunter first arrived on the scene he had been highly impressed with Macarthur's capacities, but as time went on his doubts began to grow. Macarthur was an individual who was so intensely driven as to occasionally border on the sociopathic. He had a tendency to take any snub or rebuff as a good excuse to launch furious vendettas. He did exactly this when Hunter questioned some of his practices. Hunter and the NSW officers (the ones who sided with Macarthur at least — others continued to remain very close to Hunter) were soon at each other's throats.

Hunter looked around for allies and found that the angry Evangelicals, Johnson and Marsden, were ready to step into the new feud. Hunter invited them to send examples of monstrous excess that the NSW Corps officers' regime had committed to the Colonial Office. The reverends were more than happy to oblige. More outraged reports about the corrupt, debased and much abused state of the colony of NSW followed.

In 1800, Hunter was recalled to Britain in mild ignominy — his administration had proved largely inept. Worst of all, he hadn't cut expenses. Getting approval from the reverends didn't alter the impression of a governor with no real control and with many of the NSW officers against him.

King Came, King Saw, King Conquered — Kind Of

In 1800, Hunter was replaced by Philip Gidley King, who swept a new broom through some of the colony's more rank practices. He tried to make trade and production more diversified, hoping the colony itself would provide the market for the more varied products that would be produced. Less successfully, he also tried to end the rum trade.

Vigorous cost-cutting measures were also the orders of his day, so King introduced a system whereby some convicts were granted conditional freedom on arrival if they had the skills, capital or connections to ensure they could support themselves.

Diversifying trade and production

Like Hunter, King was a veteran of the First Fleet, and so had burned on his memory the original hardships and squalor of the foundation years. He arrived with one very strong official injunction — Cut Down Costs. The colony, said the Colonial Office (and this is only slightly paraphrased), is costing a bomb. Do something about it.

Which King did. For a start, he stopped assigning so many convicts as free labour to private farmers. He also re-established public farms so he was no longer forced to purchase foodstuffs to feed those convicts still being kept by the government.

King attacked inflation and the ruinously high prices being charged in the colony by effectively managing the government store. King developed the government store into a real alternative to the stores run by the emancipist (ex-convict) traders, some of who were charging frankly extortionate prices. King's attack on inflation was also helped by a glut of incoming commodities and imports. Prices dropped naturally, but at least he was putting in place structures that could permanently assist the settlers.

King also vigorously championed a more diversified economic life in the colony, figuring that if everyone was a simple small-scale farmer (as Britain's original plan had it), there'd be no-one to buy the surplus crops that the farmers produced.

Having people involved in a range of different industries actually helped those tilling the soil, because they provided a market for what the farmers grew. Not rocket science maybe, but a bit of a conceptual breakthrough. King encouraged entrepreneurs to set up local manufactures, and to further explore trading possibilities in the Pacific region.

LIFE DOWN UNDER

King, a keen fan of economist and philosopher Adam Smith's writings about free trade and enterprise, encouraged the development of new industries wherever they looked like becoming profitable. Under his watch, trade with the South Pacific — in pork, sandalwood, and the occasional human head — all flourished, even though King was also tasked with enforcing the East India Company's trade monopoly, and countering the highly devious and admittedly quite brilliant ruses employed by the mostly ex-convict businessmen to get around these regulations. King also did much to ensure the whaling grounds near Port Jackson (which American boats were discovering and exploiting at the same time) were actively developed, as well as heavy sealing in Bass Strait. Local industries were encouraged as well; weaving, ship building, leather tanning, textile weaving and dying, pottery and glassblowing, as well as the manufacture of shoes, hats, blankets, soap and candles, all expanded dramatically as traders, forced out of the easy profits to be had from selling high-priced imports, began to think more laterally.

Ending the rum trade (well . . . points for trying)

King went into battle against rum importation and trade, but his actions here were mostly counterproductive. He attacked the grog trade by turning away shiploads of spirits and outlawing private distilling. This, contrary to King's expectation, actually made things worse — cutting back on grog allowed in or made locally only drove the price up, and it didn't stop people drinking it. The prohibition also encouraged smuggling in contraband and illicit distilling.

These restrictions meant that if you were a farmer and had, say, a surplus crop of peaches, you weren't allowed to distil them into liquor, but had to throw them away or feed them to the pigs. This was profoundly irritating.

LAYING A CLAIM IN VAN DIEMEN'S LAND

Although Abel Tasman sighted the coast of Tasmania in 1642, he was too modest to call it Tasmania — that name didn't happen until the 1850s. Instead, he called it Van Diemen's Land. He didn't stop for long, though, passing on to other explorations.

British settlement in Van Diemen's Land began in 1803. Governor King of NSW got worried about the continued interest the pesky French seemed to be showing in the region, and sent off a small party to establish a settlement there. The British Government were getting the same idea, and sent out their own settlement party under David Collins. Soon the towns of Hobart and Launceston were established on the south and north coasts of the island, and Collins got to enjoy the unique experience of being largely ignored by both NSW and Britain. Hardly any ships were sent with further supplies and, as with the first years of NSW, starvation threatened. Collins gave many of the convict and other settlers weapons to go off into the ranges and hunt kangaroos to bring back for food. Unsurprisingly, plenty of the armed roo-hunting convicts decided life out beyond the confines of settlement ranging the bush was preferable to starvation with Collins, and didn't come back. They took to raiding huts and isolated farms, and soon enough a new word emerged to describe this phenomenon — bushranging. (You can follow some of the individual bushranging exploits in Van Diemen's Land in Chapter 6.)

Pardoning convicts

King instituted a world first in punishment — he began letting convicts go free, conditionally, before their time had expired. This was the first time that what would become known as parole was experimented with anywhere in the world. In NSW, it was called *ticket of leave*. He also introduced conditional pardons, which were valid in the colony only. King's rationale for initiating these pardons was again illustrative of the chief priority in these early years: Don't worry about reforming the blighters, or punishing them either, just save us some money.

King wanted to get as many convicts off public rations as quickly as possible, and if a convict with skills turned up on the incoming shipload — a carpenter, say, or a builder, or a bookkeeper — or had connections and capital, then King would free him or her with a ticket of leave instantly.

LIFE DOWN UNDER

In the early years of the colony, no-one cared about making sure convicts were actively punished after they were transported — the prevailing view was let them start earning money and look after themselves. The transportation itself, the act of exile, was seen as the major punishment (until word started leaking back to Britain that convicted felons were getting rich and doing what they wanted). As long as the convicts were transported, kept out of the way for the period of their sentence, and didn't cost too much, no-one cared too much about how exactly they spent their time Down Under.

King offered his resignation in 1803 (the stresses of trying to maintain order in an unruly colony seemed to age him considerably) and his resignation was duly accepted.

Fixing up the mess

Thanks to the efforts (and, sometimes, lack of efforts) of various ambitious convicts, the NSW Corps and Governors Hunter and King, the new colony was starting to thrive. However, some of the methods used to create the new productivity had been, let's say, questionable. On top of that, the convict and ex-convict populace seemed to be placing an exceedingly low priority on decency and decorum. Thanks to the outraged Evangelical reverends and missionaries based in NSW, word had gotten back to Britain about these questionable methods and the unruly state of affairs. No-one was pleased.

The British Government thought they needed a man to set everything — and everyone — straight. Instead, they got someone who quickly set about putting everyone's noses out of joint.

Choosing Bligh for the job

The missionaries had their great patron — William Wilberforce — and he was close to Sir Joseph Banks. Banks was someone who'd long liked to think of himself as the special patron of this colony and the settlement he'd advised (refer to Chapter 3). At the same time, Whitehall was complaining how incredibly expensive this convict colony was still proving to be. They contacted Banks and asked him if he could suggest anyone who might be suitable to go out and bring this colony back into line, destroy this terrible rum monopoly that everyone's talking about, and put some morality back into this depraved sink of fallen humanity.

'Actually, yes', Banks says (or something like it). 'Come to think of it, I've got just the fellow. A naval protégé of mine. Been in some scrapes, got a bad reputation for having crews mutiny on him (happened twice so far, once the infamous *Bounty*, the other time closer to home). But for a case like this, it's probably not such a bad thing — he certainly won't stand any nonsense. Fellow by the name of Bligh.'

REMEMBER

Britain had started out with only a vague idea of what sort of shape the colony was going to take. Self-sufficient farming was to be the order of the day for the mass of urban criminals being transported from London.

In sending William Bligh out to Australia, and in instructing him to crack down on various ad hoc practices that had sprung up in the absence of any workable instructions or assistance coming from Britain, the powers that be were working with a set of mistaken assumptions:

>> They didn't expect a society to have so quickly and spontaneously grown out of the dregs that had been deported. But it had.

>> They didn't expect it to be so modern, or so mercantile, or to consist of anything other than convicts and self-sufficient yeoman (peasant-like farmers). But it was and it did.

>> They fully expected it to be a moral cesspit, thanks largely to both ingrained attitudes about the moral depravity of the criminal underclass, and to the bad press the colony had been given by the Evangelicals — Reverends Johnson and Marsden, and missionaries who'd arrived in NSW in the 1790s. But it wasn't.

Bligh gets down to business

In came Bligh. He knew he'd been chosen by Sir Joseph Banks as the man to bring an unruly and disobedient colony back into line, and that if some serious kicking of heads was in order, those back in the Colonial Office would be fine with that.

Bligh arrived in the colony in 1806 with a very set idea of the sort of place NSW should be. The original vague idea of convicts becoming a self-sufficient rural peasantry had stuck fast in his mind. The problem, however, was that it had never been like that, and it was never going to be like that. By trying to force NSW to revert to a kind of pre-modern self-subsistence economy and society, rather than assist it in its continued adjustment to the mercantile and commercial realities it was part of in the early 19th century, Bligh was trying to force back the tide. The place was not, and never had been, what these original government orders had told it to be. The place, as one historian put it, was 'born modern'.

Bligh was not the sort of individual to be disconcerted when reality didn't conform to what he insisted it ought to be. To his grim satisfaction, he found no shortage of felons and ex-felons on the make, with men and women (both free and unfree) involved in 'dubious' enterprises such as trading and buying and selling. So Bligh got to work.

One of main problems Bligh focused on was the favourite form of incentive payment and extra wage: Rum. He attacked the distillation and rum retailing industry, which the officers had already left and was by this time dominated by soldiers and ex-convicts. The inhabitants of Sydney, who at this point made up more than half of NSW's total population, were livid; the main populace, made up of convicts, ex-convicts and soldiers, particularly so.

Not content, Bligh then went further. He declared that some who had leases and property rights in the township would have to be evicted to fit in with his new town plans. At the same time, Bligh made it clear that he despised the NSW Corps soldiers, claiming they were no better than the convicts and, because many of them were ex-convicts themselves, couldn't be trusted. Then he finished it nicely by calling them 'wretches', 'tremendous buggers' and 'villains'.

Removing rum as payment

Bligh began by outlawing the use of both rum and promissory notes as mediums of exchange. Rum was still the usual form of payment for many workers and traders. Promissory notes were IOUs that passed from one hand to another and could be traded in and redeemed by the individuals who had first released them.

Both rum payments and notes of exchange had sprung up because Britain had failed to provide the colony with any form of currency in the first place. (After all, why should convicts living as happy self-supporting peasants need something so complicated as money?) These became the common mode of making exchanges and payments throughout the colony.

If rum and promissory notes could be replaced as forms of exchange, well and good, but Bligh didn't replace them, he just outlawed them. No established business owner in the colony could do business without these forms of pseudo-currency. Without them, the wheels of commerce and daily life would grind to a halt.

Quashing all dissension and threatening eviction

When three ex-convict entrepreneurs (Lord, Kable and James Underwood) sent Bligh a (relatively mild) protest letter, he jailed them. Bligh declared the letter insulting.

Then Bligh started threatening Sydney residents with eviction, because he wished to do with the town layout what he was trying to do with the economy — push it back to Phillip's period. Bligh didn't like the colonial mess he was being confronted with, and he certainly didn't like the sprawling, mercantile shanty metropolis of Sydney that had just grown up without, as he put it, 'any particular design'.

HISTORICAL ROOTS

The mess that was Sydney was actually the source of the colony's greatest strength. No strictly military area of the settlement, no ex-convicts ghetto and no free settlers area existed, and only one convict jail to restrict convicts to was established. On the land and in the town, convicts lived with settlers, both free and emancipated.

Bligh launched a campaign against colonial disorder. He had 'plans which I had formed for the improvement of the town', and put the fear in people badly by telling them colonial leases may have no legal meaning.

IN THEIR WORDS

In trying to implement his reforms, Bligh wasn't helped by his own language and demeanour. He reacted badly to being questioned or disagreed with. When someone brought up the laws of England, he exploded: 'Damn your laws of England! Don't talk to me of your laws of England: I will make laws for this colony, and every wretch of you . . . shall be governed by them; or there [pointing to the jail] is your habitation!'

Bligh's end

It's hard to find a historian who doesn't take sides on Bligh, on whether he was either:

>> A noble but misunderstood, valiant governor trying his best to get rid of that pernicious officer trade cartel, and help out the little guy

>> A serial buffoon given to violent threats and outbursts who managed the almost impossible — uniting all the warring factions and overcoming the seething animosities that Sydney was riven with, by bringing everyone (soldiers, ex-cons, officers, traders, house owners and renters) together against him

Either way, it's impossible to ignore the one really big event of his tenure, and the only violent overthrow of established government in Australia's history — known (since the 1850s) as the Rum Rebellion.

Soldiers and common populace join forces

The 20th anniversary of NSW's first settlement (26 January 1808) saw the majority of the population uniting as one — to arrest their own governor! At the desperate urging of ex-officer John Macarthur (who had just escaped from being jailed by Bligh), Major George Johnston led his detachment of the NSW Corps to Government House where Bligh lived. After a few hours of searching and ransacking the house high and low, the marines found and arrested Bligh.

That night bonfires were lit, people got drunk and it was difficult to find anyone in Sydney who didn't think that the arrest of the blustering, unpredictable governor was a very good idea indeed. And if they didn't like the idea, they (understandably) stayed fairly quiet.

Most historians will tell you that the arrest of Bligh by the NSW Corps was all about the big players — bold, bad Bligh versus Macarthur. And so on. Some have described Johnston as a 'puppet' of Macarthur who did his bidding in arresting Bligh.

But the real cause of the Rum Rebellion is to be found in the fact that the ordinary soldiers and common people of Sydney had become utterly meshed with each other, to the extent that the soldiers couldn't be relied upon to do the Governor's bidding. In a functional sense they formed a common interest.

If Johnston was a puppet it wasn't of Macarthur, but of the common soldiers and ordinary populace.

LIFE DOWN
UNDER

The soldiers who deposed Bligh were in day-to-day life practically indistinguishable from the ex-convicts in both social and economic background. Most of them had been in NSW since the early 1790s. They had married or entered into de facto relationships with convict women, had children, set up businesses and established farms. The NSW Corps had 'gone native' in the 18 years or so since its first formation and arrival. The Corps was no longer a reliable arm of the Crown and could no longer be trusted to impose the British Government's will on the local population.

Major George Johnston, at his trial for mutiny in England three years later, explained how the NSW Corps was inextricably involved with the people of Sydney: 'The soldiers are not at Sydney kept in a state of separation from the people, but mix, marry and live among them, and are in all respects identified with them. They hear their grievances, and would with infinite difficulty, if at all, in a matter of great public concern, be brought to act against them'.

Sorting out fact from legend

The name 'Rum Rebellion' actually does more to confuse than clarify understanding of what actually happened. Rum had little to do with it, and the notorious 'rum monopoly' that the officers of the NSW Corps had established in the colony had been dismantled ten years previously (refer to the section 'Ending the trading monopoly game' earlier in this chapter for more on this).

And neither was the disturbance a rebellion, or mutiny, even though that's what the British Government decided to call it when they put Johnston, one of the rebellion's leaders, on trial for mutiny. Rather, it was a revolt, supported by almost the entire township of Sydney — soldiers, convicts, ex-convicts alike — by those down on the low rungs of the social ladder as well as just about all the established entrepreneurs and businesspeople in the colony who weren't working for Bligh directly as officials.

Chapter **5**

A Nation of Second Chances

Within 20 years of the establishment of NSW as a colony, it had become a place of second chances — a place where people who had made a mess of their lives in Britain could wipe the slate clean and start again. For convicts, this was the reality of the colonial world that they'd been living in almost since 1788 — ever since the first few nightmarish starvation years — but this wasn't what the Colonial Office, and most of the powerful people in Britain, wanted the colony to be.

The Colonial Office sent out a series of governors (such as Governor Bligh) to try to fix up the mess, but it didn't end well for any of them — particularly Bligh, who ended up being arrested by the NSW Corps (refer to Chapter 4).

After the Bligh fiasco, the Colonial Office figured they had a troublesome colony on their hands — after all, you don't arrest the governor unless you're a rag-tag rebellious lot, right? So the next governor to arrive — Lachlan Macquarie, veteran of the American War of Independence and various skirmishes in India — was told to expect a colony gone wild, full of rapacious profiteers, angry and drunken ex-cons, and a place ripe for rebellion. Macquarie's instructions were to quickly restore some order.

But something strange happened when Macquarie turned up in NSW in 1810: He liked what he saw. Then, to top it off, he went rogue. Macquarie wasn't particularly interested in punishing convicts, or in making the place so brutal that it scared Britain's would-be crims into behaving themselves. He embraced the fact that the colony gave convicts a second chance and made it official policy to reward people who had turned their lives around. If they succeeded and became prosperous, influential or simply useful, Macquarie wanted to know them. This was in complete opposition to what the Colonial Office believed official policy should be.

In the end a stern-faced commissioner was sent out from England to inquire into Macquarie's rule, and it was found wanting. Macquarie returned to Britain and died a few years later, bitter and unappreciated. But in Australia the mark he left was deep. He ruled New South Wales for 11 years — from 1810 to 1821 — and when they buried him they inscribed his tombstone with the words, 'Father of Australia'. The colony was already a nation of second chances before Macquarie arrived. But he was the first governor to try to make it official.

In this chapter, I cover the wide-ranging effects of Macarthur's rule, and the outside forces (and one Commissioner Bigge) that brought him down.

Macquarie's Brave New World

Governors in this period of British colonial rule generally turned up at the various tin-pot little outposts they'd been assigned to, imposed His Majesty's will as much as they reasonably could, then got out (with hopefully a promotion), and headed off to the next assignment. The list of governors who began to identify with the interests of the colonists, against the British Government's orders, is about as short as your little finger. Shorter even.

To start with, Macquarie seemed to have had no intention of varying this pattern. Having spent 30 years with the military, and seen postings that took him from New York and Charleston in the American Revolution through Jamaica to various battles and cities in India, his chief concern when being assigned to NSW was that such a distant and unimportant posting would mean he'd be overlooked for any upcoming promotions. But then, after arriving, the bizarre happened. He fell in love with the place, with the new kind of world that people were making in NSW.

Converting Macquarie

After Bligh, and because of the bad press circulating from various disgruntled Evangelical Christians and people of influence (refer to Chapter 4), Macquarie arrived in NSW fully expecting a crime-ridden, chronically inebriated nightmare hellhole. Instead, he found a social experiment that had been bubbling along for some 20 years. Starting out with the maligned 'dregs' of British society, the unplanned experiment seemed to show that if you took even criminals and misfits and gave them

>> A chance to start again

>> In a new place entirely

>> With plenty of chances to get ahead

Lo and behold, people often did succeed.

LIFE DOWN UNDER

Since 1788, the feckless, the jobless, the impulsive and just plain foolish, not to mention the cunning and nasty, had been extracted from their usual habitations and haunts and used to begin a new society. Remarkably quickly, they filled out practically all the social and economic niches of 18th-century Britain that were available for the taking in a new world. By the time Macquarie arrived, ex-convicts were landholders, farmers, traders, tradesmen, retailers, ship owners, manufacturers and professionals such as doctors and lawyers.

IN THEIR WORDS

One ship's captain, reporting back to Sir Joseph Banks with some contempt on the improved situations of two ex-convict businessmen, stated: 'I am informed they each have handsome houses at Sydney, keep their gig [carriage], with saddle horses for themselves and friends, have two sorts of Wine, and that of the best quality on their Tables at Dinner . . .' Banks may have despised this but Macquarie thought it was wonderful.

As well as the very successful, there was everyone else — the skilled and unskilled labourers, the servants, the publicans and innkeepers, the dozens of professionals, clerks and administrators, the jailers and constables. Many of them, from top to bottom, were the classic 'lower orders', who in Britain had comprised the bulk of the soldiers and the criminal classes. Out here in the colony, they were filling practically every social role and occupation (including, of course, the drunks and repeat offenders — but these hard cases Macquarie didn't mention quite so often). All in all, the social and economic world of Sydney and its hinterland, and soon enough in Van Diemen's Land also, was starting to take robust shape.

Macquarie's stroke of genius was to recognise this world order and seize upon it — not try to turn it back to what the original planners or current ministers in London expected, insisted or wanted it to be. Instead, he chose to fast-track it. He recognised the positive outcomes of this (accidental) social experiment, and began to champion it.

HISTORICAL ROOTS

Early on in his governorship, Macquarie decided that the convicts, ex-convicts and others who were making a go of it in NSW weren't the problem — they were the purpose of the place. Rather than treat the colony as simply an outpost of Britain's imperial will, he began to see it from the convicted criminals' point of view. The colony was a land of opportunity for the people living there, and it should be governed with their interests in mind. With a policy of part goodhearted benevolent patron, part authoritarian despot, he endeavoured to make sure that generations of convicts' descendants who came afterwards would remember him warmly.

This went against express instructions from the Colonial Office and general British opinion.

Living under the Macquarie regime

Macquarie believed in giving ex-convicts 'every equality', which he started pushing for in his official correspondence from quite early on. He gathered successful ex-convicts around him and gave them prominent positions, making them magistrates, police superintendents, surveyors and architects — and even making one a poet laureate. They were all warmly welcomed into 'society', invited by the Governor and his wife to receptions and dinners at Government House.

Macquarie also believed in treating newly arrived convicts as if their slate was cleaned of past behaviour. In this he was helped by the fact that, like previous governors, he had precious little information about the crime or character of those getting off the boat: A note about the sentence, a behaviour report from the hulk he or she had been transported from, and that was about it. This bureaucratic inoperativeness worked in Macquarie's favour. The way he saw it, things started over when you arrived as a convict in Australia. Your behaviour, your diligence and (most of all) your usefulness was what counted most. The chance for convicts to start again was the priority.

FLINDERS GOES INVESTIGATING AND FINDS THE NAME AUSTRALIA

In 1803 the explorer Matthew Flinders circumnavigated the Australian continent in the *Investigator*. The only thing was the continent wasn't called Australia. The western side of the continent had been named New Holland in the 17th century (which you can read more about in Chapter 2), while the eastern side of the continent was named New South Wales by Captain Cook after he'd sailed up along it in 1770 (refer to Chapter 3). Now that Flinders had gone around charting every nook and cranny of the continent, people could say for sure that no gulf or strait separated the two.

But what to call it? Flinders quite liked the Latin name that had been used in ancient Rome — *Terra Australis*, or 'southern land'. But the Latin seemed a bit old fashioned. So he changed it to Australia. Not everyone liked it — Sir Joseph Banks (the botanist on Cook's voyage and powerful patron of the settlement thereafter), for instance, thought it sounded terrible. So strongly did people not like it that when Flinders published his book in 1814 (just before he died), it was titled *A Voyage to Terra Australis*, rather than *A Voyage to Australia*. But in the intervening decade (between Flinders circumnavigating the continent and publishing his book) the name Australia had begun to stick with ordinary people living in the colony of NSW. Macquarie liked it, and in 1817 he formally requested that the name be used in dispatches and official correspondence. The Governor who came after Macquarie, Thomas Brisbane, liked the name so much that he called his daughter Eleanor Australia.

Macquarie's Main Points of Attack

Macquarie wasn't content with just occupying the colony — he wanted to push outward past and through previously impassable geographic barriers (like, say, the Blue Mountains; see the sidebar 'Getting through the Blue Mountains blues').

Macquarie also wanted to put Indigenous relations on a better footing. Macquarie figured that if he could act like an all-powerful chief with white colonists, he could act like a benevolent chief with the local Aboriginal people as well. The idea of having annual tribal gatherings, where he dispensed gifts and authority, and opening a school for Aboriginal children to be taught reading, writing and the various skills of European civilisation, appealed to him a great deal.

When it came to the convicts, while Macquarie was surprised and pleased at how successful convicts had become (refer to the preceding section), he also wanted them to behave in a more orderly, less raucous fashion. He did his best to make this a reality too.

Pushing expansion

Macquarie was keen to get the colony of NSW moving even faster, pushing the expansion of both settlement and the economy. Declaring new townships at the drop of hat, he was also big on road construction and public buildings. This was the Macquarie vision: To not simply cut costs and keep things quiet, but to build the place up.

Expanding settlement

Macquarie encouraged expansion of settlement by establishing new peripheral settlements in the colony, such as Windsor, Wilberforce and Liverpool. But the biggest challenge to expansion was the Blue Mountains, which essentially lay in a ring around the settlement. Various attempts had been made to penetrate the forbidding range since the first few months of the First Fleet's arrival at Port Jackson, but so far none had been successful. The arable land available in the settlement was by now nearing exhaustion and Sydney was in danger of becoming a permanent 'limpet port' — a small-scale settlement that clung to the side of an unknown continent, depending solely on its maritime flow, ready for abandonment if and when the British Government decided to give up the project as a bad exercise. People didn't even know what lay on the other side of the mountains. Desert? An inland sea? Or, as some convicts continued to believe, China?

HISTORICAL ROOTS

In June 1813, three settlers — Gregory Blaxland, William Lawson and William Wentworth — and their convict servants finally found a way over the Blue Mountains, discovering enough grassland on the other side to 'feed all the stock in the colony for thirty years'. Macquarie sent his surveyor, George Evans, to investigate and Evans returned greatly impressed with what he had found: 'I cannot speak too much of the country. The increase of stock for some 100 years cannot overrun it'.

A new vista of what Australia might become opened up, and Macquarie set to work building a road out along the route through the mountains and proclaimed a new township — Bathurst.

GETTING THROUGH THE BLUE MOUNTAINS BLUES

For the first 25 years of white settlement, the Blue Mountains were a big problem. They formed a ring around the NSW settlements at Sydney, Parramatta and on the Hawkesbury River. If a way wasn't found through the mountains, the colony would never reach its full potential.

The Blue Mountains weren't like the regular 'ordinary' mountains the European settlers were used to. In order to cross European mountains, you found the valleys that went between the peaks and followed them. But this wouldn't work with the Blue Mountains because their geological formation had been completely different. Rather than being peaks of land that had been thrust up by subterranean forces, the Blue Mountains formed part of a range that had originally been a plateau. Formed from sandstone rock, countless aeons had worn down most of the plateau, forming gorges and gaps between other parts that had retained their height. This meant that if you followed the valleys you wouldn't go between the peaks, but would just find yourself running into walls and dead ends.

Between 1793 and 1804, numerous attempts were made to cross the Blue Mountains, with no success. The attempt in 1804 was made by George Cayley, a young protégé of Sir Joseph Banks (refer to Chapter 3 for more on this rich botanist who had fingers in just about every Australian pie). Cayley reported back to the governor at the time, Governor King, that it was useless to try to cross such a 'confused and barren assemblage of mountains'.

King agreed with Cayley. Moreover, he was worried about the rumours that kept inspiring convicts to run away: The distant view of the purple-blue mountains (which, of course, is how they got their name) was so inviting that convicts kept running away, believing that on the other side was a land where everything was perfectly lovely. King said this was stupid, and forbade people to try any further mountain crossings. And there, for the next ten years or so, is where the matter rested.

However, in 1813, Governor Macquarie, who liked the idea of pushing the settlement outward, hopefully discovering more fertile land and finding new outlets for the increasing population, encouraged a new attempt. Gregory Blaxland, a gentleman settler, William Wentworth, native-born youth, and Lieutenant Lawson set off from near Penrith. They tried a different strategy to the other explorers — rather than follow the valleys and try to hoist themselves over the ridges, they climbed up onto a ridge and kept following it. This way they got past and through the mountains, and happily reported on the fertile land on the other side.

The group hadn't actually managed to get all the way through the bigger Great Dividing Range — that happened a year later with surveyor G W Evans — but they penetrated far enough to show how it could be done, and got a fair share of public acclaim for doing it. Finally, the colony could begin to properly expand into the Australian continent.

Expanding the economy

Massive economic expansion went with settlement expansion, as Macquarie ordered the building of roads, public buildings and even parks to be commenced.

Shortly after arriving in the colony, Macquarie wrote to Britain, asking for more convicts to be sent out. Previous governors had asked for specific trades (for example, 'Send more carpenters!') but Macquarie was the first to ask for more, full stop, arguing, 'The prosperity of the Country depends on their numbers'. He also abandoned government farming, thinking economic improvement was more likely with private settlers. (He would be forced to bring government farming back later in his administration, due to circumstances outside his control; see 'Coping with the deluge following Waterloo' later in this chapter.)

Under this scheme of rapid economic expansion, the skilled manual labourers — masons, builders, blacksmiths, sawyers, splitters, fencers and carpenters — continued to be the worker 'aristocracy', earning exceedingly good wages. The unskilled variously became house servants, wharfies, quarry-workers, farmhands, assistants in offices and warehouses, or workers in the small manufacturing workshops that were proliferating.

Conciliating (and pursuing) Indigenous Australians

Macquarie was keen to make his mark with the Aboriginal community as well.

In October 1814, Macquarie wrote to Lord Bathurst in the Colonial Office, suggesting an Aboriginal school be established in Parramatta as part of an endeavour to win the hearts and minds of the younger Aboriginal generation, and to persuade the parents to allow their children to learn some of the European ways, of cultivation, literacy and sedentary 'civilised' society. On receiving Bathurst's approval, the school was soon in place. (Parents, however, removed children from the school after they realised its aim was to distance the children from their culture and families.)

Macquarie's attempt to conciliate Aboriginal peoples was also manifested a few months later, when he held the first of what would become an annual 'gathering of tribes' in Parramatta. Here, Macquarie played the 'big chief' (he fancied himself as a bit of a Scottish Highland chieftain), handing out gifts and good humour to Indigenous Australians who travelled up to three hundred kilometres to attend the gathering.

Macquarie wanted all those beneath him to prosper — both convicts and Aboriginal people — as long as they acknowledged they were beneath him in rank and authority. Macquarie wasted little time mounting punitive military expeditions when some Aboriginals seemed set to continue their 'perverse' hostility to his good intentions and the settlement at large. In 1816, after Aboriginal attacks on farms on the outskirts of the Sydney settlement, Governor Macquarie sent a party to arrest the offenders. This resulted in an attack on an Aboriginal camp at Appin, and the killing of 14 Aboriginal people, none of them known to have been involved in the initial incident.

Macquarie declared individual Aboriginals as wanted outlaws when whites and blacks clashed, and declared martial law on both Aboriginals and bushrangers when needed in regions where conflict was most rife.

Re-ordering a town, re-ordering convict behaviour

Macquarie may have been impressed with the industry evident in the new colony of NSW, but he still believed things should be done in a certain (ordered and moral) way. Although not really in the way instructed by the Colonial Office, Macquarie did introduce some order to the settlement.

Introducing order to Sydney's layout

Macquarie proved himself different from the previous governor (Governor Bligh) when he was able to refashion the town of Sydney without residents threatening him with revolution. Unlike Bligh, who called into question ordinary people's property rights and threatened them with summary eviction (refer to Chapter 4), Macquarie was able to impose change in a way that seemed orderly rather than arbitrary.

In October 1810, a new town plan was introduced for Sydney, which included new street names, washhouses, widened roads — and the creation of a certain Macquarie Place. A month later, it was announced that a brand new hospital was to be built (for the price of a five-year rum trading monopoly to the three men who promised to build it — pragmatism in action!). A year later further plans were introduced, including a new animal pound and a turnpike on the Parramatta Road. These were followed by a lighthouse on South Head, a new fort, and plenty more churches — with a very large fountain in Sydney topping it all off.

Macquarie ensured that whatever came next in the colony, no-one was going to forget him in a hurry. His mark would be evident everywhere, on maps and on buildings, roads and other structures. As a result, the shanty metropolis began to show a lot more orderliness.

HELLO NSW: CALL ME LACHLAN, AND I'LL CALL EVERYTHING MACQUARIE

Macquarie made a lasting impact on life in Australia — and on maps in Australia. He made sure he was remembered by naming things after himself, and encouraging others (explorers, surveyors, builders and designers) to do the same. Here Macquarie didn't stint.

In Australia today you can find Macquarie

- Lakes
- Rivers
- Lighthouses
- Harbours
- Piers
- Hills
- Fields
- Passes
- Marshes
- Islands
- Pubs

You name it — Macquarie's name will be on it.

Introducing order to the population's behaviour

Macquarie was keen to introduce orderliness to all aspects of colonial life, and so he encouraged the general population to settle down in their behaviour and lives.

Hundreds of men and women were living in 'common-law marriages', or what are known today as de facto relationships (and what shocked Evangelical ministers at the time called the keeping of 'concubines'!). Macquarie tried to get men and women to make it all official, in a church, with the registry. This was part of his plan to make the whole colony more settled, along with his building of churches and encouragement of schools.

Macquarie was also strict in his treatment of convicts. Even though he liked nothing more than helping ex-convicts attain the social prominence that their material wealth and industrious activity had (in his eyes at least) earned them, that didn't mean he thought convicts should be allowed to do whatever they wanted.

In 1814, Macquarie declared sternly that convicts could no longer swap between masters. If a neighbouring settler offered you a better deal, more free time or more pay, tough — you had to stick with the master you'd been assigned to.

Macquarie took his control of convicts further in 1819 when, to groans from convicts all round, the Hyde Parke Barracks opened.

In a pretty clear illustration of the power dynamics in the early colony, Macquarie couldn't just order the convicts into the new barracks. Many convicts would have preferred to continue living wherever they'd already found lodgings — staying with their mates or a nice landlady perhaps. So Macquarie threw a big feast — offering the convicts a party, with plenty of rum — and the convicts fell for it. In they went, with the big door locked behind them.

For those who Macquarie coaxed into the Hyde Parke Barracks, there was no more task work and knocking off when the job was done at about midday. Now work would continue from sunrise to sunset, with two short meal breaks. Finally, 30 years after the so-called prison colony was founded, something resembling a prison to put the convicts in was opened. Convicts were still allowed out on weekends, and they made the most of it — thefts and arrests for drunkenness rose steeply at the end of each week.

Becoming a Governor Ahead of His Time

Macquarie may have said that he only wanted to let ex-convicts be readmitted to their previous rank in society, but everyone could see it was much more than that. To Macquarie, your previous 'rank' in the British social hierarchy didn't matter. If you made a great success of yourself and your operations in NSW, Macquarie welcomed you. This would cause problems for Macquarie among the 'Exclusives' within the new colony and, eventually, with the Colonial Office in Britain.

Stirring up trouble with the free folk

Most of those who'd arrived free in the colony mingled, cohabited and married with the convicts and ex-convicts without any real worries. But a small minority (there's always some . . .) went out of their way to hold themselves aloof and 'exclusive' (which became their nickname) whenever possible.

The *Exclusives* were a small group of free colonists who had kept themselves separate from close social involvement with the convicts and the emancipated. They were a handful of families who, although themselves from generally humble or low-class backgrounds, had made it very rich in the colony. But while they had all had close business involvement with convicts and ex-convicts (it was impossible to get anything done otherwise), they had made sure to marry and socialise with those others who had no taint of past criminal conviction. This made for very small tea parties, and a great deal of social anxiety.

With the arrival of Macquarie, the Exclusives found themselves dealt a governor who not only insisted on appointing ex-convicts along with Exclusives to positions of responsibility — as magistrates, for example, or as fellow board members on public trusts — but also enjoyed their company so much he invited them to receptions at Government House, to pleasant Sunday dinners and christenings.

This was exciting stuff — for everyone bar the Exclusives. For these people it was frightening. The stigma of coming to a convict colony was bad enough. If word started getting back to Britain that felons and free settlers intermingled easily throughout society, just think of the disgrace! They feared social contamination. And, more than that, they thought, strongly, that if you'd committed a crime and been transported, it just wasn't right that afterwards you'd be treated like everyone else.

Creating outrage back home

The Exclusives in NSW sent impassioned letters about the state of affairs under Macquarie to various people in power and with influence in Britain. And most people in Britain completely shared the Exclusives' attitudes.

HISTORICAL ROOTS

Although Macquarie and people in NSW might have thought it perfectly reasonable that an emancipated convict shouldn't be forever marked, socially and legally, by their previous crime, in Britain it was shocking. There, a person convicted of any of the various larcenies, embezzlements, forgeries or assaults that those transported had committed was ejected forever from respectable society. There could be no coming back. And your legal status was forever altered too — even after serving time, a convicted felon couldn't give evidence in court or hold property.

LIFE DOWN UNDER

In NSW, the economic and legal order would simply collapse under the regimen upheld in Britain — convicts owned more than half the wealth in the colony, frequently used the courts to sue and protect their various rights, and were involved with just about every economic transaction that took place. Different realities had bred different attitudes, which Macquarie discovered and then championed.

While the Exclusives were the singular minority in the colonies, their attitudes reflected what most people thought back home. Members of the British Parliament, and readers of popular periodicals, were duly outraged when they heard and read that a society made up largely of ex-criminals had so lost its sense of respectable decency that ex-thieves not only enjoyed the most luxurious mansions in Sydney town but also served as magistrates and dined regularly with the governor. Had the whole colony gone completely mad?! This was a world too topsy-turvy for good sense.

Big World Changes for Little NSW

Trouble was brewing for Macquarie among the Exclusives in NSW and those in power in Britain. The situation was then made worse by forces largely outside Macquarie's control — in particular, the end of the Napoleonic War.

Coping with the deluge following Waterloo

If Macquarie might have learned a moral from his time in NSW, it might have been a rueful 'Be careful what you wish for'. His request for more convicts to keep the engines of prosperity and growth turning over had been roundly ignored for the first five years of his administration. However, from 1816 it was answered with a deluge to make up for the scarcity of the last 25 years.

HISTORICAL ROOTS

In 1815, the Duke of Wellington combined his British forces with Prussian and other forces at the Battle of Waterloo to defeat Napoleon's French Army and end, finally, the French Revolutionary and Napoleonic Wars. These had been raging, on and off (with more on than off), for some 25 years. Just as an outbreak of peace in the early 1780s led to a rapid rise in crime from returned soldiers and sailors in Britain (refer to Chapter 3) so here, too, the defeat of Napoleon meant 400,000 soldiers found themselves *demobbed* (stood down from their jobs). They returned to a Britain of stagnant economic growth, with few jobs on offer. A dramatic spike in the number of convictions and transportations ensued, as ex-soldiers took to crime.

LIFE DOWN UNDER

Macquarie found himself dealing with three or four times the annual number of convicts that previous administrators had received, while simultaneously being dealt an almost biblical set of ecological catastrophes: Droughts, floods and caterpillars destroyed much of the harvests after 1816. He had little choice but to put most convicts back on the public store (for work on public projects) and re-establish large-scale government farms and projects to soak up the surplus convict labour. The increased expenses charged back to Britain reduced Macquarie's standing with the Colonial Office even further.

TECHNICAL STUFF

Male convicts under government charge tripled between 1817 and 1819, while those in the private sector halved between 1818 and 1820.

Britain starts paying attention again (unfortunately!)

The end of the Napoleonic War meant Britain start paying attention to the penal colony again but, curiously, this wasn't really a good thing. Scrutiny of the far-off colony of NSW started to increase — and for Macquarie, and most of the convicts and ex-convicts in NSW and Van Diemen's Land, this scrutiny didn't bode well.

The extended period of neglect previous to 1815 had proved to be largely benign for most colonial inhabitants. In this initial period, no-one insisted that NSW was meant to function as a place of punishment — it was just a place to get sent off to. Once here, governors were mainly concerned with keeping costs down and were quite happy to give convicts conditional freedom if they could pay their way or had a decent trade that was in demand.

With the end of the wars and the beginning of a long period of peace, Britain began to experience increased economic depression and social turmoil. Increased crime led many to begin asking questions about the current system of crime prevention and punishment. They weren't greatly impressed by the answers.

Bringing back terror

The strange thing about NSW was that it was begun as a place of punishment, yet for many convicts who arrived in the period up to and including Macquarie's rule, it had proved to be a place of freedom and opportunity. Macquarie's idea of a society of second chances (building on the reality he'd found on his arrival and undoubtedly popular in a colony chiefly made up of convicts and ex-convicts) cut less mustard in Britain, where the late 1810s saw greater scrutiny and debate about the nature of life in NSW.

In the House of Commons, a parliamentarian denounced the rule of Macquarie for being both expensive and chronically slack. The story of D'Arcy Wentworth, last seen leaving England after being caught as a highwayman and now the Chief of Police in Sydney, was repeated with anger.

Originally, the general impressions most people in Britain had of NSW and Van Diemen's Land were vague, hazy ones based on the idea of a Botany Bay hellhole. NSW and, later, Van Diemen's Land, were assumed to be places of hard labour, little food 'and constant Superintendence'. This made the place 'an object of peculiar Apprehension'. Now, however, the real stories were getting back — about thieves, pickpockets and highwaymen being freed on arrival and going on to achieve wealth and respectability unlike anything they'd had before.

Earl Bathurst, running the Colonial Office, decided to send out Commissioner John Thomas Bigge, ex-chief justice of Trinidad, to conduct an inquiry into what was really happening in NSW. Bathurst's instructions outlined the problem as he saw it.

Transportation, the second worst punishment aside from execution, was now being explicitly requested by those convicted of even minor crimes. And transportation only worked as a deterrent, clearly, if people didn't want to be sent. Something had to be done to make transportation once again 'an Object of Real Terror to all Classes of the Community'. Bigge's job was to work out what, and how. Bathurst warned him to avoid letting any 'ill considered Compassion for Convicts' lessen transportations main purpose: The all-important 'Salutary Terror' that would keep potential British crims in check.

Big Country? Big Ambitions? Bigge the Inspector? Big Problem!

Commissioner Bigge arrived in Australia in 1819 with a remit to find out all that was necessary to change NSW back into an object of 'Salutary Terror' for would-be crims in Britain. As such, Bigge was always going to clash with Macquarie, who had long decided that the purpose of NSW was not as a stern deterrent against crime in Britain but as an opportunity for convicted felons to start again, in a new land with a clean slate.

The first flashpoint between Bigge and Macquarie took place over Macquarie's promotion of ex-convict William Redfern to magistrate. Macquarie had appointed ex-convicts in previous years, but in those years no other candidates were available for the post. This time, however, other choices were possible, but Macquarie ignored them to give the appointment to a man who many considered to be an old Macquarie favourite.

This, thought Bigge, was insupportable and he gave Macquarie an ominous warning: Giving Redfern the job was a move that the British Government would 'regard as a defiance of their Authority and Commands'. And Governors who defy His Majesty's Authority and Commands tended not to last long in their careers.

IN THEIR WORDS

Macquarie's response was to make a spirited defence not simply of the Redfern appointment (where he probably thought he was on shaky ground anyway), but of his entire policy. He put it to Bigge that when he first arrived in NSW he'd, naturally, had no plans or desires to start raising convicts in society. The only thing he expected to do with convicts was control them. To his surprise, however, 'a short experience showed me . . . that some of the most meritorious men . . . who were the most capable and the most willing to exert themselves in the public service, were men who had been convicts!' And so, he argued, he'd developed a plan to encourage men and women according to merit (and material success) rather than past criminal conviction. The future of the colony, Macquarie told Bigge, was convicts and their children. He then went further, asking Bigge to 'avert the blow you appear to be too much inclined to inflict . . . and let the Souls now in being as well as millions yet unborn, bless the day on which you landed on their shores, and gave them . . . what you so much admire . . . Freedom!'

A little verbose maybe, but Macquarie got his point across. More basically: This country belongs to them; don't take it away. But more than that it was a plea to a man who had more power than any other to shape the future trajectory of the colony to not condemn the social edifice he'd been creating.

IN THEIR WORDS

Bigge's response was as measured and terse as Macquarie's plea was flowery and sentimental. He pointed out he represented not only the 'respectable' opinion in the colony, but also that of the British Government. Bigge said that he was willing to try to 'subdue the objections which must arise in the breast of every man' whenever they were forced to associate with convicts and ex-convicts 'but I also think with Lord Bathurst that this feeling may be carried too far; that there is a very wide difference between indulging a compassionate consideration towards convicts and rewarding them with honours or investing them with Magisterial Trusts'.

And Bathurst, ultimately, did agree with Bigge on Redfern's appointment, saying ex-convicts certainly couldn't be turned into magistrates. And, when Bigge finally published his reports on the colonies of NSW and Van Diemen's Land after he returned to England, it turned out that Bathurst agreed with Bigge on just about everything else as well. (See Chapter 6 for the effects this had on colonial Australia and the system of transportation.)

Recognising Macquarie's Legacy

Macquarie left NSW in 1821, with large crowds lamenting his departure. He endured a cold and hostile reception on his return to Britain, just as the highly critical Bigge Report was published. He died in 1824, feeling bitter, misunderstood and misrepresented. But despite how he came to be viewed by most people in power in Britain, Macquarie created a legacy, something beyond the innumerable Macquarie Streets, Macquarie townships, Macquarie Harbours, and Macquarie Rivers, fields and hills which he so delighted in naming.

Australia was now known as Australia, and it was Macquarie who got the continent's official name changed from New Holland (refer to the sidebar 'Flinders goes investigating and finds the name Australia' for more on this). And for the first time in Australia's history, the man in power decided that this new society was being built not for the officials, the officers or the few free settlers, nor for the

British Government to use as simple dumping ground or receptacle for punishment. Australia was here for the convicts and ex-convicts themselves, their children and descendants.

In the decades that followed Macquarie's rule, a new tone became evident in colonial debate and discussion, as the mass of colonials began loudly declaring: 'This country belongs to us'.

Exactly why Macquarie promoted this idea is hard to say. He was no progressive, wanting to innovate and change society's structures and mores. His actions were the product of no revolutionary new social code or progressive movement. He was a classic, gruff, 18th-century old-style Tory conservative, who believed in hierarchy, obedience, respect and order. He wanted to combine kindness with firmness.

Perhaps the chance to play benevolent patriarch and to preside, Scottish-chieftain-style, over a flourishing and vibrant new colony simply brought out a strong element in his character that had previously not had such scope to express itself. It's not every day you get appointed autocrat over a whole colony, after all. Regardless, because of Macquarie, the sense of Australia began to shift significantly — and it's why he's the only governor or leader from these early years to have inscribed on his grave the epitaph, 'Father of Australia'.

2

1820s to 1900: Wool, Gold, Bust and then Federation

Understand why Britain belatedly tried to introduce more order, efficiency and discipline into the convict system and colonial life in general in the 1820s — and why in the 1840s Britain began getting out of the whole convict thing, and transportation to NSW ended.

Find out more about the newly self-governing Australian colonies hitting the gold jackpot — pulling the colonies out of the chronic slackness of the 1840s global depression, triggering a long boom that lasted more than 30 years, and transforming the shape and nature of colonial society.

Discover how the 1850s to 1880s saw rapid expansion in cities, settlement, exploration, transportation and technology — and a growth in 'larrikinism' and bushranging.

Examine the factors that led to Australia being christened a 'workingman's paradise' — until the boom stopped and, in the new austerity, people started thinking about nationhood.

Chapter **6**

Getting Tough, Making Money and Taking Country

The 1820s and 1830s were a period of massive territorial expansion in European settlement in Australia. Australia's 'fertile crescent' — the stretch of land that goes in a curve from southern Queensland, continues through modern NSW and Victoria, and ends in the region surrounding Adelaide in South Australia — was occupied in this period, changing everything.

Meanwhile a massive penal reform was being implemented by the Governors Ralph Darling in NSW and George Arthur in Van Diemen's Land (modern-day Tasmania). The new instructions from Britain were to get tough and to systematise, and that's exactly what Darling and Arthur set about doing.

By the late 1830s, demand for wool was going through the roof as Britain's industrial revolution kicked into gear, and factories and wool mills began producing commodities at a greater rate and for cheaper prices than had ever been seen before. Australia, with newly opened up grasslands and pasturage, was perfectly placed to take advantage of this. Investors with capital in London, Edinburgh and Manchester began channelling funds into Australian properties.

In this chapter, I cover Britain's attempts to make the punishment of convicts in Australia more systematic and consistent (and more of a punishment). I also look at the impact of the developing wool trade on the riches of the colony and on the settlement of newly 'acquired' land (and British attempts to control this frantic settlement as well).

Revamping the Convict System

In 1819, Earl Bathurst of the Colonial Office in London sent Commissioner John Thomas Bigge (ex-chief justice of Trinidad) to Australia to report on the state of affairs in the Antipodes. By this time, word had made its way back to Britain that life in New South Wales wasn't too bad, and that the new colony could actually be a land of second chances — if you played your (sometimes randomly dealt) cards right. Because of this, convicted criminals began requesting transportation (refer to Chapter 5 for more on this, and for more on Commissioner Bigge's trip Down Under). So, as well as a rundown on what was happening, Bathurst wanted ideas on how to make the punishment of transportation to be a real deterrence again — and Bigge delivered.

**HISTORICAL
ROOTS**

Over the next two decades, a new system was implemented — one that tried to eliminate the perks, inconsistencies and arbitrariness that had been a feature of the previous form of transportation. Being sentenced to transportation would again evoke fear in the hearts of would-be criminals, and the system would have a *system* — convicts would be rewarded for good behaviour and signs of reformation, and punished for further crimes or bad behaviour.

At the Colonial Office, Bathurst also starting offering enticements (in the form of land grants and free convict labour) to free settlers, hoping that an influx of non-convict immigrants would tip the moral scales of the colony into a more 'respectable' tone.

To make sure his new regime was implemented effectively, Bathurst then sent out his enforcers — Governors Darling and Arthur.

Putting the terror back into the system . . . and the system back into the terror

Under Bathurst, and based on Bigge's recommendations, the new priority was ironing out old loopholes, freedoms and indulgences. The hope of easy money and free land should no longer be an enticement to England's criminals.

Bigge and Bathurst's new, more systematic, regime included:

>> **No more special deals for convicts when they arrived, regardless of what sort of work they could do or what sort of connections they had:** This also meant convicts would no longer be automatically assigned to their spouse (if they were already here and being assigned convicts) on arrival.

>> **All convicts to work for no wages.**

>> **Tickets of leave to be given out only after serving a minimum sentence, and only if the convict was well-behaved:** These indulgences (established under Governor King and kind of like instant parole) would no longer be given out to save money, or as a sign of the Governor's favour, but only as a special reward.

>> **When assigning convict labourers to settlers, the new free immigrant arrivals would have priority:** Ex-convicts were no longer considered to be fit 'masters' to oversee the reform of criminals, and convicts being assigned to convicts (on ticket of leave parole) was eliminated completely. (Not using ex-convicts as convict 'masters' proved impossible to implement — too many of the bosses and land owners in the new colony were ex-convicts.)

>> **New hellish punishment places to be created for those who continued to commit crimes after their arrival in Australia:** These included settlements on Moreton Bay, Port Arthur, Macquarie Harbour and Norfolk Island.

Under these changes, transportation became a thing to legitimately fear again.

Bringing in the settlers

During the 1820s, a new emphasis at the Colonial Office was on encouraging wealthy free settlers to emigrate to Australia. This was meant to achieve two things. Firstly, they would help 'grow' the pastoral and agricultural economy, giving NSW an export industry that would help it become less of a drag on the British Treasury. Secondly, they would provide the right 'tone' of respectability to help balance the regrettable low class and unruly nature of NSW society.

**LIFE DOWN
UNDER**

CHAIN GANGS AND FLOGGINGS — WELL, FOR SOME

The popular images that we have today of what the convict system was like — resembling a horrible gulag on the Russian steppes, with convicts herded together, chained up in gangs, and imprisoned in remote and inhospitable locations — result from changes brought in under Darling and Arthur.

The image is nothing like what convict life was actually like under all the previous governors, from Phillip through to Macquarie. Even under the new regime implemented by Darling and Arthur, the majority of convicts never experienced chain gangs or terrible penal settlements. Generally speaking, no more than 20 to 25 per cent of convicts found themselves in road gangs or sent to the hard-core penal settlements. But a minority *did*, and places such as Norfolk Island, Hell's Gates (at Macquarie Harbour), Moreton Bay, Port Arthur and even the whole colony of Van Diemen's Land acquired their ugly reputation during this period, and frequently for good reason. The terrible images of what some experienced during this period have crowded out all other ideas of what convict life was like for most.

Workers would be provided by transportation, but they weren't encouraged to later become established employers or successful businessmen or landowners. The free settlers arriving with ample capital received the lion's share of land grants and the convict labour, rather than the convicts and emancipists (ex-convicts) or their children, who were known as 'the native born'.

Bringing in the enforcers

A lot of Bathurst's changes were first announced while Governor Macquarie's replacement, Thomas Brisbane, was in charge of NSW and Lieutenant-Governor Sorrell was in charge of Van Diemen's Land. But Britain remained unhappy with the convict system — it still wasn't inspiring enough dread. Two tough-minded military officers were chosen to come out as replacements — Ralph Darling for NSW and George Arthur for Van Diemen's Land.

Darling and Arthur had both served in the Napoleonic Wars, and both had proved themselves as not just tough officers but also extremely able administrators — order, efficiency, discipline and a liking for absolute control featured prominently on their respective CVs. Both men took over the changes that had been begun under Brisbane and Sorrell, and quickened the pace, working hard to increase the order and — where they thought necessary — the severity.

Getting Tough Love from Darling

Ralph Darling arrived in Australia in 1825, and he came with the clear idea that a convict colony couldn't expect to be treated like a normal free society. People who still had warm memories of the close paternal involvement taken by Governor Macquarie (and his memory was still toasted at annual dinners to mark first settlement day on 26 January) were in for a rude shock with Darling's manner.

Darling was the new breed of officer. Cold, calm, aloof and rational, he had a strong belief that British colonies should do what they were told. He worked hard at reforming the colony's administration, the allocation of land, the quirky banking, bartering and IOU system (refer to Chapter 4) and, most of all, the convict system.

None of this was easy. Firstly, this was because of practical reasons and constraints — such as administrative positions being staffed by convicts and ex-convicts, with no-one else willing or available to take their place. Secondly, the very entrenched belief in the colony was that this place was here for more than just punishing convicts, and had other ends to serve beyond the wishes of the British Government.

In the new colony, the press had more freedom than the press in Britain (and much more than Darling would like) and weren't afraid to take advantage of this. Darling also had little interest in new requests being put forward by ex-convicts and native-born Australians for a more representative assembly and for trial by jury.

In a word, the colonials were getting uppity again, and Darling had the devil of a time trying to iron it all out.

Running into staffing issues

The practical constraints Darling found himself confronted with arose because, to implement most of the changes he wanted to make to NSW convict society, he had to try to convince the convicts themselves to help him. Before Darling arrived, most of the clerks working in the civil service were convicts. This meant that most of the sensitive administration — noting down how many years a convict still had to serve, for instance, or how much land should be granted to individuals — was in the hands of men whose professional integrity wasn't exactly above reproach.

LIFE DOWN UNDER

Instances of people bribing officials to get a convict's sentence surreptitiously shortened as the paperwork went from hand to filing cabinet occurred so often that by the time Darling arrived standard rates were in place — so much for getting your sentence shortened from life to 14 years, so much for halving it from 14 to 7, and so on.

Darling naturally wanted to eliminate corruption and remove convicts from administrative positions, but then found, to his annoyance, that he couldn't — it wasn't possible to staff the administration with free immigrants only. Convict society was being run by convicts because no-one else was around to do the work. Darling did what he could to change the system but he also had to make do with what he had.

Going head-to-head with the press

When Darling arrived in NSW, he was aghast to find a press operating with greater freedom than in Britain — with convict journos! And ex-convict editors! In a penal colony! This he thought was crazy, especially when two newspapers — *The Australian* and *The Monitor* — began waging pubic campaigns against him, taunting and denouncing him at every opportunity. (See the sidebar 'Two soldiers and the son of a highwayman' for more on *The Australian*'s campaign against Darling, under the editorship of William Wentworth.)

Darling tried to cripple the press by imposing a stamp duty on newspapers through introducing a Newspapers Duty Bill. However, just before he had arrived, a new Legislative Council had been formed, with members to be nominated by the governor to advise him. Darling thought that because he was the governor sent by Britain and those in the Council were only there because they'd been nominated — not elected — they wouldn't oppose him. In other words, he should have a free hand in reshaping NSW, without having to bother unduly about the rule of law. Chief Justice Francis Forbes begged to differ and overturned the bill, describing it as 'an excessive instrument of suppression'. (Forbes was not only NSW's sole judge, but also an official member of the Executive and Legislative Councils, and all colonial legislation had to bear his certificate that it was not 'repugnant' to the laws of England.)

Coming up against calls for representation

Darling's clash with the press was soon used by Wentworth, as editor of *The Australian*, to create wider implications. According to Wentworth and his supporters, not only was Darling an 'unjust, despotic' governor but the whole form of government in the colony was also equally unfair.

TWO SOLDIERS AND THE SON OF A HIGHWAYMAN

A particular thorn in Darling's side was William Wentworth, the son of D'Arcy Wentworth, a doctor with aristocratic relations and a bad habit of paying for gambling debts by moonlighting as a highwayman. D'Arcy arrived on the Second Fleet in 1790, and soon after had a son — William — with a convict woman. William had grown up in the colony without any real awareness of social stigma — plenty of respectable people had children with convict women, and no-one mentioned his father's shady past. Having won plaudits for his part in crossing the Blue Mountains in 1813 (refer to Chapter 5), he went back to England to finish his education and set up as a barrister.

While in London, Wentworth found out about his father's past, and in the most embarrassingly public of fashions. A parliamentarian in the House of Commons, H G Bennett, indulged in a long denunciation of the terrible slackness of Macquarie's administration. As illustration of the madness of Macquarie's policies, Bennett mentioned the fact that a 'notorious' highwayman, D'Arcy Wentworth, was now Chief of Police in Sydney! Wentworth demanded a duel for this calumny (or slander), but then found out that the calumny was true. Others might have been chastened by this humiliating revelation but that wasn't really the Wentworth style. He swore to make such a success of himself and his life, and the country of his birth, that every previous blot or slander would be completely cancelled out.

This, as it turned out, was bad news for Darling. Wentworth arrived back in Australia a confirmed ally of the emancipists, and became one of the leading promoters of the idea of Australia as a country for the convicts and those born in it rather than for the use of Britain. He set up *The Australian* to push this cause as well as promote the interests of the 'native born', the generation of children of convicts who were just arriving at maturity.

Wentworth set out to nail Darling as an arbitrary military despot and, because he wasn't averse to a bit of cheap sensationalism, went further to declare him a cruel and vindictive tyrant. In doing this, a case involving two privates of the 57th Regiment, Joseph Sudds and Patrick Thompson, came in handy. These two had pulled a stunt that spoke volumes about how unterrifying life in NSW was. While stationed in NSW, they committed a robbery hoping to get caught so they could be discharged from the army and could make the most of life in the colony. Their actions seemed to show the opinion of many that (in the words of Chief Justice Forbes) 'the condition of a Convict as superior to that of a soldier . . .'

(continued)

(continued)

For Darling, this seemed to be a pretty clear example of exactly what Bathurst had sent him out to eradicate — the attitude that convict life wasn't that tough. He intervened in the judicial process to sentence Sudds and Thompson to seven years in chains working on the public roads. This he thought would be a lesson not just for them but for any other soldier who might be getting any bright ideas about life in the convict colony.

Unfortunately for Darling (to say nothing of the misfortune for the poor ex-soldier), Sudds was ill, and died five days after the governor's order was put into effect. This, you might think, didn't look good. And you'd be right. Wentworth leapt on it, and used *The Australian* to denounce the governor daily. On top of that, he sent long dispatches back to the Colonial Office demanding the governor's impeachment. All dispatches had to be sent and read by the governor — in this case, Darling, who was surely by now white with rage.

Despite the overturning of the Newspapers Duty Bill (refer to the previous section), the Legislative Council in NSW wasn't much more than a rubber stamp. Wentworth demanded a representative government and the right to trial by jury for everyone, a sentiment shared with varying degrees of enthusiasm by the convict and ex-convict population. This wasn't quite radical democracy — Wentworth blithely assumed that naturally only those with property and wealth should be represented. But it was a lot more than the British Governor or the colonial Exclusives were willing to countenance.

REMEMBER In the early 1820s, the majority of those with wealth and property in Australia were those who had previously been convicts, and the concept of giving them effective power in a colony that the Colonial Office was still trying their best to make terrifyingly severe for would-be crims in Britain wasn't tenable.

Putting it all down to a personality clash

Darling was picked by Bathurst to come out to Australia and be tough, and in this Darling performed exactly as asked. The problem was Bathurst's vision for Australia as punishment and deterrent was at odds with the vision of most of the people living in the colony.

IN THEIR WORDS Darling wrote off his clash with Wentworth: 'As to Young Wentworth, he is a Demagogue . . . a vulgar, ill-bred fellow . . .' But people of import at the Colonial Office were beginning to conclude that at least half the problem might be Darling himself.

As complaints and controversies kept rolling in, James Stephen, the Permanent Under-Secretary in the Colonial Office, concluded that Darling's 'great unpopularity' in the colony had been caused in significant part by 'the exercise of his authority by a severe temper and ungracious manners'. The 'deep-rooted antipathy' towards him meant that no peace could be had 'so long as General Darling is Governor of NSW'. Ominous words.

After a new reformist liberal Whig administration took power in London, Darling, the stern conservative Tory, was recalled to Britain. His recall was put down to 'misunderstandings and dissensions' which had made his tenure in the colony untenable. Darling did his best to take it on the chin.

IN THEIR WORDS

If he'd done wrong, Darling said, then he asked his new boss, Viscount Goderich (Bathurst's replacement at the Colonial Office), to bear in mind the sort of material he'd been forced to work with: 'Habitual Drunkards, filling the most important Offices, Speculators, Bankrupts and Radicals, while I (and I only state the fact) have exerted myself strenuously to promote the views of His Majesty's Government and maintain His Majesty's Authority.' Deep sigh. *However* — 'If it be Your Lordship's will that I should be the Sacrifice, I must submit . . .'

Enduring Tough Times from Arthur

While Darling was doing his level-headed best to implement big changes in the way NSW was run from 1824 to 1831 (refer to the preceding sections), George Arthur was doing the same down in Van Diemen's Land until 1836. Like Darling, Arthur was an army officer with a background in administration, and he also had an unswerving view that the colony he was administering existed for the purpose of serving British rather than local needs.

Arthur oversaw the conversion of Van Diemen's Land to a colony completely devoted to punishment and made the recording of this punishment more systematic. He couldn't devote all his time to the convicts, however — he also had to deal with some pesky bushrangers and work on the Aboriginal 'problem'.

Concentrating on punishment and reform

In 1824, just as Governor Arthur was arriving, Van Diemen's Land (known as Tasmania these days) was made a separate colony to NSW, and given a more particular purpose than what it had previously had. Rather than just a colony of free settlers and convicts, it started to become more definitively the British Empire's chief receptacle for many of the worst criminals. Over the next three decades, Van Diemen's Land became the place where punishment and reform of convicts became the chief preoccupation of government. Arthur was the perfect choice to attempt bringing this change about.

Arthur, even more than Ralph Darling, had almost untrammelled powers as governor of Van Diemen's Land. Advised but not much influenced by a nominated Legislative Council, and hostile to ideas of colonists having trial by jury or a representative assembly, Arthur suffered no anxiety that Van Diemen's Land existed for any other reason than to serve as a place of punishment and reform for convicts. If this was the colony's purpose, he figured, you couldn't choose to settle there and then complain that it lacked a free press or other ordinary British freedoms. (Some newspaper editors argued strongly with him on that score, but they generally found themselves jailed.)

IN THEIR WORDS

Arthur's opinion of Van Diemen's Land as a place of punishment and reform was fully shared by the Colonial Office. James Stephen in the Colonial Office talked of it as 'a Colony set apart for the discipline and reformation of the scowerings [sic] of our Gaols'. The best approach to take towards such a colony was, he joked, the same as dealing with a young child — 'Be good Children and dutiful and quarrel with us as little as you can help and we will be very tender and considerate Parents'.

Arthur was in place to make sure that the child colony stuck to its lessons while the parent nation was busy on the other side of the world.

Recording punishments in the system

From very early on Arthur started monitoring all the administration of convict life, keeping detailed records of each convict: His or her behaviour, crimes, and progression or regression under the penal system.

Under Arthur, the punishment system had a series of different grades, or rungs on the ladder:

>> The lowest rung was for repeat offenders who had committed further crimes upon arriving in the colony. They were sent to isolated penal settlements and subjected to rigorous punishments — hard labour, treadmill and solitary confinement.

>> The next rung was for convicts who were assigned to government work, generally on road gangs.

>> The third rung was for convicts who were assigned to settlers.

>> The final rung was for convicts who were granted conditional freedom via the ticket of leave (refer to Chapter 4).

As you behaved in the colony as a convict, so you made progress or otherwise. Gone were the good old days of possibly scoring an easy second chance, and gone too was the chance and randomness of the previous regime, where connections could get you out of serving time.

Fighting bushrangers and Tasmanian Aboriginals

Aside from evolving better ways to classify and punish convicts, Arthur's two great challenges in 1820s Van Diemen's Land were bushrangers and Aboriginals. He did well on eliminating the bushrangers, but not so well in ending the 'Black War' then raging between whites and blacks.

Breeding bushrangers

Van Diemen's Land has the honour of being the first breeding ground for the stock figures that would later be embraced as folk heroes — bushrangers. Bushranging in Van Diemen's Land began in the hungry years following first settlement on the River Derwent in 1803, when rations ran so low that convicts were given guns and dogs and told to go out and shoot kangaroos to bring back for food.

Many convicts didn't come back at all, preferring life in the ranges, living on roo meat, clothing themselves in roo skins, and trading both items for anything else they wanted. They weren't folk heroes at this point, though, and weren't above theft and assault on easy prey — small farmers and solitary travellers on the back roads.

Arthur managed to bring Van Diemen's Land's incessant bushranger problem under control by turning the island colony into one of the most heavily policed countries in the world. He created a field police force, three-quarters of which was made up of convicts. They were under the control of paid police magistrates, who were answerable to Arthur personally. Arthur's solution was incredibly heavy-handed — and it worked a treat. Bushranging was quickly eliminated as a social problem.

Fighting the 'Black War'

While the bushranger problem was largely over within the first year of Arthur's rule, the ongoing armed struggle between Indigenous Tasmanians and white settlers — which included murder and rape on the side of settlers, and retaliatory spearings on the side of Aboriginals — was far more protracted.

HISTORICAL ROOTS

Arthur was a man of strongly pronounced evangelical religious views, and at this time it was the Evangelicals who were the most vocal opponents of the British slave trade. Previous to coming to Van Diemen's Land, Arthur had been administrator of Honduras, and made enemies of the slave owners who dominated local society by exerting himself in the interest of the welfare of slaves and indigenous tribes.

TASMANIAN DEVILS

LIFE DOWN UNDER

Van Diemen's Land began life as a peripheral settlement to the NSW colony in 1803, and for the first couple of decades had to struggle along with little trade or contact with the outside world. The hinterland contained ranges and rugged bushland that made for perfect terrain for convicts to escape into and live as outlaws. These were the first bushrangers.

Michael Howe made a name as being the most rugged of the bushrangers. Having deserted the army, he was found guilty of highway robbery and arrived in Van Diemen's Land in 1812, aged 25. He took off the next year and soon made himself the leader of a gang. Here he felt secure enough to write a letter to the colony's lieutenant-governor and signed himself 'Lieutenant-Governor of the woods'. Given amnesty, he soon took off again, and disappeared even deeper into the ranges, becoming in appearance at least like some kind of mythic character — dressed in skins, with his hair and beard overgrown, matted and bushy, he was a wild man who wrote his dreams down in blood, listing the flowers he could remember from his childhood in Yorkshire. Howe's escapades didn't end well. Caught once, he escaped by killing those who'd captured him. A year later he was cornered and beaten to death, with his head cut off and carried as a trophy to Hobart.

Matthew Brady was more the gentleman highwayman, known for consideration towards women but, like Howe, he seemed almost congenitally incapable of putting up with even the suggestion of servitude. In the four years he was held as a convict until 1824, he was lashed upward of 350 times for attempts to escape and various forms of insubordination. Exiled to the most remote settlement on the island — Macquarie Harbour, on the mostly uninhabited west coast — he and some others stole a small boat and sailed it back to Hobart, where they dumped the boat and took to the bush. He then pulled off the added publicity coup of holding up an entire town, and taking prisoner a set of respectable citizens who had just sat down to dinner after a day of fruitless searching for the bushrangers. Around this time, he also posted up notices offering a reward for Lieutenant-Governor Arthur's capture. Injured and informed on by fellow gang members, he was eventually captured by bushman John Batman, future co-founder of Melbourne (see the section 'Opening up Australia's fertile land', later in this chapter), and was hanged in Hobart in 1826.

And it wasn't just convicts. Mosquito was an Indigenous Australian who was born on the north shore of Port Jackson in NSW, a member of the Eora tribe. He took up armed resistance in the young NSW colony, leading raids on the Hawkesbury settlers. Handed over by local Aboriginal people to the authorities, he was exiled to Norfolk Island and then sent to Van Diemen's Land with the rest of the settlers when Norfolk Island was evacuated in the early years of Macquarie's rule. There he won praise as a tracker — he was one of those who traced Howe to his hideout — and stockman. After his ticket of leave was granted, he got permission to return to NSW. Instead he went bush, joining the Oyster Bay tribe in guerrilla resistance, leading raids on farms. Captured after being wounded by an Indigenous boy, he was hanged in Hobart in 1825.

Arthur arrived in Van Diemen's Land with the strong support of powerful Evangelicals both inside and outside the Colonial Office, all of whom agreed that conflict with native peoples constituted a blot on the reputation of British settlements. He set about trying to reconcile the interests of black and white, but found hostility so entrenched on each side as to be immoveable.

Relations between black and white got so bad that Arthur figured the Indigenous Tasmanians had to be brought in for their own good — and everyone else's. Removing Aboriginal people seemed to him the only way to stop the ongoing bloodshed of the 'Black War'. There was nothing for it, he thought, but to send roving parties out to capture Tasmanian Aboriginals.

This proved far easier said than done. The roving parties met with little success. One of the party leaders, John Batman (who had captured Matthew Brady three years before this — refer to the 'Tasmanian devils' sidebar, earlier in this chapter) was admonished by Arthur when he attempted capture of Aboriginal people by sneaking up and firing on them, and then shooting two of the captured men because they were too wounded to keep up.

Eventually Arthur turned to George 'Black' Robinson, who had the novel idea of trying to make friends with the natives without trying to grab them or shooting at them (see the sidebar 'Trekking around Van Diemen's Land').

Meanwhile Arthur organised the settlers into what would become known as the 'Black Line'. Conducted in October 1830, it involved practically the entire white male population of Van Diemen's Land marching steadily across the south-east of the island in a long chain with the aim of capturing or at least herding the Aboriginal people in the region onto a peninsula. Arthur himself rode round exercising his usual hands-on supervision.

TREKKING AROUND VAN DIEMEN'S LAND

George Augustus 'Black' Robinson was a self-educated, self-important, very brave brick-layer from London who was the first British settler to go out into the Tasmanian bush to establish contact with Indigenous peoples while completely unarmed. Robinson had grown up in London, and was also seriously religious. From 1829 to 1834, Robinson embarked on a series of remarkable treks around and across the island.

He walked almost the entire west coast of the island, through terrain that even today is incredibly difficult and remote. Here he encountered Aboriginal people who had hardly seen any settlers before, and began contact. Later he would win praise from Governor Arthur for helping end the 'Black War' when he convinced the remaining Aboriginals to come in to Hobart. This has subsequently been variously described as either a great act towards the Tasmanian Aboriginal people or their worst betrayal.

In the short term, it proved an unmitigated disaster; only two Tasmanians were captured — an old man and a very young boy. Everyone else had slipped through the chain without anyone noticing. Ultimately, though, it was effective as a potent example of just how much in the way of resources and manpower the white settlers could draw on.

A full sense of just how unequal the conflict was dawned on the remaining Aboriginal people and, after Robinson promised them he would support their rights to the land, they agreed to come in. Perhaps misunderstanding occurred, perhaps they'd simply been duped and conned, but once the Aboriginal people surrendered, they were transferred to Flinders Island in Bass Strait. Here, away from their home country, most quickly sickened and died.

Hitting the Big Time with Wool and Grabbing Land

The settlements that would become the states of Queensland, Victoria, South Australia and Western Australia all got their start in the 1820s and 1830s. (See Figure 6-1 for how settlement really exploded in the 1820s, and then continued through the 19th century.)

Some settlements began haltingly, as small outposts that were meant to precede greater settlement (such as Queensland and Western Australia). Others came into being as the result of the overwhelming expansion of settlers and livestock, against the express rules and laws that were meant to limit this settlement (most particularly in Victoria). And one new settlement came about because people in London were alarmed at the unplanned, ad hoc nature of colonial life, put their heads together and came up with some decent 'planned settlement' (see the sidebar 'No convicts, please, we're South Australia', later in this chapter).

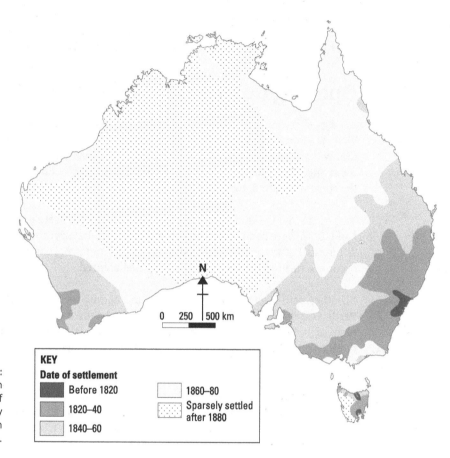

FIGURE 6-1: European settlement of Australia really expanded from the 1820s.

KEY
Date of settlement

███ Before 1820	░░ 1860–80
▓▓ 1820–40	∴∴ Sparsely settled after 1880
▒▒ 1840–60	

The 1830s, economically speaking and land-invasion speaking, were huge. Building on the steady progress and expansion of the 1820s, momentum took off. The reason behind both the economic explosion and the massive land grab was the same: Wool.

LIFE DOWN UNDER

As pastoralism emerged as the dominant factor in colonial life and land was taken up — taken off Indigenous Australians, that is, with a mixture of guns, cajolery, grog and sheer numbers — for the burgeoning wool industry, governors and the British struggled to contain settlement within the previously demarcated limits of administration and law. Settlers kept moving past the limit, squatting on land and occupying it without permission from the government or the traditional Indigenous owners.

To begin with, these settlers were those who were finding it harder to get land — such as native-born Australians (the children of convict parents), ex-convicts and assorted disreputable types. Soon enough, however, every class was in on the act, taking herds and flocks out in search of good pasturage, and carting back wool and hides in such quantities that they constituted the bulk of the colony's wealth.

Opening up Australia's fertile land

In 1835, three men converged on the region of Australia that is now the state of Victoria and contributed to the establishment of the main settlement in the area that would eventually be named Melbourne. One was Thomas Mitchell, a government Surveyor General, another was John Batman, a bushman and grazier, while the third was John Fawkner, a pub-owner, newspaper editor and townsman.

Two of the men — Batman and Fawkner — came separately from Van Diemen's Land. Both were sons of convicts, but in just about everything else they were very different. Between them (although personal enemies), the seed of what would become a future capital city and colony was planted.

HISTORICAL ROOTS

All other settlements that became future capitals — Sydney, Hobart, Adelaide, Perth, Darwin, Brisbane and Canberra — were begun as a result of official government acts. Melbourne, however, began as an 'illegitimate' and illegal establishment of private settlers, capitalists, squatters and traders.

John Batman was born in Parramatta in NSW, and as a young man moved to Van Diemen's Land and became a pastoralist, running livestock, capturing a bushranger, and leading a roving party against Aboriginals in rugged terrain. In June 1835 he arrived in Port Phillip Bay (in modern-day Victoria) looking for more grazing country for a syndicate of pastoralists. He struck an agreement with the Wurundjeri tribe, passed near the future site of Melbourne, declared 'This will be the place for a village', and soon after started bringing over stock from Tasmania.

Fawkner arrived in Van Diemen's Land with his convict father under David Collins' first settlement of the island in 1804 (refer to Chapter 4). He grew up to be a jack-of-all-trades, and soon after Batman's return from Port Phillip sent over his own party to begin a settlement.

Meanwhile, Major Mitchell, Surveyor General of NSW, established a route down into the new Port Phillip region from NSW, along which countless new settlers would travel. When not surveying he did a lot of exploring, and was one of the first to use Aboriginal place names for various places that he was putting on maps. (His rationale being that when the next whites to pass through the area wanted to go to a place, they could ask the local Indigenous people and they could direct them there — requests to see places like 'King George's Hill' tended to provoke blank looks.)

Travelling across modern-day Victoria, Mitchell was so impressed with the quality and fertility of the soil he called it 'Australia Felix' — Latin for 'Australia the Happy'. The soil was so soft that the cart wheels made ruts in the ground that in following years new settlers would also follow: 'Mitchell's Line'.

Adding sheep, making money

Australia, with its vast hinterland ready for occupation by men, women and sheep, was in the right place at the right time. The British woollen industry was going into overdrive — thanks to the world's first industrial revolution, demand from factories for raw commodities such as wool was going through the roof. If you're looking for a moment when Australia's famous (or infamous) moniker as the 'lucky country' becomes relevant, then it lies here.

The raw numbers speak for themselves. In 1830, exports from Australia of various fishery products (such as whale and seal) were nearly double that of wool. By 1840, wool exports were nearly triple that of the maritime industries. Land on the other side of the Blue Mountains (west of Sydney) in the 1820s and further south and north in the 1830s was very quickly turned to the production of high-quality wool, and by 1840 Australia was the dominant player on the global wool market, knocking off Germany (who had knocked off Spain, who earlier had taken care of England) as the leading wool producer in the world.

TECHNICAL STUFF

The development of merino wool in Australia combined the qualities of robust English wools with finer Saxony wool, making it perfect to meet the new fashion for soft and fine cloths after the end of the Napoleonic Wars. The British Government reduced duties on colonial wool in the 1820s after it began winning medals for quality, and an 1828 Select Committee declared Australian wool better even than German wool. And it actually cost less for wool to get to Britain from Australia than it did from southern Germany (where the bulk of Saxony wools came from). Australia's share of the wool trade went from 8.1 per cent in 1830 to 47 per cent in 1850, while Germany's slumped from 75.8 per cent to 10.6 per cent.

Thanks to NSW and Van Diemen's Land being such an eager market for imported goods and commodities, plenty of ships were already making the run to Australia by the 1840s. Now they had a staple product to put in their previously empty holds for the homeward journey.

LIFE DOWN UNDER

RIDING THAT SHEEP'S BACK (AND THE LIVING'S RELATIVELY EASY)

The beauty of the wool industry lay in how little extra development had to be done for it to be successful in Australia. New settlers didn't have to massively alter or work the land. With convicts as 'assigned servants' they didn't even need fences, because the convicts worked as shepherds (free men could work as shepherds too, but they generally didn't want to, preferring jobs that were better paid). Settlers had to find the land, stock it with sheep herded from (an often far away) settlement, put up some bark slab huts for shepherds tending separate sheep flocks, and they were away.

Of course, the wool had to be sheared and the transported on bullock-drawn carts (something that could involve journeys of hundreds of kilometres). Then it needed to be stored in a warehouse, and transported onto a dock and then a British-bound ship. But production required no great infrastructure developments, no exhaustive training and no elaborate organisation. For a young, raw colony, wool was perfect.

Far removed from the established centres of European civilisation and settlement, the squatters themselves, whether native-born men or new arrivals from Scotland, England and Ireland, often found themselves acting more like clan chiefs than capitalist bosses. They were generally at the front of the party that settled the land in the first place, and then set up operations. Their houses for the first years were often little more than huts, and they had to be able to ride, track lost sheep, fight 'hostile blacks', win over 'friendly natives', and oversee the welfare of their various sheep flocks and workers.

For the shepherds themselves, life was quiet, generally monotonous and peaceful. Sitting under a tree (if one was available) and staring at a flock of sheep all day may not sound like much, and it wasn't, but it sure beat prison, and most of the shepherds in the industry were convicts who had been assigned to settlers. Often enough the convicts were even paid incentives by settlers, such as money, tobacco, tea and grog.

And even though the reformation of convicts was very low down on the list of settler priorities, the private assignment of convicts to settlers on the land was a kind of accidental reformation, producing a much better effect on criminals than other forms of punishment. Assigning convicts to work on the land dispersed them away from their old circumstances and habits in the town and the city, and gave them the space to gradually readjust to ordinary life before receiving a ticket of leave.

Clashing with the locals: white pioneers, black pioneers

White settlers during the 1840s and 1850s were written up in history books in the years to come and glorified as part of a 'pioneer myth'. The myth had a lot of basis in fact — these first waves of settlers were intrepid, resourceful and brave. What the pioneer myth left out, though, was 'the other side of the frontier'. Violence and confrontation erupted as the new occupiers swept in and took country that had been held and lived in by Aboriginal peoples for pretty much forever (in human terms, at any rate). Indigenous Australians grappled with this new implacable reality in a number of ways. The range of their responses, and the resourcefulness with which they dealt with these forces of destruction, dislocation and transformation, absolutely earns them the right to be considered black pioneers.

Probably unsurprisingly, this explosion of territorial expansion by white settlers didn't go unresisted by Aboriginal peoples already in occupation and possession of the country they had called their home for millennia.

A rolling frontier zone accompanied the expansion of British settlement of eastern and southern Australia across these colonial decades. Disputes and confrontations sprang up between Indigenous clans and the interlopers wherever contact occurred. The confrontations were often violent, with reprisals, killings and payback killings, and sometimes massacres — such as the one at Myall Creek (see Chapter 7).

Again and again conflicts took place over:

>> Water access

>> Land access and ownership

>> European possessions and new commodities

>> Indigenous women

REMEMBER

Describing this rolling frontier zone as violent conflict and resistance only is a misrepresentation. Indigenous Australians grappled with the fact of the newcomers, adapted wherever they could, made the most out of new opportunities, and resisted and retaliated where they felt they had no other choice. They were experiencing the dislocation of an established order of being human, and of human relations, which had prevailed for more centuries than historical time normally reckons in. Their stories altered and were modified as they did so, and so kept alive. Indigenous Australians survived the diseases that swept through (almost like an advance force, killing many before the settlers even turned up). They survived violence and dislocation. And those who did acquired new languages, new skills and new practices.

In frontier society, Aboriginal people became:

>> Shearers

>> Herdsmen, stockmen and boundary-riders

>> Blacksmiths

>> Sawyers and fencers

>> Cooks, child-carers and housekeepers

In the words of a famous historian of Indigenous–settler relations, these were 'black pioneers', even if the history books being written up until recent decades didn't actually record them alongside and among the white pioneers.

For more on how Aboriginal people dealt with, and adapted to, the rolling frontier zone of white settlement, see *Indigenous Australia For Dummies*, 2nd edition, by Larissa Behrendt, Wiley Australia Publishing.

Fighting the land grab

During the 1820s and 1830s in Australia, the economy was going gangbusters. For the authorities, this created one big problem: People, known as squatters, were grabbing land in all directions. The British Government was strongly against this dispersed settlement — it was hard to police and made it difficult to keep people under proper authority — and felt it had to be stopped.

HISTORICAL ROOTS

At the start of the 19th century, Britain was a small island where in rural areas an intricate social hierarchy still existed — from the squire down to the farm-hand, everyone knew where they fitted in the social mosaic. Land was finite, owned predominantly by the wealthy, and the Church was on hand in every country parish to provide sermons about the need for deference and social order. The very idea, then, of practically limitless amounts of land spreading off in all directions, being populated without any order or control by people of all classes, with large herds of their own livestock, did something profoundly disturbing to the English imagination. Just as many in England in the 1800s and 1810s had been horrified at the news of ex-convicts becoming highly successful (refer to Chapter 5), so now many were distraught at the thought of this uncontrolled settlement.

The British tried to put the convict upstarts back in their place, and to restrict the allocation of land. Ultimately, however, their efforts were unsuccessful.

Putting convicts in their place

The British elite were greatly concerned about the relatively open nature of society in Australia. If you had initiative, talent or money, you could start getting ahead, regardless of what your class background or upbringing might be. This had to be rectified!

In 1826, Governor Darling began placing tight restrictions on settlement spreading further out from Sydney. In 1829, he declared the 19 counties that surrounded Sydney were the only places where settlement would be permitted. Everything else was trespassing. But settlement outside these boundaries continued.

In one of the most beautiful ironies of Australian history, the answer to this great perceived problem was devised by a man who was himself a prisoner but who had never been to the colonies. Edward Gibbon Wakefield was serving time in Newgate Prison in 1829 (for abducting a schoolgirl heiress) when he began writing a series of essays that would eventually be published as *A Letter From Sydney*.

Wakefield's idea of how to solve the problem of too much dispersal was very simple. Closer settlement could be enforced by limiting the amount of land freely available and by making the land that was made available more expensive. This would create a couple of benefits:

» Members of the lower orders would no longer be able to afford to become landholders straightaway. The high prices would attract investors from Britain who had plenty of capital, while people from the lower orders would be forced to work for their betters for a long time as they attempted to save enough money to buy land for themselves. All the while, everyone would be living near each other, and would therefore remain under the benevolent thumb of social order and authority.

» Money would quickly fill the government coffers (from the land, see), which could be used to bring out male and female free labourers.

In government circles, it was quickly agreed that settlement would have to be more restricted and not allowed to spread beyond certain demarcated boundaries.

In 1831, Viscount Goderich at the Colonial Office (and soon to become the Earl of Ripon) followed Wakefield's recommendations and introduced new land regulations. The minimum price of land was raised to stop just anyone being able to buy it (to not less than five shillings an acre). Part of the proceeds from the auction would then be set aside to subsidise immigration, and so begin weaning the colony of NSW off convict labour. (For more on Wakefield's influence, see the sidebar 'No convicts, please, we're South Australia'.)

Quietly accepting the inevitable

The British, through Wakefield, Goderich and Governor Darling, did their best to control the allocation of land in Australia, but the settlers themselves largely ignored their regulations. They kept on spreading right out and government was largely powerless to stop them. What were they going to do? Build a big fence and arrest anyone who crossed through it? In 1835, Governor Bourke (who replaced Governor Darling) sternly warned off all the new arrivals at Port Phillip (in modern-day Victoria) as 'trespassers and intruders' — then quietly advised Secretary of State for the Colonies, Lord Glenelg, that they may as well give up trying to limit settlement.

IN THEIR WORDS

Bourke told the Colonial Office, as politely as he possibly could, that 'the vast tract of fertile land lying between the County of St Vincent's and Twofold Bay [in NSW]' was already used as pasture by 'flocks and herds, attended by shepherds and stockmen'. Restraining dispersion might be a smart idea in other places, Bourke said, but these pastures were sustaining the flocks that provided the wool that made the substantial bulk of the productive wealth of the colony, and would continue to do so into the foreseeable future. 'The proprietors of thousands of acres already find it necessary, equally with the poorer settlers, to send large flocks beyond the present boundary . . .' Aside from all of which was another simple fact — 'the Government is unable to prevent it'.

NO CONVICTS, PLEASE, WE'RE SOUTH AUSTRALIA

Whalers, sealers and their Aboriginal women had established themselves on Kangaroo Island (just off the coast of modern-day Adelaide) after 1810, but in the first decades of the 1800s no official settlement had been made anywhere in what would become modern-day South Australia. Then in 1830, explorer Charles Sturt charted the course of the Murrumbidgee, Darling and Murray Rivers down to where the Murray enters the sea, and proclaimed the coastal region rather a fine one for settling in.

This attracted the attention of a group of reformers and speculators who planned a colony on the principles of Edward Wakefield (refer to the section 'Putting convicts in their place', earlier in this chapter). They got the attention of the British Government, which in August 1834 passed an Act to create the colony of South Australia, a colony that was meant to do everything differently to the ad hoc, largely unplanned development of the colonies of NSW and Van Diemen's Land.

Various administrations in both NSW and Van Diemen's Land had given large, almost despotic, amounts of power to the government executive, almost randomly assigned parcels of land in grants to people as they saw fit, and utilised convict labour as a workforce. South Australia would be an experiment in modern, logical, 'systematic colonisation'. Land would be sold at a set price by the South Australian Company, the price of land would be high (to ensure labourers would remain labourers rather than acquire cheap tracts of land themselves and disperse into the countryside), and the expense of shipping the free labour force out to Australia would be paid by the revenue from the land sales.

This best-laid plan didn't work so well, however — at least in the first few years. Initial squabbling among officials was followed by speculative land sale bubbles, followed by (the annoying ignominy of it all!) the completely unplanned settlement of Port Phillip (which became Victoria) rocketing right past them in power, wealth, population and influence.

Rather than simply issuing diktats that everyone promptly ignored, Bourke suggested it might be better to acknowledge the settlers who were already squatting on land outside the restricted areas. He also suggested more dispersed settlement might be encouraged, to provide 'centres of civilization and Government, and thus gradually to extend the power of order and social union to the most distant parts of the wilderness'.

The following year, Lord Glenelg agreed that Bourke could introduce a licence system for those beyond the established boundaries. An annual rent of £10 gave squatters the right to keep doing what they'd been doing for a while now, although it didn't give them ownership of the land.

In 1846, The Waste Lands Act was passed in the British parliament. For the first time, it gave squatters security of tenure beyond the annual licences. While not giving in to squatter demands to own the land outright, the Act gave longer leases of up to 14 years, with rights of *pre-emption* (first right to buy land) and renewal.

REMEMBER

The British Government spent a lot of time and energy in the late 1820s and early 1830s telling settlers in Australia to stop spreading out and taking land without permission — but they didn't mean permission from Indigenous peoples. The British didn't think Aboriginals owned the land and they also didn't think settlers squatting on their own initiative could be said to own the land. They said *they* owned the land — the Crown. Even today, in Australia public land is called Crown Land.

Aboriginal peoples had been denied sovereignty over the land because, in the eyes of European and British arrivals, they didn't work the land intensively. This was the same description applicable to squatters, who didn't engage in agriculture, build big structures or visibly alter the environment. (However, the pitter-patter of millions of hooves on soft feathery top soil would have enormous long-term effect.) In later decades, subsequent arrivals would accuse the squatters of taking up the good land without doing anything substantial with it — the squatters hadn't introduced any cultivation or heavy settlement. (See Chapter 8 for the struggle between squatters and new gold rush arrivals.)

Chapter **7**

Economic Collapse and the Beginnings of Nationalism

The first 50 years of white settlement in Australia saw economic growth and territorial expansion — at first slowly, then rapidly, and in the 1830s, maniacally. The boom came shuddering to a halt in the 1840s when an economic depression hit and the bottom dropped out of the British market for wool, Australia's main export. Although in the long term the effects were beneficial — pastoralists were forced to improve their techniques, and new products and industries were developed — the short term made for serious economic pain. For the first time ever, unemployment became a big problem, and bankruptcies and bank collapses occurred everywhere.

Meanwhile, the main reason for the original settling of Australia — convict transportation — came to an end on most of mainland Australia in the 1840s. In the late 1840s, however, the British Government changed its mind, and began to dabble with the idea of sending convicts out again. The colonists were furious, and promptly set about organising a movement to counter it.

As the Australian colonies developed through the 1830s, the British Government became more concerned about the treatment of Indigenous Australians. It created new policies to try to ensure that Aboriginal people in frontier areas were treated with less brutality than the treatment they'd previously received from the settlers. The new laws were largely ignored by settlers.

In this chapter, I look at how, despite a cataclysmic economic crunch, the colonists began thinking of their interests as shared and unique in a way that hadn't occurred previously — creating the first stirrings of nationalism.

Bubble Times: From Speculative Mania to a Big Collapse

The 1820s and 1830s saw a pastoral boom in Australia, as more land was opened up and wool started to be exported (refer to Chapter 6). However, by the late 1830s, all this success started to go to people's heads. Credit was easily available, imports greatly outweighed exports and land started to be bought for purely speculative reasons, with the purchasers quickly turning the land over for a sometimes massive profit.

As they say, all good things must come to an end and, in the early 1840s, the bubble popped — loudly. Many people were wiped out, and insolvency and unemployment were widespread. However, the new colonies proved to be resilient, with industries emerging stronger once the dust had settled.

Working the market into a frenzy

Certain things came together to make for a perfect storm of market bubble and speculative frenzy in the mid- to late 1830s. The main forces were the following:

>> **An industry in boom conditions:** Pastoral Australia was providing the wool for the British industrial revolution, which really began with the mechanisation of the textile industries. This led to an explosion in demand for and production of textiles in woollen mills and factories — so demand for Australian wool was practically insatiable. Even though wool prices peaked in 1836, then dropped by 25 per cent in 1837 and kept falling thereafter, investment capital kept flooding in to NSW.

>> **A vast mass of fertile grassland:** Thanks largely to Indigenous peoples' patterns of firestick farming for previous millennia, the land the new settlers

took over in the 1820s and 1830s was fertile grassland that could very easily be converted for highly productive use running sheep and growing wool.

>> **The British financial market was beginning to loosen up:** Previously, any number of restrictions had been placed on investments in far-flung colonial settlements. In the 1830s, however, as Britain finally emerged from the post-Napoleonic War slump, the banking sector was substantially liberalised. A great deal of capital started floating around, and a lot of it headed to overseas investments. London banks entered the Australian market in a major way — all the high interest rate investment opportunities made it difficult to resist.

LIFE DOWN UNDER

Soon things started to go a little crazy. More land kept being explored and settled, thereby increasing the demand for labour. Convict servants had been filling the breach for the entire history of white Australian settlement, but demand was now sucking up more convicted British felons than could be conveniently manufactured. Besides, influential people both in the colonies and in Britain were starting to go off the idea of using transported convicts as a labour force (see the section 'Moving On from Convictism', later in this chapter). Convict and self-funded migration began to be supplemented by government-subsidised schemes. Private individuals were also encouraged to nominate and sponsor individuals to be immigrants out to Australia, with the government then reimbursing them with a 'bounty' payment.

These new 'bounty' migrants weren't cheap to bring out. The new governor, George Gipps, who took over from Richard Bourke in 1838, turned to the best money-earner he had — land. From 1839 he began fixing the 'upset price' (or minimum price) of town lots throughout NSW far above the minimum previously possible in the market, often ignoring the more modest set price suggestions made by the Surveyor General, Thomas Mitchell (the same Mitchell who established a route down into the vast pastoral country of the Port Phillip district in 1835; refer to Chapter 6).

Investing in land with easy credit

After the liberalisation of the British banking sector in the second half of the 1830s (refer to the preceding section), English banks began to transfer funds from Britain to lend in Australia. Previously, money coming into Australia came through largely unofficial channels — immigrants bringing in cash and goods, and people drawing bills individually from agents in London. Now the new banking system in London began to have its effects in NSW and Van Diemen's Land, and the newly established English banks gave out loans freely. The pre-existing Australian banks — the Bank of NSW, the Commercial and Union Bank and the Bank of Australasia — were stunned into action, setting up branches in the hinterland and using bank deposits to loan out funds.

Settlement kept spreading, and more and more investment capital kept coming in. So much credit was flooding into the colonies that it was given to practically anyone who asked for it (and plenty who didn't — starting to sound familiar?). Extravagant consumption of luxury imports became the norm.

Land prices were particularly affected. They were high enough in the booming colony, but after Governor Gipps massively raised the set price of town lots throughout NSW (refer to the preceding section), combined with the availability of easy credit, prices went into overdrive. Land rapidly became people's favourite commodity to buy and sell.

LIFE DOWN UNDER

At the heart of the newly opened pastoral and squatting country, Melbourne was the epicentre of the real-estate madness. A block of land in the newly surveyed township was sold in 1836 for £150. Given that the annual wage for a skilled tradesman at this time was about £150, you might think fair enough. But that block of land, like surrounding blocks of land, multiplied sixty-fold in value over the next three years, selling in 1839 for £9000.

The land speculation was a market bubble of monumental proportions. Business in Britain was flat, so investors kept coming for the high returns offered by London-based colonial banks to British investors, even as the wool price was heading south due to oversupply and an economic downturn in Europe (see the following section). In Australia, the continued flood of loan capital meant money was available for more and more imports. For the first time in living memory, inflation was becoming a real problem. The madness couldn't last, and it didn't.

LIFE DOWN UNDER

COMBINING PROPERTY SELLING WITH THE COCKTAIL HOUR

Champagne breakfast, anyone? These became the stock-in-trade of auctioneers and business agents, who would take prospective clients out from newly established towns such as Melbourne to gaze, boozily and delightedly, at the surrounding country.

One fly-by-night real estate broker must have swallowed a thesaurus (and perhaps a few brandies) before writing out the first lines of an ad placed in a Port Phillip paper: 'The teeming powers of this beauteous land has been opened to the industry of enlightened minds but a short period. Its establishment will be an epoch of time . . .' and even *that* sold land. Much of the land was being bought by speculative investors, who borrowed big-time to purchase, planning only to sell it on again in a few months' time when prices had risen still higher.

Ducking for cover as the economy collapses

Around 1840, the incredibly high rate of return on investing in land that had been sustained for most of the 1830s started to fall away. Land prices stalled, and then began falling precipitously. Credit dried up and confidence took a tumble.

Apart from a seriously overheated market, the economic collapse was caused by a number of factors:

>> Settlers reached the limits of the immediately productive land in the fertile south-east Australian crescent.

>> Drought hit various regions through the late 1830s.

>> Europe experienced an economic downturn.

British investors, already skittish with their own stock exchange crises and various economic downturns, started to pull out. Soon practically zero capital was coming into the colonies and Australian businesses and farms. Local banks started, belatedly, curtailing credit. A complete collapse in confidence threatened. Soon enough it was actual.

By 1841, the economy was in a serious downturn. In 1842, a complete market collapse took place. Wool prices slipped down still further. Sales of Crown land fell away significantly, and an alarmed Governor Gipps lost a large chunk of his revenue base. He took a knife to his administrative expenditure, which was cut by an incredible 64 per cent. The number of people going bankrupt skyrocketed. Unemployment became seriously endemic for the first time in the Australian colonies. Destitution was widespread and all-pervasive.

IN THEIR WORDS

Governor Gipps reported to Colonial Secretary Lord Stanley that insolvency was rife 'amongst all classes'. In Melbourne an interested observer observed gloomily that there was 'no money, no credit, no trade, nothing but failures. Even the lawyers can scarcely succeed in getting paid. Land is worthless, and cattle and sheep little better'.

Newly assisted immigrants had kept on arriving — disastrously, their numbers peaked just as economic conditions were at their worst. In 1841, some 20,000 men, women and children climbed off the boats in Sydney and Melbourne, only to find no jobs and no livelihood. In 1844, angry mobs of unemployed men confronted Gipps in Sydney's Hyde Park. Nervously, he promised to do something about it all, but the road to recovery would be long, slow and painful.

Picking up the pieces after the implosion

The economic pain of the 1840s cut deep but, ultimately, it did a lot of good. For starters, it achieved what a much later prime minister (Paul Keating, in his role as treasurer in the 1980s) would have laconically described as a 'de-spivving': Most of the speculators and shady dealers were eliminated. But more than that, the old elite, the Exclusives, were largely wiped out.

A growth in exports led the recovery. In 1844, exports actually exceeded imports for the first time — a big improvement on the unsustainable extravagances of the late 1830s when practically everyone enjoyed luxuries, and all the luxuries were imports. Conditions actually improved for workers and labourers in this decade, too, once the intense unemployment lifted. Wages went down, but not nearly as fast as the prices did and, on the whole, the cost of living improved.

Meanwhile, the brash young upstart squatters (read more about them in Chapter 6) had their ranks thinned mightily but emerged stronger at the end of it all, as the pastoral industry kept expanding to make up for the shortfall in prices. They achieved their long-sought aim of security of tenure on their leases, and pre-emptive rights of property purchase when the British Government passed their Waste Lands Act in 1846 and in subsequent Orders-in-Council.

A furious political opponent of the squatters (Robert Lowe) pointed out that while the government was still refusing to sell any land — even 'the most barren rock' — for less than £1 an acre, now most pastoral lands were being almost permanently locked up for squatters at the low price of 'a fifth of a penny per acre'. The 'waste lands' of Australia 'are to be a sheepwalk for ever!'

By the end of the 1840s, with many in the colonies pushing for self-government, the squatters began aspiring to be the new landed elite of the colony. In the early 1850s, one of the leaders of the Pastoral Association, William Wentworth (who appears in more detail in Chapter 6), declared that the new colonial legislature should have an upper house of landed lease-holders, and be given hereditary titles.

Another opponent of the squatters (Daniel Deniehy), poured vitriolic scorn on this idea, claiming most of those who had gone on to amass great fortunes and large land holdings in the colony had done it through dodgy deals, grog selling and disreputable trade. What sort of hereditary aristocracy would the colonial upper house have? 'A bunyip aristocracy!'

The idea to create the upper house got laughed out of town. But the large-scale squatters continued to dream of holding all the reins of power. (See Chapter 8 for more on what happened in the squatters' plans for power in the 1850s — when gold was discovered and thousands more people arrived.)

These dreams of grandeur aside, the colonies were again headed in the right direction.

Moving On from Convictism

Transportation was providing the bulk of the labour force to most pastoralists in Australia in the 1830s. Plenty of people wanted to get rid of the convict system — though many more in London than in the colonies.

Eventually, these voices of dissent were heard, and transportation of convicts to NSW ceased in 1840, causing all sorts of problems in Van Diemen's Land.

British calls to end convict 'slavery'

Those against transportation in London were humanitarians and Evangelical reformers.

HISTORICAL ROOTS

Although sarcastically referred to as 'the Saints' (for their patronising, 'holier than thou' attitude), the seriously religious Evangelicals had a big achievement to their credit in the 1830s — they led the campaign that successfully banned the institution of slavery in the British Empire. The elimination of slavery in the 1830s affected the whole mood of the age.

The system of *convictism*, or of transporting criminals as convicts to the other side of the world and then assigning them out as labourers, had been used by Britain since settlement of Australia. With its implication of a master having control of the life and labour of a convict, convictism came to be seen as a horrific form of modern-day slavery — it was necessarily brutal and brutalising. This was especially the view taken by those in London and Britain, who didn't have any day-to-day understanding of how the convict system actually worked (refer to Chapter 6 for a description of the realities of convict life for most assigned convicts in this period).

Being a convict was a form of slavery, the Brits argued, because the prisoner was the victim of every whim of a master. Even a good master couldn't help but be a kind of tyrant. If the British claimed to be the upholders of freedom (and they did), then, like the notorious slavery practised on Caribbean sugar plantations, convict transportation had to be abolished.

In the Australian colonies in the 1830s, few people had any issues with transportation. The only ones who really had a problem with it were the free folk, who had to put up with the stigma of shameful association whenever they returned to Britain. At the time, if you told people in Britain you'd been making money in NSW, they'd look at you funny — and then check their pockets to make sure you hadn't pickpocketed them. The real colonial outcry against transportation began in the 1840s, after the British Government had already halted transportation to NSW and then tried to reintroduce it using a different system. (See the section 'Feeling the First Stirrings of Nationalism', later in this chapter, for more on this.)

Ending transportation to NSW

In the 1830s, the British Parliament appointed a Select Committee on Transportation (also known as the Molesworth Committee), which, giving its final recommendations in 1838, condemned transportation wholeheartedly. They concluded that, thanks to transportation, NSW was now composed of 'the very dregs of society'. (This offended no end the upstanding, respectable types in the colonies.)

The view of Australian society as degraded was by now an entrenched British opinion. In the Colonial Office, James Stephen reflected this attitude when he brooded darkly that the well-intentioned British Empire had 'converted Australia into a den of thieves'.

On top of this, which private settler a convict was assigned to (and most were assigned out) was a game of pot luck — you could get assigned to a generous and easygoing settler, or to a regular tyrant, regardless of what your crime had been.

In Australia, Governor Bourke's opinion was a little more nuanced. He criticised the effects of the convict system among the settlers — but only on the men who were *masters* of convicts. The effects on the convicts themselves he thought mostly beneficial, or at least largely harmless.

In November 1837, Britain tried to dampen down the outcry by issuing instructions that convicts in Australia would no longer be available for private settlers to use. It wasn't enough, however, and orders were soon given for transportation of convicts to mainland Australia to be abandoned completely. In November 1840, the convict transport the *Eden* unloaded the last convicts transported to NSW.

The transportation of convicts wasn't abandoned completely, however — the plan now was that convicts would be sent to Van Diemen's Land until they could all be put in gaols in the UK.

Feeling the effects of ending transportation

The cessation of convict transportation produced two immediate effects in NSW:

>> Self-government, something the emancipist movement had been advocating for a long time, now became possible. Previously, there was (not to put too fine a point on it) no way in hell the Colonial Office or respectable British opinion would countenance self-government while a steady stream of convicts continued to arrive in the colony.

Instead of a governor and his officials ruling, from 1843 a partially elected Legislative Council was established.

>> The political divide between the Exclusives (free settlers, who thought only people who had never been convicted should have any say in government) and the Emancipists (ex-convicts), which had become more and more intense during the 1820s and 1830s as increasing amounts of free immigrants arrived, collapsed. Leading members of each group (James Macarthur, son of 'pure merino' John Macarthur — or the exclusive of the Exclusives — and William Wentworth, son of a convicted highwayman, being but two examples) came to appreciate their common interests.

In the new council, only those owning or renting substantial property could vote — which meant about two-thirds of adult men didn't qualify. Exclusives had always feared being overwhelmed by a more representative government, and had desperately fought for a purely nominated council. Now, however, the new body's voting franchise was so limited that this wasn't a problem.

'What's so "representative" about a government that two-thirds of men can't vote for?' the radicals and popular advocates wanted to know. 'Well, it's a very select sort of representation,' replied the newly combined Exclusive and emancipist elite rather comfortably. 'Sort of "invitation-only" representation, don't you know. Now . . . run along. The important people have important work to do.' In this new environment, the old social and political divide between Exclusives and emancipists seemed, well, a bit inconsequential.

Van Diemen's Land hits saturation point

While the debate over representative government raged in NSW, in Van Diemen's Land big problems were brewing. Because more convicted felons were now being sent to Van Diemen's Land, the island quickly reached saturation point. They had more convicts than they knew what to do with, especially when a new policy shift to the *probation system* occurred in 1842.

LIFE DOWN UNDER

The probation system was meant to replace the assignment system that had previously been used for the mass of convicts, whereby convicts would get assigned to private settlers. Private settlers had been notoriously blasé about whether convicts actually reformed — all they wanted was good workers, and they weren't choosy about how they got the convicts to play along. Bribery, incentives, cajolery, abuse and threats — all were used by different settlers in their attempts to get good labour out of their assigned servants.

The new probation system took the entire punishment process out of the hands of private settlers and placed it squarely under government control. This, it was thought, would be a more impartial and closely calibrated form of punishment. New convicts would be placed in government gangs for probationary periods, after which they could, behaviour permitting, qualify for conditional freedom within the colony.

This proved very unpopular with settlers, especially when it became clear that they were still expected to pay for the upkeep of these government gangs in the probation system.

Feeling the First Stirrings of Nationalism

By the 1840s, most people in the colonies of NSW were against any further convicts being transported to Australia. In Van Diemen's Land, this came to a head when settlers, angry at having to pay for the upkeep of convicts without having any control over their management, formed the Anti-Transportation League in Launceston (a large town in the north of the island).

At first the League was a local affair, but when Britain threatened to resume sending convicts to NSW, its appeal spread — especially among townsmen, traders and the labouring classes. Soon league meetings were being held throughout the colonies — in Brisbane, Adelaide, Melbourne and Sydney — making it Australia's first federal organisation. (See the sidebar 'Going federal with anti-transportation protests' for more on the influence of this movement.)

Britain tries turning the convict tap back on

In 1846, six years after transportation of convicts to mainland Australia had ended, word started getting out that transportation might be resumed, and in October the first public meeting was held to protest against this possibility. In Britain, the then Secretary of State for Colonies, future Liberal prime minister Gladstone, gave a pre-emptory rebuke, saying that when it came down to it, it didn't matter what the colonials thought — if the British national interest demanded transportation, so it would be.

GOING FEDERAL WITH ANTI-TRANSPORTATION PROTESTS

HISTORICAL ROOTS

Although many people tend to assume that the first proto-national sentiments began with the Eureka uprising at Ballarat in 1854 (covered in Chapter 8), the Anti-Transportation League actually represents a more accurate origin point. Starting in Launceston and quickly spreading through the mainland, the Anti-Transportation League became Australia's first trans-colonial organised political movement.

The flag the league adopted, featuring the Union Jack and the Southern Cross, was practically identical to the design that would become the Australian flag in the 20th century. But more than that, the sentiment that participants in the movement voiced showed that they were more than willing to countenance political separation and independence from Britain if their very strong feelings on the transportation question weren't listened to.

Gladstone had his problems — Van Diemen's Land (which was now taking all the transported convicts) was stuffed to the gills with convicts — and he refused to rule out mainland transportation options.

REMEMBER

Even though Evangelicals and humanitarians had been against convictism in the 1830s, they didn't run the Empire — they could only apply pressure. Sometimes they were successful, other times not. This was one of the *not* times.

IN THEIR WORDS

Gladstone declared (a bit dismissively), 'Her Majesty's Government hold it indispensable that within the Australian colonies receptacles should be found for all the convicts and exiles who may be sent from this country . . . This is so momentous an object of national policy that we can acknowledge no conflicting motive . . . of sufficient importance to supersede it'.

Gladstone's statement didn't particularly improve anyone's mood, but then, in 1847, the new Secretary of State for Colonies, Earl Grey, announced the new policy — the official end of transportation to NSW. Wild cheers all round (except the squatters, who began muttering darkly that now the government would start bringing in Indian 'coolie' labour instead).

Britain offers exiles instead

Soon after Earl Grey's announcement of the official end of transportation, however (refer to the preceding section), the waters started to muddy considerably. Earl Grey asked the governor of NSW, Charles Fitzroy, who had succeeded

Governor Gipps in 1846, whether he thought Australians might like it if a new form of transportation were introduced. This time, the proposal involved not bringing out convicted criminals *per se*, but sending convicted criminals who had served their time as prisoners already and were now not being transported but, having finished their sentences, exiled to Australia. They wouldn't be convicts — they'd be exiles. Fitzroy said he'd check.

Either Fitzroy didn't check very thoroughly, or he asked only one set of people, because he reported back in early 1848 that NSW would be quite fine with this, so long as an equal number of free migrants was sent out also. As it turned out, however, the people of NSW — Melbourne, Sydney and Brisbane especially — were very, very far from being fine about any of this. They saw the plan as a slur against their whole community. The colonies continuing to take convicts would continue to be a 'stain' that people could throw in their face whenever they returned 'home' to Britain to see friends and family — and brag about what great lives they'd been building in Australia. If Australia was to be what one colonist called 'a New Britannia', with all the rights and liberties any 'freeborn Englishman' could expect to enjoy, then a large caste of unfree women and men didn't help. Rights of free speech, to hold property, to get fair treatment at the hands of the law, and also the right to govern oneself — they had to apply across the board.

In the meantime, the British Government had responded to Fitzroy's report by saying, in effect, 'Oh, great. We'll just revoke the old order-in-council abolishing transportation to NSW, and start sending you exiles'.

In 1849, the first of a small number of ships carrying exiles — including the *Hashemy* — arrived in Australian waters, and all hell promptly broke loose. Massive protests took place in Sydney and Melbourne, with people threatening that if Britain continued ignoring the colonists' most heated wishes like this, they would react by firstly refusing to have any business or trade with those squatters who accepted the exiles, and secondly by getting some guns and rebelling against the mother country, as had happened in America.

IN THEIR WORDS

At public meetings held by the Anti-Transportation League, speakers declared the colonists could become, if needs be, 'a free and independent people. Let us have a council of our own, and a Senate of our own'. Whereupon voices in the crowd called out amid the cheers, 'Yes, and an army of our own'.

IN THEIR WORDS

'The British Government has done away with black slavery,' a speaker at an Anti-Transportation League meeting held in Melbourne said (an ex-convict himself), 'but they manufactured white slaves and sent them out here. I am an advocate for trying all legal means first, before I shoulder my musket or rifle, but I'll be found as ready as any of you when every other means have failed'. To some extent this was bluff and bluster, but even if so, it's telling of just how angry people were getting about it.

A LITTLE HELP, PLEASE: CONVICTS IN WESTERN AUSTRALIA

The Swan River Colony was established in Western Australia in 1829. Like South Australia, the colony was founded as a convict-free settlement, but things didn't really get off to a booming start. The land wasn't particularly good (too sandy) and the colony was unable to attract enough willing immigrants as labourers.

In early 1849, at the same time as the anti-transportation campaign was reaching fever pitch in the eastern towns and cities, a public meeting in Perth requested that the Swan River settlement in WA begin receiving convicts.

Earl Grey didn't have to be asked twice, and convicts were transported to WA until 1868, when the last convict shipment arrived in Western Australia on the *Hougoumont*.

In Melbourne, Lieutenant-Governor La Trobe prudently ordered the ships carrying exiles to sail on to Sydney. They did so, only to be met with a similar reaction. Here Governor Fitzroy, just as prudently, ordered them up to Moreton Bay in modern-day Queensland. The matter continued to dog colonial–imperial relations, with Earl Grey insisting

>> Most of those against transportations were themselves wealthy ex-convicts, so the system couldn't be *that* brutal, and they shouldn't stop other convicts from being given the same chance as they themselves had been given.

>> He was the minister for the colonies, dammit, and they were the colonies, so he could do what he darn well liked with them. So there.

The only thing that finally settled the matter of transportation once and for all was the discovery of gold in NSW and the newly separated Victoria in the early 1850s (see Chapter 8). Now, in the middle of a gold rush that saw hundreds and thousands of men and women desperate to get to Victoria and NSW and head straight for the diggings, insisting on transporting criminals (or ex-criminals) to Australia for free seemed like a really silly idea. The mineral wealth lying beneath the Australian soil dealt the Colonial Office a *fait accompli*, and after Earl Grey was no longer in charge of the Colonial Office, no-one bothered talking about transporting British criminals to the east coast of Australia again.

Van Diemen's Land continued to be treated as a sort of specialist convict terminus for criminals, receiving convicts throughout the 1840s and up until 1854. On the other side of the continent, Western Australia bucked the trend and actually requested convicts (see the sidebar 'A little help, please: Convicts in Western

Australia' for more on this). In total, about 164,000 convicts were transported to the Australian colonies between 1788 and 1868 on 806 ships.

Protecting Indigenous Australians — British Colonial Style

Without doubt, black–white relations were the ugly side of the pastoral expansion. Reports and rumours of frontier killings and deaths were frequent. While, technically, Australian Aboriginal peoples were British subjects, deserving of all the protection and rule of law as others, in reality, and far from any central supervision or authority, new settlers shot Aboriginals down as if they were (in the words of an early 20th-century historian) 'wild ducks'.

HISTORICAL ROOTS

The mistreatment of Australian Aboriginal peoples was happening at a time when public opinion in London was particularly sensitive to the condition of 'natives' in imperial domains. The 'Age of Reform' had begun in 1830, when a new Whig Government shaped new Reform Acts that enfranchised the middle classes and gave seats in parliament to new cities. Vigorous campaigns conducted by humanitarian and Evangelical groups to outlaw slavery in British colonies had proved successful. Those parliamentary reformers who had been successful in banning slavery now turned their sights on the condition of 'natives' and 'Aborigines' in British colonies. And they didn't like what they saw.

The British set about introducing new measures meant to protect Australian Aboriginals — without budging from the view that the land Aboriginal peoples inhabited was Crown land. They refused to recognise a treaty that was worked out between Aboriginals of Port Phillip and John Batman, but insisted that the perpetrators of a massacre at Myall Creek, where stockmen and convict shepherds killed 22 Aboriginals, be punished.

Attempting to protect Aboriginal peoples

Through the efforts of various Evangelical and Quaker philanthropists in London (in particular, Thomas Foxwell Buxton, the noted anti-slavery campaigner), the Aborigines' Protection Society was formed in 1837. To the Society, the condition of free Aboriginal people 'who may be termed British' was dire to the point of disgraceful.

According to the Society, 'our imported diseases produce frightful ravages; our ardent spirits deprave and consume their population; our unjust laws exclude them from enjoying that first element of well-ordered societies — judicial protection, as well as from the possibility of a timely incorporation with the Colonial communities; while, in addition to all these evils, our neglect of suitable methods of improving them, prevents their adopting the civilised manners and customs to which they are inclined'.

In August 1837, the Select Committee on Aborigines in British Settlements tabled its report in the House of Commons. The report suggested reservations of land should be set aside for Aboriginal people for them to hunt and live peacefully within until they eventually came round to the idea of tilling the soil. The report also suggested more money for missionaries and education, and that special 'Protectors' should be appointed who were able to prosecute whites who interfered with Aboriginals.

In January 1838, a new Aboriginal policy arrived for Governor Gipps from Lord Glenelg at the Colonial Office in London. Glenelg, himself an ardent Evangelical and strong humanitarian who had previously voiced deep misgivings about the effect that unsupervised pastoral expansion was having on Indigenous Australians, now lost no time in establishing new rules. The newest squatting district south of the Murray River — Port Phillip, at this stage still part of NSW — was divided into four provinces. A Chief Protector of Aborigines was appointed, who had four assistants. The Protectorate was to be paid from local revenue.

The Protectorate was not a success. Reports of outrages continued to filter back from the frontier zone of contact. The Chief Protector and his assistants were resented by settlers, who thought that the government seemed more concerned about protecting Aboriginal people from white attacks than protecting settlers from black incursions. The assistants, four lone and underfunded men, had no hope of policing the vast pastoral frontiers, especially when the majority of the squatting population was given no incentive to try to positively engage with Indigenous clans and tribal groupings in the regions they were overrunning.

The Noongar warrior Yagan was quoted in a contemporary Western Australia newspaper, describing the motivation for his resistance: 'You came to our country — you have driven us from our haunts, and disturbed us in our occupations. As we walk in our own country, we are fired upon by the white men. Why should the white men treat us so?'

ABORIGINAL RESISTANCE AND SELF-PROTECTION

The Aboriginal Protectorate established in Port Phillip by well-intentioned governors, bureaucrats and missionaries was not the only form of Aboriginal protection.

In many parts of Australia, Indigenous Australians played a role as 'black pioneers' adapting and adjusting to this new alien society being imposed upon them (refer to Chapter 6). This sort of adjustment was a type of autonomous self-protection. In many parts of Australia the self-protection also took the form of violent resistance.

Indigenous resistance leaders who fought against the expansion of British settlement in the colonial era include the following:

- **Pemulwuy**, an Eora man like Bennelong (described in Chapter 3), who took an almost exactly opposite path to Bennelong. He began his resistance to the settlement at Sydney at about the same time that Bennelong was getting on a ship with Governor Phillip to visit Britain. He led guerrilla-like raids on settlements throughout the 1790s, before being killed in 1802.

- **Windradyne**, a Wiradjuri man in the Upper Macquarie River region of NSW, who was a leading warrior during the 'Bathurst War' conducted between Indigenous people, settlers and soldiers during the 1820s. He led raids on settlers' crops, and was involved in clashes that resulted in the deaths of convict stockmen. He was eventually wounded in a tribal fight, and died of his wounds in Bathurst Hospital.

- **Musquito**, also an Eora man, who was involved in conflicts with settlers on the Hawkesbury River in the early 1800s. Captured and exiled to Norfolk Island, he eventually found his way to Tasmania (then called Van Diemen's Land). He won renown as a tracker of bushrangers before joining the still 'wild' Oyster Bay Tribe, leading raids on stores and killing settlers before eventual capture and execution in 1825. (Refer to Chapter 6 for more about Musquito in Tasmania.)

- **Yagan**, a warrior of the Noongar People in south western WA, who resisted the settler influx after the establishment of the Swan River colony in 1829 (refer to the sidebar 'A little help, please: Convicts in Western Australia', earlier in this chapter). Yagan saw the settler influx, as in so many other parts of Indigenous Australia, as a type of invasion. He was eventually captured and exiled (like Musquito had been) on the other side of Australia. He escaped from his exile and returned to Western Australia, but was shot and killed after a large bounty had been placed on him.

- **Jandamarra**, like Yagan, a Western Australian Indigenous man, but from the far north-west corner, whose resistance occurred at the end of the 19th century. Jandamarra was an initiated warrior of the Bunuba People, but one who had also grown up working and living extensively with white settlers. He organised and led an armed insurrection in the 1890s, in what constituted practically the last full-scale frontier conflict of the Australian continent.

New possibility on Merri Creek

The new regulations sent by Lord Glenelg, which set up protection zones for Aboriginal people, were diametrically opposed to the alternative mode of concili-ation that had been suggested by the Port Phillip Association (a handful of Van Diemen's Land pastoralists, businessmen and entrepreneurs).

In 1835 John Batman crossed Bass Strait from Van Diemen's Land to Port Phillip on behalf of the association. Like any other prospective squatter in the mid-1830s, he was on the lookout for good sheep grazing country — but he tried a completely different method of acquiring it.

In a bold move, Batman followed the practice that was being adopted in agree-ments with Maori people in New Zealand. On the bank of the Merri Creek (a trib-utary of the Yarra River), Batman struck an agreement and then signed a treaty with the local Wurundjeri people, a clan of the wider Kulin nation.

IN THEIR WORDS

Batman, as representative of the Port Phillip Association, promised to keep other settlers from overrunning the country if members of the Association were allowed to graze livestock throughout the region. He told the Aboriginal people that he had 'come in a vessel from the other shores to settle amongst them' and that he was 'although a white, a countrymen of theirs [Batman was a native-born son of a convict], and would protect them'.

Plenty of people, both at the time of the treaty and since, have criticised the treaty as nothing more than a scam — that Batman used classic trinkets such as beads, knives, tomahawks and mirrors to trick the 'gullible' natives into giving up their land. But this misses the significance of the act, and the possibilities it entailed. Settlement predicated on reaching good relations with local Aboriginals, aiming to maintain those relations on a localised family, clan and sheep-station level, and underwritten by the pledge to keep further arrivals out, was something entirely new.

HISTORICAL ROOTS

Squatters acting as protectors may seem preposterous, but Batman's treaty had one great advantage over the Protectorate plan that was eventually adopted at the urging of humanitarians and Evangelicals in London: The treaty combined self-interest with the best interests of Australian Aboriginals. If given official endorsement, it would have given settlers themselves real incentive to establish workable relations with the clans local to the regions they were moving into. If black–white relations were to be in any way sustainable in the immediate future, the two groups had to be mutually reconcilable.

If Batman's treaty had been officially recognised, it could have profoundly altered the subsequent nature of Australian settlement. But it wasn't recognised. Glenelg scotched it, reminding everyone that Indigenous Australians didn't have ownership of the land to begin with — the Crown did. Therefore, they couldn't strike agreements about access to it. The Protectorate plan became official policy. White and black were to be treated as warring tribes that had to be kept apart at all costs.

Same old tragedy on Myall Creek

If the Port Phillip Association's attempted treaty was a short-lived and optimistic example of what might have been, the tragedy of Myall Creek and its aftermath is a powerful example of how bad things actually were.

In June 1838, a mere six months after Governor Gipps had received Glenelg's new instructions and regulations for protecting Aboriginal people, a group of stockmen and convict shepherds at Myall Creek in the New England District of NSW retaliated against a series of cattle and sheep spearings by shooting, beating and knifing to death some 22 Aboriginal men, women and children from the local Wirrayaraay tribe.

At first this was likely to be just another 'outrage' that came back to Sydney in the form of unverified rumour. But Governor Gipps heard of it, had it investigated, and ordered 11 men to be arrested and tried for murder. When they were acquitted in the Supreme Court, Gipps refused to let it be. He ordered a retrial. This time seven men were sentenced to death.

This produced outrage throughout the colony. Petitions demanding reprieves and clemency poured in at Gipps's office. But Gipps, strengthened by the recent orders and regulations from London, held firm. In December 1838, the men were executed. The Colonial Office backed Gipps's actions.

Gipps, and the Colonial Office, won the battle — the guilty men were hanged — but lost the war. The executions seemed to only harden hostility in the minds of most white settlers. Killings on the frontier continued — but now they were better hidden.

IN THIS CHAPTER

» **Discovering gold and witnessing the biggest population explosion in Australia's history**

» **Recognising the assertiveness of Australian workers**

» **Allowing tensions to boil over in Eureka**

» **Welcoming more representative government**

» **Demanding land be made available for all**

Chapter **8**

The Discovery of Gold and an Immigration Avalanche

The Australian colonies emerged from the great economic crisis of the 1840s battered but stronger. Shorn (excuse the pun) of its late 1830s boom-time mania, the wool industry became robust and profitable. And townsmen, traders and the labouring classes had united to stave off the reintroduction of convict transportation in the late 1840s.

By the time the 1850s rolled round, things were looking steady and quietly prosperous, if perhaps a little unexciting. Most people assumed that the Australian colonies would continue to be the wool-source for the British manufacturing industry and not much else. Far away from the European centres, and with the United States much closer for prospective immigrants, Australia was a peripheral player in the global scene and, it was assumed, would continue to be so.

But then, in 1851, gold was discovered and the effect was stupendous. Within weeks, every spare ship was re-routing itself to Australia, and men and women from all walks of life were cramming themselves on board, more than happy to endure the four-month trip to the other side of the world on the basis of a glimmering hope that a pot of gold would be found at the end of it.

In this chapter, I cover the discovery of gold in Australia and the wide-ranging effects this had on colonial life — including the Eureka uprising, the expansion of male suffrage and the breaking down of the squatters' stranglehold on arable land.

You want gold? We got gold!

The impact on colonial society of the discovery of gold was volcanic — it ranks as one of the great 'game-changers' in Australian society, and quickened elements already in evidence. A gambler's ebullient optimism often prevailed in business ventures from the 1850s on, and an almost religious-like faith in progress and what the future entailed was born. The old social hierarchies were overturned. Labourers, both on the goldfields and off, found themselves with more power than ever before, and much more than they could have hoped to have gained in Britain, Europe or America.

Discovering gold (and going a little crazy)

For the first 50 years of settlement, colonial governors and governments hadn't wanted to know about gold. General consensus among the governing administrators was that the effects of the discovery of gold on a convict society would be dire.

IN THEIR WORDS

In the early 1840s, Governor Gipps of NSW told someone who showed him a recent unearthed piece of the ore to put it away at once — 'or we'll all get our throats cut!' (The authenticity of this line is actually a little doubtful, but it gives you the idea of attitudes at the time.)

Then, in 1849, a gold rush began in California. Before it knew it, the government was faced with men deserting the Australian colonies to get to the new goldfields. The government quickly changed its tune about discovering gold in Australia, and declared a reward for anyone who found any of the precious metal.

In March 1850, William Campbell at Clunes, situated in what the following year would be Victoria, found gold, but kept quiet about it (no doubt hoping to keep all the possible riches to himself). The following February, near Bathurst in NSW, Edward Hargreaves found gold, was very un-quiet about it, and claimed the reward. In May, the government released news of Hargreaves's find, and by the end of May 1,700 men were concentrated at the site of the find, which Hargreaves had named the Ophir Goldfield.

In June, a new rush occurred when news of gold on the Turon River, also in NSW, leaked out, and the Kerr Hundredweight nugget was found by an Aboriginal Australian in nearby Meroo Creek. Containing about 40 kilograms of gold, this nugget was bigger than anything found in California, and when news reached Sydney the town was quickly deserted as men grabbed or bought picks, crowbars, pans, tin pots, wash basins and colanders (and whatever else was handy) and took off up the road through the Blue Mountains to the hinterland.

This, however, turned out to be no more than the preview to the main event.

In mid-1851, Victoria separated from NSW to become a colony, with its own governor and government — and this new government faced an immediate challenge. With men walking off sheep runs in Victoria to go to the NSW goldfields, the Victorian Government also announced rewards for local finds to try to coax people back into the colony.

Some false starts occurred, with some small finds in Clunes in early July 1851. Then came the big ones: Major finds near Buninyong and Ballarat. And then the news got even better. In this part of Victoria, gold could be found close to the surface, just beneath the topsoil — unlike the 'creek-wash' gold in NSW, which was buried deeper underground.

Then, just when everyone was probably thinking it couldn't get much easier, it got easier. In late 1851, gold was found in the scrub beneath Mt Alexander (near what became Castlemaine in Victoria). Here, unbelievably, gold could be picked up by whoever got there first from the very surface of the ground and from out of the topsoil.

If you think this sounds like a fairytale, you're in good company — that's how the rest of the colonies and, when they found out about it, the rest of the world, reacted also. The greatest gold rush yet seen in history had begun, and its effect on people was such as to send the whole country collectively mad.

COMING DOWN WITH A BAD CASE OF GOLD FEVER

Few people were immune to the gold fever that spread through the colonies. In September 1851, the Melbourne newspaper the *Argus* reported that 'The whole town of Geelong is in hysterics' after news of the Ballarat finds first filtered through. 'Gentlemen [were] foaming at the mouth, ladies fainting, children throwing somersaults' from the news that 'splendid treasure' had been found 'imbedded in the light blue clay'.

A few weeks after the discovery in Ballarat, Charles La Trobe, Victorian governor, reporting to Earl Grey in the Colonial Office, announced that the streets of Melbourne were deserted, that men of all classes — everyone from common 'idlers' through to labourers, shopmen, artisans, clerks and mechanics — had run off to the diggings, and substantial amounts of men from 'the responsible classes' had gone with them. 'Cottages are deserted, houses to let, business is at a standstill, and even the schools are closed. In some of the suburbs not a man is left'.

The only thing to be done now, La Trobe concluded grimly, was 'to let the current spend itself', and hope the collective madness would soon subside and people would return to their ordinary minds and day-to-day occupations. Meanwhile, government would have to 'see as far as possible it is kept within proper bounds'.

Introducing order and hoping for calm

In 1852, gold-seekers began arriving from the rest of the world — including Europe, the US, Canada, South America and China. As one English visitor put it, in the ports and towns these new arrivals found 'wild Backwoods-looking fellows' striding up and down the streets, in rough coats, dirty boots, broad hats, long wild hair and shaggy beards. 'Almost every man had a gun, or pistols in his belt, and a huge dog, half hound half mastiff, led by a chain'. And the 'rage for gold' seemed to pervade 'everybody and everything in the colony'. Clearly there was little time to lose.

In 1853, the Victorian Government introduced uniform gold claims — 144 square feet for individuals and 576 square feet for groups. The allocation wasn't much room to dig in, but with so many thousands of new diggers arriving each week, it was best to ensure that everyone had a fair share. The size meant, however, that an individual's claim could be quickly exhausted, making mining populations prone to packing up and moving off en masse at the merest rumour of a new find or goldfield being opened up.

Governor La Trobe also introduced licences — if you wanted to dig for gold you had to pay the fee, regardless of whether you found any gold or not. La Trobe liked this idea because he thought it would clamp down on the enthusiasm and quickly force unsuccessful diggers, and those without money, to leave the goldfields and return to sober industry and ordinary jobs.

He had a long wait in store. (And the subsequent governor had trouble to come from the licensing system — see 'That Eureka Moment'.)

Adding a gambling mentality to the mix

If an entire society can be said to suffer an instantaneous collective seizure, then gold rush times in Australia was it. Everyone seemed to go a little crazy. Gold mining was a lottery, particularly after the first early finds, and, like any lottery, the odds were stacked against you. And yet that didn't matter. The manic search was on.

IN THEIR WORDS

When in Australia, the English novelist Anthony Trollope described the logic that seized hold of the committed gold-seeker who came out to try his luck. The digger knows most will miss out on the great prize — the welcome nugget, the big fortune — yet 'something tells him . . . that he is to be the lucky man'. Every man hustling up to the diggings was telling himself that same thing. Yet 'in truth he has become a gambler, and from this time forth a gambler he will live'.

HISTORICAL ROOTS

A distinctive element was being added to the Australian mentality here: The propensity to gamble. By gambling I don't simply mean the obvious forms — horses, boxing, two flies walking up a wall and so on. I also mean the gambling that was evident in people's approach to business and life. The reason many people were coming out to Australia was to make a fortune, as quickly as possible. Most of them didn't make a big fortune, and instead stuck around and settled down, but they remained willing to speculate financially on various daring adventures — in mining companies, in real estate, and in all sorts of smaller businesses. This kind of gambler's ebullient optimism meant more failures than in Britain — bankruptcies for individuals and businesses were common events in the 1850s and 1860s — but also a greater number of successes as well. Men and women arrived in the colonies with very little but then established themselves in all kinds of profitable ventures. They then began to widely populate colonial society and (for the men at least) its parliaments. The tenor of the colonies, like these men and women, was brash and ambitious, full of hustle and hustlers rather than deference and decorum.

Working Towards the Workingman's Paradise

In the early 1850s, Australia acquired the nickname 'the workingman's paradise'. It had a great climate (although arguably, compared to Britain, this wasn't the toughest competition), good work and high wages. 'Meat three times a day!' declared migration advocate Caroline Chisholm (see the sidebar 'Threats of revolution in Britain? Try the Australian safety-valve solution'). Chisholm, and others like her, conjured up an image of prosperity that was both, in strict terms, accurate (in Australia, if you wanted to, you *could* have meat three times daily), and, for workers emerging still a little shell-shocked from the 'Hungry Forties' in Britain, Ireland and Europe, unbelievably luxurious — it was the stuff of 'land of milk and honey' dreams.

When gold was found in the Australian colonies, angry radicals and hungry workers didn't need any more encouraging or assisting. They'd already heard the stories and read the reports about how good life could be in the colonies; the discovery of gold seemed to assure everyone that finally all their dreams could come true.

These radicals and workers flocked out to Australia in their hundreds and, soon, in their thousands, bringing with them their dreams — and their ideals of how society could be reformed.

IN THEIR WORDS

Visiting English novelist Anthony Trollope observed how gold 'upheaves everything, and its disruptions are those of an earthquake'. He went on to describe the effect of gold on the 1850s workman: 'He rushes away from his old allotted task, not to higher wages, but to untold wealth and unlimited splendour, to an unknown, fabulous, but not the less credited realm of riches. All that he has seen of worldly grandeur, hitherto removed high as the heavens above his head, may with success be his . . . His imagination is on fire, and he is unable any longer to listen to reason. He is no longer capable of doing a plain day's work for a plain day's wages. There is gold to be had by lifting it from the earth, and he will be one of the happy ones to lift it'.

HISTORICAL ROOTS

Plenty of things were transplanted without any great difficulty from Britain to its Australian colonies — language, laws, styles of houses, habits, tastes and customs, ways of farming, institutions of government and authority — but the social hierarchies of the British class system wasn't one of them. The relatively fluid and open nature of Australian society, the high value placed on mateship and equality (even as everyone busily does their best to make money) was already evident in colonial society before gold was discovered. Its discovery meant these elements were magnified, and this had immediate effects on day-to-day behaviour and on how people acted towards one another.

THREATS OF REVOLUTION IN BRITAIN? TRY THE AUSTRALIAN SAFETY-VALVE SOLUTION

Before gold was discovered, the vast Australian hinterland was already considered an ideal place to send the starving and discontented workers of Britain, but not for completely altruistic reasons — the people making these recommendations also feared these workers, if left in Britain, would foment revolution.

Caroline Chisholm — married to an officer in the East India Company, a convert to Catholicism and a keen advocate of social reform — was horrified by the Irish famine of the 1840s, and feared the influence of working-class radicals on British society. She and her husband established the Family Colonisation Loan Society to assist and encourage emigration among the 'lower orders'. In Australia, she declared, there had recently been discovered 'a vast, magnificent tract of country, rich in pasture, intersected by fine rivers, untrodden by European foot'. Australia was just the place for displaced poor and their large families to go to.

Chisholm wrote to Earl Grey, asking him, as Secretary of State for the Colonies, to provide assistance for the prospective emigrants. Earl Grey, however, thought people who chose to emigrate from Britain generally weren't worth assisting, so wasn't much help. Then she teamed up with the most famous and popular writer of the 1840s and 1850s: Charles Dickens. Together they did their best to encourage emigration as a way of dealing with the frightening prospect of violent working-class insurrection.

In a March 1850 edition of Dickens's paper, *Household Words*, Chisholm and Dickens collaborated on printing 'A Bundle of Emigrants' Letters', which included an excerpt from a letter from an angry radical who had emigrated to NSW. Once in this land of plenty, good wages and regular employment had made him renounce his previous wrong-headed radicalism.

Another writer and publicist, Samuel Sidney, whose books advised people on the best way to emigrate and who was being published at around the same time, explained the purpose behind his books: He wanted 'to enable my labouring fellow-countrymen to exchange their state as ill-paid, ill-fed workmen in England, Scotland and Ireland, for that of comfortable freeholders in Australia'.

IN THEIR WORDS

The 'social betters' noticed the alarming lack of deference and respect first, and were not in the least amused. Reverend Polehampton noted 'the independent manner, and *who cares for you?* bearing of everybody'. Heads had been 'completely turned' among the traders and shopkeepers — 'sudden riches had the usual effect of making vulgar people insolent'. Servants deserted their masters to go to the diggings. Masters headed to the diggings themselves, and often ended up grateful if they could find work as a cook to their ex-servants! 'In fact . . . a regular saturnalia [unrestrained revelry] was going on'. But this behaviour didn't bother everyone — especially not the gold diggers. One traveller described the diggers: 'They have no masters. They go where they please and work when they will'. Another writer noted 'a jauntiness of manner and a look of satisfaction' on people more properly subservient. A third traveller reported 'Diggerdom is gloriously in the ascendant here . . . every servant in this Austral Utopia thinks himself a gentleman'.

The social world down on the underside of the globe was in danger of being reversed, of turning classes upside down. The coming precedence of the working man in colonial life was widely anticipated.

LIFE DOWN UNDER

The assertiveness of working people wasn't limited to labouring men and shopkeepers. Female domestic servants displayed the same behaviour to dismayed respectable families. Maids attended table not dutifully but as if they were doing their employer a big favour, one resident observed. After luncheon the servant could be expected, 'if so inclined', to go out to shop for herself, 'or make calls without the embarrassing ceremony of asking permission. If mildly remonstrated with for not being home in time to prepare for dinner, it was then the invariable custom for well-bred servants to give immediate notice'. There was, concluded the frustrated writer, no choice but to submit to this 'menial tyranny', as finding a replacement could take weeks.

In significant ways the labour market had tilted dramatically (and alarmingly) in favour of the worker.

That Eureka Moment

As more and more people kept rushing to Victoria in search of gold, Governor La Trobe and, after him, Governor Hotham needed revenue to deal with the sudden influx of people, and it seemed fair that the diggers should provide it. La Trobe introduced a licensing system to regulate the gold-seekers, but it became increasingly resented as seasons passed and the gold search became more difficult.

Tensions continued to grow as some miners tried to avoid paying the licence fees, which led to a pretty unsophisticated crackdown from local police. Everything came to a head at the now infamous Eureka Stockade.

Rumblings of discontent

As the first flush of discovery faded in Victoria, and fewer people were finding gold, many people started to question the licence system. In December 1853, tensions were further increased when the Goldfields Management Act was tightened up and a new scale of fees introduced: £1 for one month, £2 for three months, £4 for six months and £8 for a year. Most miners, not finding gold, not flush with funds and optimistically hoping that a month's digging would be enough to secure a great fortune, went for the one-month fee. This was the cheapest option, but still more expensive than charges in NSW, where the licence fee had been reduced to 10 shillings per month.

By 1854, the easy finds in Victoria were over. Mining shafts needed to be sunk deeper and deeper as the surface alluvial gold began to be exhausted, and deeper reefs were what miners began to hunt for. This wasn't easy work, and the deeper you went the more dangerous it became.

LIFE DOWN UNDER

Not meeting with any luck, many miners avoided paying the licence fee, hiding down shafts or running off through the trees when police made periodic sweeps of the goldfields to check for licences. The police, a pretty rough and raw lot, responded by cracking down. Anyone found without a licence on them — even if they'd left it back in their tent while going down a water-soaked shaft, for instance — was arrested and carted off to the lockup. If no lockup was nearby, they could just be chained up to a tree and left there for hours, or overnight.

To say this infuriated the miners is to understate the case significantly. They figured they were now British subjects in a British colony — just because they'd sailed halfway round the world to get there didn't mean they could be deprived of their rights, and have punishment such as arbitrary imprisonment inflicted on them.

The fact that they were paying taxes to a government while being unable to have a say in the make-up of that government also began to rankle. 'No taxation without representation' began to be bandied round as a slogan, something that the large number of Americans on the goldfield would have been familiar with, seeing as it had inspired their own revolution and push to secede from Britain some 70 years earlier.

Tensions boil over

Early in 1854, La Trobe's replacement, Governor Hotham, made a tour of the goldfields. At the goldfields, many diggers made a point of proudly showing Hotham the success they'd had in their digging, hoping that he'd give them more respect as a consequence. This backfired badly — on his return to Melbourne, Hotham decided the diggers had it too easy and ordered that licence searches be stepped up!

A group of miners, led by ex-Chartists and Irish firebrands, decided they'd had enough. (See the sidebar 'The Chartists arrive' for more on this group.) By the start of December, at Eureka lead (a deep lead of gold near Ballarat), they'd built a wooden stockade to retreat into the next time the officers swept through the diggings, had unfurled the Eureka Flag (based on the Southern Cross) and had begun drilling miners in quasi-military formations for self-defence. The leader of the miners was 25-year-old Irishman Peter Lalor (who went on to be elected to the Victorian Legislative Assembly and eventually ended up the Speaker of the House).

On Sunday morning, 3 December 1854, 152 infantrymen, 30 cavalry riders, and 100 mounted and foot police stormed the barricade. While about 1,000 men and women had been inside the stockade on Saturday night (enjoying themselves and drinking a lot of whisky, chiefly), most had wandered back to their own tents and huts to sleep. No more than about 150 miners, mostly asleep, were left in the stockade when the troops and cavalry swept in. The ensuing struggle was nasty but short. Within 15 minutes the soldiers had taken the fort, and 34 miners and 6 soldiers were dead.

While dramatic enough, the real significance of Eureka lies not in the Sunday morning skirmish but its aftermath. Four days after the stockade was broken, Governor Hotham appointed a Gold Fields Commission to inquire properly into conditions on the goldfields. They reported back within months, recommending that the governor

» Abolish the licence fee

» Replace it with an export duty on gold

» Open up the Crown land for diggers to acquire small holdings to live on and cultivate

» Pass an Act to exclude or at least cut down on Chinese diggers on the fields

These recommendations largely reflected the original demands being made by the Ballarat Reform League, the local Chartist-inspired organisation (see the sidebar 'The Chartists arrive'). This group had also wanted all (white) men in the colony to be given the right to vote — what they termed 'manhood suffrage'. While they had to wait for this representation to be granted, it was only for another two years (see the next section). The radicals in the colony seemed to be winning the public fight over Hotham's (and other's) insistence that obedience and good order must come before all else.

Then, early in 1855, the ringleaders of the resistance at the stockade (those who had been caught, anyway) were tried for treason in a Melbourne court. The jury refused to convict them. The freed men were received in the street outside the court by a rapturous crowd and carried away.

Hotham may have won the battle, but the longer war went comprehensively against him. The attitude of the colony, and of the period itself, was running in the opposite direction.

THE CHARTISTS ARRIVE

In the 1850s, people came to Australia for gold — to strike it rich; to rapidly amass stupendous amounts of wealth. The bulk of those coming from the working and lower-middle orders of society in Britain were also coming out as economic refugees. A prolonged economic depression in a society experiencing the world's first industrial revolution had made for material deprivation. Out of this, a resurgent political movement for the working classes of Britain had emerged — the Chartist movement.

The Chartist movement gained its name from the People's Charter of 1838, which set out the social and political reforms the movement was hoping to achieve — the main ones being the extension of universal suffrage for all men over the age of 21 (middle-class males had already been given the vote in 1832) and an end to the need for a property qualification to run for parliament.

In Britain, workers' attempts to gain a say in parliament via the Chartist movement through the 1830s and 1840s had been rejected with contempt by the governing classes, and with some very real fear. The enfranchised minority feared mob rule of the violent and bloodletting kind, as seen in the excesses of the French Revolution only 50 years previously. (In England in the 1840s and 1850s, you couldn't call yourself a democrat, or argue for the right of all men to vote — manhood suffrage — without being accused of preferring the guillotine as a political problem-solving device.)

The people who signed the petitions of support for the Chartist movement in the 1840s were, predominantly, the same people getting off the ships docking in Melbourne and Sydney in the 1850s. Once here, they were completely unrepresented politically. However, manhood suffrage was introduced in most colonies in the late 1850s through not much more than a fait accompli — because suffrage was granted based on ownership of property. The effect of inflation on prices after the gold rush, and increasing rental and property values meant that most men in the colonies could already vote. The vast majority of newly arrived immigrant men (workers, radicals and the plain uninterested) found that they could vote in elections for the first time in their whole lives.

The Arrival of Self-Government

The influence of gold fever brought a tremendous change not only in Australian society but also in Australian politics. New immigrants brought new ideas and new expectations, just in time for a change in British law that gave the Australian colonies more say in their own governments.

Increased rental and property values meant practically all colonial men could vote for the lower houses of the new colonial parliament, while the upper houses maintained a more restricted franchise. This meant that the squatters, who had assumed they would become the new political elite once the governors stopped running local colonial affairs, were in for a rude shock.

Votes for a few men

In the 1820s, a Legislative Council was set up in NSW to assist the governor in governing, but it was made up entirely of individuals selected by the governor himself. In 1843, the first voting began when two-thirds of the Legislative Council was opened to individuals voted in by electors. But those given the right to vote (the franchise) were a select minority. Only those owning or renting substantial property qualified, excluding most of the working class. This partly elected council continued to work in conjunction with the governor.

The big money men — the squatters and pastoralists, the merchants, the bankers — were the men who were elected to the Legislative Council in the 1840s, and they had fully expected it would be them who would form the governments from colonial parliaments as soon as self-government was granted. But they were swept out of power as soon as they had a chance to gain it, reduced to maintaining surly resistance from the more elitist upper houses, blocking what legislation they didn't like whenever they could. But the governing went on without them, in spite of them, and often against them.

Votes for many men

In 1852, the British Government granted self-government to all the colonies except Western Australia (and Queensland, which hadn't been separated from NSW yet; that had to wait until 1859). (See Figure 8-1 for the establishment of Australian colonies, up to 1851.)

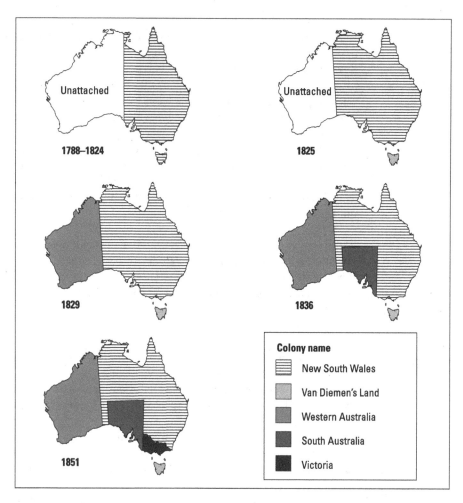

FIGURE 8-1:
The establishment
of Australian
colonies, up to
1851.

Map labels:
- 1788–1824: Unattached
- 1825: Unattached
- 1829
- 1836
- 1851

Colony name
- New South Wales
- Van Diemen's Land
- Western Australia
- South Australia
- Victoria

The big external questions — who to invade, who to threaten diplomatically, who to strike trade treaties with and so on — were still in the hands of London. However, all the day-to-day business of running the colonies was now in the hands of the soon-to-be-elected governments. These new governments would be able to make laws on questions of revenue, how to distribute Crown lands, and how much to spend on infrastructure and services such as roads, railways and ports. (The constitutions for these new governments were drafted by the old Councils.)

In NSW, the older hands who'd established themselves in previous decades tried to establish themselves as a political elite. William Wentworth (read more about his influence in Chapter 6) tried to institute a new form of aristocracy in the colony, an aristocracy who would have the major power in government. This aristocracy would be made up of people like . . . well, him: Men with large amounts of property and established wealth.

In a colony where everyone's fortune had been made in generally quite unaristo-cratic endeavours, and oftentimes dubious circumstances, it was difficult to see how this would work. The idea was laughed out of favour.

The longer the great gold decade went on, the more impossible the idea of any kind of hereditary aristocracy, or even a limitation on the franchise (right to vote), seemed to be. These kinds of ideas went against the essential mood of the place. In stark contrast to the mood in Britain (refer to the sidebar 'The Chartists arrive'), the whole spirit of the colonies was an essentially democratic one.

The idea of universal manhood suffrage became more and more popular through-out the Australian colonies.

REMEMBER

While the workers and radicals in colonial Australia were arguing for universal manhood suffrage — that is, the extension of the right to vote to all adult males — they didn't really mean all males. Manhood suffrage would be granted to British subjects only. Other immigrants would continue to be excluded, as would Aborig-inal men in most cases (with Aboriginal people not being granted the right to vote federally until 1962).

In 1856, the new government in South Australia granted all male British subjects over the age of 21 the right to vote. Victoria followed in 1857 and in 1858 NSW joined these colonies in instituting manhood suffrage. (Women would have to wait a while longer for the right to vote — see Chapters 11 and 12.)

IN THEIR
WORDS

Given that in Britain at this time only one in five men could vote, the Australian colonies granting manhood suffrage was a leap into the democratic dark. Much of the politics in the colonies at this time reflected this new democratic and populist turn — suddenly the men forming colonial governments weren't wealthy land-owners like William Wentworth. Liberals, radicals and workers started getting voted into the crucial lower houses — which is where governments are formed. So governments began to be formed by small business people, shopkeepers, auction-eers, grocers and publicans rather than the big money men.

Many working people who had supported the great Chartist cause in the 1830s and 1840s (refer to the sidebar 'The Chartists arrive') now saw a chance to push for further changes — such as the enforcement of an eight-hour working day, pay-ment for politicians and the ending of the property qualification needed to run for parliament. They also saw they would be able to push for these changes in a soci-ety that didn't have the 'drag' effect of old established hierarchies and outdated institutions. A new radicalism became accepted among politicians, newspaper editors and stump orators alike.

Suffrage goes rogue

After manhood suffrage had been granted in the Australian colonies (refer to preceding section), it seems the new taste of power went to the heads of the workers, and they began issuing all kinds of 'outlandish' demands.

Demanding an eight-hour day — and getting it

During the gold rush and the sustained economic boom that followed, demand for workers was so strong that workers themselves, alongside calls for manhood suffrage, were able to push for improved hours and conditions well in advance of the rest of the world.

In 1856, stonemasons at work constructing the university quadrangle in Melbourne downed tools and marched to Parliament House to demand an eight-hour working day — a long-held but unrealised Chartist ideal. They got it (see Figure 8-2), and it spread to other skilled trades and other colonies soon after — with a Factory Act in 1873 even going so far as to limit the working hours of women to eight hours too.

FIGURE 8-2:
A banner commemorating the achievement of an eight-hour working day.

EIGHT HOURS WORKING LEAVES MORE TIME FOR PLAY (AND PARADING)

The 'eight hours work, eight hours rest and eight hours recreation' principle had been advocated by the occasional radical in Britain since the 1830s but had never come close to being realised. From 1856, it was a reality in Australia and workers ranked the achievement so highly that they insisted on turning the anniversary of the achievement into a public holiday, with an 'eight-hour day procession' to go with it.

An English observer described 'the eight-hours demonstration' in the large cities and towns of Australia to his bemused British audience by comparing it to what they might see at the Lord Mayor's Show in London. Different trades all marched through with various banners, all dragging floats — the blacksmith float with a shoeing forge, for example, and the bakers with big bread loaves. There were printers and news-boys, biscuit manufacturers throwing out various sweets, tobacconists throwing out small plugs of tobacco and, occasionally, a brewery would run a float with a huge beer barrel on it. Perhaps not surprisingly, the beer float was always very popular, with 'beer drawn and handed to thirsty souls in the crowd'.

LIFE DOWN UNDER

The gaining of the eight-hour working day had further ramifications in colonial life. Thanks to the enforcement of shorter working hours, Charles Don, a stonemason, could run for and enter parliament. As parliamentarians still weren't paid, workers previously hadn't been able to run for parliament. Now Don was able to work for eight hours until four in the afternoon, and then make his way to the Legislative Assembly (the lower house) where he represented the good people of Collingwood in the evening.

Demanding the opening up of arable land

In 1857, and again in Melbourne, a Land Convention was formed as an alternative unofficial parliament, where different Victorian townships and goldfields sent delegates to debate what changes should be made to the colony. Members of this convention began meeting in the Eastern Market of Melbourne to discuss how best to take the land off the pastoralists (who held vast blocks of land leased to them as squatters) and throw it open to all the new arrivals. In 1858 they marched on parliament with a brass band playing 'La Marseillaise' (or 'the Marseillaise Hymn' — which had been the song of the French Revolution), waving a banner that declared 'When Justice is denied, allegiance ceases to be a duty'. A riot ensued. (For more on moves to open up the land to more people, see the section 'Unlocking the Arable Lands').

Demanding higher trade protection

In 1859, a Tariff League was born. The league argued against the prevailing *laissez faire* free trade economic orthodoxy then current in Britain, insisting that in the colonies a heavy customs duty should be used to keep imports out and encourage the growth of local manufactures and industry (and with it, jobs).

The first protectionist tariff introduced in any Australian colony was in Victoria some seven years later (in 1866). The new tariff placed duties of 10 per cent on goods such as watches, jewellery, glass and blankets coming into the colony, and added similar rates to various fabrics and textiles. The tariff proved popular — by 1877, Victoria was placing a massive 30 to 40 per cent tariff rate on many goods, and after Federation tariffs became the dominant policy for Australia, and stayed in place into the 1980s.

Unlocking the Arable Lands

The vast majority of gold-rush migrants didn't find gold. Many returned to the major cities of Sydney and Melbourne and the old trades and jobs they'd previously had in Europe, America or Britain. However, they also declared that if they couldn't get gold, the next best thing was a life on the land. A little plot of land, with a small cottage, some livestock, a crop (and maybe even some bees) and they'd be quite contented. But first there was a problem — the arable land was taken up by squatters, who had secured long-term leases in 1847 (refer to Chapters 6 and 7).

Moving the squatters

The 1850s immigrants most enthusiastic about 'unlocking the lands' were:

>> **The urban middle classes:** The town-based traders, shopkeepers, school teachers and bankers all reckoned that the denser the settlement throughout the colony, the better the opportunities for making money from trading goods and services. The squatters with their (to English eyes) enormous pastoral runs were taking up good land that could be better used by putting far more people on it in smallholdings and closer settlement schemes.

>> **The working classes:** These immigrants had arrived in Australia with high hopes for a new life of big fortunes and gold. Not finding these things, they turned to another dream they'd long cherished — of owning land, being their own master and growing their own food. Coming from Britain, they'd grown up in the most advanced economy in the world. Agriculture was no longer the

mainstay of their lives, as it still was in more traditional parts of Europe and the rest of the world, but it had been for their parents or grandparents (or failing that, great-grandparents . . . a long time ago at any rate). They wanted to recreate a cherished vanished dream.

Before these immigrants could settle, they faced the problem of getting rid of the squatters. This never happened fully — wool was the most profitable industry possible on the Australian hinterland at this time, and it was the squatters who controlled this industry. Aside from gold, wool, and so squatters, was the mainstay of the Australian economy.

But the opponents of the squatters also had a couple of other realities to face.

Those who spoke out against the squatters said they were a new pseudo-aristocracy — a tiny elite who got to dominate the upper houses of colonial parliaments. But squatters, much as they themselves might try to pretend otherwise, were no landed aristocracy. They were from all sorts of backgrounds, and the properties themselves weren't sealed off in the hands of one social group or class in colonial society.

Ownership of land held by squatters was fluid — there was high turnover, and many people who arrived in the 1850s and went on to make money (including grocers, publicans and cabinetmakers) found themselves investing in squatting runs as a profitable enterprise.

The next problem was that the dream of being contented small-time farmers was a tad unrealistic, given that the bulk of those trying for it in the 1850s had been townspeople and city-dwellers.

REMEMBER

The dreams of being a proud independent *yeoman* (in English cultural tradition, a yeoman was a self-supporting small-scale farmer, and so was a cut above the peasantry) may have been a reaction to the realities of the modern capitalist, urban and industrial life these immigrants had grown up in, rather than growing out of a realistic knowledge and understanding of agrarian living. These immigrants hadn't been yeomen before coming to Australia — many of them had never been *any* kind of farmer. Some very sweet dreams were about to run smack bang into some annoying reality.

Despite being based on unrealistic dreams, the demands for land to be taken off squatters and opened up to selection by more people continued.

Making new laws for new farmers

From the early 1860s in both NSW and Victoria, the 14-year pastoralist leases granted by the British parliament (refer to Chapter 6) began to expire. Legislation began to be passed in the new colonial parliaments to assist people who wanted to be small-time farmers. These were the Land Selection Acts, and they were intended to allow people to select small blocks of land for agricultural use. A whole series of them were passed because they had the annoying habit of creating more problems for the would-be farmers than they solved — which meant that a new Act would have to be designed to deal with the problems caused by the previous one, which had been brought in to deal with the unholy mess created by the earlier one, which . . . well, you get the idea.

LIFE DOWN UNDER

In NSW, land was made available for 'free selection' with the radical Robertson Land Act of 1861. Amazingly, this Act meant people could just wander onto a pastoralist's holding and stake out their claim, much like when digging for gold, and the squatter couldn't do anything immediate about it. The selector had to pay a deposit to the Lands Department, and then could buy the land over a three-year period. They didn't need to wait for surveyors to mark out the land first — the selector could just turn up, peg some land, pay a bit of money, and become the owner-in-waiting. The squatters didn't take this super-well, and resorted to all sorts of ruses and tricks, such as buying select pieces of land (those with water access, for instance) and so making the surrounding land not worth having, and paying 'dummies' to select on their behalf.

In Victoria, the land-selection movement was more powerful and radical than in NSW, thanks to all the Chartist radicals turning up for the gold rush (refer to the sidebar 'The Chartists arrive'). But the upper house of the Victorian Parliament, the Legislative Council, had a very restrictive franchise, and members of this house managed to find loopholes and hobble much of the early legislation. This meant it was only in 1869 (with the Grant Act) that Victorians were finally granted free selection before surveying.

Dealing with squatter problems

On the face of it, the life of a squatter would appear to be not that great in the colonies in the 1850s and 1860s. Holding leases that were about to expire, in colonies where universal male suffrage had been granted and where the majority of voters overwhelmingly approved of the idea of setting up small-scale farms on land that the pastoralists had held previously, you'd expect most squatters to be getting a little worried.

But the first selection Acts passed in NSW and Victoria (refer to the preceding section) generally had the *opposite* effect of what the mass of legislators and voters had intended. Squatters actually used the new laws to strengthen their hold on the land.

Squatters did this by:

>> Creating as many loopholes in the Acts as they could (made possible via their control of the upper houses in colonial parliaments), and then exploiting every loophole available.

>> Employing 'dummy' selectors. These were men and women who were paid off by the pastoralist to front up and select the land before anyone else, live on it for however long the minimum occupancy period required by law was (generally three years), and then 'sell' it to the squatter in question.

>> Purchasing land at public auctions themselves. Public auctions, which often forced the price of land beyond the reach of new immigrants, were being held at the same time as the Selection Acts were coming into effect.

>> Arranging for public reserves to be declared on crucial areas of land — say, areas with river frontage — so they could continue using it for their stock but selectors weren't able to settle on it.

But many of the pastoralists got their comeuppance by the end of the 1860s. Not only did the Selection Acts tighten up considerably, as legislators ironed out the flaws, but the squatters had also overextended themselves financially. They had often borrowed large amounts of capital to buy up all the land they felt was at risk of selection, and they were then hit by a bad drought in the second half of the 1860s.

Facing up to non-squatter problems

Most selectors came from the major towns and cities of a highly industrialised Britain, and lacked a background and expertise in rural pursuits. Without enough capital to establish a viable and profitable farm in the modern, industrialised, sense, yet lacking knowledge and expertise in the traditional practices required to make a successful self-sustaining non-profit venture, many failed in these early years, walked off their selections and returned to the towns and cities.

Selectors would have a much better chance in the 1870s. New Selection Acts finally ironed out a lot of the previous loopholes and problems and, most important of all, the railway lines began to penetrate the hinterland. For the first time, goods and produce could be freighted from farms direct to the big markets in the towns and cities. (For more on the introduction of train networks in the colonies, and the effects this had, see Chapter 9.)

WHAT THE ITALIANS, GERMANS AND CHINESE SHOWED COULD BE DONE

A strong contrast to the broader failures of British selectors in the early years of selection can be found in the success that was made by some of the other working-class arrivals during the 1850s and 1860s — such as the Italians, Germans, Swiss and Chinese. Coming from countries and regions where rural traditions hadn't been eliminated by various agricultural and industrial revolutions, they fared much better.

Italians and Swiss immigrants established themselves in Daylesford and Hepburn Springs in Victoria, and Germans played an instrumental role in establishing viticulture in South Australia's Barossa Valley. Italian soil was generally unpromising land, so reclaiming and improving substandard soil was part of their agricultural tradition. Australian soil was similar to Italian soil and wasn't suited to intensive agriculture, so Italian immigrant farmers benefitted from the knowledge they brought with them. German settlers were frequently from peasant communities, and so brought with them practical traditions. Lutheran Protestants were frugal, hardworking and pious, believed in work for work's sake, and were noted for their industry, application and quiet perseverance.

And for the rest of the century, Chinese immigrants and sojourners (those who had got past the prohibitive poll taxes and restrictive entry laws) were to also show how possible it was to grow vegetables and other crops if you came from a culture that was still agriculturally literate. They would provide the bulk of the greens and much of the fruit that colonials ate in the second half of the 19th century.

These small European and Asian minorities remained the exception, but they showed what was possible given the right background, cultural traditions and approach.

IN THIS CHAPTER

» Exploring what the big fuss was about when it came to explorers

» Dispelling — and creating — exploration myths with Sturt and Leichhardt

» Entering the great intercontinental race with Stuart versus Burke and Wills

» Getting established on the land with selectors and bushrangers

» Bushranging with Ned Kelly and the Kelly Gang

» Heading towards nationhood with telegraph and trains

Chapter **9**

Explorers, Selectors, Bushrangers . . . and Trains

Explorers and bushrangers have the biggest claims to being the first 'heroes' of colonial Australia. Even though explorers were celebrated by their contemporaries as being the outriders of civilisation while bushrangers were decried by many for being at war with society, both groups had something in common. They were both active in the remote or rural hinterland of the Australian continent, which most colonial arrivals had remarkably little contact with.

Even though the emerging mythology of the Australian colonies featured explorers traversing wilderness, and bushrangers performing bold highwayman-like deeds in remote rural areas, the majority of colonial Australians were urban, living in the towns and cities that clung to the coast. It took the arrival and expansion of the train networks for the rural areas of the colonies to be brought more closely into the familiar experience of most colonials.

In this chapter, I cover the major players in the exploration and bushranging businesses, the myths that built up around them, and the impact these activities had on colonial life. I also cover the expansion of the telegraph and train network in Australia, which allowed an exploration of a different kind.

Explorer Superstars

In the 19th century, explorers in Australia were treated in a similar way to our modern-day sports stars. They pitted themselves against the elements and other explorers as they competed for the great prestige that came with achieving certain feats. (These feats included first to cross the continent, first to cross the continent and not *die* while doing so, and first to find a non-existent inland sea.) Public subscriptions subsidised the various expeditions, and explorers' exploits were recounted in intricate detail in the newspapers (all with the excited tone of 'This just to hand . . .'). They received rapturous welcomes if they returned alive, and solemnly impressive martyr-like funerals if they died in the attempt.

REMEMBER

Colonial Australians were predominantly urban. In the second half of the 19th century, more people in Australia lived in towns and cities, proportionately, than anywhere else in the world: More than the United States, more than Canada, more than Britain, more than anywhere in Europe. With the exception of a small cluster of gold towns in Victoria — such as Castlemaine, Bendigo, Beechworth and Ballarat — practically all the significant towns and cities were clinging to the coast, sending staple exports and receiving imports and immigrants. The farms and the bush weren't where most people lived. Most long-term colonial residents wouldn't have seen a bushfire, an Aboriginal or a kangaroo.

Seeking thrills in the 'great unknown' . . .

Colonial urbanisation helps explain why explorers in this period became the big heroes of Australian life — it was through following the exploits and stories of the explorers that colonial Australians got some sense of contact with the Australian interior. Plus, compared to most humdrum lives, the world of the explorer was undeniably exciting — head off into the interior and there was a good chance you might die. Starvation, scurvy, spearing, drowning or just plain disappearing: Plenty of opportunity for adventure arose.

. . . Then making the unknown known

As well as being admired as adventurers, the explorers were also lauded as 'men of science'. Many had scientific training and backgrounds, had worked as surveyors, and did the work of civilisation — encountering what was unknown to Europeans, topographically surveying it, reducing great mysteries to the realm of the known, and putting it all on maps. These explorers found land that was new to the colonial Australians — some of it immediately useful for graziers, agriculturalists and settlers, much of it not, but it all became *known*. The explorers were taming the wilderness and creating new knowledge, as 19th-century scientists prided themselves on doing.

HISTORICAL ROOTS

The Victorian Era (from around the 1830s to the end of the century) was big on progress. People had all these new inventions — such as steam, telegraph, electricity, telephone and trains — which transformed what was possible in the world, improved standards of living and completely changed the way people lived. The acts of the explorers seemed to be a very dramatic and bold example of the more general mood of British progress and 'civilisation': The explorers were the 'advance guard' of progress and civilisation. Within this mood of general advancement, the whole continent was going to be drawn into the dominion of colonial Australians, and this was an unalloyed good thing. Very few people at the time questioned its impact on Indigenous Australians, and even fewer noticed how assistance from Aboriginal people was often vital to the explorer's survival in difficult environments.

Sometimes the wilderness beat civilisation, as when Burke and Wills died, Leichhardt disappeared, or Sturt's long-cherished dream of a vast inland sea surrounded by fertile land was found to be dry and stony desert (see the sections later in this chapter for more on all of these explorers). Other times, progress was the winner over wilderness, as when Sturt found land that would become South Australia or when Stuart completed the herculean labour of finding a viable way through the centre of the continent (which the Overland Telegraph would later follow). But always the story was a good one. Explorers, successful or otherwise, were seen and spoken of as the outriders and the trailblazers of settler society's inevitable advance. And some of them looked rather spiffy on camels.

See Figure 9-1 for the routes travelled by Sturt, Leichhardt, Burke and Wills, and Stuart.

FIGURE 9-1:
The routes
travelled by Sturt,
Leichhardt, Burke
and Wills and
Stuart in the
19th century.

— · — · — · —	Sturt 1829–30
— — — — —	Leichhardt 1844–45
· · · · · · · · · ·	Burke and Wills 1860–61
—————	Stuart 1860, 1861, 1862

0   300   600 km

Sturt and Leichhardt Go Looking

Charles Sturt and Ludwig Leichhardt were two explorers whose most prominent exploits took place in the 1840s. Sturt, courteous, good-hearted and decent, dispelled a long-standing myth that had grown up in previous decades — the existence of an inland sea. Leichhardt, brooding, enigmatic, German, didn't dispel a myth — he *became* one. He pulled off the greatest exploratory feat to date when he led a party from Moreton Bay (in modern-day Brisbane) to Port Essington (north-east of modern-day Darwin). A couple of years later he set off to cross the continent . . . and disappeared completely.

Sturt — have boat, will walk

Charles Sturt was born in India, the son of an East India Company judge based in Bengal. At the age of five he was sent to England to live with relatives, be educated and to follow generally the established pattern for the sons of the British in the Indian colonies: Harrow at 15, then Cambridge, then the military.

HISTORICAL ROOTS

Arriving in Sydney with his regiment in 1827 and placed in charge of convicts, Sturt became interested in the work done by John Oxley and Alan Cunningham in charting rivers that seemingly all headed inland. In 1828 he was given the job of tracing the course of the Macquarie River, which led him to the Murrumbidgee River. In 1829 he followed this river into the Murray River, which took him to the Southern Ocean. His published accounts of the land he found around the mouth of the Murray River led to the establishment of a new colony: South Australia. In 1838 Sturt himself overlanded cattle to the new colony, and found himself pleasantly surprised at the admiring reception he received on his arrival in Adelaide. Once settled in Adelaide, he joined the public service.

Even after Sturt's tracking of various rivers, the great mystery of what exactly lay in the middle of the continent was still unsolved. Sturt liked the idea of an inland sea and was so confident in it becoming a reality that in August 1844 he led an expedition off into the interior — carrying a boat.

Initially, Sturt and his party followed where the rivers were going. But this turned out to be fruitless — they kept petering out into marshes or small lakes. Further on and further into the interior, the party found themselves stuck in dry, hot, stony country in the middle of summer, and had to bunker down until fortuitous and heavy rains arrived in July 1845.

They kept going, still hopeful of finding an inner sea (at least Sturt was — some of his fellow travellers were having serious doubts), only to run into the Simpson Desert. With the second–in–command dead from scurvy, the party had to retreat to find water. Sturt then had the bright idea of heading off on what would have been a 724-km journey to the still-unseen centre of the continent. His party managed to talk him out of this final act of death-and-glory-style heroic, and they began to retrace their steps to Adelaide.

IN THEIR WORDS

The whole endeavour was, Sturt said, 'a fearful but a splendid enterprise . . . if I fell my name would stand in a list I have always envied'.

The whole thing took 16 months. Instead of a vast inland sea, Sturt had found barren, stony desert. On the plus side, he'd lived to tell the tale.

Leichhardt also walks . . . right off the map

If no Germans had come to the Australian colonies in the 19th century, not only would Australia have lacked for the beginnings of a serious wine industry (courtesy of Germans who settled in the Barossa Valley), but also a significant number of all colonial scientific endeavours mightn't have been attempted so early.

HISTORICAL ROOTS

German education and science throughout the 19th century was at the forefront of progress, while British science education lagged behind. Prussian schools and universities pumped out botanists, naturalists, astronomers, physicists, artists and explorers while British institutions tended to produce fluent speakers of Latin and ancient Greek. Australia, and the Australian frontier, as a 'new' country for the western world, required scientists, naturalists and artists to help people gain an intellectual grasp of this largely alien continent they lived in. A vital proportion of this scientific and artistic reconnaissance was carried out by arrivals from Germany. The most famous example of this was Leichhardt, soon to be renowned as the lost explorer.

Having studied at Berlin University in philosophy, classics, biological sciences, mathematics and anatomy, Ludwig Leichhardt travelled throughout Europe, meeting and becoming close friends with Englishman William Nicholson. Under Nicholson's influence, Leichhardt came out to Australia.

In August 1844 (the same month as Sturt was leaving Adelaide to search for the inland sea), Leichhardt left Sydney and travelled north to Brisbane. In October 1844, he then set off on an expedition to the far north of modern-day Queensland. A year and two months later, and some eight months late, he and his party reached Port Essington (north-east of modern-day Darwin), with everyone having already given him up as lost. Although late, Leichhardt had managed the opposite of Sturt's venture: As he travelled through the interior but parallel to the coast, he had found fertile, well-watered country. Leichhardt thought it 'magnificent country', and everyone thought he was wonderful. He received a tumultuous reception on his return to Sydney, and the explorer cult went stratospheric.

For his next trick, Leichhardt attempted to cross the continent, from east to west — which had never before been achieved. Leichhardt tried once and failed. He tried a second time and disappeared, along with his party, without trace. His career, and dramatic end, has been inspiring poems, novels, paintings and plays ever since.

The Great Race — Stuart versus Burke and Wills

The late 1850s saw increasing colonial rivalry for the honour, prestige and publicity that would result from sponsoring great exploratory expeditions — not to mention for news of any great untapped resources in the interior of the continent that might be ready to plunder.

HISTORICAL ROOTS

In 1860, both South Australia and Victoria got caught up in the race to cross the continent for the first time. The ostensible purpose of exploration (science, knowledge, blah, blah . . .) took a back seat as colonies sent men out with the express purpose of just getting to the other side — as quickly as darn possible, please. The results were sometimes tragic, sometimes farcical, and very occasionally useful.

While Robert O'Hara Burke and William John Wills of Victoria made it onto the big disaster list, feats of endurance and survival helped John McDouall Stuart's endeavours as part of the South Australian contingent join the growing list of stirring explorer adventure tales.

Seeing the back of Burke, losing Wills

Robert O'Hara Burke was many things: An Irish ex-army officer with a thirst for glory; a Castlemaine police superintendent with a mad crush on a Melbourne bombshell actress. He was also a man of persuasive charm, as is evident from the fact that he managed to convince the Royal Society of Victoria to appoint him leader of the expedition to the north coast of Australia, despite not having any exploration experience.

The expedition's chief purpose was not so much scientific or geographic — the cashed-up gold rush colony of Victoria just wanted the honour and glory of being the first colony to sponsor an expedition that crossed the continent. Time was an issue too, because South Australia had John McDouall Stuart, a veteran of Sturt's earlier expedition, itching to do the same (see the following section for details of Stuart's expeditions). It was going to be what Victorian Governor Barkly called a 'glorious race across the continent' between two great rivals: Victoria and South Australia.

IN THEIR WORDS

Burke's expedition left Melbourne in August 1860, and confidence was more than high, it was soaring: 15,000 enthused Melburnians turned out to see them off. 'Where the camel pioneers the way, telegraph and railway will in due course inevitably follow', said *The Age*. The exploration party was more like an advance force of Victorian conquest, the article continued, and great cities would surely rise up 'beside the now lonely waters of Carpentaria'. Nowadays 'there is nothing improbable, much less impossible . . .' and Burke and his party are just the men to reveal new territory that will succumb to settlement, commerce, trade, railways, telegraphs and all the rest.

Burke's party was far from modest — it consisted of officers, a camel-master, several Afghan camel drivers, a surveyor-meteorologist (William Wills), two German scientists (never leave home without them), one foreman and nine assistants. The provisions packed bordered on the ridiculous (actually, they breezed past that border). All initially considered essential for the trip, supplies packed included oak tables and chairs, rockets and a Chinese gong.

Their original progress was more like a slow victory parade, but things began to speed up as Burke grew more impatient and began dumping supplies (some of which would turn out to be essential, such as sugar), splitting the party up, and arguing with various other party members. Wills was made second-in-command after Burke quarrelled with the first holder of this position. By the end of 1860, a base camp had been established at Cooper's Creek (in South Australia) and Wills, Burke, Charles Gray (an ex-seaman) and John King (a young Irish ex-soldier) then made a dash for the Gulf of Carpentaria.

This smaller party was in luck with the weather — heavy rains that season temporarily converted the Stony Desert (which Sturt had discovered) into one big garden dotted with lily ponds, and finding water supplies, normally the biggest problem in the Australian interior, was no hindrance. But such was their haste that navigation readings were inaccurate, and they didn't stop to hunt for much-needed fresh food — the overwhelming goal was beating Stuart to the north coast.

The goal was reached, just — the party turned back after sighting a sludgy tidal channel in mangrove swamp near the Gulf — but they were now very far from home.

Camels were dying and more equipment was abandoned. Gray died, and Burke, Wills and King spent a day scratching out a shallow grave to bury him. This proved fatal — they got back to Cooper's Creek, more than a month overdue, to find the main party had left that morning. On arriving at the camp, they failed to see the tree marked 'Dig', directing them to precious supplies. Then, as they gradually starved to death, Burke fired on local Aboriginal people who had been providing food to the main party. Four search parties were sent after them, and King was eventually found being sustained by Aboriginals. Burke and Wills, however, were both dead.

CAMELEERS OPENING UP AUSTRALIA'S INTERIOR

Cameleers from modern-day Afghanistan, Pakistan and India made possible an entirely new era of transport in the arid and semi-arid regions of the Australian continent. They opened up NSW, Queensland, South Australia, the Northern Territory and Western Australia, playing key roles in nearly all sectors of transport and exploration. They supplied homesteads and mining camps, carting ore, wool, provisions, timber, firewood, stones, water, railway sleepers, roof tin, rails, nails, insulators, wire, telegraph posts, and so on, and on.

The cameleers were not only a vital component of Australia's internal infrastructure in the 19th century, without which internal settlement and commerce was unthinkable, they were also the first Muslim immigrants. They brought with them a distinct set of religious and cultural practices that flourished in the various 'Ghantown' settlements in many of the major interior townships. While ethnically diverse — coming as they did from Afghanistan, Baluchistan, the Punjab, and the Kashmir and Sind provinces in modern-day Pakistan and India — they were almost all Muslim. They built permanent mosques in Adelaide and Perth, while all outback 'Ghantown' settlements featured rough shelters as bush mosques.

While many Afghanis remained workers, some rose to prominence to become significant business owners and community leaders. The camel-driving industry was not simply a case of cheap foreign labour being brought into Australia to carry out a necessary and unpleasant task. It was a vital industry that, by the time it was most needed during the 1880s and 1890s (as the WA goldfields of Kalgoorlie and Coolgardie were opened up), was chiefly in Afghan hands.

In January 1863, the remains of Wills and Burke were given a state funeral in Melbourne. The city streets were packed with 40,000 people in a public farewell of what the local paper called 'two gallant but unfortunate men'. The funeral procession took three hours to weave through the thick crowd. Overall, the project had cost an astronomical £60,000 (including the cost of monuments to commemorate those who had died), and seven lives.

Super Stuart — just a pity he's drunk

John McDouall Stuart was an intense Scot given to drinking. He arrived in South Australia (SA) in his early 20s, at about the same time that Charles Sturt overlanded some cattle there from NSW (refer to the section 'Sturt — have boat, will walk', earlier in this chapter). Stuart accompanied Sturt on the 1844 expedition into the interior, and was the companion Sturt chose near the end of the trek to join him on an insane 724-km journey to the very centre of the Australian continent (fortunately both Sturt and Stuart were talked out of it).

Apart from nearly dying in a hare-brained scheme, Stuart benefitted mightily from the Sturt expedition. He'd watched a pro in action, and become accomplished at topographical mapping and survey work. Unlike the Burke and Wills expedition, the subsequent journeys he took were clearly navigated and mapped.

Stuart's expedition to the centre

In the 1850s, Stuart worked as a surveyor, and led successful expeditions in SA in search of gold, grazing country and stock routes, and became the first to cross the salt lakes that had hemmed settlement in. He was, therefore, the prime candidate when in July 1859 the SA parliament offered a £2,000 reward for the first expedition to successfully cross the Australian continent.

By April 1860, Stuart was camped at the centre of the continent, and next day planted the Union Jack flag at what he named Mt Sturt in honour of his mentor (but which was afterwards changed to Mt Stuart to honour the discoverer himself).

IN THEIR WORDS

Stuart wrote in his journal that 'we . . . gave three hearty cheers for the flag, the emblem of civil and religious liberty . . . may it be a sign to the natives that the dawn of liberty, civilization, and Christianity is about to break upon them' (lucky fellows).

Stuart continued north, reaching Tennant Creek (pretty much the centre of what we now know as the Northern Territory) and beyond before being stopped by impenetrable scrub. He made it back to Adelaide, and was received with public banquets and Government House welcomes — some of which he was sober for.

Stuart's expedition to the north

At the end of 1860, with Burke and Wills making indecent haste to cross the country and reach the Gulf of Carpentaria (refer to the section 'Seeing the back of Burke, losing Wills', earlier in this chapter), SA parliament agreed £2,500 should be spent on funding another Stuart expedition to the north, and he left practically the next day — in January 1861. This time Stuart made it through the previously impassable scrub, but couldn't get beyond the plains that lay on the other side. Provisions down to practically zero, clothes shredded, his party barely made it back to Adelaide.

Stuart was still game for more punishment, however, and left once more in October 1861, perhaps strangely emboldened by the news that Burke and Wills had died in their own attempt. This time he met with success. On 24 July 1862, Stuart and his companions stood on the sand on the north coast of Australia.

This time Stuart made it back in even worse shape. Scurvy riddled, nearly blind, carried in a stretcher, he made it back to Adelaide in December 1862, but such was his woeful state the city had to wait until the end of January before holding a public holiday to celebrate, with crowds, banners and streamers ornamenting the streets.

A grateful SA Government awarded Stuart £2,000 for the achievement, but then, worried he'd drink it all, allowed him to access only the interest accrued from the sum rather than the capital. This improved Stuart's mood not one bit, and in 1864 he left the continent he'd been first to cross, kept drinking, and died two years later.

SA gained a lot from this monumental achievement — the state secured the contract to build an overland telegraph line across the continent to connect to the rest of the world, and the line largely followed Stuart's tracks. Stuart became retrospectively lionised as one of those heroic martyrs who sacrifice their lives for the spread of civilisation.

Selectors and Bushrangers

In the rural areas of Australia, two main groups really established themselves in the public's consciousness during the 1850s, 1860s and 1870s: Selectors and bushrangers.

Selectors were small-scale farmers who had selected land for cultivation and, overall, they became more successful through the 1870s, thanks partly to their own improved efforts after the failures of the 1860s (refer to Chapter 8), partly to improved legislation, and partly to the arrival of rail. *Bushrangers*, on the other hand, became the definitive bad boys of colonial Australia, and were indulged, adored and reviled for that reason. Bushrangers went in for adventure, money, fast horses, gorgeous women, fancy clothes and, oftentimes, revenge against society (and especially police). Selectors went in more for next season's harvest. Bushrangers were sometimes selectors — although they were happy to rob selectors.

Myths sprang up about each group. One myth said that bushrangers robbed from the rich and gave to the poor. (Untrue — they robbed from *everybody*, and mostly gave to their mates, who also tended to be their criminal associates, and to their immediate families, girlfriends and wives.) Another myth said that selectors were forever doomed to be ground down and oppressed by bad legislation and predatory squatters. (Also untrue — by the end of the 1870s, selectors were beginning to establish farms with a rate of success and accumulation of profit that defied selection failures of the previous decade.)

Moving on from the selectors' dust heap

In the early 1860s, many gold-seekers had tried their hand at becoming small farmers as new Land Acts were passed by colonial parliaments. Many failed in their first land selections. Coming from modern Britain, they often had little or no experience of life on the land — being town or city dwellers to begin with. Frequently, they lacked the money to start up and successfully establish a farm, even if legislation allowed them to select land to live and work on. On top of that, most of the rural colonial hinterland could only be used for wool-growing until railways began to fan out from the main metropolitan centres, offering cheaper freight costs to markets in the city and overseas. (Chapter 8 describes these difficulties and failures more fully.)

By the 1870s, however, things were starting to improve significantly. While NSW pastoralists had been successful in restricting selection, in Victoria and SA better legislation aimed at getting rid of old loopholes proved successful. As well as this, the colonial parliaments, keen to do everything possible for their selector voters, created special boards to oversee the administration of these Acts. Land departments made sure legislation and its regulations weren't abused. It had taken them a while, a good decade in fact, but they'd learnt.

Simultaneously, the selectors too had learnt. Those taking up land in the 1870s had often had previous experience farming on other selections and had begun to develop intelligent strategies for Australian conditions.

The railways were also now arriving with a vengeance. The squatters' great declared enemies, the radical liberals, were in government (see Chapter 10 for more on Colonial Liberalism), and the Victorian Government, in particular, made a point of building railway lines out to all areas featuring dense selector settlement before building lines out to areas of traditional squatter strongholds, such as the western district of Victoria. The modern wheat belt, which developed in South Australia and northern Victoria during this time, was predominantly made up of smallholders who could make use of these new train lines. (See the section 'It's raining trains' later in this chapter for more on the impact of the expanded rail network.)

While come election time the old terms of political abuse would still be wheeled out against the great class enemy the squatter, the reality closer to the ground was far less polarised. Both pastoralists (many of whom were squatters) and selectors were surprised at the extent to which their needs and interests could overlap, and the extent to which they could all integrate into a localised rural community. Getting a railway put through your region was in both pastoralist and selector interest. Ditto good roads and decent postal services. Droughts, floods and sudden climate shifts were common enemies and dangerous to both groups.

LIFE DOWN UNDER

A shop owner, storekeeper or pub owner would generally try to keep friendly with both pastoralists and selectors. If a pastoralist wanted to get voted onto the local council or for mayor or into parliament, it was the majority of small-scale farmers he'd have to woo. Their children went to the same local schools, and intermarriage rates were high — the marriage choices of the daughters and sons of selectors and pastoralists had a pattern of confounding expectations. Selectors would often ask pastoralists to be godparents to their newborn, thinking of them more as the prominent local figure rather than the eternal class enemy.

Bushranging nation

Statistically, a higher degree of criminality occurred in the Australian colonies in the 1850s than during the same period in Britain — mostly because of that certain proportion of ex-convicts still in the colonial population with a propensity for crime.

But the gold rush world of 1850s Australia provided many more *opportunities* for crime. Society was now largely made up of new arrivals living in unfixed and free-floating circumstances, where staggering amounts of wealth could be seen — with diggers who had got lucky flaunting their wealth down the street, and *gold escorts*, who carried large fortunes between gold fields, towns and cities, becoming numerous. This situation made for many people taking matters into their own hands. Bushranging flourished during the 1850s and 1860s, and experienced a brief renaissance in the late 1870s when the most famous and notorious gang of all — the Kelly Gang — reigned.

When the Gardiner Gang comes together . . . look out!

The 1850s bushrangers and highwaymen were generally men who had arrived freely in the gold rush, while most of those operating in the 1860s were 'native-born'. These native-born were like the city-based larrikins who were exciting notice and censure at the same time, in that they were a new generation quite different from their parents, who had mostly arrived as immigrants from Britain.

The bushrangers of the 1860s had either been born in Australia or arrived very young, and had grown up in the bush and rural districts.

The Clarke brothers, Frank Gardiner, Ben Hall and John Gilbert formed the nucleus of a gang that operated in the southern tablelands region of NSW between Yass, Bathurst and Forbes, an area uniquely rich in both goldfields and rugged mountain country — offering a remote and inaccessible refuge. For a brief period in the 1860s, they led the police and authorities on a merry dance and pulled off enough bold robberies and violent deeds to inspire the next generation of native-born youths who would come along after them.

The biggest exploit was the Eugowra gold escort robbery at Coonbong Rock in 1862. Planned by Gardiner, featuring the involvement of Gilbert, Hall and others, it netted a massive sum — some £14,000. Soon after, Gardiner narrowly avoided capture, decided a quiet life was better than a short and glorious one, and headed up north with his girlfriend. They ran a grog shanty and store near Rockhampton till tracked down by police two years later, after which he was arrested, tried and sentenced to 32 years' hard labour.

Gilbert, meanwhile, became Hall's right-hand man as they embarked on a crime spree of truly impressive proportions. Robbing travellers on the Melbourne–Sydney road, they carried out over 600 robberies, with the record being 60 travellers in one day — impressive, no? Gilbert and Hall had stolen racehorses, rifles, double-barrel shotguns and revolvers in abundance, while the police, riding on old nags and stuck with single-shot muzzle-loading cavalry pistols, had a problem: They couldn't ride them down, nor could they outshoot them. Plus the gang had an extensive support network consisting of everyone from small-time squatters to big property owners and even officials in the local region, all working as a 'bush telegraph' and keeping them abreast of police whereabouts.

REMEMBER

Even though the Gardiner Gang robbed all and sundry without compunction — including children, selector farmers, recently lucky (now not so lucky) gold diggers, shearers, an old shepherd, a mail-coach driver and a toll-keeper — and were well known to cheerfully let their prize horses graze on small farmers' crops, they pulled off enough grandiose exploits to win a lively public following. Often enough, they favoured daring hold-ups that would humiliate and taunt police over exploits that would simply score them big loot. The gang raided Bathurst in broad daylight, and took over the entire town of Canowindra for three whole days, but ended up taking no money or property.

Larrikins on the streets of Sydney let out big 'hurrahs!' when news arrived of policemen being shot by the gang, young stock riders thought it sounded fine, and shearers and station hands didn't ever intervene if a pitched battle between bushrangers and police happened to be taking place nearby. Verses and songs started circulating, and the colonial pastime of laughing at police being fooled and humiliated (a tradition cherished since convict days) went from strength to strength in the 1850s and 1860s.

MEETING THE MEMBERS OF THE GARDINER GANG

The Gardiner Gang may have acted together to pull off some big robberies, but individually they had each already got up to some real mischief. Here's a summary of their main exploits in the lead-up to them joining forces:

- **Frank Gardiner:** Reportedly the son of a free settler father from NSW and an Aboriginal mother, when Gardiner began his highwayman career he acquired the nickname 'Darkie'. Arriving in Victoria in 1850 aged 20, he was quickly convicted for horse stealing and sentenced to five years' hard labour. The next year he escaped Pentridge prison and made off back to NSW. In 1854 he was convicted of two charges of horse stealing in Goulburn. Given a ticket of leave in 1859, he soon broke his parole and went to the Lambing Flat goldfield where he opened a butcher's shop. Soon after he began carrying out robberies on the road, and formed a gang to carry out sundry 'daring outrages'.

- **Ben Hall:** Native-born, with parents who were ex-convicts but considered respectable, Hall grew up around Maitland in NSW and became a stockman, leasing a pastoral run and becoming a squatter. Dashing, funny and courteous to women, he had a propensity for crime, and was often found in the company of bushrangers and armed men up to no good. Hall was involved in armed robberies and was caught and charged. Although acquitted, he had to sell his squatter's lease to pay his legal fees. He then experienced the police harassment *coup de grace* when the local police inspector burned his house down on very flimsy pretext. This made Hall angry enough to go full-time as bushranger — and he joined Frank Gardiner's gang.

- **John Gilbert:** Arriving in Melbourne from Canada in 1852 and aged 10, Gilbert soon after became a stableboy in Kilmore, Victoria. From here it was a short trip to the Victorian goldfields, where he fell in with card sharps and crims. Wearing his hair long 'in the native-born style', he started dressing 'flash' — and the authorities started to have strong suspicions the source of the wealth for all the fine clothes wasn't legitimate. By now 18, Gilbert took off to NSW where in 1860 he met Frank Gardiner on the Kiandra goldfields.

The Gardiner Gang meet their (mostly) grisly ends

The bulk of settlers in the regions where the Gardiner Gang was operating stayed quiet. Some were actively colluding with the gang, but most stayed passive and didn't take sides. Partly this was fear — the bushrangers intimidated, assaulted and burnt down the property of those who acted as informants or witnesses, or who actively assisted the police. Partly it was just attitude. The ex-convicts didn't have much respect for the law, and squatters who had expanded beyond the boundaries of settlement in the 1830s and 1840s (refer to Chapter 6) were used to a world where central authority was weak. You looked after your own property, kept your guns loaded, and minded your own business.

But gang members were starting to get shot — not so much by policemen but by homeowners when they began raiding homesteads and pastoral stations.

HISTORICAL ROOTS

In November 1864, the Gardiner Gang robbed the Gundagai–Yass mail coach. A battle with police took place and Gilbert shot a sergeant. In April 1865, the Felons Apprehension Act was passed. All citizens could now shoot a bushranger down on sight.

In December 1864, Gilbert was shot by a constable and buried in a police paddock at Binalong. He was 25. Hall was betrayed by an informer, ambushed and shot by police on the Yass plains. His body was riddled with bullets, shot by police who could finally have their revenge after being made to look like fools for so much of the past few years, and paraded through the town of Forbes in grisly triumph.

Gardiner, meanwhile, was still doing his time after being arrested in Rockhampton (refer to the preceding section). Eight years into his sentence, in 1872, people started submitting petitions pleading for mercy, saying he was both chronically ill and a reformed character. These petitions began to have an effect on the NSW Governor, and in 1874 Gardiner was let out of jail. (This led to a public outcry and the fall of the government of the future 'father of Federation' Henry Parkes, but no matter.) Because one of the conditions of release was exile, Gardiner headed off to Hong Kong, and then to San Francisco. Once there he ran a saloon, and eventually died, aged 73, in Colorado in 1903.

HISTORICAL ROOTS

Between 1863 and 1867, six bushrangers were killed, including the aptly named and psychopathic 'Mad Dog' Morgan, and the Clarke brothers. In the same period, seven policemen died. Looking only at these bald facts, the numbers don't seem to add up to much. But enough robbery, adventure and ostentatious showmanship had taken place to reinvigorate an old folk myth. Colonial Australians now had their very own highwaymen, transplanted and flourishing as bushrangers. The next generation of native-born youth was inspired.

Getting in on the action with the Greta Mob

While the Gardiner Gang had been wiped out by 1867 (refer to the preceding section), a small criminal subculture was flourishing in the Greta area of Victoria in the 1860s and for much of the 1870s. In this group were professional stock thieves who preyed on selector and squatter alike; the core group was called the Greta Mob.

LIFE DOWN UNDER

Most of those in the Greta Mob were part of the native-born generation who were born to migrant gold rush parents in the 1850s. In the Greta area of Victoria, stock theft was abnormally high — more horses were stolen there than in any other part of the district. The Mob numbered about 40 and its members had a conviction rate of 56 per cent, mostly related to horse-stealing charges. They were part of a generational phenomenon that was acquiring the new term 'larrikin' — flash thieves and petty crims who were confident, cocky, self-assertive and entirely at ease in this colonial world that they'd grown up in. They were prone to drinking, fighting, gambling, stealing and racing very fast horses.

From this group emerged the most well known bushranger of all: Ned Kelly.

Ned Kelly: Oppressed Selector's Son? Larrikin Wild Child? Stone-cold killer?

Few individuals in Australian history have polarised opinion as effectively as Ned Kelly — and this includes the opinions of historians as much as those of the wider public. Admire him or otherwise, the acts Kelly performed during his short life and two-year outlaw career compel attention.

Kelly was a horse thief, and when the police pursued him for this he 'went bush'. Search parties went after him, police got shot, and Kelly and his mates — brother Dan, Joe Byrne and Steve Hart — were declared outlaws.

Kelly showed the usual, run-of-the-mill bushranger behaviour:

>> Shooting policemen

>> Robbing banks

>> Having a final shootout with police

But his more outlandish behaviour went beyond that of the ordinary bushranger type:

>> Authoring two massive public letters, each bloodcurdling and lyrical in turn, detailing all the changes he was going to wreak on the colonial social and political landscape

>> Trying to derail an entire police train and shoot all survivors

>> Clothing himself and his three fellow gang members in iron armour

Kelly's key events

Kelly makes it difficult to put what he did into perspective, largely because so much of what he planned and carried out managed to defy all perspective. But here's my attempt.

From 1877 to 1880, Kelly planned, executed and was involved in a series of escalating crimes, robberies and murders, starting with horse theft in 1877 and culminating in the Glenrowan showdown in 1880.

Euroa Bank hold-up — 9 to 10 December 1878

On Monday 8 December, the Kelly Gang rode into Younghusband's pastoral station at Faithfull's Creek, a few miles outside the town of Euroa. They took prisoner everyone who was on the station, locking most into a large storage shed. That night Kelly stayed up with the prisoners, keeping most of them awake until dawn, narrating the events that had turned him outlaw. Meanwhile, Joe Byrne wrote out two good copies of a letter to be sent to Donald Cameron, a member of parliament.

The next day, three of the gang rode into Euroa. Arriving just before closing time, the three held up the National Bank of Euroa. Picking up just under £2,000 in cash, 30 ounces of gold, property documents, two revolvers and a box of cartridges, the gang returned to Faithfull's Creek station with the bank manager and his family in tow. The gang then left at 8 pm, with Kelly having threatened to track down and shoot anyone who left within the next three hours.

Holding up Jerilderie — 9 to 10 February 1879

Arriving in the NSW town of Jerilderie late on Saturday evening, the gang approached the police station, whereupon Kelly shouted, 'Mr Devine, there's a row on at Davidson's Hotel! Come quick, or there'll be murder!' Constables Devine and Richards stumbled out onto the verandah only to find themselves staring down the barrels of some serious guns. The police were placed in the lockup for the night. Next day, Kelly forced Richards to lead them around town (dressed in police uniform), introducing them to townspeople as police reinforcements on their way to take part in the pursuit of those dastardly Kelly boys in Victoria.

About midday on Monday, Kelly took charge of the Royal Mail Hotel, which was next door to the Bank of NSW. Using the bar as a depot for prisoners, Kelly and Byrne robbed the bank, netting about £1,400.

LIFE DOWN UNDER

Through all his antics in Jerilderie, however, the man Kelly most wanted to find was the local newspaper editor, who he wanted to print and publish his second great public letter (his first not having got much further than a rather bewildered Donald Cameron). The editor had gone to ground, and Kelly had little choice but to leave the document with the bank's accountant, who promised to see it published (he was to promptly hand it over to police).

IN THEIR WORDS

Kelly returned to a now full and captive bar at the Royal Mail Hotel and gave a farewell speech. Leaning against the bar, he placed his gun next to his glass and said with a loud voice, 'There's my revolver. Anyone here can take it and shoot me dead, but if I'm shot, Jerilderie will swim in its own blood'. There weren't any takers.

Showdown at Glenrowan — 26 to 28 June 1880

After the shooting of police-informer Aaron Sherritt (by Kelly Gang member Joe Byrne) in June 1880, the police sent through reinforcements in a special 'police train'. The train was expected to pass through Glenrowan train station early on Sunday morning, and on Saturday evening, Kelly, having had four suits of iron armour built for the occasion, oversaw the tearing up of railway tracks just past the station. 'I'm going to shoot every one of the bastards', Kelly promised as the tracks were being torn up. The train, however, didn't arrive on Sunday.

By early Monday morning, the gang was preparing to leave, and Kelly was giving his typical 'lecture' to the prisoners who had been gathered in the Ann Jones Hotel, when the sound of an approaching train became apparent. Instead of whistling through Glenrowan station and off broken tracks and plummeting down a steep precipice, however, the train slowed to a halt, before steaming slowly into the station. The gang disappeared into the back room of the hotel, and returned in armour.

In the subsequent shootout between the Kelly Gang and police, Dan Kelly, Hart and Byrne were killed. Kelly was brought down as he emerged from the scrub at dawn, trying to shoot his way back into the hotel to save his mates.

IN THEIR
WORDS

At his trial, on 29 October Kelly was found guilty for the murder of Constable Lonigan, and hanged on 11 November 1880. Some reports have him sighing 'Such is life' as his last words. They've become an iconic Australian phrase voicing a weary and slightly cynical acceptance that the world works as it works and there's little a rebel can do to change it.

The man in the iron mask

Many historians have argued that Ned Kelly was an Australian version of an international sociological phenomenon — the 'social bandit'. These bandits were individuals who took up arms against the law and received widespread support from groups or classes who saw themselves as having been oppressed by the law and the bandits as representing their interests.

In the Australian context, Kelly is often seen as a representative of the poor selectors in the north-east region of Victoria, small-time farmers who were victims of the hold that squatters had established both in the law and on the land itself. In this version of events, Kelly was the guy who stood up to the squatters and their puppets — the police and public officials.

REMEMBER

When it came to land settlement in the Greta area, where Ned Kelly came from, no great squatter obstruction existed. Selectors in this region were largely part of the 'second wave' of selectors who had taken up land in the 1870s after the Grant Land Act of 1869 (refer to the section 'Moving on from the selectors' dust heap', earlier in this chapter). Selection conditions had vastly improved by this time, and the selectors themselves had often gained valuable previous colonial farming experience before trying their hand in the north-east region. This led to an eventual selection success rate of 70 per cent. The public officials themselves were generally of the same generation and period of arrival as the selectors, and were often more sympathetic to selectors' claims against pastoral tenants.

The war Kelly was conducting was not on behalf of selectors, but of the group of professional stock thieves known as the Greta Mob (refer to the section 'Getting in on the action with the Greta mob', earlier in this chapter). The Greta boys walked (and talked themselves up) as 'fearless, free and bold', and were largely contemptuous of the selector farmers plugging away, trying to establish their holdings on the land. They all wore the kind of 'flash larrikin' uniform that Kelly wore to the last stand at Glenrowan (underneath his armour): Strapped moleskin trousers, gaudy waistcoats and flashy riding boots. This group formed Kelly's active support base once he became an outlaw.

Growing Towards Nationhood . . . Maybe

Two technological developments in the latter part of the 19th century worked to bring the disparate and self-governing Australian colonies into closer orbit with each other — the telegraph and the railway. The telegraph brought the world much closer to the colonies, demanding more immediate and coordinated responses. The railway brought the separate colonies much closer to each other.

A telegraph to the world

At 12:10 pm on 22 August 1872, two ends of wire were touched together, connecting the Australian telegraph line extending across the continent from Adelaide in South Australia to Palmerston (modern-day Darwin) — and to the rest of the world.

IN THEIR WORDS

Someone who worked on the construction team that built the telegraph line across Australia later recalled how, the moment the wires were finally soldered together, 'South Australia touched a key and spoke to the British Empire', and 'harnessed the world'. At a banquet held in Sydney to celebrate, people went even further. The NSW Governor called it 'by far the most wonderful event that has ever occurred in the history of this country'. NSW Premier Henry Parkes declared the telegraph 'a magical business, uniting us hand in hand . . . with the parent land'.

Now news and information could travel to Australia in hours rather than weeks and months. The thin wire promised to be a thread to the world that might help Australians overcome the overpowering sense of isolation they so often felt as a people who (along with their culture) had been transplanted from one side of the world to the other.

The telegraph dramatically drew the Australian colonies more directly into the flow of the world's events, demanding immediate colonial responses. Previously, the great events, threats and disasters from the outside world, arriving after a significant lag, were often resolved or reacted to well in advance of news of it arriving in Australia, so a colonial government could leave the problems of the rest of the world to London to resolve. Now the outside world began to impinge — it wasn't that the telegraph line had harnessed the world for Australia, but that Australia had been itself lassoed.

In 1883, Queensland, fearing German designs on the island to its immediate north, annexed New Guinea. Informed of this by telegraph, it took the British Government not much more than a few hours to perform an unholy smackdown on its presumptuous colony for thinking it could decide and then implement what was, in essence, British imperial policy in the Pacific region. In previous decades, the British wouldn't have found out until the annexation was well advanced, making things far messier for the government in London (not to mention the people of New Guinea), but leaving the colonial periphery a good deal more freedom of action.

In February 1885, news arrived in Australia of the death of Britain's General Gordon in Sudan (where he'd been sent by the British government to help evacuate British-Egyptian forces from Khartoum). The news was current on its arrival and the effect it produced instant. City streets filled with people shocked and angry at the news, demanding that the colonies do something to revenge Gordon's death. The next day, the NSW Government announced it would be sending a volunteer force to Sudan, which the British Government accepted four days later on 15 February, and the contingent left Sydney on 3 March. None of this could have happened without the telegraph. News from the world was now arriving so quickly that Australian colonies lost the luxury of inaction. The world's events were becoming more and more Australia's events, demanding reactions and actions that couldn't help but involve Australia in global affairs.

It's raining trains

Trains were the 'it' thing for the second half of the 19th century. Big gleaming metal behemoth monsters that promised to deliver whole towns, suburbs and nations into a new age. 'There is nothing so extraordinary in history as this modern march of "progress"', said the Melbourne *Argus* at the opening of the first big hinterland railway line (to Ballarat from Geelong) in 1862. And the steam engine was widely accepted as 'the most important lever' of progress.

In Australia, railways were expected to continue the trail-blazing work done by explorers in taking the modern world into previously (to the colonists at least) unknown country. As construction began in 1850 on the first Australian railway line (from Sydney to Parramatta), the company manager said rail would help create 'a civilized community in the wild and unpopulated parts of our country'. Fourteen years later, plans were becoming more comprehensive. The *Argus* said the 'network of railways' was 'destined in the fullness of time . . . to bisect the Australian continent'.

Building up a good head of steam laying train lines

Railway lines first began to poke tentatively out from the hubs of colonial cities in the 1850s, as the gold explosion brought seismic shocks to what the colonial mind could conceive of as possible. New volumes of revenue and population meant everything in the modern world could and should be had at once, and the great train love affair began.

The first railway line to open in Australia was in Victoria — it was opened in September 1854, and ran from Flinders Street in Melbourne to Hobson's Bay at its port. (The Sydney to Parramatta line opened in September 1855.) In June 1857, Geelong was connected to Williamstown; in October, Adelaide and the town of

Gawler were connected in South Australia. The major projects in the 1860s were the lines built from the burgeoning Victorian goldfield towns to Melbourne and Geelong on Port Phillip Bay, and lines built from Sydney and Newcastle in NSW to their respective nearby hinterlands.

When trains really took off, however, when it looked like the 'network of railways' across Australia was really going to become a reality, was in the 1870s. As this decade progressed, the bulk of the Australian population gained ready rail access:

» In 1873, the north-east line opened from Melbourne to Wodonga on the Murray.

» In 1876, the Great Western Railway was opened from Sydney to Bathurst (following the route Wentworth, Blaxland and Lawson had taken in 1813 — refer to Chapter 5).

» In 1876, a line opened from Brisbane to Ipswich.

» In November 1876, a line from Hobart to Launceston opened (as even Tasmania got in on the act).

» In 1878, the Great Southern Railway began operating from Sydney to Wagga Wagga, and three months later the Great Northern Line began from Sydney to Tamworth.

The construction of the railways was labour-intensive, requiring the services of

» Architects

» Builders

» Engineers

» Labourers

» Planners

» Quarrymen

» Surveyors

» Timber cutters

Between 1870 and 1890, the amount of railway line laid down in the colonies went from 1,657 to 15,290 kilometres, a staggering near-tenfold increase.

Trains bring (politically motivated) growth

The effect of all this immense railway-line-laying activity was powerful. For the first time, the bulk of small-time farmers who had either bought land or taken out selections were able to freight their produce to the major markets in the capital cities at reasonable cost. Wool ceased to be the only viable industry in the colonial interior. A wheat industry began to emerge in the Wimmera and northern plains regions of Victoria and the Riverina in NSW. Previous to this, the only viable wheat industry was in South Australia, in parts of the colony easily accessed by coastal shipping.

LIFE DOWN UNDER

As the train network was extended in the 1870s, concentrated settlement and more intensive agriculture away from the coast and the goldfields got serious. And thanks to near-universal manhood suffrage (refer to Chapter 8), governments built the railway lines where the mass of voters wanted them rather than where the most profitable industry was.

The western region of the colony of Victoria was the stronghold of the hated and demonised 'squattocracy', the wool-baron pastoralists. To the north-east, were plenty of men and women taking out selections under a new Land Act to farm land. The 1873 north-eastern railway line that opened from Melbourne to Wodonga was built well in advance of the line to the Western District of Victoria, where the wool industry was based. The lines went where the votes dictated, not where the money wanted — a case of rampant pork-barrelling (with projects created purely for personal and political gain) or democracy at work, depending on whose side you were on.

LIFE DOWN UNDER

In Australia, railways expanded very differently from the way they expanded in other parts of the world. Europe had a high density of settlement, so private companies could count on building railways and having immediate custom. But Australia, like the United States, had a vast interior without much settlement, so companies couldn't rely on a pre-existing pattern of settlement to make the new railways immediately profitable. In the United States, this was solved by governments giving private railway companies large tracts of land along their railway routes, thereby providing a good profit source to the company. This would never have worked in the majority of the Australian colonies, however, where most colonial governments were campaigning with policies to take the land off pastoralists, and then divide it up for ordinary people to select and to make farms and live on. The task of constructing railways, therefore, became the job of the state. Governments raised the loans to get the money for construction, and gathered the revenue to pay off the loans if receipts from the railways were not enough (often via high customs duties called tariffs).

REMEMBER

In the last decades of the 19th century, critics of the railways being in government control thought too many lines were being put down simply to meet the demands of various electorates. This may be so but, nonetheless, colonial governments *did* ensure that travelling and freighting goods via the railway was considerably cheaper than in Britain. In the 1890s, at the end of the railway explosion, first-class tickets were being used by people who in England would be riding third class. Governments took on the job of building as many railway lines as possible, raising loans to do so on the London Stock Exchange, and the mass of voters seemed well pleased.

Chapter **10**

Work, Play and Politics during the Long Boom

I n the 1850s, Australia acquired the nickname 'the workingman's paradise'. It had a great climate (although arguably, compared to Britain, this wasn't the toughest competition), good work opportunities and high wages.

Most of the middle- and working-class immigrants who made the move to this paradise in the 1850s and beyond were full of the rhetoric of self-improvement, personal liberty and free enterprise. Generally, their great ambition was to set themselves up as economically independent, with their own business, farm or enterprise. In this they largely failed: Most ended up earning wages rather than paying them.

But the desire of the immigrants to be treated better than they had been in Britain was a strong one, and the intention of enjoying markedly better conditions at work and in life (and, eventually, politically) didn't go away. In this they *did* succeed, thanks partly to very favourable conditions caused by the long boom that lasted from the 1860s to the 1880s. This boom was caused directly and indirectly by the massive gold finds of the 1850s (refer to Chapter 8). Their success was also partly due to their own attitudes and political leanings, and partly to the preexisting colonial culture where arrivals of 'humble' and 'obscure' origins found little impediment to making a newly upward way in society.

In this chapter, I cover the distinctly Australian attitude to work and play that emerged during the sustained growth of the 1870s and 1880s, as well as the distinctly Australian political force that emerged, which became known as Colonial Liberalism.

The 'Workingman's Paradise' Continues

The majority of people arriving during the 1850s inrush stayed on in the colonies even after the gold yield peaked in 1856 and began to decline. Unemployment and a relative drop in wages occurred in the 1860s, as miners went from digging for gold to other areas of work and industry, but in the 1870s things picked up as new parts of the economy grew strongly.

LIFE DOWN UNDER

During the 1870s, full employment was approached in Australia, with little in the way of inflation to eat away at the good wages. Conditions were so good that the colonies began to attract significant and steady streams of labourers and workmen from Britain, who often chose Australia despite getting here being so much more expensive than passages to Canada or the US. The 'workingman's paradise' might have in part been hyperbole (any place that touts itself as paradise is probably not telling the whole truth), but compared to conditions for workers in the rest of the world, life for the working man and woman in Australia was about as good as it gets.

Growth brings jobs

Largely, the agreeable working life that was created in Australia had to do with the great economic diversification that had followed in the wake of the gold explosion. With a massively enlarged population, plenty of new industries became viable, and it was these burgeoning industries that ex-gold miners moved into after they gave up looking for gold.

The railway industry had an intense demand for labour. (For more on the growth of this industry, refer to Chapter 9.) Workers were needed for the construction of lines, the manufacture of steam engines and carriages, and the maintenance of the lines and stations once the trains were up and running.

In the pastoral industry, increasing amounts of work on sheep stations had to be done — fencing was replacing shepherds and someone had to build them; ditto the dams and artesian bores that began to be constructed. Seasonal work such as shearing and harvesting was also lucrative.

RICHARD TWOPENY'S TWO CENTS

In his book *Town Life in Australia*, published in 1883, Richard Twopeny had this to say about conditions in the colonies: 'Those who are industrious and careful in a very few years rise to be masters and employers of labour, and are at all times so sure of constant employment that it is no wonder they do not care about undertaking odd jobs. If their manner is as independent as their character, I am far from blaming them for it, though occasionally one would wish they did not confound civility and servility as being equally degrading to the free and independent elector. But when you meet the man on equal terms in an omnibus or on other neutral ground, this cause of complaint is removed. Where he is sure of his equality he makes no attempt to assert it.'

Another big growth industry as the initial gold boom faded was the construction industry — busy both in building and rebuilding the cities and townships that had sprung up everywhere, and in the building of private residences.

**LIFE DOWN
UNDER**

In the gold rush 1850s, Melbourne and gold townships had the appearance of various shanty metropolises — jerry-built, thrown up overnight, with people living and sleeping in tents, huts, lean-tos, sheds or wherever else they could. By the 1860s, those who were still here had decided they were here for the long haul. The original assumption of only being in the colonies long enough to score a fortune and make off home to Britain, Europe or America had faded. And they figured that if they were going to live here, they might as well live in semi-decent houses. House-building numbers shot up by 50 per cent in the early 1860s as a consequence. Then manufacturing followed — clothes, shoes, hats, metal and leather goods, coaches, wagons, carriages and furniture all began to be produced for the local market.

Workingwomen's paradise too

An odd thing happened to working women in late-19th-century Australia. They stopped being servant girls. And those who did stay dropped much of the obedient and subservient air that had long been expected of servants.

**LIFE DOWN
UNDER**

Young working-class women during the 1870s and 1880s far preferred work in the factories and shops that the new manufacturing industries were establishing in the inner-city areas. They preferred the freedom of not being cooped up and under orders and supervision 24 hours a day, as they were as servant girls. They liked that they could take their pay at the end of the week and go off to do what they chose with their evenings — often mingling freely with plenty of young men. Shocked respectable moralists thought this was outrageous — young women meeting up with men after work and hanging out on streets and beaches, in pubs and parks? Unheard of! Two kinds of culture were at war here — the respectable and the rough — and many working-class women voted with their feet to show why Australia could also be a bit of a working woman's paradise.

IN THEIR WORDS

Like working men, the freely available work meant working women could pick and choose, as Richard Twopeny highlighted: 'There is a feeling in existence amongst them that in some way or other household labour is menial occupation, and that to undertake it is to lose caste in the class to which they belong'. Being in domestic service was degrading, while 'the sewing girl or the shop-woman has certain business hours, outside of which she is as independent as her employer, and as little amenable to control'.

Workers' Playtime

One of the distinctive things about the workers in colonial Australia was their clear choice of leisure over pay. Time and again it was made evident that those earning good wages preferred to earn enough to pay their necessary living expenses, but not much more. Instead, the extra hours were used for leisure — sports, games, drinking, sleeping, eating and talking, and play.

MELBOURNE CUP GETS GOING (RAUCOUSLY)

IN THEIR WORDS

Horse racing was popular in colonial Australia — the first Melbourne Cup was run in 1861, won by the Sydney outsider Archer (with his owners pocketing a big bag of 710 gold sovereigns and a gold watch). By 1873 the popularity of the day was such that 70,000 were at Flemington to watch Don Juan romp it in.

But the influx of people didn't please everyone. As one newcomer later wrote: 'At Cup time Melbourne is not the most moral city on the face of the globe. There is an influx of undesirable citizens from all parts of the colonies. Bourke Street at this time of the year is a sight almost without a parallel, more especially on the eve of the Cup. So dense is the crowd of people, that it is well-nigh impossible to move about, and it is with difficulty that tramcars run'. Some might say the scenes these days in Flemington at the end of Cup day aren't that different.

Pubs, streets, back paddocks and front yards, and music and dance halls all featured various pursuits of the mass of colonists, but the development of cricket and the various codes of football casts most light on the distinctively Australian traits that were emerging in the colonies. In cricket, Australians had the opportunity of pitting themselves against England, to prove that they were still made of 'the right stuff'. In football, they made the most of a relative abundance of leisure time in the 1850s, 1860s and 1870s to develop a code of their own.

Beating the English at cricket

Like many pursuits, cricket took off in Australia in the 1850s, with different colonies forming teams to play against each other as well as taking on touring English outfits.

In 1868, a team of Aboriginal cricket players toured England, making them the first organised tour by Australian cricketers. The two big 'proto-national' moments came in 1877 and 1880, when Australia's best 11 beat England's best at first the Melbourne Cricket Ground and then the Oval in London.

LIFE DOWN UNDER

Colonial Australians were thrilled about beating the English at cricket because it helped deal with that nagging doubt many still had about the questionable origins of Australia as a convict dump. Beating the English at their own game helped dispel insinuations about 'bad stock' and was, given that Britain was the global superpower at the time rather than a funny little island in a chilly part of the world, a big deal.

HISTORICAL ROOTS

The way Australians played cricket against the English also reveals something distinctive about colonial society. In England, two categories of players existed, which mirrored the class system — the workers and their 'betters'. In cricket, the workers, those who were paid professionals, were classed as 'players'. And their betters, who were wealthy enough to not need to be paid and were amateur, were 'gentlemen'. Everyone who played for Australia, or for the colonies, was ranked the same (as long as you were white, of course) — the English categories of 'gentleman' and 'professional' had collapsed in the colonies. In Australia, the place you occupied on the social and economic ladder was far more fluid and mobile than in Britain. Further, practically everyone had come out to Australia with 'professional' rather than 'gentlemanly' aspirations — that is, to make a fortune or at least set themselves up in life.

New codes of football

Australian Rules Football was first developed in the late 1850s in and around Melbourne (and was then called Victorian Rules). From there, it spread to the colonies of South Australia, Tasmania and Western Australia. New South Wales, meanwhile, adopted an English code of play — rugby — in the 1870s, as did Queensland (and across the Tasman Sea in another British colony, New Zealand).

LIFE DOWN UNDER

It's telling that Victoria developed its own game of Australian Rules Football in the 1850s while NSW opted for the British importation of rugby. In the second half of the 19th century, thanks largely to the gold rush and the enormous economic and social kick it delivered, Victoria was renowned as the 'Yankee' colony — ambitious, pushy and independent-minded. NSW, meanwhile, was seen as more staid and traditional, and more likely to follow English precedent. This is an almost exact reversal of the reputations that Victoria and NSW, and Melbourne and Sydney, would occupy in the 20th century (see Chapter 11 for more on how this role reversal occurred).

Victoria, with its independent 'Advance, Victoria!' attitude developed its own structured football code early, while in Britain other codes — soccer, rugby, Gaelic football — were still in the planning stages of drawing up their own particular rules and practices. In the 1870s, NSW finally settled on the full book of rugby rules, adopted straight from Britain.

But the codes adopted in both colonies shared a preference for a more flowing game style. From its development, the Victorian game showed an emphasis on an open free-flowing contest. NSW also adopted the more open and flowing form of rugby — on the whole opting for 'league' rules over union. And the spectators loved it. In the mid-1860s crowds showing up to watch a Victorian Football League game numbered about 1,500. By the mid-1870s this was closer to 10,000, and by the mid-1880s it had doubled to 20,000.

HISTORICAL ROOTS

SPORTING AND CULTURAL DIVIDES

Even today, the same Australian states by and large still follow the same codes that were adopted between the 1850s and 1870s. This works as a kind of freeze-frame of which colonies had greatest influence where during this time. South Australia, Tasmania and Western Australia, where Victorian football was adopted, all formed part of the Victorian orbit. NSW's influence was felt strongest in the territory that ran up the east coast of the continent, and across the Tasman Sea in New Zealand — all areas where rugby league was adopted as the dominant code and continues to be popular today.

As the adoption of sporting codes shows, the Australasian colonies had two different cultural hemispheres at this time, which would prove to be one of the major obstacles against federation. The cultural divide can be seen to this day, where someone from Perth can have an animated work conversation with someone from Hobart about Australian Rules Football, while most Sydneysiders, Queenslanders or recent Auckland arrivals in the vicinity are left shrugging in bored incomprehension.

The crowds at sporting events in the colonies were vociferous and fierce — they became known as 'barrackers'. Originally, 'to barrack' was a term used to describe someone hurling abuse, but in the Australian context it simply came to mean vocally offering support, and regular spectators became known as barrackers. And from the beginning players and crowds were a freely mixing lot. As in cricket, no 'professional' and 'gentleman' distinction for the players existed, and in football crowds men and women of all classes mingled easily — bankers, larrikins, clerks, laundresses, shop owners and factory girls all jostled together. The Victorian Football League, emerging in the 1890s, took as its motto the Latin *Populo Ludis Populi* — 'the game of the people for the people'.

The Big Myth of the Bush: Not So Rural Australia

The pattern of urban and suburban living was laid down very early in Australia. This pattern was a distinctive trait of colonial life well before it became the norm in other parts of the world, and still holds true today. Australia is a big country, but that doesn't stop most of its people clustering in and around the major cities.

In 1850 colonial Australia, 40 per cent of people lived in towns of 2,500 people or more. (By comparison, at this time, the US had an urban population of 14 per cent and Canada 12 per cent.) On the face of it, this seems bizarre. The major industry was wool production, a rural sector. Yet it was a rural industry with a minimal workforce — some station hands, some shepherds, some shearers in the right season, and that's about it. The bulk of people lived and worked in or near the port towns where the wool got taken to and shipped from, where the imports arrived, where business exchanges took place and where the money got spent. All the service industries (everything from brothels and hotels through to tailors and haberdasheries) clustered around the main port towns in each colony, encouraging a concentration in urban living.

The growth in population during the gold rush of the 1850s (refer to Chapter 8) only served to continue the trend of highly urban living. The capital cities continued to be the port conduits of all export and import industries and, with the acquisition of self-government in 1852, became serious administrative capitals as well. The productive goldfields soon had large and thriving townships growing up around them.

The only real exception was Brisbane, wedged in at the bottom south-east corner of Queensland. A far smaller urban outpost in a large colony with a whole series of port towns up its coast, the Queensland capital was about a tenth the size of

Sydney and Melbourne, and in 1871 held only 13 per cent of the overall population of the colony.

By 1891, even Brisbane was showing the same classic colonial capital expansion signs — it contained just under a quarter of the Queensland population. Melbourne, meanwhile, had reached an astounding 41 per cent of Victoria's population, Adelaide touched 37 per cent and Sydney reached 35 per cent.

Partly these urban rates point to the fact that railways in all the colonies except Queensland had fanned out from the central capital cities, increasing the hold of the urban centres over their respective rural hinterlands. 'The mighty bush', wrote Henry Lawson, 'with iron rails is tethered to the world'.

Moreover, most new arrivals tended to go to where surroundings felt most familiar. Rural Australia continued to be something of an alien landscape, whereas the towns and cities were remarkable in their similarity to urban areas of Britain and America. An English arrival in Melbourne remarked it was as if 'a slice of Liverpool has been bodily transplanted to the Antipodes, that you have landed in England again by mistake'. Plenty of new arrivals got off in the port city capital, found work in the port city capital, and stayed in the port city capital. The majority of colonial Australians never saw a bushfire or an Indigenous Australian.

The urbanisation of Australia also helps explain why bushrangers and explorers so quickly acquired such a strongly romanticised edge, to be followed later (from the 1890s on) by shearers, jackaroos and other bush workers. People tend to naturally romanticise what seems alluringly strange and different from their common experience, and the bush heroes and outback pioneers were people who lay largely outside the everyday experience of most colonials.

Marcus Clarke, the English-born author of *For the Term of His Natural Life* (a novel set in Van Diemen's Land and taking in most of the more gothic aspects of Tasmania's convict past), was aware of Australia's tendency to urban clusters when he said in the 1860s that future Australians would be a 'fretful, clever, perverse, irritable race'. And visiting London journalist Francis Adams saw it too. In Melbourne, he said that 'the look on the faces of her inhabitants is the metropolitan look. These people live quickly; such as life presents itself to them'.

Rearranging the Political Furniture

In the decades from 1850 through to the 1890s, colonial life was dominated by a new breed of politician and political ideas. The political movement of the newly emerging middle classes in Britain — Liberalism — encountered the radical working-class movement that had in Britain been violently suppressed — Chartism (refer to Chapter 8).

Out of this encounter was born a distinctive new thing — Colonial Liberalism — which was unlike anything in either Britain or America. This hybrid was the dominant movement and political creed until the 1890s. It dominated most colonial governments, and instituted often quite radical and distinctive changes to education, trade, workplace relations and economic development.

Charting new colonial directions

In Britain in the early 1850s, Liberalism, the political theory favoured by the middle classes, and radical Chartism, favoured by the tradesmen and working classes, were often at variance with each other (see the sidebar 'Liberals versus Chartists'). Middle-class Liberals argued for the pre-eminence of the individual, fearing the unreasoning mob and a bloody revolution if the vast mass of workers were given a direct say in running the country. The Chartists, coming from the 'lower orders', didn't have quite so much faith in the free play of market forces. They preferred the power of 'the people', bonded together with a common charter, over separate, freely associating individuals.

LIFE DOWN UNDER

During the gold rush, the upwardly mobile elements of the working classes and the aspiring lower middle classes formed the great mass of arrivals to Australia, and within a few short years they had self-government and near-universal male voting rights (refer to Chapter 8).

In these conditions, Chartism and Liberalism began to meld and fuse in unexpected ways, producing a distinctive new progressive political philosophy. Called Colonial Liberalism, or (later, by its detractors) Colonial Socialism, it soon overpowered the more established elements in colonial governments, taking root in most popularly elected governments in Victoria, NSW and South Australia, with other colonies following later.

Creating Colonial Liberalism

Colonial Liberals believed, like Liberals in Britain did, that established hierarchies and authorities — aristocrats, the established church, the military officers and the standing army — shouldn't be allowed to maintain a monopoly on power. But, unlike the British Liberals, they also came to accept political rights should be granted to more people, and to believe that government should freely interfere with the economy and people's lives in order to make things fairer and to encourage growth and prosperity.

The Colonial Liberalist view was cruder than the classic Liberal vision, but not without its own logic — government exists for the people; if the people need something and government intervention could help that need be realised more quickly and easily, then government should go right ahead and do it. Colonial Liberals believed that

>> Land should be made cheaply available for the people rather than used in an industry (such as wool) that was highly profitable only for a select few.

>> Railways should be built that offered cheap freight costs.

>> Agrarian industries, such as wheat and dairy, should be developed and encouraged by state involvement on the part of smallholders.

>> Customs duties should be levied against most imports to ensure that local manufacturing industries develop and non-rural jobs on offer continue to diversify and grow.

TECHNICAL STUFF

LIBERALS VERSUS CHARTISTS

Liberalism was a political philosophy that came to prominence in Britain in the middle of the 19th century. Liberals argued in favour of free trade between countries, and of freedom for the individual to use the calm order of reason to decide the best course to take in life and the world, not to be the slave of established authorities, certainties or traditions. They believed it was the individual, not the government, nor tradition, who was best-placed to make decisions for the individual.

Names such as Adam Smith, Thomas Macaulay and John Stuart Mill were touchstones for a view of the world that saw free markets and freedom of individual conscience and actions as the key ways forward for civilisation. For too long, society had been hindered by institutions, superstitions, practices and beliefs that maintained an outmoded social and political order.

Chartists preferred the power of people acting as a group rather than individually. They were working-class people who had been involved in a mass movement in the 1830s and 1840s to gain representation and other rights (which they called a charter) in Britain. Their movement failed abysmally, in large part due to the middle-class Liberals. The middle classes of Britain had used working-class support to pressure the British Parliament into passing Reform Acts in 1832, which gave the middle classes access to power. However, the middle-class Liberals then shut the door on requests from Chartist working-class activists for the same rights. Many ex-Chartists ended up in the colonies from the 1850s on, and soon began influencing Australian politics.

This made Colonial Liberals almost a contradiction in terms for 'classic' Liberals in Britain, who believed fervently that the market should be allowed to freely operate and, through this freedom, would find the most efficient ways of getting things done. The chief exponents of this new contradictory form of Liberalism were found in the gold rush colony of Victoria.

LIFE DOWN UNDER

In NSW, which had been less overwhelmed by 1850s arrivals, they stuck with free trade. But voters in the other colonies, the main powerhouse of Victoria especially, proved on the whole to be more than happy with this turn of events. Partly due to the mass arrival of disaffected British Chartists in the 1850s, classic Liberalism had less traction — the new arrivals were much less attached to arguments about unsullied free trade and markets. The idea that government was there for them began to dominate, and many progressive and radical Liberals began to follow this new direction being taken in the colonies.

Taking on the squatters, but not the conservatives

When Liberals arrived in Australia in the 1850s, they arrived accustomed to fighting against the established conservative forces of society — only to find in Australia that these conservative forces were practically non-existent.

IN THEIR WORDS

In an electioneering speech in 1856, the Victorian Colonial Secretary contrasted the situation with England. There, 'radical' and 'conservative' actually *meant* something. There were things — institutions, practices, established protocols and hierarchies — to conserve. In Australia, however, 'we have nothing to preserve, and nothing to destroy. We [have] landed on a naked shore to form, to found, to create. Nobody could possibly be opposed to progress here.' Thirty years later, another colonist wondered 'what could we ever have done at home with a dead weight of wealth and privilege hanging over us?'

To be a conservative in the Australian colony seemed to be a contradiction in terms. Everything was so new; traditions belonged to the mother country. In Australia, the golden age was widely thought to lie not in the past but in the future, and the old clamps on society had been taken off.

HISTORICAL ROOTS

The squatters, pastoralists and banking men who were the elite and who expected to become the big political power with the advent of self-government (but who didn't — refer to Chapter 8 for why) weren't what you could call 'conservatives'. No established traditional institutions existed for them to conserve, and they themselves were upstarts who had seized land and made money in the 1830s and 1840s.

With the granting of self-government and almost universal manhood suffrage through the 1850s, the crucial lower houses of colonial parliaments were controlled by liberals, radicals and workers. The upper houses, which maintained a more restricted franchise, were mostly controlled by the men with big money, and these became the main reactionary force the Colonial Liberals had to take on. (Refer to Chapter 8 for more on the granting of self-government and manhood suffrage, and its effects.)

Gaining power for the Colonial Liberalists

During the 1850s, near-universal manhood suffrage was granted throughout the Australian colonies. For these newly enfranchised voters — workers, radicals and the lower-middle class — the Colonial Liberals were speaking their language.

HISTORICAL ROOTS

Colonial Liberals were in charge of governments in NSW, Victoria and South Australia by 1860, and the movement would remain dominant until the 1880s and 1890s. Individuals such as John Robertson, Henry Parkes and George Reid in NSW, George Higinbotham, Charles Pearson and Graham Berry in Victoria, and, later, Charles Kingston in South Australia were politicians who helped develop various strands of this distinctive new political movement, promoting the continued development of prosperity for the working and middle classes, which constituted the vast bulk of the colonial populace.

Under the influence of Colonial Liberal politicians, Australian governments

>> Established state schools for all

>> Happily took on the role of raising money to invest in and build big infrastructure projects

>> Passed laws to try to establish small-scale farmers on the land, allowing them to pay less than market prices

>> Established customs taxes on imports to encourage the growth of local industries and raise crucial revenue without using income tax

HISTORICAL ROOTS

Colonial radicals and Liberals who seized power and tapped into mass public support through the 1870s and 1880s were the people who laid down the planks of a newly emergent dynamic society that would eventually become the Federation of Australia, with its democratic institutions, its aggressively egalitarian streak and its insistence that a decent society owed everyone a 'fair go' in life — a good education and a chance at decent work with good wages.

GETTING ALL WORKED UP IN PARLIAMENT

When ambitious laws ran into opposition (often in the upper houses of colonial parliaments, where the wealthy were often the only ones with the right to vote) intense debate and vitriolic public anger was often triggered.

The flashpoint was Victoria, which at this period was the most radical and progressive colony (having attracted the bulk of ambitious and radical young men and women in the 1850s gold rush), yet saddled with a quite reactionary upper house. In Victoria in the 1860s and again in the late 1870s, popular measures were blocked in the upper house, and public demonstrations and anger reached such heights as to threaten varying degrees of civil disorder.

The rhetoric of politicians in the colonies was often far more violent than that used back in Britain. Denunciations of 'the squatters', 'the rich bankers' and any others who would seem to stand in the way of the popular will were often extreme. Paradoxically, travellers from Britain suggested this was because the social order of the colonies was quite harmonious.

Because colonial life was relatively open, fluid and meritocratic, and most workers, labourers, tradesmen and working women had had little trouble in finding various degrees of material prosperity and success, nothing like the sort of tensions that resulted from the more rigidly stratified British society arose.

This meant politicians could appeal to 'the people' to unite against 'wealthy exploiting interests' with much more freedom than in Britain, where such rhetoric ran more risk of causing conflagration. In the economic and social spheres, class conflict was negligible, so political confrontations could go ballistic.

This doesn't mean that overblown political denunciations couldn't and didn't risk conflagration, however. At various moments — Victoria in the mid-1860s and late 1870s especially — the brinksmanship and ferocity of agitation and denunciation on either side risked dragging the whole society into aggressive confrontation, with the Colonial Office in Britain, and with the bankers and pastoralists who held large chunks of land and made up an obstructive power bloc in the upper house (the Legislative Council).

The political hacks and visionaries — grocers, drapers, wine merchants, bankrupts, toy makers and radical lawyers alike — who grappled with new democratic life and self-government from the 1850s on were at least as extraordinary and unique a colonial phenomenon as the bushrangers and explorers (which you can read about in Chapter 9), but are nowadays less well known.

Intervening in the economy

One of the key debates in Australian politics, even in the mid-1800s, was how much say the government should have in the economy. If government could be made to raise money in London to build railways with extra-cheap freight costs, to create land departments that would try to engineer and oversee the mass settlement of ordinary people on small farm selections (refer to the preceding section), then why not use government intervention to build tariff walls to help build local industries and keep everyone in a good job?

REMEMBER

Classic economic theory that was accepted in Britain in the mid-1800s held that the market could flourish if you eliminated state interference, and allowed the 'invisible hand' of market forces to realise the most effective and intelligent outcomes for all concerned. In Australia, that orthodoxy largely went out the window. Instead, the state began intervening extensively in the economy.

Colonial governments began to supervise land settlement, irrigation projects, the construction of public works and the implementation of tariffs. These governments secured half of the total foreign investment of capital into the colonies, investing it in rail and communications (telegraphs and post), water, funding education for all children and (eventually, when the smell and cholera deaths got too bad) on sewerage and sanitation. By 1900, the largest enterprises in the economy were held by the colonial governments.

Trains — Colonial Liberal style

With government involvement, railways expanded rapidly throughout the long boom decades. Unlike America, which had a similarly vast interior without much white settlement, the expansion of the railways was not handed over to private companies. In Australia, colonial governments were the big sponsors and organisers of railways — for most of the colonial period the biggest governmental department, and certainly the biggest source of contracts and jobs, was the Railways Department.

Workers at manufacturing companies, foundries and railway workshops found themselves gainfully employed producing engines and carriages. On the government payroll were

>> Administrative staff

>> Attendants

>> Conductors

>> Drivers

>> Maintenance crews

In the 1880s, railways began to fan out through newly developing suburbs in the major cities and into the surrounding rural areas. One classic (and notorious) example was the Victorian Railway Act of 1882 initiated by Thomas Bent, which boasted 52 lines — one for each electoral constituency! (For more on the expansion of the colonial railways, refer to Chapter 9.)

Tariffs

One of the best examples of the way the free-trade Liberals of Britain had to change their stripes when they adopted Colonial Liberalist ideals was in their adoption of customs barriers and excise taxes. Beginning in Victoria in the mid-1860s, and followed subsequently by most of the colonies apart from NSW, these tariffs were brought in to protect and encourage local industry, and to raise revenue.

Called 'Protection' (as opposed to free trade), one of its earliest proponents was David Syme, the owner and editor of *The Age* newspaper in Melbourne. Syme was later given the moniker 'Father of Protection', and it's highly unlikely the protection movement would have ever have been translated into colonial legislation and law if Syme hadn't devoted the energies of the cheap newspaper (only one penny a copy! Even in the 1860s that was remarkably cheap) with its vast circulation.

The argument made by Syme was that the conditions of colonial economic life were very different from those of established European societies. Therefore, the colonies should be treated differently. Free exchange might be the best philosophy in the wider context, but on the colonial periphery where new societies and even newer industries were struggling to emerge, different rules should apply. In his 1876 book, *Outlines of an Industrial Science*, Syme went further, arguing not just for protection but for active state intervention in economic life.

Syme's argument was pitched to appeal to the working men and women who wanted jobs in the cities, in manufacturing and other related trades. And in Victoria it worked. In 1871, the tax rate in Victoria was lifted by then-Treasurer Graham Berry to 20 per cent on imports to encourage local manufacturing — boots, clothes, shoes, furniture, coaches and wagons, metal and leather goods. Victorian farmers were also protected from cheap produce arriving from other colonies or countries.

The protection argument didn't work as well in NSW. This is because NSW had an alternative that Victoria lacked. The other purpose of the tariff was to gather revenue to fund the big projects colonial governments were often involving themselves in. No tax on incomes or property was levied in colonial Australia, and if governments were going to continue to pour investment into infrastructure projects and public works programs, they needed the money to come from somewhere. Often the money came from large loans raised by colonial governments on the London money market, but the loans had to be paid back. In NSW, they could gather revenue from selling Crown land. Victoria, being much smaller, had much less land to sell. They needed another revenue source, and no-one liked the idea of an income tax, so tariffs it was.

LIFE DOWN UNDER

Protection's long-term social impact was probably best described by James Service, a Victorian politician who had actually stayed an advocate for free trade. In 1889, 25 years after protection laws had first been brought in, he said that free trade produced more wealth, but protection meant it was distributed more evenly throughout the community. The preference of most colonies for protection over free trade showed the emerging attitude that would become known as egalitarianism. An equal share for most people seemed a better deal than cheaper goods for everyone combined with no attempts to establish and expand new industries.

HISTORICAL ROOTS

The historical impact of the protection argument begun in the 1860s by David Syme — one newspaper editor in Melbourne — was prodigious. The policy of tariff protection against external imports was adopted after Federation by the Commonwealth Government, and the rules surrounding it were actually made more rigorous so that the benefits of industry protection were passed on to workers in the form of sufficiently high wages. This became part of the Australian Settlement, which you can read more about in Chapter 12, and made the country a kind of economic fortress until the tariffs finally began to be dismantled in the 1970s and 1980s. That's one very long shadow cast by one newspaper editor!

Education – for everyone

The movement to refashion education tapped into a desire to make a new society in Australia that abolished the old class distinctions: 'This being a new and free country, let us leave behind us all the superstitious nonsense of the old world', declared Edward Cohen to the Victorian Parliament as it finally passed the 'Free, Compulsory and Secular' Education Act in 1872. South Australia followed in 1876. Henry Parkes's Public Instruction Act in 1880 did the same thing in NSW. State assistance to denominational (or religious) schools ended.

IN THEIR WORDS

Not everyone was impressed with the new education laws introduced in Australia in the 1870s. The Catholic Archbishop of Sydney attacked Parkes's Bill, saying the new schools were 'seedplots of future immorality, infidelity and lawlessness, being calculated to debase the standards of human excellence, and to corrupt the political, social and intellectual life of future citizens'. But others were enthusiastic. In Victoria, future Premier Graham Berry enthused that 'under the present system undesirable social distinctions are being annihilated. . .' and the abolition of old class distinctions was more important than any potential religious divisions that might open up, because it was the class differences 'which are the great barrier to true democratic progress'. Another future Victorian premier, James Service, stated emphatically 'Let our motto be, Equal rights to all, Special privileges to none!'

MELBOURNE THE (MOSTLY) MARVELLOUS

The 1880s was the decade when Melbourne was the dominant centre of Australian life. Melbourne was the largest city on the continent, and the go-to place for trade, business and pleasure.

In the 1880s, nearly 25 per cent of all of Britain's overseas investment went to Australia, and most of it went through Melbourne banks. As Melbourne became the financial centre of the whole continent's expansion, so too its central city area got rebuilt as a banking district. The new buildings said something particular about the general attitude of the place, said Francis Adams — 'movement, progress, conscious power'. It was 'a city into whose hands wealth and its power is suddenly phenomenally cast'.

In 1885, George Augustus Sala toured Australia and was impressed with Melbourne, then at the height of its prosperity, financial clout and social influence. Getting back to London, he tagged it 'Marvellous Melbourne', a nickname that Melburnians found, well, marvellous.

However, Melbourne acquired another nickname during this frenetic decade — Smellbourne. While building great edifices and making money had for decades been high priorities for the municipal councillors and legislators of Victoria's capital, doing something about all the build-up of sewerage, rubbish and filth attracted much less urgency.

The problem began shortly after the gold rush began, as the numbers converging on Melbourne mushroomed alarmingly. In 1852, the report from the Select Committee on Melbourne's sewerage disclosed, 'in the backyards and enclosures, more astounding accumulations of putrescent substances and rubbish of all kinds, than I ever inspected in the very worst parts of the dirtiest English or Continental towns: or that I should have thought could have ever occurred in a civilized community. Many of the foundations of the buildings are greatly injured owing to the saturation of the subsoil by liquid excrementitious matter'. One place in the city grid revealed 'a green putrid semi-liquid mass, partly formed by the outpourings of surrounding privies', and other parts of the city were in a similar state: 'a fetid putrescent mass of tenacious mud, exhibiting on the surface masses of fly-blown putrid meat, entrails of animals, bones, discarded wearing apparel, and other unsightly rubbish'.

By 1870, another observer could describe how, 'there, before me, were very wide gutters, one on each side of the street, along which ran the liquid refuse of Melbourne . . . where before the eyes of the public, a foul-looking and still more foul-smelling fluid runs the daily and appointed course'.

The general filth and unsanitary conditions continued to be largely ignored by the Victorian Government, until the late 1880s saw an escalating death rate due to cholera and other bad-sanitation diseases. In 1890, the Melbourne Board of Works was established and a system of proper sewerage was begun.

The schools were not just for those who couldn't afford private schools, but for children of all classes. Middle-class children, working-class children, and even some of the few upper-class children who lived in the colonies, all passed through the same school gates together, producing a strong sense of shared identity for the generation of 'native-born' Australians who were growing up as children of their largely immigrant parents.

HISTORICAL ROOTS

To begin with Catholic parents (mostly Irish) were quite willing to send their children to the local state school, but the Catholic hierarchy felt strongly otherwise. Even though space in the curriculum was set aside for separate religious instruction for children of different denominations, Catholic prelates and bishops found this dangerously secular. They demanded that Catholic children go to separate schools and continue to receive state aid. The colonial governments flatly refused this, and an impasse ensued . . . which lasted another 90 years, until 1964, when state aid to private schools was resumed (via the federal government).

LIFE DOWN UNDER

While the bishops and parliamentarians dominated the newspaper headlines, another, more profound, revolution was quietly taking place. With the institution of compulsory education for school-age children throughout colonial Australia, child labour largely came to an end — although it wasn't until the 1890s that the compulsory attendance clauses were implemented strongly enough to eliminate all forms of child labour in the colonies. Because children had to be in school, it was no longer permissible for young boys and girls to go straight into jobs. This alone gives the Acts a significance beyond simple education.

Chapter 11

The Economy's Collapsed — Anyone for Nationhood?

The 1890s saw the biggest changes in Australian society since the gold strikes of the 1850s. Australia had seen 30 years of economic good times that had sustained decades of colonial expansion, and during which colonial Australians had enjoyed the best standard of living of anywhere in the world. The long boom ended dramatically and a long trough began, featuring higher unemployment, slower economic growth and very little immigration. (The big exception to this was Western Australia, where gold was discovered in the early 1890s.) The trough in most of the country would last until a second long boom began, after World War II in the late 1940s (see Chapter 18).

The great crash and subsequent 1890s depression had profound effects, both direct and indirect. Violent strikes were one effect, with a new organised political wing of the union movement — the Australian Labor Party — emerging from the comprehensive defeat of the unions in these industrial conflicts.

Another was the movement for nationhood itself. The federation of all the self-governing Australian colonies had been kicked around as an idea, on and off, for some 50 years before the 1890s. But the dominant wave of endless economic expansion and political progress had sustained colonial ideas and ambitions for four decades, putting all other ideas on the backburner. This was torn to bits in the economic and social strife of the early 1890s. The future could no longer be taken for granted. A new dream was needed. The idea of a new profound unity — 'a nation for a continent', 'one people, one destiny' — suddenly became a lot more compelling.

In this chapter, I cover the profound effects of the economic collapse of the 1890s, including the birth of the Australian Labor Party and the creation of Australia as a newly federated nation.

From Boom to Bust

Australia in the 1880s had achieved a high level of prosperity that had spread through all levels of society. Among other effects, this meant:

>> The real value of wages was high, as were consumption levels.

>> Many regions had functional full employment.

The demand for labour and for labourers had reached a peak in the 1880s because of big infrastructure projects and various construction booms — including the redevelopment of metropolitan centres, the continued expansion of the rail network and the expansion and consolidation of properties in the rural areas. (Refer to Chapters 8 and 9 for more on these construction booms.)

The suburban dream of home ownership was becoming a new reality for workers and for a new generation of Australians: The children of the gold-rush immigrants who were now reaching adulthood.

But as credit became more freely available and natural growth began to slow, Australia was heading from boom times to bubble times — and from there, it didn't take long for the bubble to burst.

The bubble before the pop

The growth in infrastructure and construction had given good bargaining power to workers, and attracted large numbers of (mostly British) migrants from overseas. Some short-term trouble spots cropped up, such as South Australia, where development lapsed, or NSW and Queensland in the middle of the 1880s, but as some sectors finished their boom, others would begin. Colonial residents were remarkably fluid in their movements, often travelling from one colony to another, based on wherever the best wages, conditions and chances for making good money were.

LIFE DOWN UNDER

With the sustained prosperity, houses were built and occupied by the owners. Home ownership became a possibility for a majority of the population. Workers put their savings in high-interest accounts in local building societies, and new suburbs began to radiate out from the metropolitan city centres.

At the same time as new migrant workers were saving money and having houses built, a generation with ambitions of home ownership was also coming to maturity. The 1850s gold-rush immigrants had themselves settled down and had children, and by the 1880s these children, Australia's first baby boomers, were reaching adulthood, getting married, having children and setting up new homes. Put it this way: It was a good time to be a property developer.

HISTORICAL ROOTS

The dream in the 1850s among gold-rush arrivals had been of land ownership — small farms and a life on the soil. For various reasons, this had proved a non-starter (refer to Chapter 8). Now, 30 years later, the dream of land ownership had transformed into the recognisably modern Australian suburban dream — the quarter-acre block.

The real estate market then entered an insane speculative frenzy phase: In January 1888, transactions on the Melbourne Stock Exchange passed the £2,000,000 mark. By July, Melbourne properties were selling for £1,500 per square foot — more than the prices for property in London. Land investment companies started declaring dividends for investors even before they'd sold any land. Between January and September, £13,000,000 passed hands in land sales. By the start of 1889, Melbourne banks and financial institutions had advanced a grand total of £113,000,000.

Think of Wile E Coyote in the *Road Runner* cartoon, shooting off a precipice. His feet keep whirring in the air before gravity hits and he plummets to earth. Australia by the late 1880s was in that moment after shooting off the ledge — its legs were churning faster and faster, but there was no solid ground beneath, just empty air. What came next? A dawning moment of realisation — 'Uh-oh' — and a very hard crash. Just ask Coyote.

And now for a big collapse

After a good 40 years of boom times, the 1890s depression hit. The big collapse was caused by three broad causes:

>> **A stalling economy:** In 1889, a collapse in the housing market, a crisis in the wool industry and a natural end to the expanding railway network all occurred.

>> **Investment in freefall:** A crisis in London capital markets in 1890 meant that British investors in foreign markets needed all their money back to prop up their own banking system.

>> **A massive crash in the banking sector:** Practically all the major banks had to suspend operations in the early months of 1893, and many had to shut down permanently.

Stalling economy

The 1880s building boom was based on unprecedented levels of borrowing and foreign (mostly British) investment. Australian colonies had become flavour of the investment month in British capital markets in the 1880s, as investors queued up to put money into Australian ventures. From the Australian point of view, this meant that ambitious expansion projects that would have otherwise been curtailed as natural growth slowed could continue and build to still higher levels.

However, the growth came with a very big *but*. In the midst of all this economic sunshine, the foundations were shaky. The real growth rate in the 1880s had actually trailed right off, because the massive demand for new housing coming from the children of gold-rush immigrants who had come of age, married and started families had, by the late 1880s, largely been met. But not many people noticed. So much foreign investment was coming in — the amount borrowed by colonial governments nearly trebled in the 1880s, from £36,000,000 to £90,000,000 — and so many money-making projects were roaring along, that slowing demand was bad news that was easy to ignore.

A crisis was also brewing in the wool industry, with the international price dropping and a series of droughts wiping out many farmers' stocks.

Decreasing foreign investments

In 1890, the Barings Bank in London nearly collapsed after its investments in Argentina ran into trouble. (Barings was only saved after a bailout from a consortium that included most of the major London banks.) This close call made all British banks a bit nervy about their massive investments in similar southern-hemisphere colonial regions, and they started dragging their investments out.

Banks crashing loudly

In October 1888, a belated halt to the Melbourne real estate frenzy had been called when Victorian Associated Banks agreed not to lend out any further money in overdrafts for speculative land purchases. This came as a bit of a shock because everyone had become quite *used* to overdrafts and speculative investments — buying things, generally land, purely in order to sell them on when they increased in value in a very short time.

The shock got worse when land stopped appreciating in value and started bottoming out. Then the international wool price collapsed (refer to the section 'Stalling economy', earlier in this chapter). In 1890, British investors began to withdraw their large deposits (refer to preceding section), and banks began calling in their loans. Plenty of people were in deep, and weren't able to pay off their debts. Banks foreclosed on pastoral properties, because many owners had taken out large loans to develop their properties, relying on the high price of wool to pay it off. Pastoralists began losing their properties to the banks.

The banks couldn't recoup their losses on the sale of properties that had dramatically dropped in value and, as British investors continued to withdraw their funds, couldn't cope with having to pay the money back so quickly.

LIFE DOWN UNDER

In the second half of 1891, financial institutions collapsed in droves, not just in Victoria but across Australia. The worst of the increasingly severe economic depression, however, was felt in Melbourne. In January 1893, the prestigious Federal Bank of Australia, based in Melbourne, ran out of money and closed. In April 1893, the Commercial Bank of Australia, one of Australia's largest, suspended operations, and 12 other banks soon followed. Understandably, depositors started to panic, and decided they wanted their money back. Thousands of small-time investors and depositors began to converge on their banks and demand their deposits be returned. Gold coins made their way into mattresses and private safes in households everywhere.

Then the National Bank of Australasia — established in 1853 and one of the oldest, soundest, most careful and conservative banking institutions in the country — suspended payment, 'with the view of reconstructing the bank upon a basis favourable to the altered conditions of the money market'. The panic got worse. On the last day of April 1893, a Sunday, the Victorian cabinet met and decided to close all banks for the following week as they tried to deal with the financial crisis. On Monday, only three banks remained open.

IN THEIR WORDS

The next day, two major banks, the Union and the Australasian, were paying out and, in the words of one reporter, on the footpaths of Collins Street, Melbourne, all day 'an eager mob surged'. 'The people stood about in the street and on the opposite side of the way outside the Bank of Australasia till it looked more like the betting ring on a racecourse than anything else, whilst on the stairs of the bank, men at first literally fought with each other to get inside'. Another writer described central Melbourne as 'like a disturbed ant-hill, men running hither and thither with their money, not knowing in whom to believe'.

THE MELBOURNE PERSONALITY SPLIT

Melbourne, the city that had been known as cocky and confident, the centre of just about all business ventures in Australia, became conservative, cautious and fearful as a result of the economic collapse of the early 1890s.

In 1880, Melbourne had been described as a phenomenon, 'a city of a generation'. The proofs of colonial progress and achievement were seen in 'the elegance of its shops and the costliness of the wares within, the beauty of the numerous parks and gardens by which it is environed . . . the thousand and one comforts and conveniences afforded to its enterprising and industrious residents'. In the 1890s, after the crash, people who kept living in extravagant fashion were for the first time in Melbourne's history accused of 'bad taste'. Large mansions and houses were sold off, abandoned and boarded up, while in the working-class suburbs, many were reduced to destitution as they lost work.

In 1904, Henry Gyles Turner, a banker who had himself been sucked in by the 1880s boom, wrote a history of Victoria. In this, he turned the 1880s — 'the era of extravagance' — and the lean 1890s that followed into a kind of morality tale. During the madness of the 1880s, he argued, many foolish things had been done. In the sober 1890s, 'by the exercise of a spartan economy the lean years which followed the crisis were lived through . . . with a wholesome avoidance of any new schemes for capturing Fortune'. Fortune, luck, and the gambles made on business investments and the like had been a kind of god in colonial Melbourne, particularly from the 1850s gold rush onward, and had provided the incredibly expansive energy of the place.

In the aftermath of the great 1890s crash, dour and sober Melbourne was born. The city experienced an almost complete personality change, so dramatic was the crash and fall. Now it began to seem like the only kind of fun to be had was a rather dull one — 'the satisfactory feeling of living within one's means'. The 'city of a generation' had become a place that didn't seem to want to do much of anything at all. Sydney overtook Melbourne in population as people left the colony in great numbers, and became the new cultural centre as well — the painters and writers who had been active in Melbourne during the boom years now went to Sydney. Other Victorians went overseas, and some headed to the goldfields in Kalgoorlie (in Western Australia) to try their luck there.

The economic collapse of the 1890s had a number of long-term effects. The metropolitan cities — Melbourne and Sydney chiefly, but also Brisbane and Adelaide — were now seen as corrupt, decadent, soulless, heartless and artificial. For the first time, the bush, the outback and its workers — shearers, jackaroos, station hands, drovers and stockmen — became the embodiment of the 'true' Australia, and the bush legend was born.

Three strikes and we're out — industrial turmoil

The biggest effects of the 1890s depression were felt by the working classes. After the economic and banking collapse of the early 1890s, depositors and investors lost their savings and investments. Workers lost homes. Businessmen weren't able to pay their overdrafts and huge unemployment loomed for most members of the working class.

LIFE DOWN UNDER

The 'workingman's paradise' (refer to Chapters 8 and 10) was coming to an end. In this new environment, it was no longer the worker who had all the bargaining power — now the business owners called the shots as they tried to cut costs. Bosses began to take on the unions.

Workers dealt with these attacks head-on — through a series of major strikes. Ultimately, these strikes would be unsuccessful, as the government intervened on behalf of the business owners and pastoralists.

Strike 1: Maritime strike, 1890

In 1890, wharfies and other maritime workers went out on strike for five months (from August through to December) to fight for what they saw as a basic right — their right to form effective unions. In industrial action that threatened to shut down industries and city lights across the country, more than 5,000 workers in both Melbourne and Sydney stopped much of the vital traffic in and out of the ports. Coal miners, transport workers, shearers and station hands throughout Australia all backed the maritime workers and staged sit-downs and strikes of their own.

When employers hired non-union labour, the government sent in police to protect them. The minister in charge of maintaining civil order in Victoria was Alfred Deakin, self-described 'ultra-radical' (and future prime minister and Federation founder — see the section 'New Nation? Maybe. Maybe Not', later in this chapter). Deakin declared that 'The first duty of a Government is to preserve order . . . to stop at nothing to protect the community'. Informed that violent riots were being planned, he sent in 200 Mounted Rifles, as well as the Victorian Rangers and all available cavalry.

IN THEIR WORDS

Deakin wasn't messing around when he sent in the troops, and neither was the commander of the Victorian Mounted Rifles, Colonel Tom Price, who had the following to say to his men: 'If the order is given to fire, don't dare let me see one rifle pointed up in the air. Fire low and lay them out. Lay the disturbers of law and order out, so that the duty will not have to be performed again. Let it be a lesson to them'.

The order to fire on the strikers never had to be carried out, however, because the violent riot didn't eventuate. The strike was eventually broken and the maritime union's power crushed as they ran out of funds to maintain the action. The wharfies went back to work, and the progressive government and the middle classes showed that when push came to shove, they were on the side of 'order'.

Strike 2: Shearers' strikes, 1891 and 1894

The shearers' strikes of the early 1890s had their origins in the mid-1880s.

In 1886, shearers' unions began to form, first in Ballarat in Victoria and later the same year in Bourke and Wagga Wagga in NSW. In the middle of a wool boom, their bargaining power was good and they could force sheep-station owners to keep paying high shearing rates, even as the international price of wool began falling. However, sheep farmers began forming their own associations and tried to cut shearers' wages. The stage was set for an almighty confrontation.

The first minor scuffle occurred in May 1890, when the Pastoralists' Union of Graziers and Farmers decided to employ only non-union labour on one large property station. This was a clear attempt to break the hold of unions on the labour force. The attempt failed. Maritime unions in both Australia and Britain refused to handle the wool.

The fight was far from over, however, with the major showdown beginning in January 1891. Pastoralists, themselves pressured by the collapsing wool price, tried to cut wages. Shearers wouldn't have a bar of it. Pastoralists tried to get around union demands by employing non-union labour — often Chinese labourers — which infuriated the shearers intensely. Shearing disturbances — such as work stoppages, attacks on property and assaults on non-union labour — began on a wide scale, on and near stations throughout a vast area covering Queensland and NSW down through the Riverina area to the Victorian border. In NSW, 28 per cent of the entire police force was sent to the districts affected.

LIFE DOWN UNDER

When it came to policing the civil disturbances caused by the shearers, the police had a problem. The maritime strike had been huge but it was concentrated at the wharves and docks of the major port cities. The police knew where the trouble spots were, and where to find the trouble makers threatening insurrection. With the shearers' strikes, the police had difficulty in knowing whether to break their force up to protect every shed that was trying to use non-union shearing labour, or to concentrate their forces where the major shearing camps were. It was a nightmare.

Many unionists were arrested during the 1891 shearers' strike, with 12 put in jail. Property was destroyed and gunfights broke out as the police and army were called in. The union representing shearers in this strike was ultimately forced to capitulate when, like the maritime union in 1890, it ran out of money and lost the support of the majority of the population. The bulk of the press and most of the public saw the conflict as a question of anarchy versus order, and of potential insurrection versus civilised society.

In 1894, shearers went on strike again against pay cuts. Non-union labour (mostly unemployed men who were happy to do any work for some pay) was brought in as the Queensland Government passed a Peace Preservation Act, which gave it emergency powers to deal with any threats to order.

Strike 3: Broken Hill miners' strike, 1892

At Broken Hill in NSW in 1892, the mine owners reversed a previous wage agreement, and then brought in non-union labour. A strike followed.

Future prime minister Edmund Barton (see the section 'New Nation? Maybe. Maybe Not' later in this chapter for more on Barton) was acting premier of NSW at the time and resisted demands to send in the army — he sent in plenty of extra police instead.

Leaders of the miners' strike were arrested and charged (and some were convicted) with conspiring to 'incite, move and persuade great numbers of the liege subjects of our Lady Queen to riots, tumults and breaches of the peace'.

Birthing the Australian Labor Party

The industrial strikes and turmoil of the early 1890s had failed to ensure worker demands were met. But it wasn't all bad news. This failure encouraged the emergence of a centralised political party to act on behalf of trade unions. The logic was that if the government had used the law to come in on the side of the bosses in the three strikes of the 1890s (refer to the preceding section), then the best thing to do was to take control of government itself, and change the laws.

The resulting party was the Labor Party, and it was in luck. Such was the decimation of all the small craft-based unions, and the overwhelming defeat of the shearers, wharfies and miners in the industrial conflicts of the early 1890s, that the politicians in the Labor Party were able to steer the direction of the workers' movement for the next 25 years. New 'super unions', such as the Australian Workers' Union, were, like the new Labor Party, centrally organised with less participatory involvement from the majority of members. Labor politicians in these unions were prominent.

Much of the original aims of the industrial workers' unions in Australia had been aggressively militant, with the main aim being to create a socialist society (where no-one had private property and no-one was out of work or had to work too much). But the political leaders of the new Labor Party moderated these early aims to come up with a 'fighting program' that they could put to voters. This program was much more moderate — and much more successful. Members of parliament received what was, for workers, good pay, so Labor politicians didn't have to worry about extra paid work just to earn enough to live on. They used their free time well, travelling (for free!) on trains throughout the colonies preaching their political cause. These politicians formed what was the first recognisably modern political organisation.

From little things . . .

On 1 August 1890, the first general council of the Australian Labour Federation began sitting in Brisbane. At this council, a parliamentary program, or 'platform', was drafted that all Labor politicians had to commit to.

The first Labor Electoral League in NSW was set up in March 1891 in the Sydney suburb of Balmain, and later in the year other leagues were set up in nearby industrial suburbs of Sydney. The agreed political platform now included an eight-hour working day, elected magistrates, support for the federation of the colonies of Australasia (meaning New Zealand too), and land nationalisation.

In June 1891, the Labor Party entered NSW parliament, with a staggeringly successful 35 members elected to the Legislative Assembly (of 141 total seats). For the rest of the decade, ruling NSW governments would have to do deals with the Labor Party.

Two Australian halves of a Labor story

The Labor Party had more of an immediate effect in NSW and Queensland than in other colonies. This was for two reasons:

» Queensland and NSW received the lion's share of new British immigrants in the 1870s and 1880s. Most of these new immigrants were hardened by class conflict in Britain, and brought new aggressive agendas to Australia.

» Victoria and other colonies had already produced a kind of ultra-radicalism of their own, with the highly state-interventionist Colonial Liberalism being fostered by the gold-rush generation. (Refer to Chapters 8 and 10 for more on political radicalism in the gold-rush generation.)

In Victoria, a trade union convention formed the Progressive Political League, which helped get 10 members voted to the Legislative Assembly in 1892. But they didn't think of themselves as Labor only — they thought of themselves as radicals with Labor links. An unimpressed Trades Hall Council said this wouldn't do at all, and formed a United Labor Party of Victoria in June 1894, but even then things stayed fluid in the political sphere. At elections, Labor candidates often agreed not to run against radicals and progressive liberals such as Alfred Deakin, Henry Bourne Higgins and Isaac Isaacs (all of whom get talked about more in Chapter 12).

Labor politicos and Labor unionists — the struggle begins!

Because the 1890s depression had destroyed so much of the previous union power and so many of the small locally active unions, a new set of Labor politicians filled the power vacuum, with a centrally organised political machine. Later in the decade, when unions began to put themselves back together, they were absorbed into and organised by the new Labor political machine. Men with no previous union experience but with a lot of Labor political experience took charge of reorganising unions.

The best example of this is Billy Hughes (a future Labor prime minister you can find out more about in Chapter 13), who had a huge role in re-establishing a national wharf labourers' union in 1899. The wharfies union had previously had their power crushed in the 1890 maritime strike (refer to the section 'Three strikes and we're out — industrial turmoil', earlier in this chapter). Now it was a Labor politician coming in to set them back on their feet.

This kind of thing worried a lot of unionists. They figured that the Labor Party had been built up to get political power for the union movement. But now it seemed like the political tail was wagging the union dog. For the moment they kept quiet about it, though (see Chapter 13 for more on when the conflict really heats up). In politics, Labor was proving an instant hit, getting seats in parliament, negotiating with different sides to get the best deal for workers and, for a few weeks in Queensland in 1899, even taking power. This was better than any Labor political movement in the world had done so far.

GOING OUT WEST — KALGOORLIE GOLD

The biggest gold discoveries since the 1850s strikes in Victoria and NSW took place in Western Australia (WA) in the early 1890s, at first at Coolgardie and Southern Cross, and shortly after at Kalgoorlie.

In Coolgardie in 1892, nuggets and lumps of gold began to be found in shallow soil. In the first few weeks after first discovering gold, 3,000 ounces were dug up by the first few hundred (highly excited) diggers to arrive. Apart from the lack of water, it was a gold prospector's paradise. By 1898, Coolgardie was the third-largest town in WA behind Perth and Fremantle.

But Kalgoorlie was destined to become bigger. Gold was first discovered here the year after Coolgardie, and by 1898 Kalgoorlie was producing 500,000 ounces of gold compared to Coolgardie's 150,000. But the gold in Kalgoorlie was harder to get at. Rather than lying in shallow alluvial soil, it was embedded deeper in the ground in reefs. This required large-scale machinery and engineering expertise to dig down and extract the gold from the rock. Here, the miners became workers not diggers. If Coolgardie was the prospector's paradise, Kalgoorlie was the paradise for joint-stock companies, mine vendors, engineers and mining companies.

In the middle of the 1890s depression, WA was the only colony that could raise money on the London Stock Exchange for ambitious development projects, and promptly did so for the water pipeline to the Kalgoorlie goldfields. Thanks to London money, a pipeline soon began pumping five million gallons of water per day to the WA goldfields. Between 1892 and 1896, more than 700 WA mining companies were floated on the London Stock Exchange, attracting investment that governments and companies in the eastern colonies of Australia could only dream about. People in the eastern colonies were left to 'live within their means' while WA expanded and developed in a manner similar to eastern Australia in the four decades prior to the 1890s crash.

For thousands of men in the eastern colonies who were without work or had lost all their savings, news of the new gold rushes couldn't have come at a better time. A massive exodus to the western edge of Australia took place, and WA found itself, like Victoria in the 1850s, suddenly catapulted into wealth and importance in the national scheme of things.

Without the gold finds in Kalgoorlie and Coolgardie, Western Australia would never have joined the Commonwealth of Australia. For so long a small unimportant colonial backwater, WA had only achieved self-government in 1890, and didn't much like the idea of giving that away to join a federation. But the gold rushes meant that WA was swamped with 't'othersiders' — men and women from the eastern colonies of Australia. And as of 1893, near-universal adult male suffrage operated in WA, and from 1899 most women were also allowed the vote. (Aboriginal people were still excluded from voting in WA.) Without the sudden inrush of eastern colonials seeking gold, most of whom were pro-federation, there would never have been a majority in favour in WA's referendum to join the Federation in 1901.

New Nation? Maybe. Maybe Not.

Colonial Australians in the 1880s enjoyed the highest standard of living in the world, as well as some of the most democratic governments. Colonies were self-governing, meaning Britain didn't interfere in internal matters (although Britain still set foreign policy for the colonies). A little over ten years later the prosperity was gone, and the self-governing colonies had decided to form together into a new political entity: A federated nation.

Why Federation happened

Through the 1870s and 1880s, colonies in Australia operated like competing city-states, each with a central dominant capital as the main port and each tapping their respective vast interiors with separate railway systems. Each was self-governing, had established customs houses on their various borders, and trained their own defence forces such as local navies.

REMEMBER

The main areas that could have created problems for the colonies were internal trade and centralised defence. But these could have been solved without a federal form of government. One big problem with internal trade was that, when the states had developed their various rail networks, they'd used different *rail gauges* (or widths for the tracks), so the lines didn't link up between the states. If you wanted to travel, or ship goods, by train between NSW and Victoria, for instance, you had to change trains at the border. But a centralised body could have been set up to determine a standard gauge and organise the laying of new tracks. If the push for internal free trade was strong enough, all that was needed was a customs union. The other area of potential problems was defence, with concern focused on whether forces needed to be centrally coordinated (as visiting English experts advised in 1884). Once again, however, a special body could have been set up to provide this coordination, without going to all the extra bother of creating an entire extra layer of government and a new nation.

However, in the 1890s, colonial economies crashed and burned, and the pitch 'One Continent, One People' became increasingly persuasive in the aftermath of strikes and chronic social disturbances.

The collapse of the old dream

The decades before 1890 had been sustained by a belief that the colonial way of life 'had it right'. Progress and prosperity would continue to increase inevitably. While this was happening, the rule of 'if it ain't broke, don't fix it' applied.

IN THEIR
WORDS

Even *The Times* of London agreed with this approach, arguing in 1888, 'The prosperity and sense of security experienced by the colonies have tended to repress the desire for federation . . . [the colonies] will doubtless continue to make the same wonderful progress that [they have] done up to the present'.

At the start of the 1890s, the prosperity and sense of security came crashing to an almighty halt, and the terrible vision of intense class hatred appeared.

IN THEIR
WORDS

During the crash of the 1890s, Alfred Deakin lamented that 'selfishness and shams, cant and materialism rule us, up and down and through and through'. Evidently a new dream was needed, something that would convert divided people into a single national community, turn 'jarring atoms' of divided colonial societies into 'a united organism'.

Significantly, it was only after the great bank crashes and the maritime, shearers' and miners' strikes of the early 1890s that the movement for federation began to get real.

In late July 1893, the Corowa Conference, the first of the 'people's conventions', took place. It was here that the idea of taking the federal idea and a constitution direct to the people in a national referendum was first taken up. Also significant is the fact that for as long as Victoria was pre-eminent as Australia's leading colony and the prime mover for federation, there wasn't a hope that NSW would join. After the great crash, though, with Victoria's expansive economy crippled, NSW had less reason to fear sinister takeover plots from the colonists south of the Murray River.

Railing against second-rate 'colonial' status

In the 1880s, the children of the gold-rush immigrants reached maturity. They, unlike their parents, suffered under the weight of colonial birth. At this time, to be colonial was almost by definition to be inferior. However, this generation turned it into a badge of pride, declaring that their Australian birth and upbringing actually made them *superior* to those born in Britain.

HISTORICAL
ROOTS

Although many of their parents came from working-class British origins, the native-born children benefitted from their parents' hard work and good economic fortune during the long boom to move into more middle-class professions. They also benefitted greatly from the new system of compulsory education brought in during the 1870s and early 1880s (refer to Chapter 10), which meant they began reading and writing and forming public opinions with vigour. The best example of this were the founders and writers behind *The Bulletin* magazine who, although they didn't support federation (they wanted a republic completely separate from Britain), aggressively pushed the idea of Australian superiority, arguing it was 'against the worship of imported habit and belief that the Australian must rebel'. (See the sidebar 'Maverick Archie and *The Bulletin* school' for more on this magazine.)

MAVERICK ARCHIE AND *THE BULLETIN* SCHOOL

LIFE DOWN UNDER

Jules Archibald was the man behind a new magazine that began coming out in the 1880s called *The Bulletin*. With it, a new style of writing began to emerge — irreverent, laconic, shorn of unnecessary rhetorical flourishes, and always ready to puncture British conceits and class distinctions. Many of the best writers of the period — Henry Lawson, A J 'Banjo' Paterson and Joseph Furphy — all made their names publishing poetry and prose in the magazine, and often found their writing styles being shaped by Archibald's editing pen.

The Bulletin was published from Sydney but pitched itself to a widespread 'bush reader-ship' of labourers and itinerant bush workers (many of whom had acquired literacy from the compulsory schooling of the previous decade — refer to Chapter 10). The magazine established itself by taking advantage of free newspaper distribution then being offered by the NSW Government.

Archibald was (in the words of Banjo Paterson) 'about the first Australian to "call" the English bluff'. He was the son of a Warrnambool policeman who began his career at the *Warrnambool Examiner* aged 15. A stint in Melbourne at the *Herald* preceded a move to Sydney. Establishing *The Bulletin* was no picnic — printing crises and libel suits ensued, and Archibald was sent to jail for six weeks. By 1883, Archibald, suffering depression, sailed to England. There he became even more certain that Australia needed to develop differently to Britain. He hated the British class system, and the misery of the urban underclass didn't impress him greatly either.

Returning to Australia with renewed zest, he began a series of ferocious attacks on the links between Australian colonies and Britain. Significantly, even though Australia was by now close to the most highly urbanised place in the world, *The Bulletin* encouraged prose about bush life, especially stories and poems that emphasised those elements of bush life that coincided with the new ideal of Australian nationhood. Archibald wanted material that was clearly Australian. Lawson described taking a story to him once and being told, 'Yes, that's a very good little thing, old man, but it might have been written in Greenland. We want Australian stuff — we want the Australian atmosphere'.

This was a bold new direction in Australian sensibility. Previously, the arbiters of quality literature and art were the gold-rush generation of British immigrants. They felt more British than Australian. Now for the first time, a new attitude was springing up in the next generation, the native-born intelligentsia, who pushed a sense of Australianness as the crucial thing in their identity. Archibald, more than any other individual, harnessed this, inspired this, encouraged this, and gave it an outlet.

By and large, native-born Australians felt the only way to prove themselves as equals to the British, and to stop being treated as 'second-rate' colonials, was to form the Australian nation through federation. Practically all leaders at the 1897 to 1898 federation conventions were either native-born (like Alfred Deakin) or had arrived in Australia in early childhood (like Samuel Griffith). Without the native-born generation, federation wouldn't have happened.

How Federation happened

Federation, as they say, didn't happen overnight, but it did happen relatively quickly. Just 12 short years passed between the first tentative steps and two new houses of a federal parliament and a constitution being in place.

In this section, I outline the major steps in the process.

Tentative first steps at Tenterfield

In 1889, in a speech at Tenterfield in NSW, NSW Premier Henry Parkes declared that it was time to stop messing round — basically saying, 'Let's get serious; let's federate'. According to Parkes, the time had now come 'for the creation on this Australian Continent of an Australian Parliament as distinct from a local Government'. Seeing as most other colonies and their leaders had already been kicking federation ideas around in the 1880s, only to have Parkes and NSW pour scorn on the idea and stop it short, Parkes's speech got things moving nicely (although other premiers still objected).

Convening for Constitution

In March and April 1891, Henry Parkes held a National Australasian Convention in Sydney. Key players were statesmen Samuel Griffith, Edmund Barton (discussed in the 'Three men who made Federation happen' section, later in this chapter), Charles Kingston and Andrew Inglis Clark, who wrote a constitution — the idea being to get it passed by colonial parliaments, then British parliament and passed into law. The Constitution and the idea was heavily criticised in NSW for not being democratic enough. Parkes dropped the idea and, again, federation looked to be a non-starter. It was, in the words of one gleeful NSW politician, 'as dead as Julius Caesar'.

Getting real at Corowa

Popular federation leagues, made up of farmers, shopkeepers, business owners and ordinary citizens, formed in the 1890s to agitate for federation. For two days late in July and early August in 1893, delegates from these leagues converged on the town of Corowa on the Murray River (and the border between NSW and

Victoria) in what became known as 'the people's convention'. The conference decided to follow the idea of John Quick, a delegate from Bendigo. Quick! said Quick — to the people! Have a popularly voted convention, draw up a new constitution, and then take it back to the people in a referendum. One of the big opponents of the previous federation plan, George Reid of NSW, liked Quick's idea. With NSW in, the idea took off.

People's delegates attend conventions

Late in 1897 and early in 1898, three conventions took place in Adelaide, Sydney and Melbourne attended by ten delegates from each colony — except Queensland. A new Constitution was painstakingly formulated over many long nights, and prepared for the referendum. NSW Premier George Reid didn't like it, though — he thought the proposed Constitution wasn't democratic enough, and gave too much power to small states.

Referendum 1 — the people say No

In the first referendum on the Constitution, in 1898, the people said No. Well, they didn't *all* say No. Plenty said Yes — in fact, across Australia the Yes vote doubled the No vote. But NSW had failed to come over — NSW parliament decided that much more than half of their colony had to say Yes, and Premier George Reid gave it only the most lukewarm support possible. In both Victoria and NSW, the ALP also campaigned against it. Federation appeared down for the count for a second time in the 1890s.

Referendum 2 — the people say Yes!

With federation looking like a lost cause, a conference between premiers was held and a new compromise was hammered out. Concessions were given (the new capital was now to be somewhere in NSW) and some changes made to the Constitution, which was then taken to a second referendum. This time the Yes vote was overwhelming. More than triple the number of voters said Yes compared to those who voted No (377,895 votes for and 132,286 vote against) as Queensland voted for the first time.

Even WA says Yes!

Belatedly, Western Australia held a vote on federation. Thanks to the influx of eastern colonists to the Kalgoorlie and Coolgardie goldfields in the 1890s, the Yes votes were more than double the votes against — 44,800 voted Yes against 19,691 No. WA was snuck into the Federation at the last minute, with half a promise that the new federal government would build a transcontinental railway connecting the west to the rest of Australia.

Bingo! New Nation

The new Constitution made for a system and a new nation that was a curious combination of two distinct political traditions — American and British.

On the one hand, it incorporated the Westminster system of Britain's parliamentary democracy, where government is formed from a majority of members in parliament, and where government and ministers are responsible to parliament and could be questioned in parliament, criticised there and voted out in parliament. Unlike the US, if you wanted to be in government in Australia, you needed to get a seat in parliament.

But the Constitution also followed the federal model of the US, by allowing for a federation of states that retained most of their powers and providing equal representation for the states in the Upper House. The Constitution also gave the two houses of parliament the same names as those in the US — House of Representatives and Senate. The federal government wouldn't exercise overwhelming central control (as was the case in Britain or Canada). Instead, the Constitution strictly defined and limited federal powers, leaving the rest of the powers to the states.

The Constitution set up two houses of parliament, as follows:

>> **House of Representatives:** This was the lower house of legislation, with the widest possible franchise and where each person's vote had equal weight.

>> **Senate:** This was the upper house of review, which gave equal weight not to individual voters but to individual *states* (with senators still elected by individual voters).

The constitution also set up

>> A **High Court**, to decide states versus federal issues and interpret the Constitution

>> A **Governor-General**, to represent the sovereign (at that point, Queen Victoria of Britain)

The federal level of government had responsibility for

>> Arbitration of industrial disputes (when the disputes cross state borders)

>> Customs and excise taxes

>> Defence

>> Foreign trade and foreign affairs

- >> Immigration
- >> Marriage and divorce laws
- >> Postal and telegraph services

In these areas, Commonwealth laws would override state laws.

THREE REALLY BIG 1890S MOMENTS FOR WOMEN'S SUFFRAGE

The full details of the women suffrage story in Australia are provided in Chapter 12. However, three events in the 1890s were biggies, occurring at the same time as federation was being debated.

Moment 1: A Monster Petition — Melbourne, 1891

In the early 1890s, Victorian Premier James Munro was a supporter of women's suffrage, but he wanted some proof that votes for women was a big deal for women. Women's suffrage campaigners set about collecting signatures to provide such proof for Victoria's parliament in 1892.

The final petition they presented (via Munro's wife, Jane) to Victorian parliament later that year was enormous — 260 metres long, with 30,000 signatures. This was the biggest petition collected in Australia to that date. It well and truly brought women's suffrage 'into the mainstream'.

Women's suffrage legislation in Victoria got knocked back in the upper house of Victoria's parliament (which operated on a restricted voting franchise, so wasn't democratic even for men) but the issue was now on the map.

Moment 2: When sabotage backfires — Adelaide, 1894

In 1894, South Australia's parliament was considering legislation to extend the vote to women. As in Victoria, it was looking like the legislation would come to grief in the upper house. Upper houses of parliament — or Legislative Councils — were a bit notorious in colonial politics. They were mostly voted in on a restricted franchise that favoured the wealthy and established interests. One Member of the SA Council, Ebenezer Ward, thought he could put the kiss of death on the Bill. He moved an amendment to the legislation that would ensure women got the right to not only vote but also stand for election in parliament. He did this thinking that it no MP in their right minds could possibly support *that* — after building that social time-bomb into its pages, the Bill would surely be thrown out.

(continued)

(continued)

Boy, did that assumption backfire on Ebenezer. Big time.

The law got passed, and in 1895 all South Australian women, including Aboriginal women, became the first women in Australia — and the world — to be able to vote, and stand in parliament. (Women in New Zealand were granted the vote in 1893, but not the right to stand in parliament.)

Moment 3: The no-federation ultimatum — Adelaide again, 1897

Federation, the movement to bring the separate self-governing colonies together in nationhood, had its definite twists and turns during the 1890s. (You can see some of these twists and turns in other sections of this chapter.) At times, Federation looked impossible, or that it could all collapse. One of those moments happened in Adelaide, at the Constitutional Convention in 1897, and women's suffrage was at the heart of it.

The South Australian politicians who had brought in women's voting rights from 1895 were very taken with it. The reform certainly added to the colony's reputation of being at the forefront of progressive experiments. And at the Adelaide convention, men such as John Cockburn, Charles Kingston and Frederick Holder, watched on by a packed gallery of very interested women, did their best to include women's franchise in the federal Constitution. Their attempts were rejected, which brought on the ultimatum.

The South Australian delegates, the only ones voted in to the Convention by women as well as men voters, declared that if the women whose votes they represented didn't get the right to vote for federal parliament written in to the Constitution, the whole nationhood deal was off. They would walk. And if they walked, then WA, which was wavering on federation anyway, and which was separated from the eastern colonies by SA and SA-controlled Northern Territory, would also stand out. All these factors combined would mean federation falling.

This did the trick. Those delegates who had been holding out against women's suffrage, such as Edmund Barton, blinked.

Section 41 of the Constitution was the result. And it ensured that the women of South Australia would keep their right to vote *and* stand for parliament. By implication, this meant that as soon as federal parliament began, a new Franchise Act would have to be drawn up and legislated. This happened in 1902, and through it most women all over Australia gained the right to vote and stand for federal parliament. (The same Act removed Aboriginal and Torres Strait Islander people's right to vote in federal elections — unless they were already enrolled to vote in state elections.)

Three men who made Federation happen

On the road to Federation, three men were the main movers and shakers: Edmund Barton, Alfred Deakin and George Reid.

Edmund Barton — eat, drink and be merry, for tomorrow we federate

Edmund Barton was the native-born son of a broker, an early graduate of Sydney University, and permanently the clever kid in the class. Barton entered NSW parliament early, becoming the youngest ever Speaker (adjudicator) in the Chamber. Mostly, however, he liked sitting in comfy chairs in exclusive clubs, staying up late drinking and talking and generally having good times. *The Bulletin*'s nickname for him was 'Toby Tosspot'.

Barton seemed set to waste his many undoubted talents — but then Federation came along. This was the one cause he was able to throw himself into completely. He believed in the movement as a thing of destiny — coming up with the slogan 'a nation for a continent and a continent for a nation'. Catchy, no?

A key player in organising the Corowa Conference in 1893, and heavily criticised by Henry Parkes and others in NSW for being *too* democratic, he was the main leader of the federal movement in the crucial conventions in 1897 and 1898, keeping his colleagues up way too late rewriting the proposed Constitution. Campaigning in 1898 and 1899, he crisscrossed the colony, driving through the bush on a buggy, addressing remote audiences and campaigning for the cause. By the time of Federation, he was so broke that a private collection had to be made for his wife and his children's education. Things worked out okay in the end for him, though — Barton got to be Australia's first prime minister.

Alfred Deakin — crushed by the crash, redeemed by Federation

Like Barton, Deakin was a precocious young native-born talent. At 15, he got involved with the spiritualist movement, and while attending seances and running a spiritualist Sunday school, he still managed to pass his final exams for law at 21, going on to the Victorian Bar.

However, Deakin became too busy writing poetry, essays and literary criticism to handle many cases. He began writing pieces for *The Age* newspaper, and became close with the paper's editor (and political king-maker) David Syme. At 22, with Syme's backing, Deakin entered the Victorian parliament.

Deakin went on to attend the first Colonial Conference held in London in 1887, where the young colonial caused mild scandal when he had the temerity to talk back to the British prime minister, Earl Salisbury, over the issue of security in the Pacific region.

Alfred Deakin got burnt by the crash of the early 1890s. Like most, he had speculated heavily in investments during the final boom phase, and managed to lose both his and his father's savings. For the rest of the 1890s, he refused to take any further part in Victorian politics (they kept pestering him to be premier) and worked as a lawyer to pay off his debts (and also as a kind of penance — he hated working as a lawyer). Luckily for him (and for Australia), he discovered the federation campaign as a great crusading cause. He was instrumental in taking the campaign to 'the people', appealing directly to them.

IN THEIR WORDS

According to Deakin, 'Federation is like marriage; it is a lasting union. It is marriage without the possibility of divorce. It therefore is a time in a nation's history when a clear issue should be submitted to a direct vote; it is when she is entering into the bonds of permanent matrimony. It is for the people to say whether the proposal is good or not, and in their hands alone should lie the ultimate power of acceptance or rejection'.

At the first referendum in 1898, it was Deakin's passionate speech at a dinner of the Australian Natives Association in Bendigo that helped reignite enthusiasm for Federation when everyone was finding fault with the proposed Constitution.

George Reid — fat guy makes history!

George Reid was an opponent of the federation movement in the first half of the 1890s. However, as premier of NSW, Reid's opposition to and eventual support of Federation helped make it more democratic when it finally came.

George Reid arrived in Melbourne from Scotland aged seven. In his early teens, he became interested in the radical political debates taking place in Victoria, going along with his dad to see demonstrations for manhood suffrage and political reform. Moving to Sydney, he began working life as a junior clerk in a merchant's counting house, before joining the Colonial Treasury as an assistant accountant aged 19.

IN THEIR WORDS

Good with money, George Reid was even better with eating, and apparently pretty good with women too. Alfred Deakin had this to say about him: '[An] immense unwieldy stomach, his little legs bowed under its weight . . . thick head rising behind his ears . . . [a] many folded chin . . . to a superficial eye his obesity was either repellent or else ludicrous . . . To a more careful inspection he disclosed a splendid dome-like head . . . a gleaming eye which betokened a natural gift of humour; and an alertness which not even his habit of dropping asleep at all times and places, in the most ungraceful attitudes and in the most impolite manner, could defeat'.

Reid's sharp brain had him racing up the ranks in Treasury, and by 29 he was the chief clerk of the correspondence branch. In the 1880s, he shifted into parliament, made enemies with Henry Parkes and became a fierce advocate of free trade.

HISTORICAL ROOTS

Reid was very suspicious when Parkes suddenly became all enthusiastic for Federation. The 1891 Constitution he declared to be nothing more than a political ego trip — the product of 'the great ambitious statesmen of Australia'. It wasn't democratic enough, and it threatened to be a Victorian takeover — Victorian policies on tariffs and finance looked capable of overwhelming Reid's and NSW's commitment to free trade. Luckily for Federation, however, Victoria's economic, demographic and political pre-eminence got broken by the 1890s depression. Reid, by now NSW premier, could be more open to the idea of Federation.

It would still take a while for Reid to be completely convinced. While he liked the more democratic approach of taking a Constitution to referendum, he still didn't like the new Constitution — it was still not democratic enough. His half-hearted support of it in the NSW referendum (he earned the nickname 'Yes–No Reid') helped kill it off. But after further changes were made to the proposed Constitution, and NSW was given the assurance that the future capital would be in their state, Reid joined Barton in campaigning strongly for Federation in the second referendum of 1899. Because he was widely accepted as the best platform orator anywhere in the British Empire — Deakin said he aimed 'always at the level of the man in the street', using slang, crude jokes, screaming rants, and abuse to do it — his support was crucial.

So Federation was made. The decade that followed would show just how serious these nation-builders were about creating an Australian 'social laboratory', where the problems of the old world, which seemed to have caused the great economic crisis of the early 1890s, would be resolved forever.

REMEMBER

The Australian Constitution was by popular acclaim the most radically advanced and democratic document in the world in 1901. It had been written by delegates who had been popularly elected. Then the document itself was sent back to the people for their verdict. Every colony that joined had to vote Yes. Critics of the process said this was ridiculous — ordinary men and women couldn't be expected to evaluate such a complicated document. But then they went and did. On top of that, the Constitution built in a special democratic mechanism for changing the document if circumstances changed in future years. The popular vote 'referendum' was the only way the Constitution could be changed or rewritten. All of which is really great. However . . .

We should also keep in mind that the process was a pretty white middle-class male affair as well. No women took part in any of the Constitutional Conventions — although their influence could be seen in the adoption of female suffrage in the newly created federal parliament. (Refer to the sidebar 'Three really big 1890s moments for women's suffrage', earlier in the chapter.) Indigenous peoples were also excluded from the process of drafting the Constitution, and power over the lives of Indigenous people was left with the states (under their various 'protection' boards).

As with any nation, and any moment in past, present or future, you can never sit back and say, 'Well, that's it then. They (or we) have everything right now. Nothing else has to change, ever'. Life doesn't work like that, and the evolution of humans living together certainly doesn't work like that. But, if nothing else, I think you can give kudos to the all-male, all-white Constitution authors for building us a vehicle which, more than 12 decades later, we're still driving along in, and doing our very level best to drive in the right direction with.

3

The 20th Century: New Nation, New Trajectories

Examine how Australia emerged as a newly federated nation at the start of the 20th century with a serious intent to change the way society worked and deal with the major problems of the day — including intense class conflict, mass unemployment, governments taking the side of big business owners against striking workers and destitution.

Find out more about Australia's involvement in World War I, and the frictions and ruptures it faced on the home front.

Discover how the idea of 'Australia Unlimited' emerged after the war, with a focus on economic growth and increased population.

IN THIS CHAPTER

» Creating a modern society

» Debating the role of a national parliament

» Breaking ground with new laws

» Witnessing the emergence of the first 'natural party' of Australian politics

» Formalising racism through the White Australia Policy

Chapter **12**

Nation Just Born Yesterday

This chapter covers a period of time that people often tend to skip: The bit between Federation in 1901 and World War I, which began in 1914. On the face of it, it's easy to see why. People assume that not much happened during this period — no convicts, no bushrangers, no wars, no gold, no Holdens, no America's Cup, no Sydney Harbour Bridge, no Phar Lap.

But during this period, a lot of important and far-reaching stuff happened. In these years, Australians took up a belief in the value of egalitarianism and made it a core aspect of how the country was run. Many laws made during this time were world firsts. Australian political and social innovations were setting the pace that others would follow. Women were given the right to vote and stand for election to parliament. Economic protection for workers and manufacturers was established, and 'fair umpire' tribunals were set up to settle disputes between bosses and workers. The egalitarian idea of everyone having a basic right to a fair and reasonable wage was made into law. A worker's party (Labor) took complete national power for the first time anywhere in the world. On top of all that, Australia got bold and revolutionary in another way — enacting into law the racism of the White Australia Policy, which would dictate immigration policy until well into the 1960s and 1970s.

In this chapter, I cover the events that occurred between 1901 and 1914. These 14 years, from when a future English king cut some ribbon and declared the whole Australian nation thing a genuine starter, to the outbreak of a war on the other side of the world (which Labor and Liberals said they'd fight in until the 'last man and the last shilling'), proved to be some of the most crucial and pivotal that the nation has seen, before or since.

Advancing Australia: A Social Laboratory

After Federation in 1901, some big questions were asked. Australians said to themselves, 'Okay, we are now a nation. Great. But what kind of nation are we going to be? How are we going to run this place that we've just invented? What sort of rights should citizens be allowed to have? Who gets to be citizens? Who do we let in? Who do we let stay? Are we British, Australian, or both? Can you live here and be one not the other?'

The answers to these questions about what a modern, progressive and fair society should look and act like put Australia at the forefront of the world — it really was a social laboratory. The way these questions were answered showed that

» **Australians wanted a parliament that would be bold and interventionist in solving social and economic problems:** The Constitution, written in 1897 and 1898, had kept most real power with the states. But politicians — and voters — quickly showed their preference for giving the Commonwealth more power (see 'Defining the Commonwealth', later in this chapter).

» **Australians wanted an egalitarian, or classless, society:** Airs and graces seemed to be going more and more out of fashion. Pretty much everyone agreed that rigid social hierarchies and class conflicts like those in Britain and Europe weren't what a decent society should be about, and definitely not what Australia should be about. But then neither should unrestrained modern capitalism be allowed to run riot. America was seen as the pre-eminent example of what to avoid — with its great disparities of wealth and often shocking conditions for workers. New legislation was passed that reflected this egalitarian outlook (see 'Passing Innovative Legislation') and Labor, the workers' party, grabbed government and established dominance (see 'Voting in Labor').

LIFE DOWN UNDER

Curious Italian socialists, American academics and British social reformers kept visiting Australia in the years following Federation to see what the society of the future would look like. Even Lenin got in on the act, puzzling over how in Australia the future had already arrived, in that the workers had seized power, but the result was different from what Karl Marx had predicted — they had seized power without a violent revolution, they hadn't abolished private property, and they hadn't created a communist utopia.

>> **Australians wanted a White Australia:** Ironically, the same people who were so progressive and radical in their beliefs of equality for 'all' were at the cutting edge of modern debate in a less impressive way — racism. Despite some revolutionary laws also being passed (see 'Passing Innovative Legislation', later in this chapter), the first big piece of legislation passed in the new Commonwealth Parliament was the Immigration Restriction Act — otherwise known as the White Australia Policy. Name says it all really. Politicians and people of all shapes and sizes seemed pretty much unanimous that if you wanted a decent, fair and just society it needed to be kept entirely white, and British. This was in spite of the pretty clear evidence of highly successful non-white communities in Australia (see 'That Whole White Australia Thing', later in this chapter).

The period after Federation and before World War I is the pivot on which so much of Australia's subsequent history turned. The ugly stuff and the good stuff. The big arguments that took place during this period, the battles fought and won, created the Australia of the 20th century.

Defining the Commonwealth

The *Commonwealth*, also known as the Commonwealth Parliament, the Parliament of Australia and the Federal Parliament, is the legislative branch of the central government of Australia. Today the Commonwealth Government is the most powerful and important level of government in the country.

Up until Federation, however, the colonies had been self-governing, and the original Constitution's outline of the Commonwealth written in 1897 and 1898 said that it should just keep out of the way of the states and do the bare minimum for the new nation. (Refer to Chapter 11 for more on the colonies pre-Federation and the drafting of the Constitution.)

But after a national parliament was established on 9 May 1901, plenty of new debate and argument started about how powerful and how involved in people's day-to-day lives the Commonwealth should be. The two mutually antagonistic answers to the question of what the Commonwealth should do and be were

>> **Not much:** The Commonwealth should make sure no great problems emerged between the states, should represent the shared collective interests on the world stage maybe, and mediate between the outside world and Australia when it needed to project a singular front, but that's about it. Other than that, it should pretty much stay out of everyone's road, and let the states get on with what they'd been doing pretty easily for the past 50-odd years — self-governing.

>> **A hell of a lot:** If Australia was a kind of radical social experiment building a new kind of society without the ills of the modern world then, quite frankly, there wasn't much time to lose. And if the new Commonwealth apparatus was going to help to implement fair and reasonable wages for all, pass legislation that protected local industries, and keep cheap labour and immigrants out, then all to the good.

In parliament and the newly established High Court, politicians and judges argued about how much they could depart from the original Constitution's vision. The debate was largely won by the radicals and progressives — who made up both the Liberal and the Labor parties. These people argued that the Commonwealth should be able to make big changes in people's day-to-day lives. (The more conservative forces were left to take solace from the fact that while voters wanted radical governments, numerous referendums proved they didn't want the actual wording of the Constitution to be much changed at all.) This shaped the powerful Commonwealth that Australia has today.

What the judges said

The Commonwealth began life taking care not to infringe on state rights and powers. A special High Court was established to decide on questions of the Constitution and state–Commonwealth disputes. The first High Court judges, Samuel Griffith, Edmund Barton and Richard O'Connor, had the job of interpreting the Constitution and matters of state–federal conflict. They tended to follow American federal precedents, which made for strong states' rights. But then a more radical prime minister, Liberal Alfred Deakin, appointed some progressive High Court judges — Henry Bourne Higgins and Isaac Isaacs.

HISTORICAL ROOTS

Higgins and Isaacs had been involved in the debates about writing the Constitution in the 1890s, and had been disappointed that their progressive ideas were defeated when it came to writing the original document. Now they had a second chance. In the High Court deliberations, they gave interpretations of the Constitution that opened up the way for a more powerful and interventionist Commonwealth. In newly established Arbitration Courts and tribunals, they passed judgements that favoured a Commonwealth with expanded powers.

What the politicians did

Radical nationalists and progressives believed the new Commonwealth was a great instrument for actively intervening in the way things were run, and taking steps to reform and change things. From very early on in the life of the Commonwealth Parliament, it was these radicals and progressives — both Liberals and Laborites — who were in the majority against the more conservative elements, who wanted states to retain much of the power.

The upper house of the Federal Parliament was the Senate, and it had been set up to ensure state rights were preserved. As opposed to the 'one man, one vote' principle, which the lower House of Representatives operated on, the voting set-up for the Senate ensured the states with the lowest populations (such as Western Australia or Tasmania) had just as many representatives as the more populous states (such as NSW and Victoria). This was meant to ensure that the Commonwealth wouldn't ride roughshod over the states.

Just as activist judges were unravelling the initially conservative Constitution (refer to the preceding section), politicians were also changing what actually happened in the Federal Parliament. In 1901, most people still assumed that politicians from the same state would stick together to get the best deal for their particular state, but it didn't work out that way in practice. Very quickly it became clear that what mattered most was what type of politics you favoured — conservative, Liberal or Labor — not what state you came from. So the Senate, which had begun life as a house of parliament that would protect the interests of different states, instead became a battleground for national political parties.

In 1910, the Labor Attorney-General, Billy Hughes, led the charge on what the Commonwealth should symbolise: 'When we take away our powers with respect to Customs taxation and defence — we may well ask, "What is left?" . . . A National Parliament ought to deal with national matters. If our ambition aims merely at a glorified shire council uttering and re-uttering pious ejaculations [statements] concerning national sentiments about one flag and one destiny, no doubt the Constitution clothes us with more than ample power. But I take it that our desires lie in quite another direction. We desire to give legislative and administrative effect to the national aspirations of the people of the Commonwealth'.

What everyday people thought

And the people themselves? What sort of federal government did they want? Australians wanted the reform momentum to keep going rapidly forward, but they seemed to have a real aversion to changing the Constitution. Changes were put up at elections in referendums (the only way the Constitution could be changed was through a direct vote) but were frequently knocked back, even when a majority of the people supported the kinds of effects these changes would have. It was as if the people were saying to the politicians, 'You want to make the changes? Go for your life, but you'll have to be clever about it, because we're not going to be increasing your powers to do it'.

Australians liked the idea of radical changes, which is why they kept voting in radical governments, but they didn't like politicians, and they definitely didn't like giving them too much power. People were suspicious of those who tried to place themselves up above everyone else, as politicians aspiring for power inevitably did. Rather than accolades, they preferred to give them road blocks.

Australians were displaying a distinctive trait to thumb their nose at people in authority and high achievers — a trait now known as the *tall poppy syndrome*. This characteristic, inherited from cocky early convicts and native-born Australians (refer to Chapter 4) then consolidated by surly 1850s gold-seekers (refer to Chapter 8) was quite cheerfully showing its face. The intensely high value people in this period placed on equal social status was a continuation of that trait.

Passing Innovative Legislation

The pioneering laws that began to be passed in Australia's new parliament reflected the notions of fairness, equality (for some) and egalitarianism so highly valued by the nation.

The three main innovations that were passed into law during this time were

>> An Act that gave women the vote (see 'Franchising Australian women', later in this chapter)

>> A group of 'New Protection' Acts to support wages in industries that were protected from overseas competition (see 'Establishing bold new protection')

>> An Act that gave protection to workers (see 'Deciding on a fair and reasonable wage')

As well as these big innovations, this period also saw

>> Pensions for widows and the elderly

>> A maternity allowance — baby bonuses paid for each child

>> Compulsory military training for the nation's defence

>> An Australian navy established

>> A Conciliation and Arbitration Act that set up tribunals to act as fair umpires in employer-employee disputes

>> A government bank — the Commonwealth Bank — set up to protect ordinary people's savings

>> A federal land tax, developed to try to get rid of the big wealthy farms and split them up into smaller holdings

Most of the innovations in the preceding list were made by Alfred Deakin's radical Liberal Government (see the sidebar 'Hello Mr Deakin') or under Andrew Fisher's

Labor Government (see the section 'Voting in Labor', later in this chapter). However, the conservative side was also often broadly supportive, mainly because many had had previous experience as colonial premiers and politicians where such initiatives had been seen to work, and to be popular.

IN THEIR WORDS

The leader of the conservatives, George Reid, said he hoped that arbitration tribunals would show how 'even in the field of social economics Australia can win victories and set examples which will teach the rest of the world'. And for this brief period of time, Australia could and did.

Franchising Australian women

Women in the 1880s began to win the right to extended training and university education. Through the boom-time conditions, they also became more vocal and active in the workplace, demanding better pay and conditions, and reaching further into traditionally 'male' domains.

Then in the 1890s, as other big political ideals were emerging (such as the rights of unions and the push for federation), they agitated for and, in many colonies, achieved the right to vote.

Opening up economic possibilities for women

In March 1880, women became eligible to attend lectures at Melbourne University, with the first female graduating in December 1883. In 1885, Dagmar Sterne became the first woman to begin training for a medical degree in Australia, something that had previously been considered too shocking for words — a woman being allowed to medically examine naked people? Impossible! Sterne went on to get a medical degree from Edinburgh University in 1893. In 1890, the first registered female doctor in Australia, Dr Constance Stone, began practice in Australia (having already qualified at Toronto University in Canada).

In December 1882, the first organised women's trade union held a strike — more than half of the 4,000 female tailors working in Melbourne factories refused to work until their pay was raised. After two months the employers bowed to public pressure, and economic realities, and agreed to the union's terms.

LIFE DOWN UNDER

The introduction of a new communications device opened up another area of work for women in the 1880s, and even for those who came from 'respectable' families. This new device was the telephone. Telephones initially operated through all calls being made to a central telephone exchange, where switchboard operators would connect the call to the appropriate line. Women began operating these telephone exchanges — the sorts of women who came from respectable backgrounds and who would previously have few job prospects beyond becoming a governess. The first exchange opened in Melbourne in 1880, and by 1883 all Australian capital cities, with the exception of Perth, had telephone exchanges.

Taking a piece of the political action

Through both the boom-time conditions of the 1880s and the political turmoil of the 1890s, a significant minority of women went political. In 1884 the Victorian Woman's Suffrage Society opened in Melbourne. By the late 1880s, women suffrage groups had been established in Adelaide, Melbourne, Sydney and Brisbane.

But the big engine in the movement for women's voting rights was the Woman's Christian Temperance Union. They wanted to eliminate drinking from society because of all the damage that drunken men did to wives. They were a powerful movement with a lot of support, and they thought that if women had votes they could put greater pressure on politicians to change the laws.

The groundbreaking 1902 Commonwealth Franchise Act defined who could vote in federal elections. Australia became the first country where most women could vote *and* stand for parliament. Although, significantly, the same Act excluded Indigenous Australians and people of Asian, African or Pacific nationality.

MILESTONE MOMENTS: WOMEN WINNING THE RIGHT TO VOTE

When women in Australia achieved the vote and the right to stand for parliament in the 1890s and early 1900s, they finished off a democratic revolution that had begun 40 years earlier with near-universal male suffrage in the 1850s. They also achieved what women in France, the US and Britain would have to wait another 30 to 40 years for.

Beginning with South Australia, women were given the right to vote and stand for parliament in the following order:

- South Australia — 1894

- Western Australia — 1899

- New South Wales (and in federal elections and parliament) — 1902

- Tasmania — 1903

- Queensland — 1905

- Victoria — 1909

Refer to Chapter 11 for more on these state-based achievements.

LIFE DOWN UNDER

In 1903, Vida Goldstein became the first woman anywhere in the British Empire to stand for parliament. Goldstein didn't get elected, but she said she hadn't expected to. Just running for parliament was enough to make people sit up and take notice.

Australia's first female parliamentarian was Edith Cowan. Although she didn't get voted in to parliament until 1921, she had been involved in the suffrage movement since at least 1894.

A decade after Australia's women gained the vote, when Britain was mired in often violent controversy on the question of whether to grant the vote to women, both Houses of the Australian parliament passed motions to tell the British prime minister not to get so upset. Australia had given women the vote, and the social fabric was far from unravelling. In fact, it was actually turning out pretty well.

Establishing bold new protection

Protection had started out in the 19th century as a colonial solution to the problem of how to encourage new industries in a new settlement. Put simply, the protecting was done with a tax, or *tariff*, on imported goods coming from overseas. This made imports more expensive than anything made locally, protecting local manufacturers and local jobs.

The bold new protection that Federation was built on was a compromise between two opposing policies. In the 1800s, Victoria had been an enthusiastic convert to protection, while NSW held out, preferring free trade. At the new federal level of government, the Liberals, who were protectionists and led by Alfred Deakin, had routed the conservative opposition, who were free trade, by 1906 and a compromise was made. Free trade was allowed *between* states, but tariffs would be applied to goods imported from *outside* Australia.

IN THEIR WORDS

In 1906, the then prime minister, Alfred Deakin, received the chairman's report from the Royal Commission into protection, which had been set up by the previous prime minister, George Reid, to help work out a system of 'scientific national protection'. The report said that special protection was needed 'against invasion and unfair attack' by American and Canadian competition, where efficiency had been 'purchased at the terrible sacrifice of the constitutions and lives of men . . . We hope the time will never come when the fierce struggle and competition of modern commercial and industrial war will render it necessary that Australian workmen shall be reduced to such a helpless and hopeless condition'.

Armed with the Royal Commission report, Deakin initiated a far more radical set of new protection laws to go on top of the older ones. He called it . . . (drum roll) *New* Protection. And it was something dramatic and new — a tool of social and economic intervention that gave the government the right to fine businesses that didn't pass on the economic benefits of protection to their employees.

HELLO MR DEAKIN

In the first years after Federation, power and precedence had gone to the radical Protectionists, chief of whom was Alfred 'Affable Alf' Deakin. Deakin was way too dapper, witty and polite to ever be comfortably labelled a 'political colossus', but nonetheless he managed to bestride the national stage for the decade looking very much like one. A native-born Australian radical who entered Victorian parliament at the astoundingly young age of 22 in 1879, he quickly rose to prominence and was soon co-premier himself (1886–90).

Having managed to lose both his and his father's savings in the great 1890s crash, Deakin threw himself into federation with religious zeal, and it paid off. He was trusted deputy and confidant of Prime Minister Edmund Barton, then prime minister three times between 1903 and 1910, and not much of this first crucial decade in the nation's history doesn't bear his imprint. Beginning Australia's navy? Tick. Initiating compulsory military training for national self-defence? Done. Appointing radicals to the High Court to rule on Constitutional matters? New Protection? All Deakin. Setting up Conciliation and Arbitration Courts? This invention of the fair umpire used to settle industrial disputes, easily one of the most important and original Australian ideas about how a decent society should be run, began life under Deakin.

The conservatives hated this idea, and weren't backward in saying so, but Deakin's big coup was to sell the idea to Labor. Labor had always been divided about protection. But now that it was being rejigged to actively interfere on behalf of workers, Labor decided that it was a thing worth pushing. Labor started to take seriously not only New Protection, but the concept of broadened Commonwealth powers as well.

Deciding on a fair and reasonable wage

One of the most extraordinary breakthroughs in this period was the step towards ensuring that all workers (well, all white male ones at least) received a level of pay that wasn't simply the lowest amount the boss could get away with paying, but one that was 'fair and reasonable' for a person living in modern society.

A 'fair and reasonable' wage for all flew in the face of the economic orthodoxy of the modern capitalist world, and it typified the Australian 'social laboratory' approach to a tee. What people got paid was felt to be so important that it couldn't be left to the free market to decide. So Justice Higgins of the Arbitration Court (refer to the section 'What the judges said', earlier in this chapter), and Liberal Prime Minister Deakin and after him Labor Prime Minister Fisher (see the following section), gave judgements and passed laws ensuring that employers who paid less than the officially decided wage level would be fined considerably.

The idea of a decent wage for all was in its quiet way pretty revolutionary. The conflict between labour and capital, workers and bosses, had shown itself to be one of the most intractable and divisive in modern history. Here was the 'Australian Settlement' of the problem: Wages wouldn't be paid at whatever was the lowest the market would allow, but would be set by an independent umpire, neither boss nor worker, who arbitrated between the two, and decided what was fair and reasonable to pay.

In November 1907, Justice Higgins, president of the Commonwealth Court of Conciliation and Arbitration, delivered his 'Harvester' judgement. This related to a case where an employer, H V McKay, who ran Sunshine Harvester Works, was applying for exemption from the New Protection excise taxes. In preparing his judgement, Higgins had inquired into exactly what was required to pay for and support a family in the modern world, interviewing the workers and their wives. He found against McKay, and laid down for the first time the principle of the basic wage: A guarantee that all employers must pay workers enough for them to able to live a full life 'in a civilised community'. This was groundbreaking — it didn't matter whether or not the business could afford to pay the wage levels set by an Arbitration Court or tribunal, they just had to be paid. This soon became the dominant system used across Australia until 1967, with some states continuing to use tribunals until the 1980s. And the concept of a fair wage, protected by government, stuck fast in the Australian psyche.

Voting in Labor

Deakin's Liberals had set the political agenda for most of the first decade after Federation. But then something extraordinary happened. For the first time anywhere in the world, a party for workers' rights, the Australian Labor Party, took control of parliament and government. Even more amazing — they *held* government, quickly becoming the dominant party at federal elections. They held government for four months in 1904, for seven months in 1908–09, then won government for three years at the election in 1910 and then again — with massive majorities in both Houses — in 1914. Meanwhile, the Liberals and conservatives, who had been sworn enemies for most of the last 50 years in colonial and Australian politics, started wondering if they'd ever see government again. Their numbers were whittled down so much that they ended up joining together and becoming one party.

LIFE DOWN
UNDER

The Labor Party were voted in despite a lot of hostility from many newspapers and established conservatives, who did their best to whip up fears of the great threat of the revolutionary 'socialist menace'. The fear campaign didn't gain much traction with the public, however, because so much of the social laboratory that Australia was under Deakin was already fairly anti-capitalist. In government, Labor not only continued Deakin's initiatives such as New Protection and arbitration, but also set up a 'peoples' bank', a national currency, baby bonuses, and got to work on building a new capital city, to be named Canberra.

HISTORICAL
ROOTS

In its early days, Labor had suffered from an image problem. Labor was a political organisation that had begun 20 years earlier, and had grown out of the profound sense of anger and powerlessness felt by workers after broken strikes and union defeats at the hands of governments and employers (refer to Chapter 11). Being the political party for the unions and workers, Labor was open to the charge of being too class-based, interested only in the welfare of the working class rather than for the whole national community.

By developing an ingenious pitch, which was perfectly in tune with the new Australian mood of progress and desire for radical reform and nationhood, Labor seized power in 1904. The pitch went something like this: 'We're not just on about class interests; we not just about working people. No. We're all about Australia. The national community. Our radical reformist agenda makes us the *most* Australian of the political alternatives. If you like the radical social experiment that Australia's been dabbling with, then you'll love us. We've got it in spadefuls'.

Labor's pitch worked. Brilliantly. It worked so brilliantly that by the end of this period, when Australia went to war alongside Britain in 1914 (see Chapter 13), a massive majority of Australian voters decided that in a time of war the best and most natural choice of party to lead the country was the Labor Party, headed by Andrew Fisher. The party that had been born from a belief that the odds of power in modern society were stacked against the underprivileged and the mass of working people was now the overwhelming choice for most Australians in a time of war and crisis. (Labor's success had been so overwhelming that it forced the fusion of all non-Labor Parties into one Liberal Party in 1909. The non-Labor parties then continued to form various parties and coalitions of parties until the formation of the modern Liberal Party in 1944.)

Hats off to Labor.

That Whole White Australia Thing

Every great period seems to need a dark side, and the pre–World War I period in Australia had it in bucketloads. This is because one other answer to the question of what sort of nation Australia wanted to become was irredeemably clear right across the political and social spectrum — Australia wanted to be British, and white. Very British — if the percentage of Australians born of British stock dropped below 98 per cent, people started getting upset — and very, very white.

This was more than a vague wish. It was a passionate ideal that united everyone — politicians, pressmen, housewives, workers, solicitors, tradies, trade unionists, philosophers and academics, you name it. The intense desire to keep non-white people out of Australia was one of the main drivers behind Federation, and the proof is in the legislating: Practically the very first substantial legislation passed in the national parliament was to keep non-whites out of Australia (the Immigration Restriction Act) and to get rid of non-whites already in Australia (the Pacific Islanders Act). These laws would become known as the 'White Australia Policy', and would shape Australia's immigration policies — and Australia's international image — until into the 1970s.

Passing the Immigration Restriction Act

In December 1901 the Immigration Restriction Act became law, allowing the federal government to keep out unwanted arrivals and potential immigrants by applying a dictation test in any European language of the government's choosing. Because the law was made with the intention of keeping out non-whites, it very quickly became known as the White Australia Policy. Reading back over the speeches given and newspaper articles written at the time from the vantage point of the 21st century, these racist notions stick in the gullet.

LIFE DOWN UNDER

In 1908, *The Bulletin* — that radical, republican and cheerfully ratbag Australian journal that began life in the 1880s (refer to Chapter 11) — changed its motto from 'Australia for the Australians' to 'Australia for the White Man', a slogan it kept until 1960.

The obsession with maintaining white purity was emotional rather than rational, even though it had logic of a sort. The argument was that it wasn't a race thing so much as a standard-of-living issue. People from non-white countries were generally paid less money for the work that they did. Let any in, the argument went, and they'll undercut the hard-won high wages of the Australian worker.

But this argument doesn't stand up. Good evidence existed at the time (right before people's eyes, if they'd wanted to look properly) that non-British workers in Australia worked not only well but for decent wages. The Afghan cameleers (refer to Chapter 9) had, like many others, wanted to join their relevant union — the Carriers' Union. They got knocked back. Chinese furniture makers protested that they were just as interested in earning good money as the next worker. No-one believed them. You can't help but get the distinct impression that if the central problem with non-British, non-white people was *really* their undercutting decent wages, then legislators and unions could have tried just a little bit harder to ensure that *all* workers in Australia received fair and reasonable wages, not just whites.

REMEMBER

The White Australia Policy was one of the failures of the Australian social laboratory. The policy had taken some of the boldest ideas of the modern world — liberty, equality, egalitarianism — and restricted them to men and women who were white. This would take decades to undo.

Promising 'protection' — and delivering the absolute opposite . . .

The passing of Aboriginal Protection Acts is a harsh illustration of how the new nation of Australia could take seemingly innocent ambitions (like, say, protecting people they thought were vulnerable) and have the exact opposite effect. The Protection Acts are probably some of the most notorious actions in Australian history.

The Constitution had left the responsibility for Indigenous affairs with the states, so these Acts were passed by state governments. However, they were passed in the atmosphere of the federal White Australia Policy. All systematically stripped Indigenous Australians of practically every single right and freedom that makes life worth living in a democratic nation.

HISTORICAL ROOTS

In colonial times, after the violence of frontier conquest and dispute had passed, Indigenous Australians weren't subject to any special 'control' as such. It was a relatively open society, filled with people going from one place to another, trying one new occupation or job after another, and Aboriginal people found themselves able to take opportunities at the margins of colonial society. Government reserves were being established, and Christian missions, but they weren't compulsory. Aboriginal people could live on them but still largely come and go as they chose. As 'Black pioneers', Aboriginal people had taken up many different occupations (refer to Chapter 6), and this continued. Indigenous shearers, stockmen, cooks and housekeepers, respectably dressed, proud and self-confident, feature in numerous photographs of the mid-colonial period. They were clearly people who were navigating by their own lights, and making the best use of the various personal freedoms that colonial life was known by.

That changed, though.

By the late 19th century, the idea of creating a definitively 'white nation' combined with an increased belief in the necessity of using heavy government intervention to alter society, was bad news for Aboriginal Australians. Colonial governments, and then state governments after Federation, passed legislation establishing Aboriginal Protection Boards. And in this case, 'protection' meant, weirdly, stripping Indigenous people of the basic rights they'd been living with and making full use of.

This included Aboriginal people losing:

>> Freedom of movement

>> The right to own property, even the right to keep their own wages

>> Freedom of association, even the right to marry

Beginning with the Victorian Aborigines Protection Act of 1886 (more notoriously known as the 'Half-Caste Act'), Indigenous Australians began to be separated and removed from the broader community purely on the grounds of race. Aboriginal people of mixed descent — namely, those with white and black parentage — were now expelled from government reserves and from missions. This began the practice that created what became eventually known as the 'Stolen Generations': The breaking up of families, and the removal of generations of children from parents and wider kin groups.

LAYING FOUNDATIONS WITH THE 'FIGHT OF THE CENTURY'

On Boxing Day 1908, a world heavyweight boxing title fight was staged in Sydney. The fight was between Jack Johnson, an African-American boxer from Texas, and white Canadian Tommy Burns. Sydneysiders were thrilled to be hosting a global sporting event. And, in the hyper-race-consciousness era that had given birth to the practically unanimous White Australia Policy, the first multi-racial fight for the heavyweight title certainly captured attention.

But whites weren't the only Australians anticipating the fight with more than keen interest. Indigenous Australians followed the lead-up and outcome too. One in particular was Fred Maynard, at the time a young man in his twenties working on the Sydney docks.

Jack Johnson, articulate and charismatic, catalysed new possibilities of cultural pride and self-assertion for Aboriginal Australians. His triumph against Burns dismayed many whites, but seemed for many Indigenous Australians like the promise of a future triumph of racial equality.

African-American civil rights campaigns and consciousness began to permeate into newly born Indigenous activism at this time as well. In 1924, Maynard, an active wharfies unionist, co-founded the Australian Aboriginal Progressive Association in Sydney. Against the hostility of the NSW Aborigines Protection Board, this association mounted vigorous campaigns for Indigenous citizenship rights. A new direction had been set.

Excluding Chinese Australians

Chinese immigrants had been arriving in the Australian colonies en masse since the first great gold rushes of the 1850s. These Chinese arrivals were both immigrants and long-term *sojourners* — those staying for a period before moving on — and were mostly young men coming from the coastal, Guangzhou or 'Canton', regions of China.

During the 1850s and 1860s, Chinese people encountered hostility on different goldfields — anti-Chinese riots took place at Buckland River Goldfields in 1857, and at Lambing Flat in NSW in 1861. The first discriminatory racial exclusion legislation was also brought in during this period to stop the inflow of Chinese arrivals. However, in the wider community of colonial Australia, established Chinese individuals and groups became valued parts of the economy and well embedded in colonial society. They established communities in large cities and regional centres, and worked as market gardeners and door-to-door traders throughout colonial Australia.

HISTORICAL ROOTS

Whereas British migrants could only afford to return to their distant home countries rarely, the Chinese were much closer to their country of origin. They would periodically go back to their home communities, before coming to Australia again. This movement began to cause increasing alarm in the later decades of the 19th century, as social Darwinism increased racial preoccupations in western societies. The arrival of a large group of Chinese sojourners on a ship called (confusingly) the *Afghan* in 1888 sparked furore. Large protest meetings occurred, and working men's delegates swarmed colonial governments with demands that the Chinese be shut out, chiefly because of the fears that they would become a cheap labour force that would drive down the wages of all workers. (Refer to the section 'Passing the Immigration Restriction Act', earlier in this chapter, for more on these kinds of fears.)

The upshot of this was a conference of colonial premiers and ministers in Sydney, and a mutual agreement to ensure the exclusion of Chinese arrivals, even if the British Government disagreed. (They did disagree, because they had a treaty with the Chinese Government to allow for free exchange of people, money and goods between the two empires.) This agreement proved to be a precursor that was given more nationally dramatic form in the White Australia legislation passed after Federation.

LIFE DOWN UNDER

The Chinese communities continued to survive, however. Chinese communities both locally and in China had taken a strong interest in Federation. This interest centred on how democratic the process of nationhood-making had been, and raised prospects for Chinese democracy activists and would-be reformers in late imperial China. This is a large part of why Chinese-Australian communities played such a prominent role in the processions and civic festivities that greeted

Federation in 1901. They also participated enthusiastically in the procession in Melbourne the day before Federal Parliament officially opened in May 1901, including constructing a Chinese Citizen's Arch on Swanston Street in the city.

One democracy activist who was struck by the possibilities of introducing a modern, civic democracy into China was Liang Qichao. Liang toured Australia at the time of Federation, giving lectures to different Chinese communities and looking to raise funds for the Chinese democratic reform movement. He responded enthusiastically to Australia, seeing it as an example of new democratic possibilities where the people had voted on their own constitution and existence as a nation, a world first.

What did Liang Qichao think of the idea of a White Australia Policy, which dominated the election campaign while he was travelling the newly made country? Not much, as you might imagine. He described it as a throwback to old, traditional, hierarchical ways of thinking. The modern world demanded a reciprocal recognition of people's equality, he thought — equality between people, and peoples, which cut across divisions between rich and poor, between men and women, and between races.

IN THEIR WORDS

'A country is founded on equality, and love [of country] arises from the way people treat each other', Liang Qichao said. Australia's federation project had blazed a great democratic trail. But its White Australia Policy showed that in crucial ways it was failing to live up to its own high standards.

For Tang Caizhi, too, the need for true equality was obvious. Tang Caizhi was appointed as editor for the Sydney newspaper *Tung Wah News* in 1901. He threw himself into the campaign to transform Qing Dynasty China into a modern civic democracy, organised possibly as a federation of large states, similar to Australia. In his eyes, racial equality meant equality between nations, equality of citizens, and equality of social classes and between men and women.

Dealing with the 'piebald north'

The very words 'White Australia Policy' imply that Australia was, post-Federation, wholly white and that the policy was solely focused on protecting that. This was a myth — two Australias were in operation at this time. One was the predominately white British south, where most legislators and most people lived; then there was the tropical north, where the climate, the landscape and the sorts of people living in it were all quite different. Northern Australia was as ethnically diverse as southern Australia was heavily British white.

The tropical north wasn't some multicultural paradise, however; systemic discrimination and exploitation occurred. Many of the Pacific Islanders working in the cane industries in north Queensland had been kidnapped or tricked into leaving their homes — see the following section.

But non-whites were vital to the life of settlements such as Mackay, Cairns, Darwin and Broome, and together people not only survived, but also thrived. Here were settlements that weren't predominantly white, and were utterly dependent on non-white trade, labour, infrastructure and services.

The truth was that northern Australia wouldn't have been established or sustained in any viable or economically productive way without non-white participation — that is, without their labour, their businesses, and their ingenuity, expertise and enterprise. Consider the following:

>> No Japanese? The major industry of north-west Western Australia, pearl shell, collapses.

>> No Pacific Islanders? North Queensland's major industry, cane, wouldn't have got off the ground.

>> No Aboriginal stockmen? The cattle industry in northern Australia would be negligible.

>> No Afghan cameleers working the main haulage routes? No lasting penetration of Australia's intensely arid interior. No overland telegraph, no Canning Stock Route, no rabbit proof fence. No opal mining, no Western Australian gold rush — no Kalgoorlie, no Coolgardie.

>> No Chinese? Simple: Everyone gets scurvy! Most of Australia suddenly loses its capacity to grow and distribute vegetables and fruit.

All these different people made for a northern Australia that was as multiethnic as the south was Anglo-British. The south was becoming more and more aware of this, and didn't like it one bit. This was when some started describing the north as 'piebald' (an animal that displays patches of black and white or other colours) and, therefore, a 'problem' that had to be 'fixed'.

Deporting the 'Kanakas'

The Pacific Island Labourers Act was introduced in 1901 to deport Pacific Islanders ('Kanakas') who had become established in north Queensland in the cane-growing industry. Despite a series of petitions and protests to Prime Minister Deakin and others, by the end of the decade the majority of Islanders had been deported back to their original — or close enough — islands. (Some were returned to islands they didn't originally come from, and struggled to find remaining family.)

Having lived and worked in Australia for many years, many islanders didn't want to leave Australia, but they were deported all the same. Of the 10,000 islanders in Queensland in 1901, more than 8,500 were deported by the end of 1908.

HISTORICAL ROOTS

Sugarcane was the first mass staple crop in north Queensland from the 1860s and 1870s. Pacific Islanders — from the Solomon Islands, Vanuatu, New Caledonia and Papua New Guinea — provided the labour force. Originally, many of them were kidnapped from their home islands or tricked into leaving them, in a practice known as *blackbirding*. Once here, although not technically slaves, many of these workers experienced slave-like conditions, and wages paid were well below what European workers earned. They cleared forests and scrub, built rock walls, and planted, hoed, cut and transported cane for white plantation owners.

Blackbirding sounds pretty abhorrent — and it was. Tricking and then kidnapping people into becoming your labour force isn't much of a way to establish an industry. But from the point of view of the Islanders themselves, for many the wealth, prestige and material benefits — while small by western standards — proved considerable upon returning home to their own societies. Many individuals who had originally been kidnapped began bargaining at the end of their served time, often choosing to return to Australia for new, now free, contracts. But southern, British Australia, and local labour unions, decided they were a problem, and had to go. The Pacific Island Labourers Act saw to the deportation of the majority of Islanders, except those who had been living and working in Australia for 20 years or more.

Pushing 'purity'

Looked at from a 21st-century perspective, the national obsession with making the nation as 'pure' and 'white' as possible can look like a modern-day laundry soap commercial gone horribly wrong. Like some weird purity cult, the preoccupation with purity, with protecting Australia from all foreign and outside influences, bordered on the obsessive. This obsession could be seen in not only the immigration restrictions, high tariffs and deportations, but also a new image of Australia that appeared in political cartoons and advertisements at the time. Australia was depicted as a young girl, innocent, vulnerable, pure, in need of constantly vigilant attention.

She was Australia the pure and ultra-hygienic, unsullied and wholesome, not for dirty foreigners (that is, non-white, non-British) to touch. Radical reforms could fix problems, but only if the social laboratory was kept hygienically pure, unsullied and clean. Threats were seen to come from without — through foreign aggression, cheap labour, and 'filthy' and 'immoral' immigrants such as the Chinese. The need to *protect* was continually emphasised — otherwise, progress, growth and a new society were at risk.

Clearly, at the same time that Australia had been optimistically touting itself as the social laboratory to solve the world's ills, it felt incredibly vulnerable and fragile. The outside was becoming feared as a place that was largely malign, and Australia reacted by putting up walls — tariff walls, immigration walls and psychological walls.

IN THEIR WORDS

Jules Archibald, founder and editor of *The Bulletin* in the 1880s and 1890s (refer to Chapter 11), articulated these preoccupations pretty clearly when he was setting up a new magazine (*Lone Hand*) and when describing what it was going to be about: 'Its politics will be sunshine and good cooking, open air music and red umbrellas . . . an Honest, Clean, White Australia'. Meanwhile, the literary star of the 1890s, the bush poet Henry Lawson, was being heavily criticised by others for not following this new mood, for continuing to produce 'miserable broodings that are far from depicting the cheerful courage of the men and women of the bush'.

Chapter **13**

World War I: International and Local Ruptures

World War I (1914–18) marks Australia's entry into the truly modern era, for better or for worse, as Britain, Russia, France and eventually the US were involved in a war against Germany, Turkey and the Austro-Hungarian Empire.

The 'for better' part is Australia stepping onto the global stage, as a key combatant on the Western Front in 1917 and 1918, and, after the war, as a player around the bargaining table at Versailles, where treaties were negotiated and a League of Nations was formulated. Australia also developed a new brand of hero — the Anzac digger — who first began to emerge during the doomed yet heroic Gallipoli campaign of 1915.

The 'for worse' part is the sheer mass of human loss. A nation of fewer than five million people lost over 60,000 men killed, with some 150,000 wounded. This was no small thing. On top of that were the acute social and religious divisions that opened up in Australia through the course of the war. The attempt to create a new 'social laboratory' in the new nation after Federation (refer to Chapter 12) was derailed as Australia was embroiled in a global fight to the death.

At the beginning of the war, both sides of Australian politics gave enthusiastic endorsement of Britain, while many in the Australian public greeted the war as a chance to go out into the world on a big adventure; all Australian soldiers for this war were volunteers.

In this chapter, I cover the major defeats and victories that comprise Australia's war effort abroad during World War I, and some of its major players. I also cover the issues at home that divided the nation, causing splits in the fabric of political, social and religious life that would take decades to heal properly.

Gearing Up for Global War

Just prior to war being declared, both major parties declared their full allegiance to Britain and the Empire, and spoke grandly about Australia sacrificing everything for the cause. Prime Minister Joseph Cook said, 'All of our resources in Australia are . . . for the preservation and the security of the Empire'. On the same night, Andrew Fisher, the Labor opposition leader, said that 'Australians will stand beside her own to help and defend her to our last man and our last shilling'.

IN THEIR WORDS

This might seem like not much more than typical, over-the-top politician's words. Certainly most of the men volunteering to be soldiers and the women volunteering to be nurses didn't think much about the possibility of 'last man and last shilling' — they were thinking more about the chance to see the world and have some excitement. But, privately, the party leaders had some sense of what everyone was getting themselves into. Cook told his cabinet, 'If Armageddon is to come, you and I shall be in it'.

The outbreak of war, then, was not completely unexpected, and the previous Labor government, after being given the 'heads-up' from Britain, had built on Alfred Deakin's previous efforts to build up Australia's forces. Labor then used this preparation to present itself as the best party to lead the nation during the uncertain war times.

Building up Australian forces

Andrew Fisher, leader of the Labor Opposition at the outbreak of World War I, had been Australia's prime minister from 1910 to 1913 (as well as from 1908 to 1909). Like Cook, Fisher also knew that Australia was getting into something serious.

As prime minister in 1911, Fisher attended an Imperial Conference in London where for the first time ever the British shared with the various dominions — New Zealand, Canada, South Africa, Australia — some of the political secrets about their alliances with and commitments to countries in Europe. The representatives of the dominions were also given some idea of the tensions that threatened to boil over.

In other words, Fisher and the other prime ministers were told something along the lines of, 'Get ready for war. If it comes, it's going to be a big one'. The words obviously sank in, because by 1913 Labor was spending one-third of Australia's revenue on defence preparations, and compulsory military training was in place for Australian youths. In 1911, the Royal Australian Navy was formed.

Choosing the best party to lead the wartime government

The United Kingdom declared war on Germany on 4 August 1914. On 5 September 1914, Australians went to the polls to decide who would lead them in this new climate of war.

HISTORICAL ROOTS

After the war announcement, Fisher's deputy leader, William (Billy) Hughes, spent the weekend completely re-writing Labor's election manifesto. He put together a case for presenting Labor as the best choice for an Australia at war — after all, it was Labor that had laid so much of the groundwork to ensure Australia was on a good war footing, through establishing compulsory military training and throwing its energy into developing an Australian navy. Hughes's manifesto worked. Just over a month later, Labor won a stunning election victory, taking not only 42 of the 75 seats in the House of Representatives but an overwhelming 31 of 36 Senate seats as well.

Labor had established themselves as the 'natural' party of responsible national government — the party people turn to in times of crisis. Labor pitched itself as the best party to go to war with, and won comprehensively. Just three years later, the Labor Party would be split and the 1917 election would give them a defeat even more stunning than their 1914 victory. (See the section 'When Billy goes rogue — aftermath of the Labor split', later in this chapter, for more on this split and its effects.)

Why get involved?

World War I started when war was declared between European powers on the other side of the world. Why did Australia get involved? Reasons include the following:

- » **Realpolitik:** Practically all Australia's trade was with Britain, and Australia's defence and regional security depended entirely on the British, who at the time were the dominant global superpower. If Britain's power and wealth were irretrievably broken after losing this war, then Australia would be a sitting duck. Australia would inevitably come under the economic and, possibly, military domination of Germany, and could lose any real capacity to decide the future of the country.

- » **Australians *felt* British:** For most Australians, Australia and Britain weren't mutually exclusive categories. Instead, they existed as part of a continuum. The vast majority of Australians felt strongly that the Australian character was made up of intrinsically British attributes and ways of life that had been transplanted to a new environment.

- » **Australia wanted to prove themselves to Britain:** Many Australians felt anxiety about their past — the lingering sense that they weren't good enough. Firstly, a nation that begins with convict settlers is going to have to deal with a fair sense of stigma. Secondly, the status of being a colonial outpost for 120 years helped cultivate a sense of being second-best. To be a colonial was to feel, in some inescapable way, second-rate. Going off and fighting well in a big war was a way of proving that things hadn't gone that bad in Britain's colonial outpost.

Australia at War

Australia's involvement in World War I (from August 1914 to November 1918) resulted in 61,720 Australian combatants being killed, and over 150,000 wounded. Proportionate to its population, Australia had one of the highest rates of losses (with deaths equalling 1.2 per cent of the population, a rate second only to that of New Zealand). Overall, 416,809 served in the military with 331,781 serving overseas.

Australians' initial enthusiasm for war as a big adventure disappeared as the number of deaths rose, with the Australian forces suffering huge losses — battling the Turks at Gallipoli in 1915, and getting bogged down in trenches along Europe's Western Front in 1916 and 1917.

However, after repelling a massive German offensive in early 1918, news of some tremendous victories starting coming through from the Western Front, with Australian soldiers, under the leadership of General John Monash, playing a prominent part.

Through it all, Australian fighters were able to build a reputation for themselves as tough, reliable and unyielding, showing themselves to be as good as — if not better than — their British counterparts. (For a detailed coverage of Australia's involvement in World War I, and other conflicts, see *Australia's Military History For Dummies*, Wiley Australia Publishing.)

Proving ourselves to the world, part I: Gallipoli

In April 1915, Australian soldiers landed on the Gallipoli Peninsula in Turkey, as part of a combined force of Australian, New Zealand, British and French soldiers. The plan was to take the peninsula from the Turkish army in an attempt to secure a sea route for the British ally, Russia. The British thought that if they found a good way through to supply the Russians, they could also secure a way to attack Germany from the south-east. Possibly a good idea in theory, it went wrong from the start. The Turkish were better prepared than anyone expected, the wrong beaches and coves were landed on, and the peninsula proved impossible to take.

On landing, the British-allied troops were able to secure a toehold on the peninsula. Despite a number of offensives over the next few months, this toehold was never really expanded.

TECHNICAL STUFF

The Anzac area in Gallipoli was just over 11 kilometres long at its furthest point, and under 2 kilometres wide. The surrounding hills and ridges were occupied by Turks. By November 1915, 41,000 men were crowded into the Anzac area.

Fighting at Gallipoli was unlike subsequent fighting on the Western Front in two ways:

>> Very little heavy artillery was used.

>> None of the British-allied troops could escape from danger. The frontline was the entire area. Officers and administrators who were planning the campaign were also exposed to enemy gunfire.

In December 1915, the campaign was abandoned and the troops evacuated.

HISTORICAL ROOTS

Although the Gallipoli campaign was a disaster, Australia's troops performed admirably. Their conduct during the gruelling campaign became part of what would later be known as the Anzac spirit, as Australian *diggers* (originally just Australian soldiers, but now a term used to cover sailors and airmen as well) were seen to embody attributes such as mateship, courage and endurance. The day of landing — 25 April 1915 — became known as Anzac Day, the annual day of commemoration of Australia's (and New Zealand's) diggers.

AUSTRALIAN IMPERIAL FORCES AND THE ANZAC LEGEND

The Australian Imperial Forces (AIF) were formed in August 1914 at the outbreak of war. When stationed in Egypt before the Gallipoli campaign, three Australian army divisions were combined with one New Zealand division to create the (slightly cumbersome) Australian and New Zealand Army Corps. This didn't exactly roll off the tongue. A signaller needed an acronym for the wordy title, and came up with 'Anzac'. General Birdwood ('Birdie' to his mates), the British officer in command of the Corps, liked the sound of it and made it semi-official. Birdwood then designated the landing spot on the Gallipoli peninsula 'Anzac Cove'. By the end of the Gallipoli campaign, the word Anzac had gone from being an acronym to a nickname of respect, and by the end of the war the Anzac soldier, or digger, who fought as part of the AIF, was an icon.

The frontispiece of *The Anzac Book*, published in 1916, carried a quote from King George V that 'the Australian and New Zealand troops have indeed proved themselves worthy sons of the Empire'. This sense of having been tested and not found wanting pleased everyone.

As well as being renowned for their daring and courage, for their laconic humour and endurance, the Australian diggers also became known for another attribute — their egalitarianism. In the British army, the officers were renowned (at least among Australian soldiers) for arrogance. In the Australian army, even the privates carried themselves with that sort of arrogance. British officers only came from one class — the upper class. In Australian army divisions, promotions to officer class were based on merit.

As General Monash, future commander of the Australian Corps on the Western Front, explained, 'The AIF is a very democratic body, and, so far as it is possible, all Commanders make their selections for advancement of members of their units strictly on their merits and performances — very much depends upon the initiative and address of the men themselves, whether they succeed or not in bringing themselves under the favourable notice of their officers'.

Proving ourselves to the world, part II: The Western Front

After Gallipoli, the majority of Australian soldiers (the AIF) were shifted to the Western Front in France and Belgium to fight against the German army. This was where the real confrontation was — whoever prevailed on the Western Front would win the war.

On reaching the front, Australian forces suffered further losses. Casualties reached a peak in September to November 1917 when, after 15 weeks of fighting in an offensive at the Third Battle of Ypres (Passchendaele), Australian losses totalled 38,000, helping to make 1917 the worst year in Australia's history for wartime losses.

Despite the tremendous sacrifice, however, the actions of Australian forces on the Western Front helped give definitive shape to the newly forming 'Anzac Legend'. While Gallipoli was a site of valiant failure, the Australian Corps (formed from the AIF in 1918) became one of the elite shock troops that were so central to achieving victory in 1918.

For the Australian forces, the following Western Front battles were key:

>> **Fromelles — 19 July 1916:** The 5th Division of the AIF lost 5,533 men in 27 hours of fighting alongside the 61st Division of Britain, trying to hold down German reserves to stop them transferring to the battle then raging on the Somme.

Before the battle started, Australian brigadier General Harold Elliott asked a British Staff Officer how he thought the attack would go. The officer replied, 'If you put it to me like that, Sir, I must answer you in the same way, as man to man. It is going to be a bloody holocaust'. He wasn't far wrong.

>> **Pozières — July, August, September 1916:** In the summer of 1916, 23,000 men spent seven weeks trying to push through the German line on the Somme front. When the battle was over the village, fields, hedges and crops of Pozières were completely destroyed and 13,000 Australian soldiers had died. Anzac and British troops eventually took the village of Pozières, although at great cost. The German line remained unbroken.

>> **Bullecourt — April, May 1917:** Australian forces were used in an attack on a strongly defended part of the German Hindenburg Line (an extensive line of fortifications that Germany had built to protect its troops from counterattack and invasion). A new technological innovation — tanks, or 'land battleships' — was supposed to protect the infantry by moving ahead, crushing the lines of barbed wire and crossing the enemy trench lines. But the newly developed

tank technology faltered, and none of the tanks managed to reach the wire before the troops did. Moreover their steel was too thin to withstand artillery bombs. The Australian 4th Division suffered 2,339 casualties from 3,000 men. In a German counterattack to capture more territory, a force of 4,000 Australians held off 16,000.

According to Charles Bean, Australia's Official Historian during World War I, 'Bullecourt, more than any other battle, shook the confidence of Australian soldiers in the capacity of the British command; the errors, especially on April 10th and 11th, were obvious to almost everyone'.

>> **Messines Ridge — 11 June 1917:** By 1917, British military strategy seemed to become, 'If we can't fight through the German frontline, perhaps we can blow it up'. Beneath the Messines–Wytschaete ridge (which was part of the heavily fortified German line), 19 massive mines were placed after months of tunnelling and preparation. As part of this strategy, one hill (prosaically called 'Hill 60') that lay directly beneath the German fortified line was blown up by the 1st Australian Tunnelling Company. The explosion was so loud it could be heard across the English Channel and in it 10,000 Germans were killed instantly or buried alive. The battle that followed the huge explosion featured John Monash's 3rd Division following the Australian general's highly meticulous plan, and emerging highly successful (see the following section for more on Monash).

>> **Passchendaele — August to October 1917:** During the northern autumn of 1917, Australian forces were used as part of a three-month attempt to bring victory using the British commander's 'one more push' philosophy. By the end of the three futile months, British and colonial dead were between 62,000 and 66,000, with many men having drowned in the mud as the rain turned relentless.

For Australians back home, Passchendaele was the low point of World War I. The great losses on the field of battle meant that a second conscription referendum was called, this one proving to be even more divisive than the last. (See the section 'Conscription controversy', later in this chapter, for more details on the dire home front situation.)

>> **The German March Offensive:** On 21 March 1918, German troops began a large-scale offensive, using 42 new divisions — over half a million men — which they'd transferred from the Eastern Front. (Russia made peace with Germany after their Communist Revolution late in 1917.) After nine days, the Germans had regained all the ground they'd previously lost on the Somme River, and taken 90,000 prisoners. They came within 50 miles of Paris before being halted, with Australian troops being instrumental in halting the advance at the key strategic town of Amiens.

> **»** **Villers-Bretonneux — April 1918:** German troops tried to take Amiens at the start of April, sending in 60,000 men against half the number of Allied defenders. British and Australian troops were called in. At the strategically crucial Villers-Bretonneux, Australian troops got stuck into the Germans with some of the fiercest bayoneting of the war. British tanks drove back the enemy as Australian troops encircled the town in a pincer movement.

General John Monash engineers some victory

The Australian Corps was formed at the beginning of 1918 and placed under General Sir John Monash's command. This meant that for the last year of the war, Australian soldiers fought as an entirely Australian force, just as they were reaching peak performance capacity.

Some famous victories that occurred under Monash's command in 1918 include

- **»** Hamel, 4 July

- **»** Amiens, 8 August

- **»** Mont St Quentin and Péronne, 31 August and 1 September

- **»** Breaking the Hindenburg Line, 15 September

Battling for Hamel

The battle for Hamel was meticulously planned and took 93 minutes, with tanks under the control of infantry commanders, a creeping artillery barrage, air support of both fighters and bombers, and ammunition being air-dropped by parachute to machine-gun battalions for the first time in history.

Although small in scale, the battle was a sophisticated set piece, featuring all the modern forms of warfare that had been developed in the previous four years of fighting. The complete battle plan was afterwards published by the British High Command staff as an example of how to do a battle right.

Fighting for Amiens

The battle for Amiens was part of a large-scale attack across a whole series of points along the front that succeeded in seizing a large chunk of German frontline and swinging the momentum decisively in the Allies' favour. German war commander Ludendorff later called this the 'black day' after which Germany's hopes of winning the war were broken.

The Australian Corps, under Monash's command, were used as one of the spearheads of attack. The style of the battle was new, using

>> Aircraft for reconnaissance and ground attack

>> Artillery in counter-barrage (protecting infantry assaults from enemy gunfire)

>> Tanks to protect infantry and create paths through wire

Changing tactics at Mont St Quentin

After the great Amiens victory, however, new challenges emerged. The nature of the fighting changed again as the previously static trench-line stalemate was broken. General Monash's own personal character (meticulous to the point of obsessive, highly proficient at creatively abstract, organised thought) and the whole of his Western Front experience throughout 1917 had combined to make him one of, if not the, best exponent of the classic 'setpiece battle'. The taking of territory through adhering rigorously to strictly limited objectives, the classic 'bite and hold' of territory, was Monash's forte.

But the setpiece battle wouldn't win the war. As the Allied forces went on the offensive, fighting — and the thinking which shaped it — was going to be far more fluid and open than it had been for the whole Western Front campaign. This was the challenge of the attack on Mont St Quentin on 31 August 1918. Here there wasn't enough time to arrange 'creeping barrages' of precise artillery deployment, and Monash changed tack. Vigorous attacks of infantry were carried out, with Monash deciding 'Casualties no longer matter'. At Péronne, the next day, the Somme line was turned.

Holding it together long enough to make the victory march

By the late summer of 1918, the Australian Corps had been fighting continually for months. Desertion rates were higher than any other corps on the front. Moreover, the strain was beginning to show on Monash himself. His closest assistant — Thomas Blamey — watched as Monash pushed himself and his corps to the edge.

IN THEIR WORDS

Blamey wrote afterwards that Monash, along with his men, 'suffered severely from the strain of these last few months. He became very thin, the skin hung loosely on his face. His characteristic attitude was one of deep thought. With his head carried slightly forward, he would ride in his car for long periods in silence'. Monash was working his troops and himself to the extreme limits of their endurance.

Back in London, Australian Prime Minister Hughes (who had replaced Fisher in 1915), like the rest of the Imperial War Cabinet, was still assuming that the war would extend into 1919, and possibly even 1920. Hughes wanted to conserve the Australians for these imagined final battles. Monash, who like other frontline generals was beginning to sense just how hopeless the Germans' situation was, felt that no matter how exhausted and burnt out they may feel, the Australians 'should be called upon to yield up the last particle of effort of which they were capable'.

The victories keep coming, but fatigue was chronic and the casualty rate was high. The storming of Mont St Quentin and the taking of Péronne, which started on 31 August (refer to preceding section), went for 60-odd hours but Monash kept pushing, by his own admission, quite ruthlessly. Prime Minister Hughes wanted to pull the Australian Corps out, but Monash wanted to keep going — by this stage, he could almost smell victory.

Making it to the final battle: The attack on the Hindenburg Line

In September and October of 1918, the main focus of the British offensive was to break the German Hindenburg Line. To do this, they would use the Fourth Army, of which the Australian Corps would be the vanguard. This constituted Monash's biggest project, and Australia's greatest responsibility, for the whole war.

Last-minute changes to orders due to broader strategic concerns meant that Monash was unable to plan the assault in the usual meticulous, 'control everything, leave nothing to chance' way that he favoured. During the battle, an exhausted Monash refused to believe reports that the plan wasn't working. Eventually victory was won, as Australian forces captured the town of Montbrehain on 5 October, but at cost, and at loss.

In all, from their initial attack on Amiens on 8 August to their final battle of World War I in early October, Australian forces under Monash had taken 60 kilometres of crucial territory. This advance contributed significantly to the Allied victory, as well as cementing the ideal of the Anzac digger and confirming Monash's skill as a commander.

Home Front Hassles

While Australia was struggling and proving itself on the battlefields of Europe, cracks and strains were opening up on the home front. In the course of the war, fractures in Australian society began to show: The general tensions of getting the economy on a war footing, the break-up of the previous multiethnic consensus that had existed between Irish, English and Scottish Australians, the controversies over the government's attempt to introduce conscription, and the eventual Labor Party split.

Getting on the war footing

Over the course of the war, and as the financial cost of the war effort increased, the Australian Government passed a series of new laws and undertook measures that resulted in the government gaining more power and control.

On 13 September 1915, a war income-tax bill, giving the federal government power to levy tax on incomes for the first time, was introduced and tax became payable on annual incomes exceeding £156. In July 1917, the Commonwealth Government introduced a war profits tax, whereby companies' profits were compared to pre-war profits and taxed at a substantially increased rate if profits had increased during the war. This was to ensure the wealthy — and those profiting from the war — made an adequate contribution to the war effort.

But war also made good business — the demand for Australian products such as wool, wheat and other raw commodities escalated significantly. Over April, May and June 1916, the newly formed Australian Wheat Board sold nearly 1 million tonnes of wheat to the British. This guaranteed market and a good price for their wheat was great for farmers.

Frustrated at the lack of shipping autonomy, Hughes purchased on behalf of the Commonwealth 15 steamers at £2 million. These vessels became the Commonwealth Shipping Line.

Irish troubles

For the majority of colonial arrivals, the most strange and confronting thing in Australia wasn't something exotic such as bushfires or Indigenous Australians (the majority of immigrants, living and working in the main colonial cities, didn't see much of either), but the new fact of having an Irish family as neighbours, or an Englishman running your local pub. Groups with centuries of discord, conflict and enmity were confronted with each other in a way that they never had been in the United Kingdom. And, before the outbreak of World War I, they mostly got along fine.

INTRODUCING THE SIX O'CLOCK SWILL

In 1915, pubs and hotels began to be closed from six o'clock in the evening as part of a war austerity measure. The change in law was partly a response to popular feeling that pastimes and amusements (such as sport, cinema, theatre, circuses and music halls) should be curtailed while so many Australians were fighting overseas. It was also partly a response to a long-running temperance movement, which had been campaigning since the mid-19th century for the elimination of alcohol from public life.

The early closing laws and restrictions on buying alcohol from other sources resulted in the very opposite of what temperance campaigners had been hoping to bring about, however. Getting as ferociously drunk as you possibly could within a short period of time soon became embedded in the fabric of Australian culture as the 'six o'clock swill' (see accompanying figure).

Drinkers, knocking off work at 5 pm, rushed to pubs and proceeded to drink as much alcohol as possible in the next 60 minutes. Shortly after 6 pm, drunk as they could get, they wandered off home. This became part of the fabric of Australian life until the 1950s and 1960s, when early closing legislation was finally, thankfully, repealed.

At the beginning of the war, Irish Australians were as enthused as anyone else. But the Easter Uprising in Dublin, Ireland, in April 1916, and the harsh British crackdown that followed, significantly changed that. For Australia the change was far-reaching, as one of the crucial components in maintaining the pre-war national harmony, Irish Catholic Australians, now began to see themselves, and be seen, as in some intrinsic way distinct from and alien to the British Australian majority. Sectarian animosity replaced the mutual tolerance story that had been pre-war British Australia, and the rift would take decades to heal.

19th-century multiculturalism

In the colonies, the term 'British' had always been a work in progress, combining as it did previously hostile elements. Throughout the 19th century, the success of Irish settlers in colonial society became the first great 'multicultural' success story in Australia. In Australia, traditional ethnic and religious enemies — English, Scottish, Irish, Catholic and Protestant — came into contact with each other and had to learn how to cohabit.

LIFE DOWN UNDER

Throughout the 19th century, Australia had featured a significant Irish Catholic minority. Unlike in Britain and the US, Irish Catholics in Australia weren't centred in slums and ghettoes in big cities, nor were they limited to menial low-paid work. While still managing to fill more than their fair quota of those in jail (and those in the police force), the Irish spread throughout colonial society — not just geographically, but occupationally and socially.

While most Irish immigrants arrived in Australia as labourers, unskilled workers or servants, in the colonies they managed to work their way up the socio-economic ladder. From lawyers, journalists, premiers, graziers and pastoralists, to pub owners, merchants, wholesale traders and importers — every occupation had its representatives from Catholic Ireland.

As Irish immigrants were making themselves successful on the other side of the world, rumblings came from people within Australian-based Irish clubs who wanted Ireland to become like the colonies — to be self-governing but within the British Empire — and achieve 'Home Rule'. Despite huffing and puffing between fringe groups and extremist sections on either side of the traditional Irish Catholic/ Anglo Protestant divide, the majority of Irish immigrants and their children in Australia integrated themselves into colonial society with remarkable success.

Old tensions boil over

On 24 April 1916, a rebellion broke out in Dublin against British rule, and declared itself allied with Germany. The rebellion had little public or popular support, was pushed by extremists and was quickly put down. In Australia, the Irish clubs all condemned the uprising as likely to hamper the realisation of 'Home Rule'.

But the British crackdown in Dublin was brutal. The ringleaders were executed without a public trial. Irish opinion was outraged and swung in behind these new 'martyrs' to the Irish cause. For most of the next decade, a civil war was fought in Ireland before it was divided into two self-governing polities: Northern Ireland and Southern Ireland. (Following continued guerrilla conflict and then the Anglo-Irish Treaty, the territory of Southern Ireland left the UK and became a self-governing dominion called the Irish Free State, now the Republic of Ireland.)

In Australia, pledging loyalty to the British Empire as well as loyalty to Ireland became contradictory for Irish-Australian Catholics. During a war being fought in Australia's self-interest, but under the banner of Empire solidarity, this became a big problem.

The previously unified opinion on how to conduct the war split badly. An ethnic and a sectarian divide opened up between elements that had managed to previously remain integrated. After the Labor split of 1916 (see following section), the Labor Party became closely identified with Irish Catholic people, and partly as a consequence of this found itself sidelined from power because many previously loyal voters now viewed it with suspicion.

LIFE DOWN UNDER

After the war this distrust of Labor continued. In November 1919, a rally was held in Melbourne following the Australasian Irish race convention with Labor politician Joseph Ryan in the chair. This convention, and Ryan's participation, was catastrophic for Labor's electoral chances at the federal election held in December. Prime Minister and now ex-Labor man Billy Hughes used it to damage the Labor Party, linking the ALP with the Irish cause, and accusing it of disloyalty to Britain and Empire. In November 1920, Hugh Mahon, a federal MP for Labor, addressed a large Irish demonstration in Melbourne over the banning of Archbishop Mannix from Ireland by the British Government. His description of 'this bloody and accursed Empire' led Hughes to move that Mahon should be expelled from parliament. The motion was carried.

Conscription controversy

At the start of the war Australia was, on the face of it, a country quite likely to bring in *conscription* (compulsory military service). In the years previous, the new Commonwealth Government had introduced compulsory military training for youths and young men. Labor was at the forefront of this training, seeing it as an integral part of the life of the democratic nation. The basic idea was that citizens, who all lived equally in the nation, must all be prepared to fight to defend it. But everyone assumed that the kind of defending the citizen patriots would have to do would be local — it didn't occur to many people that fighting for Australia's future was going to take place in trenches in France.

In the first years of the war, this didn't matter — people from all over Australia rushed to enlist. However, this initial enthusiasm started to disappear as the number of deaths rose, despite numerous recruitment campaigns (see Figure 13-1).

FIGURE 13-1:
A 1915
recruitment
poster.

Australian War Memorial Neg number ARTV05167

Over the course of the war, Australia held two referendums over whether conscription should be introduced. Both were defeated — by the narrowest of margins — but in the process the Labor Party would be shattered.

Asking the nation once . . .

In August 1916, Labor Prime Minister Billy Hughes returned from Britain, convinced that conscription should be introduced to ensure reinforcements for the AIF. He realised that a national referendum would be needed to get around resistance from his own party. After a four-day *caucus* (internal party) debate, Hughes got enough votes to take conscription to a referendum if the required enlistment numbers weren't reached in the next month. Enlistment numbers weren't reached and a referendum was on.

LIFE DOWN UNDER

As the referendum was being proposed, many in the labour movement began to describe the war as a feud between rival capitalist bosses using working-class soldiers as fodder. And Labor unions were already annoyed with Labor politicians for not doing enough to legislate all aspects of the party's program when they got into power. As the returned soldiers leagues publicly declared their approval of conscription, the ALP's deputy leader, Frank Tudor, resigned in protest. In the end, Hughes needed votes from opposition members to get the referendum measure passed in parliament.

On 28 October 1916, a majority of voters decided against conscription, but by the tiniest of majorities — 1,160,033 to 1,087,557. Hughes was still not convinced, however, and a month later, the federal Labor Party split. Hughes led 23 supporters out of a caucus meeting, going on to form his own National Labor Party, which managed to retain office with Liberal support. In the May 1917 election, Hughes' coalition won a landslide victory, taking 53 seats in the House of Representatives compared to Labor's 22.

At the same time as the referendum was being held, further tensions began to emerge, as well as weariness with war and the way it was being allowed to affect life in Australia, and dissatisfaction with Prime Minister Hughes.

In May 1917, the Catholic archbishop of Melbourne died and was replaced by his deputy, Daniel Mannix, who was Irish, outspoken, eloquent and controversial. He voiced sympathy for Ireland's resurgent demands for home rule, and then became one of Hughes's most vocal opponents on conscription.

LIFE DOWN UNDER

Between August and October 1917, one of the most serious and widespread general strikes in Australian history crippled the country. Prices had escalated through the war, exceeding any concurrent wage rises, which made the cost of living a problem for many. This was a big change in a country that just a few years previously had boasted of having the highest standard of living anywhere in the British Empire.

Beginning with railway and tramway employees in NSW, the strike quickly spread to Victoria and became a general strike, as waterside workers, miners and unions in various essential industries joined. The strikes ended up involving 14 per cent of the workforce and 95,000 workers. Strikebreakers were used in the dispute, which served to deepen antagonistic feelings in Australian society.

Asking the nation twice . . .

In September and October of 1917, Australian losses on the Western Front became even more severe, and Hughes called for another referendum on conscription. Incredibly, this campaign was even more divisive than the first one. Returned soldiers violently broke up 'No' meetings, while 'antis' heckled patriotic women's meetings.

Anti-conscription campaigners said that conscription was a plot to flood the country with cheap, coloured labour once all the Australian workers were safely conscripted into the army and sent overseas. Pro-conscription advocates said the burden had to be shared by everyone, and anyone who tried to get out of it was a coward and a traitor.

Mannix became a lightning rod for opponents of the referendum, arguing Australia should be put first and the Empire second. Those against him said there was no difference: Australia's interest and the Empire's interest were the same. If the war was lost and the Empire fell, then Australia would be open to invasion or at the very least political and economic control by a foreign power.

On 23 December 1917, a second conscription referendum was defeated, again by narrow majority. This time the No vote defeated the Yes vote by 149,795 votes — still incredibly close, but double the majority of the first referendum on conscription.

When Billy goes rogue — aftermath of the Labor split

Two weeks after the first conscription referendum (on 28 October 1916 — see preceding section), Billy Hughes led most of the Labor ministers out of the Labor Party (just as the rest were deciding to expel him anyway). Hughes formed a 'National Labor Party' and struck up an alliance with the Liberal opposition. Although not much of a fan of the idea of multi-party 'fusion', Hughes desperately needed a party's organisation and numbers to keep government, and it worked. In the 1917 election, Hughes campaigned on a 'Win the War' platform and an overwhelming majority of voters, many of whom had recently rejected Hughes' conscription campaign at referendum, put Hughes's Nationalist Party into government.

HISTORICAL ROOTS

While Labor rose to prominence and then power by presenting itself as the party that was best-placed to continue the radical social experiment that was Australia (refer to Chapter 12), Labor politicians made themselves electorally successful by arguing their credentials as the party of Australia, not simply the working class. They were so good at this that the non-Labor parties, both the protectionist progressive Liberals led by Alfred Deakin and the free-trade conservatives, were left behind in the national debate, and soon merged into one non-Labor Party (refer to Chapter 12 for more on this).

Labor's great success fractured violently in the course of World War I. The two conscription referendums tore a hole out of Labor. The great irony was that although Labor was successful in campaigning against conscription (and against most of the country's newspapers, moneyed elite, politicians and religious ministers), it cost Labor party unity. It also cast a great doubt in the eyes of most voters as to the party's fitness to govern, and its ability to help 'our boys' who were already overseas fighting.

HISTORICAL ROOTS

Then there was the Irish thing. Part of the pre-split success of the Labor Party grew out of its ability to keep ethnic and religious tensions at a relatively low level, as was the case in Australian society at large. Many Irish and Irish-Australians became active in the emergent Labor Party at the start of the 20th century, but the party was a broad enough church to never let this one component become overwhelmingly dominant. While many workers were Irish Catholic, the Labor movement was also dominated by Scottish and English 1880s migrants. They came from a more industrially developed society than either Australia or Ireland, where the workers versus bosses conflicts of factories dominated the economic landscape. They were more experienced trade unionists and political organisers as a consequence.

The fusion of the Labor Party worked incredibly successfully until the Easter Uprising in Ireland in 1916 (refer to the section 'Irish troubles', earlier in this chapter). Labor in power was pragmatic, striking deals and pursuing policies that would prove popular with a majority of voters and get it re-elected. This approach had worked well in the prewar period but for many 'true believers' in the Labor cause, with backgrounds in the trade union movement, this seemed like betrayal. When conscription became an issue, at last there was a chance to get rid of those politicians who had already been suspected as being too pragmatic for Labor's own good.

When Billy Hughes led fellow Labor parliamentarians out of the Labor government and the Labor Party in 1916, he was in reality leading the non-Irish Catholic component out of the party. What was left was a far more strongly Irish-specific body, at the same time as it was becoming more socialist. And because some of their wilder members subsequently made speeches against the British Empire, and in support of *Sinn Fein* (the Irish political party that provided a focus for Irish nationalism), the party became seen to be even more suspect.

Moving the Pieces around the Global Table: Australia at Versailles

In November 1918, Allied forces signed an armistice with Germany and a ceasefire was declared. In January the following year, global powers gathered in Versailles, just outside of Paris, to determine the terms of the peace. Largely based on the number of war dead he claimed to be representing, Australian Prime Minister Billy Hughes managed to wrangle a seat at the table — the first time Australia had represented itself at an international conference outside of Imperial meetings.

But Hughes didn't stop there — after gaining a spot on the international diplomatic stage, he played hardball. He continued to voice the idea that Australia's proportionately high rate of losses during the war entitled it to have its demands heeded.

IN THEIR WORDS

One of Hughes's demands was that Australia be granted control of German New Guinea (previously a German protectorate, and now known as Papua New Guinea). This was in direct conflict with the view of the US president, Woodrow Wilson, who was against the idea of annexation being part of the peace accord. However, when Wilson asked Hughes whether Australia, as a tiny nation on the other side of the world, intended to place itself in opposition to the wishes of most of the civilised world, Hughes famously replied, 'That's about the size of it, Mr President'.

TECHNICAL STUFF

At the conference, Hughes secured mandate control over German New Guinea and other islands south of the equator. Although he estimated the total cost of the war to Australia to be much more, Hughes was granted £100 million in reparations. By the time payment was ceased in 1932, Australia had received £5.5 million in reparations from Germany.

The League of Nations (the forerunner to the United Nations) was also established at the conference and Australia was a founding member, with this being the first political treaty signed by Australian officials. Continuing to play hardball, Hughes prevented Japan from inserting a racial equality clause in the covenant of the League of Nations, because he feared this would put at risk Australia's White Australia policy.

Hughes returned to a hero's welcome, hailed as the 'little digger' who had stood up to the world powers to get Australia's way.

On 13 December 1919, Hughes and his Nationalist Party returned to power, although they needed the support of 11 members from a new political force: A 'Country' party, representing the interests of rural voters in the Commonwealth.

Chapter **14**

Australia Unlimited

World War I shattered the previous consensus that had prevailed in Australian life. In the 1920s, warring elements that had previously rumbled beneath the surface came much more to the forefront.

On the one hand, Australia came out of the war with a greater sense of national self-confidence and pride than it had ever experienced before. For the first time in its history it had played a significant part in global affairs, both on the battlefield and around the peace table in Versailles (refer to Chapter 13). Huge optimism also sprang from the greater level of material prosperity that the 1920s ushered in, and a period of great economic development began under the new slogan 'Australia Unlimited'.

Many returned soldiers led the spread out to suburban blocks of land, helped by a relatively new invention — the automobile — which was being taken up in large numbers by new suburban dwellers. The 1920s saw the beginnings of radio and cinema, the further spread of telephones and the growth of dance halls throughout Australia. The nation was becoming recognisably modern, prosperous and confident in itself.

However, the prosperity was brittle. High standards of living were dependent on material resources being developed and social progress being maintained — and on continued high prices for Australia's main exports, such as wheat, wool and minerals.

At the same time the nation was afraid, and beset by divisions and animosity that hadn't been seen in the pre-war Federation era. The Australian 'social laboratory' could no longer remain so insulated from troubles in the world, as the continuing civil war in Ireland and the instalment of communism in Russia made for ongoing strife in Australia. Labor turned to the political left and industrial disputes became increasingly acrimonious.

In this chapter, I cover the highs and lows of the 1920s in Australia.

Expanding Australia

In the 1920s, a shift took place in national outlook. Before World War I, the national vision had been the social laboratory — a new country organising and governing itself in order to eliminate the divisions and endemic problems of the rest of the world. After World War I, the emphasis shifted from progressive legislation to material expansion, modern development and resource exploitation. The desire for cutting-edge dynamism was still there, but it had started looking in new directions.

The 'Australia Unlimited' slogan captured the public's imagination, as did Prime Minister Stanley Bruce's 'Men, Money and Markets' campaign. A concerted effort began to build up Australia's manufacturing industries and increase population and wealth through settling Australia's interior with ex-soldiers and British migrants. However, making the interior of Australia arable proved to be a lot harder than just coming up with a catchy slogan.

Postwar Australia — from sour to unlimited

In the years immediately after World War I, Australia experienced a pandemic, an economic slump and then a recession before things started to turn around.

The pandemic was the 'Spanish flu', which actually seems to have begun in the United States in the last year of war, and then headed on troop trips to Europe. From there the virus went global, spreading in a horrific wave across each continent, and proving most devastating in Asia. In the course of the pandemic nearly 30 million people died — ten million more than died in the war itself.

Thanks to distance and comparatively strict quarantine measures, Australia kept free of the pandemic during 1918. However, the nation saw cases arrive at the beginning of 1919 as tens of thousands of returning soldiers and nurses began to return from Europe. In scenes that seem in some ways an eerie precursor to Australia's COVID-19 experience in 2020–2021, each state, each with their own Chief

Health Officer, made their own arrangements about how best to deal with the pandemic. The Commonwealth had little authority as different states shut down their borders, and decided on their own rules for mask-wearing and inoculations. Unlike the more recent COVID experience, however, this influenza strain targeted the young and otherwise healthy, rather than the old or otherwise infirm. Of the approximately 12,000 people who died in Australia, young men and women, children, adolescents and infants made up the majority of these fatalities. Worst affected were remote Indigenous communities.

Throughout the pandemic year of 1919, the economy was struggling to shift its gears back to peacetime. The great demands that war had been placing on production dropped off dramatically, and there was a lag before the more usual peace time realities could take hold (not helped by states closing their borders to each other, obviously). The inflation of the war years continued, with the added problem of wages not having kept pace with high prices, and strikes continued — in 1919 alone, 6.3 million working days were lost to strikes and lockouts.

The recession began to ease in the early 1920s (although strikes continued to be a problem throughout the 1920s), and a new surge of economic growth was coupled with big new dreams about what Australia could and should be turned into.

In the early 1920s, E J Brady, a journalist, publicist and author, created a stir when he published a glossy book called *Australia Unlimited*. In it, Brady argued that a country with an entire continent at its disposal should develop its resources and population at breakneck speed.

**HISTORICAL
ROOTS**

As Australia entered the 20th century, the demographic trend of the 19th century continued, with most Australians living in towns and cities. However, the sheer geographic mass of Australia dwarfed the area of towns, suburbs and cities where most people settled. The 'Australia Unlimited' plan tried to resolve this tension by the following:

>> Filling up the empty spaces with big rural settlement schemes

>> Continuing restrictions on imports to encourage growth in the manufacturing industry and help build up the Australian economy to be the next big America

The 'Australia Unlimited' idea took off, and came to define the ebullient, go-ahead 1920s. Ambitious projects of intensive rural settlement, sustained migration from Britain, increased customs tariffs to encourage local industry, and large development schemes were all implemented under a Liberal Nationalist Government (see following section).

The sky was seen as the limit, and possibilities of expansion and growth were seen everywhere. Many people expected Australia would soon begin to rival the US in size and power. The expectations of what Australia could and should achieve in the years to come were . . . well, unlimited.

IN THEIR WORDS

A report in Western Australia on the possibilities of settling migrants on the land gives a good sense of just how wide the horizons of the future were being seen as in the 1920s: 'It would be difficult to fix a limit to [Australia's] absorptive capacity . . . the prolific lands of Western Australia will in the future . . . richly reward every genuine effort made to win the inexhaustible treasure they hold in store for all who do their simple duty as self-reliant and self-respecting citizens'.

Postwar blues? Take the 'Men, Money and Markets' cure

Building on the enthusiasm created by the 'Australia Unlimited' plan, through the 1920s the Nationalist Government, led from 1923 by Stanley Bruce, won successive election campaigns with the slogan 'Men, Money and Markets'.

The slogan could be broken into its three parts:

>> **Men:** Increased migration inflows to build up the population.

>> **Money:** Big loans from London to fund the various migration and development projects.

>> **Markets:** Increased access to local and overseas (that is, British) markets in which to sell Australian projects.

Bruce's big thing, as a successful businessman, was doing things efficiently, logically and well. He established or developed various boards and councils to back up the initiatives promised in the 'Men, Money and Markets' campaigns:

>> **Tariff Board:** To evaluate the effects of various tariffs in encouraging local industry.

>> **Development and Migration Commission:** To help coordinate the integration of economic development and increased migration.

>> **Council for Scientific and Industrial Research:** To use scientific research for the improvement of Australian industry (which exists still today, as the CSIRO).

BRUCE! OF MELBOURNE

Prime minister from 1923 to 1929, Stanley Melbourne Bruce remains a bit of an enigma. Slightly snooty, he was simultaneously seriously good-looking (newspapers took to referring to his 'matinee idol' looks) and willing to aggressively push Australian interests both with and against Britain. He captained his school at football, cricket and rowing, before going to Cambridge and becoming a champion rower (where they nicknamed him 'Bruggins'). Dividing his time between England and Australia overseeing the family business, Bruce fought in the war as an officer in the British Army, and was wounded and received a medal for brave acts at Gallipoli.

His background was business, and his big push as prime minister in the 1920s was to run Australia along 'sound, business lines'. Many of Bruce's best achievements and worst defeats came from his desire to make Australia work in a systematic fashion. When his own business had experienced difficulties, he got out of trouble by increasing general efficiency and the rate of output; Bruce figured that the same principles could be applied to running the country.

Throughout his government, Bruce badgered both workers and bosses to concentrate more on committing to improve efficiency and output, saying this would lead to better wages and more profitable businesses. But when push came to shove, he showed himself more sympathetic to business owners than to workers, and strikes and occasionally violent clashes were a feature of the 1920s.

Although he spent most of the last 30 years of his life in England, and he was created a viscount in 1947, the title he chose for himself — Bruce of Melbourne — reveals his ultimate sense of loyalty. Significant also is the fact that after death his will dictated his ashes be spread over Canberra, the newly built city that began to be used as the nation's capital in 1927 — during his term as prime minister.

Protecting Australia with more tariffs and a Great White Train

Under the former prime minister, Billy Hughes, an Australian Industries Protection League was formed in 1919. In 1921, a new tariff was introduced, increasing the amount charged on imports brought into the country. As always, the purpose behind these protectionist measures was nation-building. Australia had been thrown back on its own resources in World War I, and many industries and manufactures had expanded to fill the requirements of the local market that Britain hadn't been able to take care of.

IN THEIR
WORDS

Massy Greene, the parliamentarian who brought the new Tariff Act into the House of Representatives in 1921, summed up its intent, saying 'it will protect industries born during the war, will encourage others that are desirable, and will diversify and extend existing industries'.

In the postwar environment of the 1920s, and with Bruce as prime minister, the idea of having a self-sufficient manufacturing industry continued to appeal. If Australia could become more self-reliant, it would also become safer. More than that, however, was the 'Australia Unlimited' ambition (refer to preceding section). If Australia was going to be bigger than Ben Hur, it needed plenty of local industries to develop. Lacking much in the way of population (Australia nudged into five million over the course of the 1920s), the local market was going to have to be 'protected' for local manufacturers.

HISTORICAL
ROOTS

On the back of 'Australia Unlimited' patriotic sentiment, the first ever 'Buy Australian' campaign developed, and in 1924 the Australian Made Preference League was formed. Based on 'sane and practical patriotism', it set out to encourage the consumer to exercise 'a little practical patriotism' in buying Australian-made goods.

LIFE DOWN
UNDER

Most spectacular of all 'Buy Australian' campaign measures in the 1920s was the *Great White Train* (clearly in the service of White Australia) — a travelling exhibition of Australian-made goods, on train wheels. In 1925, it covered over 4,000 miles (or almost 6,500 kilometres) and visited 90 NSW country towns, as an 'Ambassador of Nationhood' that would, the organisers said, 'plant the seed of a national sentiment that will yield its harvest in the progress, prosperity, and security of Australia'. A fair load for one train to pull.

Bruce used the newly established Tariff Board to develop his policy of giving full protection to industries that he thought were well-placed to flourish, while scaling back support for those industries that didn't seem likely to prosper.

At the time, Bruce's measures were met with wide agreement. Protection had been a strong part of colonial life since the 1860s and 1870s (although NSW had held out), and dominant in the Commonwealth since the early 1900s. But reports from the Tariff Board itself soon began to make clear that protection was creating problems. Although many tariffs stayed in place, Bruce's strategy meant that if you had an industry you wanted to prosper, it required government favour. If the government didn't like what you were doing, it was more often sink rather than swim.

Despite Bruce's wish for a more scientific approach to industry, his style of protection created severe imbalances in Australian economic life, the consequences of which were ignored by practically every government after Bruce until those of Hawke, Keating and Howard in the 1980s and 1990s (see Chapters 20 and 21).

Development and migration

In 1919, Prime Minister Billy Hughes, in Britain and France for postwar negotiations, was struck by the need to increase Australia's population. He cabled back to Australia: 'If we are to hold Australia and develop its tremendous resources we must have numerous population'. He thought the British soldiers being demobilised and returning to civilian life in Britain were perfect candidates.

The British liked this idea too — Lloyd George, British prime minister, with 300,000 unemployed war veterans on his hands, thought that shipping them off to Australia was an excellent idea. (Refer to Chapter 3 for more on Australia's white settlement origins and to see how this wasn't the first time Australia was thought of as a good place to ship unemployed men to after a war.) The next prime ministers, Stanley Baldwin of Britain and Stanley Bruce of Australia, agreed and a series of agreements were struck:

>> In 1922, the British Government passed the Empire Settlement Act, with the British Government agreeing to cover half the cost of transporting and settling migrants through grants or loans.

>> In May and June 1923, the Australian state premiers and prime minister agreed to establish a loan council to promote the policies behind the 'men, money and markets' campaigns — namely, to better coordinate the big sums of money that were going to be borrowed from England to underwrite the various development and migration projects that were expected to fast-track Australian growth to 'seriously major nation' status.

>> In April 1925, a loan from Britain to Australia of £34,000,000 was agreed on to fund British migration to Australia, land settlement and infrastructure development.

>> From 1925 onwards, an extra £20,000,000 per year was borrowed to promote and organise migration.

The aim to increase population was effective: Australia's population went from 5,455,136 in 1921 to 6,526,485 in 1931.

IN THEIR WORDS

Prime Minister Bruce was particularly enthusiastic about the idea of increasing Australia's population and opening up its rural land. In 1926, Bruce set up the Development and Migration Commission, saying, 'These two problems are linked together inseparably. We cannot develop unless we have more population, and we cannot absorb more migrants unless we develop'.

The Commission was put in place to advise the Commonwealth on various development and settlement schemes being put to it by enthusiastic state governments to divide up the £34,000,000 British cash cow.

The main focus of the settlement schemes would be to install the new British migrants on uncleared and previously non-productive land in the interior of the country, quickly creating more prosperity and a bigger market for Australian goods (see Figure 14-1).

FIGURE 14-1: Front cover of a handbook of farming advice for new settlers in the 1920s.

Hand in hand with the idea of increasing migration and settlement of uncleared lands (and integral to the 'Australia Unlimited' plan) was the idea of expanding Australia through increased development.

Through the 1920s, huge funds were borrowed by state and federal governments to fund development projects such as the following:

>> Irrigation systems

>> More railways

>> More roads and bridges (Sydney Harbour Bridge being a prominent example)

- >> Public buildings
- >> Sewerage systems
- >> Water supply systems

On top of this, large amounts of borrowed money went to buy land holdings to cut up for small farms. The focus was on putting farmers on the land — even before the infrastructure was in place to support them. Loans were then made to small farmers for houses, fencing and equipment.

NOT IMMEDIATELY HAPPY LITTLE VEGEMITES

Exactly how you get from a yeast extract to a cultural institution so firmly established that some even suggested it would not be out of place on the Australian flag (they were serious, unfortunately) needs some explaining. Vegemite, the truly iconic national spread, was developed largely as a result of the new initiatives of the 1920s that were designed to encourage the development of Australian manufacturing and industry.

Fred Walker was a business owner with a background in chemistry who took advantage of the new science-friendly and local-produce-friendly environment in the 1920s to develop new products for the Australian market. By 1931, he employed more food chemists than any other manufacturer in Australia, and he had university graduates engaged in research work. One of the results was Vegemite, which was produced after 18 months' research and development under the chemistry whiz kid Cyril Callister. Vegemite was to be the new 'vitamin food' that would serve as a replacement for Marmite, the popular vegetable extract from Britain.

But Vegemite bombed. As countless visitors to Australia have since testified, the taste is not instantly appealing, and Australians themselves showed little initial enthusiasm for it. The problem was that while new tariff measures might be introduced, Great White Trains might travel around the countryside showing off Australian-made goods, and Australians might show themselves to be extremely nationalist in most areas of life, their taste buds remained profoundly British patriots! People were used to Marmite. How could they tell their taste buds to shift preferences just because a new spread had been invented that was Australian-made?

Vegemite didn't take off in Walker's lifetime (an obituary in 1935, listing his various achievements, didn't mention it). It received a boost in World War II (1939–45) when it was included in soldiers' rations, but only really took off from 1950, after an advertising campaign that used Walt Disney cartoon characters and the 'Happy Little Vegemites' radio and television campaigns that began in 1954.

Scientific and industrial innovation

Like the Tariff Board, the Council for Scientific and Industrial Research (later to become the CSIRO) was first established — hastily — by Billy Hughes, but it was Bruce who dramatically increased its role and influence in Australian economic life. Bruce's main idea was to improve Australian industries and their productivity with expert advice and scientific expertise. He tracked down the best scientists available in Britain to bolster Australia's ranks, and set them to work to bring some order and intelligence to previously haphazard government attempts to improve industrial performance.

Australia Not-So-Unlimited

A lot of the big dreams and ambitions created by the 'Australia Unlimited' idea and the Bruce Government didn't actually have much detailed substance to back them up. The 1920s was a period of expansion based on borrowed money, government subsidies and empty promises made to new migrants about the possible productivity of the land they would be given — and pretty soon clear signs emerged that it would all go pear-shaped.

Borrowing unlimited for little Australia

Growth and employment in the 1920s were dependent on the government borrowing money to fund urban and rural development projects and prop up manufacture-friendly massive import tariff rates. But the value of key exports stagnated after the first few years of the 1920s, and rural settlement schemes proved on the whole to be a disaster (see following section). Servicing the overseas debt became a bigger and bigger problem — with imports exceeding exports, maintaining Australia's standard of living became dependent on the continued goodwill of overseas lenders, which couldn't last forever.

In 1927, a financial agreement was reached between the federal and state governments. This resulted in the Australian Loan Council becoming a permanent body. Under the new agreement, the Loan Council's approval was required before the states could borrow money. This, it was hoped, would slow down some of the madder development schemes that were being hatched by various state governments.

LIFE DOWN UNDER

But the Commonwealth Government, the coalition between Stanley Bruce's Liberal Nationalists and Earl Page's Country Party, were themselves not the best guardians of fiscal prudence. Imports kept overshadowing exports, as the price of wheat and wool received by Australian producers stagnated after the rapid increases of the war years and early 1920s, and the interest payments required on overseas borrowing kept rising dramatically. By 1927, the Treasurer, Earl Page, who in the early 1920s — along with the rest of the Country Party — had lambasted the policies of deficit and tariff, was now being criticised by even some in his own government for going too far with his borrowing and protection.

In parliament, Henry Gullett from the Nationalist Party declared Page was 'the most tragic Treasurer that Australia has ever known'. Page's policy of 'protection-all-round' and bolstering up weak rural industries with bounty schemes was a house of cards, Gullett said. The approach was all based on the assumption that the main Australian exports — wheat and wool — would continue to go gangbusters on the world market. But, said Gullett, those who remembered the same assumptions being made in the 1880s, and the disaster that followed in the 1890s (refer to Chapter 11), would remember 'when scores of thousands of men, down on the breadline and below it, were out of work. Knowing the seasonal uncertainties, and the variations in prices that have occurred in my lifetime, and will, no doubt, be experienced again, in the wool and wheat industries, those two supports cannot be regarded as immovable. They may fail us at any time. If they do, we shall assuredly see an era of human suffering that we have never known before . . . we cannot bury our heads in the sand'.

On this last point, Gullett turned out to be quite wrong. Australians proved more than capable of burying their heads in the sand, for another two years at least. On his other points, of course, he was quite correct. All the causes of the big crunch to come — insanely high debt level, falling export prices, unproductive rural settlement schemes, ridiculously high tariffs driving up the cost of living — were in place. But instead of being dealt with, to they were ignored wherever possible. What the 1920s sowed in wild expectations, the 1930s would reap in hard consequences (see Chapter 15).

The problem of 'Australia Unlimited' (which the 1930s Depression would soon make abundantly clear) was it was actually quite a Little Australia, dependent on capital and imports from the outside world to develop and maintain its high standard of living. This was fine only for as long as the price of exports held.

Land disasters

The land settlement scheme aimed at thousands of British migrants proved to be an almighty disaster. Beyond the grand visionary scheming, the planning on the micro-level was bad and the immigrants themselves had no knowledge of settling rural areas.

Offered little or no support, thousands of newly arrived British migrants were sent out, along with returned soldiers, to try to carve out wheat and dairy farms in virgin bush land or in mallee scrub that needed clearing. The scheme was an utter failure, resulting in bankruptcies, destitution, suicides and near-starvation. Costs skyrocketed, with little actually being achieved.

In NSW and Victoria, plans to settle 8,000 British families resulted in no more than 730 families settled on the land. The planned cost per farm was £636, but the actual cost per farm was a staggering £31,380 — which, unless you're getting gold-plated wheat bushels, isn't good value.

The assisted migration scheme was abandoned in 1929.

The scheme also managed to be a comprehensive public relations disaster. By 1928, word had started to filter back to Britain about the truth behind the promotions of sunny fields and perfect pioneering life for British men and women. Tabloids ran stories about the tragedies of suicide and financial failure, and the British parliament established an inquiry into the nature and causes of the disaster in Australia.

British newspapers reported 20,000 migrants had been left stranded after the project was packed in. A petition of 50,000 seriously angry migrants was presented to the House of Commons. The promotional propaganda had conned them, they said, and the migration agreements had been dishonoured by the Australian Government.

One migrant expressed the disappointment of many when he said, 'Englishmen who have been cramped for room and opportunities at home are encouraged to think that there is room and hope for them in Australia; they have been told that they will be assisted to travel thither, not out of charity, but because they are needed; and when at last they apply for this assistance they are only too likely to find that they are not wanted'.

Schizoid Nation

If you were looking to get a grip on the national headspace in the 1920s, it wouldn't be too much to say that Australia was showing definitely schizoid, or split personality, tendencies.

In the seeming prosperity of the 1920s, with more time and money on people's hands, sport again captured the national attention, as did new pursuits such as the beach and picture shows. New imports such as cars and radios were within reach of many people, and a new lifestyle developed around the large suburban block.

However, tensions were also evident. Returning soldiers, who had done so much to establish the ideal of the Anzac hero and help Australia position itself as an international hero, felt themselves to be removed from the rest of society, and became frustrated with empty promises of homes and jobs. The race bogey also continued to show its ugly face, this time focusing on new Italian migrants.

Sport, the beach and picture shows

As life returned to normal after the tragedy and austerity of the war, Australians wanted to enjoy themselves again.

Cricket renewed its role of expressing great national self-regard and esteem under the captaincy of 'Big Ship' Warwick Armstrong. Australia established an immense postwar superiority led by a fast-bowling duo, Jack Gregory and Ted McDonald, who were the forerunners of latter-day fast-bowling heroes Ray Lindwall and Keith Miller in the 1940s and 1950s, and Dennis Lillee and Jeff Thomson in the 1970s. The English were comprehensively beaten at their own game 5–0 in 1920–21 in Australia, then 3–0 in England. Don Bradman, a young man destined to become the statistically greatest batsman to ever play the game, made his test debut in 1928.

LIFE DOWN UNDER

Australians also began flocking to the beach in record numbers. Swimming, surfing and surf-lifesaving became popular pursuits in postwar Australia, as society began to shed some of its previous inhibitions about happily soaking up the sun and swimming in bathing suits increasingly designed to show off rather than cover up their bodies.

When they wanted to get out of the sun, Australians flocked to a new 20th-century entertainment: Cinema. By 1927, 1,250 'picture palaces' were operating throughout Australia showing silent films of British, Australian and American production. In 1928, the first 'talkies' began, and by 1936, some 3.5 million people were going to the cinema each week.

Cars, radios and Californian bungalows

In the 1920s, the average weekly wage in Australia was a third better than in Britain — 94 shillings in Australia to 60 shillings in Britain. Although the price for goods bought in Australia was often higher than in Britain due to the high tariff wall Australia had established against imports, Australians still enjoyed a higher standard of living, and had more discretionary income at their disposal to spend on some of the new developments in travel, lifestyle and communications: Cars, the suburban block of land and radio.

TECHNICAL STUFF

By 1928, over 500,000 motor vehicles were registered in Australia. Given that the population was around six million, and given that most vehicles were registered to families of an average number of four, this means that some two million Australians, or around a third, had a car in their daily lives.

When it came to lifestyle changes, the explosion of car ownership, and road construction, meant that in the 1920s large suburbs began to fan out from the hubs of

19th-century cities. Thousands of returned soldiers got married and took advantage of special purpose low-interest, low-cost bank loans to build new houses on quarter-acre blocks. This gave the construction industry a huge boost, with on average 20,000 new homes being built around Sydney and Melbourne each year of the 1920s.

LIFE DOWN UNDER

In the years following World War I, a new architectural style — the Californian bungalow — became popular. Unlike many houses built previously, Californian bungalows had no servants' quarters — servants having gone out of fashion since the turn of the century. The antecedent of the Hills Hoist — 'Toyne's Rotary Hoist' — was patented in Adelaide in 1926 to provide a new way of drying clothes above all the suburban lawns that were spreading out across the country.

In January 1924, the first radio station (2FC) began broadcasting news, music and race results from a studio on the roof of a department store in Sydney. By 1929, over 300,000 radio listeners across Australia had licences, and countless others used unlicensed 'crystal set' devices to listen in as well. (Until the early 1970s, people had to purchase a licence if they wanted to listen to the radio.) In 1932, the Australian Broadcasting Commission (ABC) was established by the Common-wealth. With 12 stations around Australia, by the end of 1936 the ABC had estab-lished permanent symphony orchestras in all six state capitals.

Returned soldiers — elite, but angry

Soldiers coming back to Australia exemplified the great extremes of the postwar Australian mentality. On the one hand, they were full of pride for what they had proved about Australian qualities while fighting in the war. On the other hand, they were in many cases scarred and traumatised by the experience, and soon made angry by the fact that the boundless promises made about what they would return to (jobs and 'homes fit for heroes!') weren't forthcoming or, as in the case of the soldier settlement schemes, were disastrous failures.

LIFE DOWN UNDER

The returned soldiers felt proud of what they'd achieved — and rightly so. Their actions had established a new reputation for Australia in the world. Although they returned to Australian society after the war, they had a strong sense of themselves as a distinct group within it. They were distinguished often by a sort of warriors' solidarity, and felt themselves superior to those who hadn't fought. For the next 20 years, not having volunteered could be thrown into a person's face as a kind of slur — Australia's future prime minister, Robert Menzies, would be denounced in parliament in 1939 by his coalition partner Earl Page for having lacked the courage to enlist and fight.

Soldiers had gone to the war being promised that jobs available would be for them on their return. When they came back, they found that many of the jobs had been taken by people who hadn't gone to war. In their opinion, government wasn't keeping its promise (see Figure 14-2).

THE RETURNED AND SERVICES LEAGUE — LARRIKINS AND HEROES

By the 1920s, the Anzac digger soldier was a national icon, and the characteristics of the previously dubious semi-criminal larrikin and of the bush worker now became the accepted characteristics of the Australian soldier — a soldier who was, it was now unanimously agreed, the finest fighting man anywhere in the world and not to be taken lightly. The characteristics that the digger inherited from the previously disreputable larrikin and rural worker were:

- Enthusiastic about grog, swearing and gambling
- Self-confident to the point of arrogance
- Not much impressed with the claims of authority and order

And the digger's great success meant that these previously more dubious characters of Australian cultural and social life acquired more respect in the eyes of the wider Australian public. It was hard to frown at the excesses of the larrikin when he and his mates had marched off to fight in war for the country.

On their return to life in Australia, and seen by all in a new light, returning soldiers worked hard to marry the exclusivity of their group with a spirit of egalitarianism.

Returned soldiers wouldn't let people who hadn't served overseas have any say in how their league (the Returned and Services League) was going to be run. And, true to the egalitarian reputation that the AIF had built up over four years of war, and unlike in the US and Britain, ranks were no longer used by returned soldiers — men went from being Major, Lieutenant or Captain back to being plain old Mr. On the memorials that began to be built to honour those who had served and those who had died, no ranks were used to order the names — the order was simply alphabetical.

In January 1919, about 200 returned soldiers forced their way into government offices in Melbourne and demanded the jobs of those 'eligibles' (that is, people who, due to their age, sex and lack of any disqualifying disability, could have signed up) who hadn't enlisted. In July, riots ended the peace celebrations in Melbourne that marked the signing of the Versailles peace treaty, and ex-soldiers were arrested. A mob stormed the state offices demanding that the arrested men be released, and the Victorian premier was assaulted. Afterwards, shaken but unstirred, the premier released a statement declaring the government would resist all returned soldier intimidation.

THAT PROMISE

'Melbourne women have been invited to enter the hitherto exclusive Chamber of Finance as bank clerks.' — News item

'Many returned soldiers complain that the promise of employers to keep their jobs open has been broken.' — News item

BANKER (to returned soldier): 'Yes, yes; possibly I DID say something about keeping your position vacant, but it has lately been capably filled by a charming young woman (to whom wages are no object); and I feel sure that you, as a soldier, will not be so unchivalrous as to ask me to discharge her to reinstate YOU!'

FIGURE 14-2:
Cartoon from 1916, highlighting what many returned soldiers felt was a broken promise.

In March 1919, returned soldiers in Brisbane attacked a meeting of trade unionists who were flying the red flag (of the communist, or 'Bolshevik', revolution). In March 1920, 500 jobless returned soldiers surrounded the doors of the Commonwealth offices in Melbourne and demanded to speak to Billy Hughes. Doubtless the 'little digger' was going to be questioned closely about the gap between promises and reality for returned soldiers. Mr Hughes, unfortunately, was 'not available'.

A new and unexpected phenomenon was taking place. Thousands of highly trained soldiers were being released back into the general community, and governments feared that they may easily become a source of civil disorder.

To try to ease the frustration felt by returned soldiers, the government introduced 'soldier settlement schemes', in which men were given blocks of land to clear and farm. This 'solution' just made things worse, for the following reasons:

>> Many of the returned soldiers didn't have farming experience

>> The land itself wasn't particularly suitable (try farming tough mallee scrub for a few weeks and see how your mood is)

>> Many returned soldiers were still harbouring various deep traumas from the war years

LIFE DOWN UNDER

HOW TO MARK THE ANZAC ANNIVERSARY — PRAYING OR GAMBLING?

In 1921, an Act of parliament was passed protecting the term 'Anzac' against commercial uses. By 1927, Anzac Day was declared a statutory holiday in all states. Exactly how it should best be spent, however, was another question entirely.

The Returned and Services League pushed for returned soldiers to have control of how to spend and celebrate Anzac Day. For them it was 'the Diggers' day' pure and simple, and if most of it was to be spent getting drunk and betting on horses and two-up with your old soldier mates, then so be it. Church leaders and women's temperance organisations weren't so convinced, and pushed to have horse racing and gambling banned and pubs closed. In the end a compromise was reached — services and marches would be held in the morning, with the afternoon free to be used for the more typical digger activities of drinking, chin-wagging and betting. The day became both mourning (for the loss of so many lives) and celebration (of typical Australian activities that the soldiers had gone off to fight for). And this compromise continues today.

The race bogey

Another thing that flourished in the schizoid national mentality of the 1920s was the race bogey. Australia was widely agreed to be necessarily a fortress in order to protect its unique social experiment in equality and progress and good wages. Heavy protective tariffs to keep out imports were meant to protect good wages for workers. The still-formidable British navy was expected to protect Australia from outside invasion. And the White Australia Policy was meant to complete the fortress, as an exclusionary immigration policy aimed at keeping out non-white and non-British potential migrants.

In the 1920s, a concerted project was developed to encourage migration to Australia for the first time in the Federation's history (refer to the 'Expanding Australia' section, earlier in this chapter). This migration scheme was specifically focused on Britain, aimed at strengthening the British–Australian link. Australians were proud to boast that they were 'more British than the British' — 98 per cent of Australians were of British ancestry or origin. And any signs that the level of Britishness in Australian might drop below 98 per cent were met with a fair degree of national paranoia.

In 1925 a new Immigration Act was passed, giving the Commonwealth new powers to prohibit from entry 'any specific nationality, race, class, or occupation' if economic, racial or cultural conditions saw an individual classified as 'unsuitable'. One source of racial fear were Italians. Whereas most other non-British arrivals were barred, a special treaty allowed Italian migrants into the country because they were allies in World War I. Out of the overall number of annual migrant arrivals, the proportion of Italian arrivals was small — in 1927 only 7,784 Italians arrived compared to 93,352 Brits — but this was enough to trigger racist outbursts.

IN THEIR WORDS

Campaigning in the 1928 election, Ben Chifley, future Labor prime minister, criticised Prime Minister Bruce for providing homes 'for dagoes not [returned soldier] heroes'. Trade unions, Billy Hughes and newspapers frequently described Italians and southern Europeans as 'the scum of Europe . . . cheap, ignorant and low grade . . . miserable semi-slaves . . . simian . . . degraded'. Not one of Australia's finer moments.

The Workers of Australia . . .

Through the 1920s, the workers of Australia watched as their political party — the Labor Party — progressively marginalised itself from any prospect of gaining power. Labor adopted socialism as a central plank of its political policy platform, which ultimately made it seem a dangerous option.

Meanwhile, unions became more militant, adopting strike measures more frequently than arbitration. Prime Minister Bruce then sharpened the conflict by pushing to remove workers' rights that had been won before and since Federation. This included trying to remove the Commonwealth Government from the arbitration process — handing it all back to the states.

Labor turns hard left

Labor split in 1916 over the issue of conscription, lost most of its parliamentary leaders, and was comprehensively trounced at the 1917 election — the first time in Australian history that this happened (refer to Chapter 13). The party shifted further left after 1917 and throughout the 1920s, until being briefly brought back to power in 1929 by moderate James Scullin.

HISTORICAL ROOTS

During Labor's long era of political dominance and power (from the early 1900s to 1916), a tension had existed in Labor between the pragmatic politicians such as Watson, Hughes and Fisher (all of whom became prime ministers) and George Pearce (defence minister for most of the period from 1908 to 1921) and the more actively socialist idealists in the trade union movement. After the split, that tension was largely gone, as the moderates and political pragmatists were diminished in number, and union officials began to rise to positions of political authority and leadership.

In 1921, the party officially adopted socialism as part of its central policy platform, which meant it pledged to put under government ownership banks, factories, major industries, large shops and businesses. The moderates, while unable to stop this going through, were able to tack on an amendment reaffirming support for private ownership. However, in a climate of fears of 'Bolshevism' and the 'world revolution' of communism, the damage was already done, playing right into the hands of critics and enemies such as Hughes who had no difficulty in stigmatising Labor as a party of extremists at loggerheads with the aims and values of the majority of Australians.

The Labor Party, however, continued its hard swing to the left, with Labor parliamentarians announcing plans for a Supreme Economic Council, which would effectively have more power than either the prime minister or parliament. Workers would be put in control of industries. Through these plans, Labor lost all chance of an allegiance with the Country Party (which had originally been open to the idea), and any hope of a vote from many of the middling classes of Australia's voters who made up the national majority.

In 1923, Jock Garden, head of the Australian Communist Party (which was officially established and linked with Moscow in 1920) and head of the Sydney Labor Council, moved a motion at the NSW Labor Party Conference to grant affiliation to the Communist Party. At the same time, communists began gradually taking many key positions in the Labor Party.

The Miners Federation Union was communist-controlled by 1934, as were various and vital waterside and transport unions. By the end of World War II (1939–45), the Communist Party dominated the leadership of 25 per cent of unions. Of the major unions, only the moderate Australian Workers Union (AWU) stayed free of communist influence.

Labor in state governments

After World War I, people kept voting in the ALP to run the state governments even if federally the party was consigned to the political wilderness. People still wanted progressive, forward-moving policy at a state level. Labor's brand of socially progressive legislation was elected to take over many of the states:

>> Joseph Lyons in Tasmania

>> Ned Hogan in Victoria

>> Thomas Ryan, Edward Theodore and William McCormack in Queensland

>> Jack Lang in NSW

>> Philip Collier in Western Australia

>> John Gunn and Lionel Hill in South Australia

By March 1928, the Labor Party held power in all states except South Australia (which had just lost its Labor government 11 months previously).

An attack of the Wobblies

At the same time as the Labor Party moved closer to a far-left ideology, the trade union movement was becoming more of a fan of confrontational strike action rather than the arbitration system.

In 1905, the Industrial Workers of the World (the IWW, or the 'Wobblies', as they were affectionately, fearfully or derisively called) had been founded in Chicago. In the pre–World War I years, they established active wings in Australia. International working-class movements influenced by the Communist Party, such as the Pan-Pacific Trade Union Secretariat, also established links with Australian trade unions. The IWW and the Australian Communist Party pushed hard for direct strikes rather than the negotiated agreements and compromises that were the hallmark of Australia's arbitration system. The IWW wanted to overthrow the government with a massive general strike, where everyone just stopped working and brought society to a standstill. The Communist Party thought revolution would be brought about by a more strategic seizure of power, led by a vanguard of Party members (more on them in the next chapter).

Prime Minister Billy Hughes blamed the Irish (Sinn Fein especially) and militant revolutionaries (such as the 'Wobblies') for much of the industrial conflict of the late 1910s and early 1920s. In December 1916, 10 IWW members were jailed for periods of 5 to 15 years for arson and sedition. Two other members of the IWW were hanged for the murder of a policeman. In 1917, the IWW movement was declared illegal. The actual Australian membership of the IWW was always quite low, but their fierce enthusiasm for massive general strikes and rulership of the world under 'One Big Union', coming at the same time as the Communist Revolution in Russia, influenced opinion in favour of 'direct action' and strike action among unions and workers through the 1920s.

Bruce arbitrates his own destruction

In the first decade of the 20th century, the Commonwealth Parliament established a Court of Arbitration and Conciliation to resolve industrial disputes between bosses and workers in the workplace. The aim was to resolve problems before push came to shove and people went out on strike. The court did something special — officially recognising the existence and legitimacy of trade unions as the organisations that represented their workers' rights. While unions were still struggling against hostile legislation and government suspicion in other countries, the Arbitration Court made for a proliferation of unions. (Refer to Chapter 12 for more on the creation of the Arbitration Court.) But things turned sour in the 1920s.

Around the beginning of the 1920s, two contradictory things happened:

>> **The field of Commonwealth arbitration opened wider:** In the High Court, Judge Isaac Isaacs gave a judgment that opened up the Commonwealth Court of Conciliation and Arbitration to workers in state-run enterprises that had previously been confined to state tribunals. In a decision in the Engineers Case that would make 1920 'a year of revolution' according to Sir Robert Garran, Isaacs produced a new doctrine when he returned to the Constitution's original wording — 'when a law of a State is inconsistent with a law of the Commonwealth the latter shall prevail' — after this, the previous doctrine of 'implied prohibitions' and 'mutual non-interference' between states and Commonwealth was effectively dead.

>> **Some militant unions, increasingly dissatisfied with what arbitration might deliver, began striking rather than conciliating:** Increased union strike activity had won some spectacular gains (for example, the coal miners in 1916 where, after a prolonged strike, miners' demands were met) and some crushing losses (for example, the general strike in 1917, where strikebreakers were used by the Hughes Government). At the same time, more revolutionary ideas were filtering through from the Industrial Workers of the World and the Communist Party, radicalising unions, and making them more confrontational than they'd been previously. Gains were made by strikes in the early 1920s, increasing the incentive.

WHAT IF YOU HELD AN ELECTION AND NOBODY CAME?

In 1922, less than 60 per cent of registered voters voted at the federal election (in WA and Tasmania, the turnout was less than 50 per cent). Previously, the normal turnout had been a healthy 70 per cent, but the political mood after the war had turned sour. The great optimistic vision of what Australia could be — the social laboratory of the world — that had dominated politics previous to 1914 had been tarnished. Australian society was more divided and unhappy with itself. Political debate became more acrimonious and bitter. Voters responded by staying away.

The politicians had a solution for this problem — make voting compulsory. Compulsory voting was instituted from 1924 and, not surprisingly, voting numbers improved. Given that compulsory military service had been rejected not once but twice during a global war less than ten years previously, politicians declaring voting compulsory, and everyone going along with it without much more than loud mutterings, sits oddly with our general idea of the typical Australian. But then the rejection of conscription in Australia was in many ways an oddity. Ever since colonial government in the 19th century (whether provided by governors or elected representatives), Australians had become used to thinking of government as a big utility that provided services and intervened decisively in ordering, regulating and legislating people's lives. The image of Australians as the great rebels against authority, ruggedly independent and impossible to order about, is misplaced. No-one queues quite as well as a bunch of Australians!

The effect of compulsory voting was mixed. Because those who tended not to vote were more often than not people with less money and education, compulsory voting made sure that everyone in society had a say in the government that would be governing them. Governments that were actively popular benefitted from having people who liked them being made to come out and vote, but governments that were stagnant and unpopular suffered from the same phenomenon. People who otherwise wouldn't have bothered to come out and vote were made to — and punished unpopular governments accordingly.

Compulsory voting does remain an oddity, though. If life in a democracy means people can freely decide who shall govern them, compelling them to decide freely seems a contradiction. And that seems to be the opinion of most people around the world — almost no other parliamentary democracy in the world actually *compels* citizens, by law, to come out on election day and vote. In Australia, though, it remains a popular rule. (Although, interestingly, it's losing popular among young people.)

So, even as federal arbitration became more accessible to more unions, many unions were losing interest. Employers started forming more close-knit organisations to counter the threat of the unions. For their part, the federal government under Prime Minister Bruce spoke about banging the heads of bosses and workers together, but spent more time kicking the workers' rather than bosses' heads, with a string of harsh laws.

In 1925, the Bruce Government called an election, and ran on law and order issues, such as security on the waterfront, and dealing with militant and aggressive unions. The campaign worked — the Nationalist coalition increased its majority from 17 to 29 seats. The Bruce Government then started passing harsher legislation:

>> In 1926, the Bruce Government brought in a new Crimes Act, which gave wider powers to crack down on militant extremists in the workplace.

>> In 1927–28, a new Conciliation and Arbitration Act was brought in. Under the new Act wages were reduced, and a 48-hour working week brought back.

The harsher legislation had an almost immediate effect in terms of retaliatory actions:

>> In 1928, strikes took place on the waterfront. Guns were used, a man was shot, and volunteer 'scab' labourers were bashed.

>> In early 1929, a strike among timber workers started in protest against the new award system. Violent confrontations took place as sawmills were set on fire.

>> In March 1929, 12,000 coal miners in the northern NSW coalfields went on strike after they refused a one shilling per tonne reduction in the award rate.

The tensions culminated in the most unexpected of ways: Bruce, having tried and failed in a 1926 referendum to have industrial powers moved entirely into the federal sphere, now got fed up. On the morning of a Premiers' Conference in May 1929, he did the completely unexpected — he sent a telegram to all the premiers saying if the states didn't get out of industrial issues, then the federal government would.

Bruce told the states, 'States or Commonwealth may be able to deal with the problem but it is impossible for both to do so at the same time. Accordingly the government is proposing to states that either they immediately give full powers to Commonwealth or that Commonwealth repeals its industrial legislation'.

The states, unsurprisingly, said they didn't much like the idea of giving up their powers on this one. Bruce, expecting this, said fine — time to abolish the Arbitration Court, keep shipping and waterside industries under the Commonwealth, but leave everything else. This meant that 149 trade unions and some 700,000 workers would lose their Commonwealth awards, and federal unions would have to deal with up to six different state tribunals.

After Bruce lost the support of some of his own side in parliament (including ex-Labor prime minister Billy Hughes), Bruce called an election on it, asking voters to decide if his solution was the best tactic. At the subsequent 1929 election, he got his own head kicked — not only did his government get swept out of office, but he also lost his own seat to a firebrand union organiser.

The election held on 12 October 1929 was the biggest landslide since the Nationalist victory in 1917, and a heavy defeat for Bruce's Government. The Labor Party, led by the moderate James Scullin (who had once said that he was committed to socialism, but was happy to wait 1,000 years before it happened), won an immense 46 seats — next best were the Liberal Nationalists with a miserable 14 seats, followed by the Country Party with 10 seats.

The downside for Labor was that the election was only for the lower house of parliament not the upper house, because the previous government was only seven months old and senators had fixed terms. So, despite having overwhelming support in the House of Representatives, the Senate would require finessing. (The other, pretty huge, downside came around two weeks after the election — and Chapter 15 shows how the 1930s Depression wasn't really the best time for finessing.)

LIFE DOWN UNDER

For Bruce, the final humiliation was losing his own seat of Flinders. From a majority of 12,000 votes, he lost by 305 votes, and the president and general secretary of Melbourne Trades Hall Council, E J Holloway, replaced him. Bruce was the only prime minister to lose his seat at an election until John Howard managed to repeat the same feat at the 2007 election. The added irony was that both elections — 1929 and 2007 — were dominated by the issue of workers' rights.

4

1930 to 1949: Going So Wrong, So Soon?

Find out more about Australia's struggles through the Great Depression, as easy dreams of rapid expansion and unlimited prosperity nosedived big-time, and politicians, bankers and bureaucrats argued about how to fix the debt problem — and what to do with the many thousands of unemployed.

Examine Australia's involvement in World War II, as it found itself directly under threat for the first time in its history and looked to powerful allies.

Find out more about the war's aftermath and the Labor Government's determined efforts to reconstruct society, and make sure nothing like the Great Depression ever happened again.

IN THIS CHAPTER

» **Crashing and burning in the worst economic depression of the century**

» **Splitting the Labor Party (again)**

» **Seeing the appeal of communism and vigilantism**

» **Emerging from the trauma: Politicians versus ordinary people**

» **Witnessing celebration and mourning 150 years after first European settlement**

Chapter **15**

A Not So Great Depression

The 1930s were a period where just about everything that could go wrong did go wrong. The collapse of international commodity prices, especially wheat and wool, meant that the huge amounts of debt run up by state and federal governments in the 1920s for all their development projects (refer to Chapter 14) were almost impossible to pay off. Experts from the Bank of England arrived with stern looks on their faces and the economy nose-dived. The result was massive job losses in many industries and a cutback in people's consumption. Suffering and deprivation, while generally localised to 'factory belts' in inner cities or particular industries (such as construction), was intense. With the main breadwinner unemployed and very little being offered in the way of government assistance, many families could no longer pay their rent and were evicted and forced to live in unemployment camps.

Governments fell. Politicians shouted. Men began drilling in secret armies in order to step in if civil unrest turned to anarchy and violence.

And yet, strangely, ordinary Australians showed themselves to be less over-whelmed than their politicians. While the politicians, the bankers and angry organisers were proving ill-equipped to agree to a solution, Australians became extraordinarily good at devising their own solutions to the problems of economic crisis and mass unemployment.

In this chapter, I cover the mismanagement and splits of political life through the 1930s, as well as the resilience of the Australian people.

Crash and Depression

The 1920s were heady days indeed, with the idea of Australia having the potential to be the next US taking hold across the nation. Massive borrowing funded ambitious development and settlement schemes. However, the dream fractured with the market crash of 1929, and Australia woke up to a huge debt and creditors knocking.

Borrowing like there's no tomorrow

Australia borrowed more than just about any other nation in the world during the 1920s, depending on high prices for their main exports — wool and wheat — to keep the money flowing in for their ambitious development projects. By the late 1920s, Australia's interest payments had increased sevenfold since Federation, and were absorbing nearly two-thirds of the government's taxation revenue.

IN THEIR WORDS

Some brokers in London reported to concerned bankers in the late 1920s that 'in the whole of the British Empire there is no more voracious borrower than the Australian Commonwealth'.

Unfortunately for Australia, the world economy was about to experience the biggest shakedown of the 20th century, in the form of the 1929 Wall Street crash and the subsequent Great Depression. Australia couldn't dodge this bullet, and the country copped it right between the eyes.

REMEMBER

At the time of the crash in 1929, protectionist taxes on imports resulted in 10 per cent inflation of all prices. Heavy tariffs made for a very rigid economic structure, meaning that costs couldn't go down in Australia as world prices for Australian exports went down.

Here comes tomorrow

In 1929, the price of wool dropped 30 per cent, and the price of wheat fell 10 per cent. By the time Scullin's Labor Party took government in October 1929, overseas debt had reached £53,000,000. Then the New York Stock Exchange collapsed, sparking global panic. How good is that for timing?

After the crash, international commodity prices collapsed, triggering a further fall in export earnings, and the overseas debt became impossible to service. Public expenditure was cut dramatically as the economy went into freefall and infrastructure projects were shelved.

TECHNICAL STUFF

In early 1930, bankruptcies rose 50 per cent on their 1920s average. After the 1920s expansion of suburbia (refer to Chapter 14), the construction industry collapsed. In Sydney and Melbourne the number of new houses being built collapsed tenfold, from the 20,000 annual average in the 1920s to a mere 2,000 — which spelt bad news for builders, carpenters, painters, plumbers and the like.

James Scullin, the Labor prime minister, raised tariffs to try to protect local industry, but it had no noticeable effect. In the factory belts of inner cities in Sydney (Redfern, Paddington and Newtown), Melbourne (Brunswick, Collingwood and Fitzroy) and Adelaide (Port Adelaide and Hindmarsh) manufacturers drastically cut back production or closed up completely. In these areas, unemployment levels reached more than 40 per cent.

LIFE DOWN UNDER

With no money coming in after mass layoffs, many people were unable to pay their rent, and the subsequent evictions led at times to violent confrontations. In June 1931, pitched battles in Newton and Bankstown were waged between police and an angry crowd as unemployed families were evicted. Evictions led to overcrowding in the inner-city *doss houses* (cheap basic lodgings). Men and families began sleeping in parks, under railway bridges and in shanty unemployment camps. In the areas of concentrated deprivation, many lived as best they could — on the support of private and religious charities, on subsidised bread and soup from soup kitchens, and the ration slips they received from '*susso*' (sustenance schemes set up to feed and pay the unemployed).

The man from the Bank (of England)

With a collapsing economy, Australia's overseas debt, most of which was owed to the London money market, was becoming impossible to service. The federal government, faced with no money in the coffers, asked for some relaxation of the loan repayments due in 1930. The Bank of England sent out its troubleshooter, Sir Otto Niemeyer, to inquire into the Australian mess and see what measures would have to be implemented.

Niemeyer arrived in July 1930, and after a month's inquiry gave his diagnosis: Australia was living beyond its means. The problem had been caused by long-term high rates of protection and heavy borrowing, which had artificially — and unsustainably — inflated Australian standards of living. And 'only Australia could save herself. It was [Australia's] business to do this and no-one else's'.

Having been clear in his diagnosis, Niemeyer was rigorous in advising the cure. Two main things would have to happen:

>> **Cutbacks:** Prohibiting and restricting imports wouldn't save the economy and nor would altering the exchange rate. Balancing the budget was the key — costs would have to be reduced and standards of living would have to go down. This would result in the retrenchment of workers but a general deflation of prices and costs would follow, and Australia would be economically viable again.

>> **Abandonment of the fantasy of Australia's unlimited potential:** This abandonment involved getting rid of what Niemeyer called 'the exploded doctrine of the enormous potentialities of Australia' also known as the 'Australia Unlimited' theory (refer to Chapter 14). The sun, it turned out, didn't shine out of the back of Australia. Time to strip away the fanciful dreams and illusions, and bring the standard of living back to parity with Australia's real trading capacity.

Part of abandoning the Australia Unlimited development ambition involved scaling back a lot of the big development schemes that had been underway throughout the 1920s. 'A country could be over-provided with public utilities' was how Niemeyer delicately put it. Australia was that country. The provision of infrastructure and services had outstripped the needs of trade and industry. 'A halt in utility work [is] necessary until the volume of trade caught up and required the services provided'.

The Melbourne Agreement

Niemeyer delivered his message of austerity to various assembled state premiers and Prime Minister Scullin in August 1930. Borrow and bust had got Australian leaders, and Australians, into this problem; now hard years were the only things that were going to get them out. As well as putting a halt on borrowing and scaling back public development projects, Niemeyer also advised cutting pensions and reducing wages. The various leaders agreed to Niemeyer's plan, but very reluctantly.

Scullin and many of the premiers were Labor, whose preoccupation was protecting and improving the rights and conditions of working people. And here they were forced into a corner, agreeing to cut pensions, wages and public works programs!

They weren't happy, but didn't see any way out of it. They signed what became known as the 'Melbourne Agreement', and had to put up with the approval of bankers, economists and newspaper editors, and the condemnation of many strong Labor supporters, trade unionist organisers and unemployed factory workers.

After signing the agreement, Scullin left the country — he had to get on a boat to go to England, to calm the bank bosses about worries over Australia's credit-worthiness, to pressure the King into letting an Australian be appointed governor-general, and to attend an Imperial Conference. He left behind his treasurer, Joe Lyons, to try to keep a lid on things. Within a few months, however, the lid was well and truly off.

A(nother) Labor Split

The challenges of meeting and solving the problems of the Great Depression proved too much for the Labor Party. Neither those who wanted more radical actions nor those in favour of more moderate approaches were at all happy with Labor's actual approach. The party ended up splitting twice within 12 months, losing much of its left and right wings in the process.

The leader of the split on the conservative side of the Labor Party was Joe Lyons, an ex-Tasmanian premier, serving as treasurer and stand-in prime minister while Scullin was in England in 1930. The leader of the split on the radical side was Jack Lang, NSW premier, and many of the NSW-based MPs in federal parliament sided with him.

REMEMBER

Even though Lang was, at the time, in politics at state level and Lyons was at federal level, the men represent the two political and philosophical ends of the spectrum of Labor's response to the Great Depression. The main body of federal Labor dithered between the two approaches, and when each man left the party, taking his supporters with him, federal Labor was left decimated.

Two different solutions for the Great Depression problems

In the early 1930s, two very different views on how best to deal with the economic crisis contended for supremacy. The widely divergent actions of Joe Lyons and Jack Lang give some insight into these opposing views.

The moderate view — triumph of the ordinary Joe

Early in the economic crisis, Prime Minister Scullin declared that he regarded the national debt in the same way he would a personal debt — it had to be paid back. When in London in 1930, he told a journalist that rather than fail to pay what was owing 'he would tax Australians to the last penny'. In a similar vein, if a little more graphic, future Liberal prime minister Robert Menzies said that rather than repudiate debt to bondholders, 'it would be far better for Australia that every citizen within her boundaries should die of starvation during the next six months'.

LIFE DOWN UNDER

The heavy words from Scullin and Menzies were partly bluster. Australia needed credit, and had to convince the world that it was still credit-worthy. However, the notion of 'saving' at this time had a great deal of meaning for people beyond the simply financial. In 1930s Australia, saving, self-sacrifice and thrift were now part of a way of seeing the world, and paying your way, balancing your books and living within your means became real indicators of character. This ethic was what it meant to be respectable. And as with individuals and households, so with nations. The notion of Australia not being able to pay what it owed struck at the heart of what people thought Australia should be.

Treasurer Joe Lyons seemed to exemplify these 1930s values perfectly. For starters, he put these principles above his political allegiance, refusing to go along with the rest of the Labor Party when they wanted to defer debt repayment, saying 'I am out for Australia and the interests of its people'. In the middle of the Depression, when people were deeply disillusioned with all parties and politicians, this struck a chord. He was a negotiator and a compromiser, not a big capitalist, nor a radical or class war agitator.

But on top of this were Lyons's other perceived values. 'Honest Joe' was lauded for being ordinary, practical, hard-working, honest, principled and incorruptible. He dealt with national problems in the way those caught up in the Depression would like to deal with their own. A newspaper approvingly described him as 'a solid, clear minded man of the people whose simple conception of right and wrong had been bred in the normal atmosphere of family life'. Lyons was seen as the man with a small amount of savings and a home of his own — the quarter-acre-block man with his family. Men just like Lyons, and their families, were Lyons's key supporters, and he spoke directly to them in countless whistle-stop tours, radio addresses and town hall meetings throughout the country.

IN THEIR WORDS

Lyons was always very clear on the best way to fix the economy, saying 'We have to go back to honest, straightforward methods . . . We must do what the ordinary citizen would do in similar circumstances'.

The radical view, as Jack saw it

On the radical side of the Labor Party was Jack Lang, and his view was that the Depression was the deliberate creation of employers and governments. In order to deal with the 'deliberately engineered' Depression, Lang said he'd borrow more money to wipe out any deficit, and fund a program of restored wages and big public works programs. Of Otto Niemeyer, the troubleshooter from England (refer to the section 'The man from the Bank (of England)', earlier in this chapter), Lang said he was no more than 'a member of the Bank of England, to which we do not owe so much as a bent sixpence'.

IN THEIR WORDS

Lang said, and plenty were found who agreed, that Australia only had financial problems because of war debts incurred while saving Britain in World War I, and the interest now being charged on these debts. Lang claimed, 'The same people who conscripted our sons and laid them in Flanders fields . . . now demand more blood, the interest on your lives'. According to Lang, Australians were being unfairly burdened with loan repayment requirements.

Lang's claim about the source of the debt, as it turns out, was rubbish. Australia's spectacular borrowing excesses of the 1920s were the dominant cause of Australia's debt problem — of the vast amount Australia owed, only 16 per cent was related to the war. But it was *highly appealing* rubbish.

HISTORICAL ROOTS

Lang was doing what the Labor Party had always said it was about doing — sticking up for the battler, the worker, the men and women losing jobs and getting evicted. Lang saw the Depression as a vast conspiracy of the terrible capitalist machine. Lang, his supporters said, was even 'greater than Lenin', the communist revolutionary who had seized power and become dictator in Soviet Russia. Furthermore, said his supporters, Lang wasn't the problem — the problem was the Labor turncoats and weak-willed politicians in Canberra who worried too much about pleasing bankers and Britain.

IN THEIR WORDS

Lang's view on unemployment was also a traditional Labor one. In 1910, Billy Hughes had written 'the unemployed man is a deliberate creation of the capitalist . . . Every industry trains many more men than it normally requires . . . In order that for one year, month or week out of every two or three, employers may have an abundant supply of labour, millions of hapless men are daily sacrificed'.

A party shoots itself in both feet

In October 1930, Jack Lang won the NSW state election by a large majority, on a platform of promising to reverse the stringent cost-cutting imposed on the government by the Melbourne Agreement (discussed earlier in this chapter in the section 'The Melbourne Agreement'). As premier, Lang immediately restored all wage cuts, established better handouts for the poor and unemployed with a new 'unemployment tax', and introduced a moratorium to delay evictions. On the downside, he pretty quickly started running out of money. He then declared that he'd reduce interest payments to English bondholders and would use the NSW Savings Bank to finance housing loans and to assist primary producers. With people fearing their deposits were at risk, a run on the NSW Savings Bank ensued, which eventually caused the bank to close its doors seven months later.

Federally, some Labor parliamentarians took note of Lang's reforms and started to think these radical policies might be a good idea. Many in the caucus began to support ideas of stimulating the economy by expanding credit and coercing the Commonwealth Bank to provide more funds. A vote was held on the issue and the majority supported this new policy direction. Acting Prime Minister Lyons was furious, saying, 'I will not do it! You have done this thing but I will not be a party to it'.

Labor's new direction didn't go down well with Australia's creditors in London. When Lyons telegrammed Prime Minister Scullin in London to tell him the news, Scullin cabled back that the Labor Party's resolution 'has demoralised Australia's stocks here, and unless rescinded will render renewal of bills here, as well as conversions in Australia, impossible'.

In a countermove to his own caucus, Lyons launched a public appeal for a 'conversion loan' to raise the £28,000,000 needed to meet Australia's debt repayment deadline. While Treasury bureaucrats said it couldn't be done — it was way too much money to raise over too short a time — Lyons organised public rallies, promotions, advertising campaigns on radio, in papers and cinema, and an 'All for Australia Day', urging everyday Australians to loan money at low interest to the government. Incredibly, it all worked. In the end, the loan was oversubscribed by £2,000,000, with much of the funds coming from small contributions of £100 or less.

While Lyons's loan-raising scheme had been very successful with the public, it was not so with Labor caucus. When Scullin returned from London in January 1931, he removed Lyons from the role of treasurer, replacing him with the previous treasurer, Edward Theodore. This didn't go down too well with Lyons, and he quit cabinet.

Theodore had become critical of the Melbourne Agreement, and suggested instead the expansion of credit to restore economic life. The governor of the Commonwealth Bank was called in to cabinet and asked by Scullin if he could give the government an extension of credit to cover the deficit and loans that were due to be repaid. The bank's governor replied, 'Mr Prime Minister and members of the cabinet, I bloody well won't'.

Back in NSW, Jack Lang topped Theodore with his own plan, one where no more interest would be paid to British bondholders and a new currency would be introduced, one based no longer on gold but on a 'goods standard' based on 'the wealth of Australia'. While Theodore's plan would be considered fairly mild by today's standards, it was hotly criticised at the time — while Lang's solution was seen as either a funny money scheme, or the greatest masterstroke since the French Revolution (depending on whom you asked).

Although federal Labor did seek more credit, they still believed the original debts should be paid back. Lang continued to ignite tensions when, in March 1931, he refused to pay bondholders any interest, saying it was more important to pay the dole in full. This was in direct conflict with federal Labor policy, under Prime Minister Scullin, and for Scullin, this was the last straw. As Lang's supporters were NSW-based, Scullin still had enough support within the Labor Party at a federal level to act decisively. Lang's supporters in federal parliament were formally expelled from the Labor Party.

In the same month, Lyons, completely disenchanted with the approach Labor was taking, resigned from the Labor Party, and took a lot of the popular goodwill that he'd built up in December 1930 along with him. Soon he formed a new party, with support coming from large citizens' organisations (the 'All for Australia' leagues) and the old opposition party (the Nationalists, begun by the last Labor renegade — Billy Hughes — during World War I).

Even though Lyons and Lang offered very different solutions, they (and their supporters) both opposed the solution proposed by the Scullin Government. For Lyons (and other moderates and also the Liberals), the solution was too extreme. For Lang and his supporters, the solution wasn't nearly extreme enough. In November 1931, Lyons and the 'Langites' combined their votes in federal parliament to force an election, and in December, Lyons's new political organisation, the United Australia Party, won, taking over the federal government.

Lang sacked and Labor in tatters

After coming to government in 1931, Lyons took action to pay the unpaid interest owed by Lang to bondholders, and Lang reacted with further extreme measures.

Lyons billed Lang for the unpaid interest, and Lang refused to pay up. In order to stop the Commonwealth confiscating state funds, Lang ordered all the state revenue being collected to be shifted into the State Treasury rather than going to the banks (where the Commonwealth could have confiscated it). Lang barricaded the Treasury and surrounded it with a security force of unemployed members of the Timber Workers Union. At the same time, Lang issued a notice to the public service seeking volunteers to enlist in a state citizens' army. This step went too far; the NSW governor decided that this activity was getting just a little too illegal — trying to start an army, for example, wasn't what premiers were meant to do. On 13 May 1932, Lang was dismissed from office, and in the subsequent election was demolished.

THE ENID AND JOE LYONS SHOW

Joe and Enid Lyons were a married couple from Tasmania. They'd both left school early, never had much money, had 12 children together and, oh, formed the most powerful political pairing of the 1930s. They didn't have to fake their ordinary, homespun style of life or approach. The great connection they had with the Australian public, communicated at town hall meetings, in newspaper columns and on radio broadcasts, was the real deal.

Joe left school when he was eight years old, thanks to his dad having had a dream about which horse would win the Melbourne Cup and betting the family savings on it. The dream prediction must have got lost in translation somewhere along the line, and young Joe found himself having to fill in the huge yawning void that had suddenly opened up in the family's finances. He worked first as an errand boy running messages around town, and then a bit later as a scrub-cutter in the bush. He managed to finish off his education in his teens and became a student teacher, and by his mid-20s had joined the Duck River branch of the Tasmanian ALP. He rode his bike all over the electorate when running as candidate in the 1909 election, and established a political style that would hold him in good stead for the rest of his life: A great face-to-face talker and listener, he was up for conversation not confrontation. This suited the style of Tasmanian politics just fine, where collaboration and 'working across the aisle' in parliament between the two main sides was the go. In his time as premier, Joe Lyons refined this collaborative approach into a fine, well-nuanced art.

A decade previous to this, he'd fallen in love with a young student teacher. Although some 20-odd years his junior, she proved to be his absolute equal in essentially all things. Enid Burnell met Joe when she went with her mother to the Tasmanian parliament, and happened to meet the Minister for Education, who happened to be Joe. She was the daughter of a timber worker, and had grown up walking 2 miles (3.2 kilometres) a day to the local school with her sister.

After marrying Joe, Enid soon found out she had a great gift for public campaigning and political life, joining in with him at public and parliamentary meetings and conversations with enthusiasm. Not even giving birth to a new child almost every year seemed to slow her down, as she herself ran as a political candidate in 1920s Tasmanian elections.

Joe moving to Canberra and federal politics in 1929, and then steering the Labor Government's response to the Great Depression financial crisis in Prime Minister Scullin's absence, took the couple onto the big public stage of national life. They soon became as familiar to ordinary Australians as Don Bradman and Phar Lap. Enid was Joe's closest confidante — essentially his unofficial chief political adviser — as he agonised over whether to split from the ALP and establish a new political party in 1931. Enid's advice in this area was emphatic — go for it. Pregnant (again), she threw herself into the United Australia Movement along with Joe, and they set out on a quasi-national tour, making the case against what they saw as the ALP's shonky finances.

On this tour, Enid admitted cheerfully, 'I'm a bit of a rabble-rouser, you know', and she became one of the star turns as the Lyons were mobbed by enthusiastic crowds in town halls, at train stations, outside radio stations and at street corners. 'Together on the plat-form, Joe and I worked like partners in a game of bridge', she said.

As well as addressing the main political rallies, Enid would address supplementary women's meetings too. Here she emphasised the importance of women participating in the national debate, for them to contribute as mothers, as wives and as homekeepers, but outside of their dominant social roles as well — not as women so much as through their identity as citizens.

Joe Lyons was prime minister from 1931 until he died in 1939, worn out from decades of stress and crisis management. Enid went on to have her own political career in the 1940s and early 1950s, and was the first woman in Australian history to be directly voted into the House of Representatives in federal parliament. She was supported throughout her career by women's political organisations such as the Australian Women's National League, the Victoria League and the Housewives Association. She wrote regular press columns and spoke often on radio.

These days, we'd label Joe and Enid the ultimate 'power couple' (possibly with a catchy portmanteau like 'Joenid'). Whatever the label, they were an extraordinary partnership of two ordinary Australians that the bulk of mainstream Australia recognised and embraced as their own.

As for the Labor Party — when Lyons left in 1931, it lost some moderates from the party and just about all of the moderate support in the electorate. Labor also man-aged to lose the majority of its NSW members when Lang left because most organ-isers, supporters and trade unionists in this state backed Lang rather than federal Labor. There would not be another Labor prime minister until 1941. The party that had been so central to shaping political life in the nation's first decades could barely muster two years of time in government (1929 to 1931) in the whole 21 years of the inter-war period.

Threats to Democracy from Best Friends and Enemies

As the Depression bit harder in the 1930s and politicians seemed unable to come up with a decent solution to the problem, many people began to wonder whether the parliamentary system could cope with the crises of 20th-century life. 'Democracy is a Great Error', declared *The Adelaide Advertiser*. A conservative politician wrote a series of newspaper articles, describing 'Why I have become a Fascist'. Many people felt a desire for a strong leader — someone decisive and compelling, similar to Italy's Benito Mussolini or the Soviet Union's Joseph Stalin. When ultra-ordinary Joe Lyons became prime minister in 1932 (refer to preceding section), it was a kind of repudiation of the dream of a strong dynamic leader that some people were pining for.

In this atmosphere, both communism and vigilantism began to have an appeal.

Seeing the virtues of communism

The 1917 Bolshevik Revolution in Russia was the first communist revolution anywhere in the world. Many idealistic people in Australia thought that now, at last, a government that abolished all inequalities and injustices could finally come into existence.

In Sydney in 1920, encouraged by the Bolshevik Council in Russia, a small group set up the Communist Party of Australia, which claimed it was committed to overthrowing parliamentary democracy and establishing a 'dictatorship of the working class'. In 1922, Jock Garden, secretary of the Trades and Labor Council, went as a Communist Party delegate to an international communist conference in Moscow. He boasted to the conference that the Australian Communist Party would take over leadership in Australia by controlling Labor Councils in the main cities, as he did in Sydney.

IN THEIR WORDS

Back in Australia, Garden said that 'the shadow of communism is over the Labour movement. All efforts to banish communism and the communists are bound to fail. The good old times of playing at politics are gone. Revolution has stepped upon the stage'.

Given that in the Labor Party the policy of socialising industry — bringing in public or government ownership of banks, factories, large shops and businesses — had already been adopted in 1921, communism wasn't seen as too great an enemy within the Australian labour movement (refer to Chapter 13). By controlling the highest councils of the trade unions, a small but committed group of revolutionaries could look to create industrial and political turmoil, seize power and abolish democracy.

LIFE DOWN UNDER

In the Depression of the 1930s, Communist Party membership numbers surged. The Communist Party's explanation for the problems — that they were inevitable by-products of capitalist society and wouldn't be resolved until a communist revolution took place — gained traction in the midst of evictions, soup kitchens and mass unemployment in the heavily industrial inner-city suburbs. Communists were prominent in rallies of unemployed people, carrying red flags and singing revolutionary songs. During the annual May Day procession in Melbourne, marchers gave 'three cheers for the revolution and the Soviet Union'.

IN THEIR WORDS

At a NSW Labor Conference in 1931, one speaker moved motions for the immediate socialisation of industry, another said that 'unemployment can't be solved under capitalism . . . [The unemployed] are going to smash the system down. The time is ripe'.

While the communists didn't succeed in overthrowing government or socialising industry, they did succeed in making a lot of people very uneasy.

Communist influence in key trade unions grew in the 1930s, giving them the capacity to cause strikes that could paralyse industry, transport and communications, and challenge the established democratic order more generally. Simultaneously, a strongly idealistic streak was evident in communist agitation. Much of the evidence in the 1930s seemed to point to modern capitalist society being plenty sick, and needing replacement. Thinkers, artists and activists were drawn to the dream of a new communist social order regenerating a sick society. Even though they planned and hoped for the overthrow of democratic government, the ambition of their hearts is harder to fault.

Forming secret armies

Fears of a communist revolution increased with the arrival of the Depression and, for most people, the most threatening part of the Communist Party was the secrecy with which it conducted its plans.

In the Labor Party, H V ('Doc') Evatt saw communists gradually taking many key positions in the party and was worried. Evatt complained that whenever communists campaigned openly for election, they were always beaten solidly so, instead, according to Evatt, they were following Lenin's advice, which was: 'A small minority, if sufficiently unscrupulous and persistent, can capture most political parties'.

Outside of the Labor Party, other people were just as worried. Taking a fight-fire-with-fire approach, these people began organising secret groups of their own, and were ready, if society began to fall apart, to maintain law and order before revolutionaries could take advantage of any chaos. 'King and Country' would have to be defended, and these fellows decided they were just the men to be defending it — deciding, in effect, democracy and open society would be defended by secret organisations.

NSW's Old Guard

The NSW Old Guard was formed by ex-army officers and businessmen who had influence in the army and police. Returned and Services League clubrooms were used to recruit ex-digger soldiers, following a district-by-district form of organisation and using a military hierarchy. They performed military drills and stockpiled weapons and, at their peak between 1930 and 1932, they numbered some 25,000 members in rural NSW, with nuclei in each region and town. In Sydney they had 5,000 members.

Members of the Old Guard saw themselves as loyal citizens defending Australia's democratic institutions — only in crisis, if Australia was threatened with a dictatorship, would they move into action. They planned to take control of government and daily administration and protect property in the event of any outbreaks of anarchy or civil insurrection.

Victoria's White Army

Similar in organisation to the Old Guard, Victoria's White Army was led by chief commissioner of police, and World War I officer, Thomas Blamey. The White Army's main plan was to protect bridges and essential services in the event of insurrection.

For them the fear peaked on 6 March 1931, when rumours spread throughout rural Victoria that an army of unemployed revolutionaries was on a rampage. They had seized Sydney and were advancing on Melbourne, marching up the nearby road. No such violent mob was on the loose and, after spending a night out manning roadblocks, the next day White Army members returned, a little embarrassed, to their homes, farms and work sheds.

Sydney's New Guard

Founded in February 1931 by fascist Eric Campbell, the New Guard quickly became popular among the middle class and ex-diggers who were most worried about Jack Lang's radical measures as premier. Lang had proposed to replace the currency and was refusing to pay interest on overseas debt, and Campbell was certain Lang was a communist (he wasn't, but at times he could certainly sound like one).

Unlike the Old Guard and White Army, very little was secret about the New Guard. They also seemed more likely to add to the turmoil the two secret armies wanted to prevent. They attacked meetings of communists, unionists and the unemployed, and Campbell threatened publicly to overthrow Lang. At their peak, Sydney's New Guard numbered 36,000 members.

IN THEIR WORDS

The New Guard's biggest publicity 'coup' was at the opening ceremony of the Sydney Harbour Bridge in 1932. Here a New Guard member, Francis de Groot, beat Premier Lang to the ribbon cutting when he unexpectedly rode forward on a horse and declared the bridge open 'in the name of the respectable citizens of NSW'.

The New Guard didn't last much longer than Lang himself (who was sacked shortly after the Bridge opening — refer to the section 'Lang sacked and Labor in tatters', earlier in this chapter), and improved no-one's mood while its members engaged in public violence and grandstanding.

HISTORICAL ROOTS

BUILDING AN ICON: THE SYDNEY HARBOUR BRIDGE

In the early 20th century, grand schemes to build a bridge that crossed Sydney Harbour weren't a new thing — as far back as Macquarie's time in 1815 the convict architect Francis Greenway proposed a bridge. After this proposal came ideas for tunnels and other bridges, but even as railways, roads, radio stations and airplanes were developed, in the early 1920s Australia's biggest city still remained divided in two halves, with ferries the main way of travelling from one side to the other.

This changed finally in 1922 when an act was passed in NSW parliament to begin work on a harbour bridge following a design of railway engineer John Bradfield. When the bridge opened in 1932, it was the world's largest single-arch steel bridge, and became an instant icon.

Coming at the height of the political and social tensions of the Depression, the planned bridge opening by Premier Jack Lang was strongly opposed by some of his more virulent middle-class opponents. Members of the New Guard had declared that Lang was a threat to the order of society and refused to let him have the prestige of opening the engineering marvel of the bridge (see the section 'Sydney's New Guard').

Regardless of who got to cut the ribbon (and viewed from the vantage point of some 90 years later, the act can't help but look a teensy bit childish — it's a ribbon cutting, people, get over it) the two halves of the Sydney metropolis were now connected with rail, road and pedestrian transport thoroughfares. And the debt incurred to build it only took another 50-odd years to pay off . . .

Mistakes and Resilience through the Crisis

Politicians spent a lot of the 1930s arguing heatedly over what might be the best thing to do in the middle of this great crisis. One solution they came up with — which had strong approval from the public — was to 'tune in with Britain', establishing even closer economic ties and allowing some British manufacturers to compete against unprotected Australian industries so Australian exports would have access to British markets. This idea offered plenty to like, but Australian politicians in the 1930s pursued it at the expense of other possible markets and ties.

Meanwhile, everyday folk got on with surviving — and managed to do so remarkably well. Although the main images we have in our collective memory about the Great Depression are the dramatic bigger catastrophes — the eviction of newly unemployed renters from their inner-city slum properties, the stories of starving men having to walk hundreds of miles in search of work in outback Australia — the vast majority of Australians in the Great Depression proved themselves remarkably resilient and highly resourceful in working out ways to get by, survive and (even) enjoy themselves.

The politicians fail

The 1930s decade can ultimately be seen as a time when Australian politicians let down the people they'd been elected to represent. The Labor Party showed itself again unable to hold the party, let alone the nation, together in a time of crisis. And the non-Labor side, while utilising Joe Lyons's capacity to unify national opinion and galvanise active community spirit in the worst of the Depression, showed itself unable to adjust to rapidly changing times.

As the 1930s progressed, politicians of all stripes failed the new task of working out exactly where Australia fitted into a far more perilous world. Australia was cocky about its international standing, and about how far it could keep using its World War I record with Britain. Australian politicians were also slow to acknowledge that the old assurances and certainties of a world largely dominated by the British Empire as sole superpower had gone. The world was now unstable and dangerous; Britannia no longer ruled supreme and, particularly in terms of trade, Australia needed to be looking for new alliances.

Doing (too) well at Ottawa

Australia had played hardball with Britain in the years after World War I, extracting maximum advantage from the kudos won and sacrifices made by Australian soldiers who had fought for Britain. Immigration schemes and easy money loans were both forthcoming (refer to Chapter 14). At Ottawa in Canada in 1932, Australia continued to play hardball and struck a trade agreement, winning just about all the trade concessions they wanted from Britain, while giving very little away.

The Ottawa trade agreement gave Australia free entry for most of its goods in to Britain (with the exception of meat). Britain in return got practically nothing. Some preference was to be given to British goods coming into Australia but at a level decided by the Australian Tariff Board (which was sort of like making the poacher head gamekeeper). Australian officials and politicians couldn't help but crow about their success.

The Australian High Commissioner in London, ex-prime minister Stanley Bruce, joked that it wasn't his job to teach the British officials how to negotiate. The British, after all Australia's talk about 'imperial family' and unity, were burned — and Australia started thinking that if this was what being a Commonwealth dominion was all about, then international life wasn't too bad after all. However, this victory damaged Australia's interests in the long run — because Australia became lazy and assumed that its trading future was entirely bound up with staying tuned in to Britain.

Britain began searching beyond its empire for other trade opportunities. 'Times have changed', said one British official. 'Australia cannot afford to continue to be as self-centred and acquisitive as she has been in the past.' But Australia was pretty slow in absorbing this fairly blunt message.

When it comes back to bite you — the 1936 trade diversion fiasco

The lessons that Australia should have been learning about the need to try to find new markets beyond Britain finally overtook them in 1936. In this year the federal government announced a trade diversion scheme, knocking back trade opportunities with the US and Japan in order to give preferential treatment to Britain. The blithe assumption was that Britain would automatically return the preferential treatment. Britain didn't.

By 1936, Japan was Australia's second biggest customer for wool, and rising. But Australia lost the entire Japanese wool market after their pro-British trade rebuff, and was shut out from the Japanese wheat and flour markets as well. In the same trade diversion scheme, Australia also increased its protective duty on motor car chassis coming into the country from America. American manufacturers were far from happy and the US withdrew Australia's 'Most Favoured Nation' trading status.

Australia complained to Britain, pointing out that Australian tariffs had been cut for British goods, and not enough preferential treatment was being given in return. The British Board of Trade, no doubt enjoying itself immensely, pointed out that Australia's tariff wall 'was so absurdly high' that plenty of tariff reduction was possible without running the slightest risk of damaging Australian manufacturers.

All in all, the 1930s didn't include the best moments for Australian politicians trying to improve the prospects of 'Australia Inc'.

The people endure

The Great Depression of the 1930s was extremely hard for many Australians, as businesses closed and mass unemployment hit some areas (refer to the section 'Here comes tomorrow', earlier in this chapter).

However, the Depression also threw Australians of all classes and walks of life back upon their own resources, and forced them to discover capacities for self-sufficiency. Most were lucky, in that the majority of Australians now lived on large quarter-acre suburban blocks. A flourishing 'black market' economy emerged, with people producing goods at home for their own consumption and trade, as well as exchanging services.

Here are some examples of what was taking place across the country:

>> Chooks and veggies replaced lawn.

>> Household items were repaired rather than replaced.

>> Bottling and preserving came into its own.

>> Clothes were made and mended.

>> Buildings were extended, and verandahs converted into bedrooms for extended family.

And the climate was good — most Australians didn't have to weather harsh winters in hardship and without heating like so many in America and Europe.

LIFE DOWN UNDER

One of the most striking things about the Depression era was that the general flow of people into cities and urban life, which had been a dominant feature of Australian life for more than 60 years, was reversed. As jobs gave out in the factories and building industries in the cities, many working-class men, teenage boys just out of school and various professionals connected with a prominent Australian social myth — the myth of 'the bush' as the heartland for authentic Australians. In the country, you could find more jobs (working for small and large farmers), more free food (fish, rabbits and occasionally free 'tucker' from homesteads) and plenty of places to camp for free. *Swaggies* (itinerant workers) became a prominent feature of the country landscape as the government provided coupons for rations of food and dole at country police stations.

The Depression brought no shortage of painful and difficult experiences — including the dramatic increase in bankruptcies and the loss of many jobs. But overall people actually got healthier. They had less money but they ate better, in terms of nutrition. Cracked-wheat porridge, jam sandwiches, rabbit stew, lots of home-grown vegetables, mashed potato, milk, butter and eggs all made for cheap and plentiful foods.

The death rate during the 1930s actually declined. The suicide rate, after a sharp rise during the first initial shock of early 1930, fell far below what it had been in the 'roaring twenties'. People crowded into cheap entertainments, such as horse races, football matches, cinemas, agricultural and flower shows, in record numbers. The worst hardships were hard, there's no doubting that, but many found that there were far worse things than being poor. Weirdly, counterintuitively, if you could get by in the 1930s, you may well have been happier than in the more affluent decades both before and since.

Celebrating 26 January 1938? Yes. Mourning and Protesting? Also yes.

On 26 January 1938, Australia marked 150 years since Captain Arthur Phillip and the First Fleet arrived in New South Wales. As with the future 1988 bicentennial, the sesquicentennial kicked off big celebrations and festivities, most especially in Sydney and Sydney Harbour. Here the original 1788 landing was re-enacted, the Union Jack flag raised, and an elaborate pageant played out for the enjoyment of picnicking citizens.

Elsewhere a new first was being marked. The date of the 150 anniversary was also the first official 'Day of Mourning' by Indigenous political activists.

IN THEIR WORDS

Indigenous protestors met together in Sydney, and declared, 'This being the 150th Anniversary of the whiteman's seizure of our country, [the Aboriginals of Australia] HEREBY MAKE PROTEST against the callous treatment of our people by the whitemen during the past 150 years, AND WE APPEAL to the Australian nation of today to make new laws for the education and care of Aborigines. . . .'. Significantly, their resolution finished with an appeal 'for a new policy which will raise our people to FULL CITIZEN STATUS and EQUALITY WITHIN THE COMMUNITY.' (Capitals here reproduced as per the original resolution.)

A new Aboriginal political identity had developed in the decades since the state-based Protection Boards had been established (refer to chapter 12). These Boards had been harsh and interventionist, often deploying the police to confine 'full-blood' Aboriginal people on government-run and supervised settlements, and stripping Indigenous Australians of basic rights and freedoms. The first generation of Aboriginal political activists first began their work in organised campaigns against these Aboriginal Protection Boards, and against their policies (which often included the removal of children from their Indigenous parents).

Older Indigenous Australians had lived at a time of greater civil freedom, when the Aboriginal Reserves were on larger regional reserves of land, and featured flourishing small towns and agriculture. Indigenous leaders such as William Cooper and Bill Ferguson mentored a rising generation of Indigenous Australians, and in the 1920s and 1930s the two generations collaborated to establish the first pan-Aboriginal political organisations.

These organisations campaigned for the end of child removal policies (which produced those who would become known in later decades as the Stolen Generations), for the abolition of the state Protection Boards, for full citizen rights for Aboriginals and for land rights as well. Groups such as the Aborigines Progressive Association and the Australian Aborigines' League helped drive the development of a new self-identity of Indigenous people as pan-Aboriginal citizens — a shared identity which extended across clans, language groups and tribal divisions.

Many men and women became prominent in the 1920s and 1930s, including the following:

>> Pearl Gibbs

>> Jack Patten

>> Fred Maynard

>> William Cooper

>> Doug Nicholls

>> Bill Onus

>> Bill Ferguson

They activists travelled from Aboriginal missions to country and city centres, and back again, looking to represent different Indigenous Australians to politicians and to the press, and sending petitions to the King of England as they sought redress.

Five days after the Day of Mourning marked the 1938 Australia Day, members of the Aborigines Progressive Association and William Cooper, leader of the Australian Aborigines' League, went in a deputation and met with Joe Lyons, Australia's prime minister and his wife, Enid. They called for the Commonwealth to take control of Aboriginal affairs away from the states, and for the recognition of the equality and rights of Australian Aboriginal people with all other Australian citizens. These were long campaigns that would take decades to realise, but they begin here, in 1938.

CREATING LEGENDS: PHAR LAP AND BODYLINE

In the 1930s, a New Zealand horse and a disreputable tactic in games of cricket produced national myths and controversies at a time when the people desperately needed some diversions and heroes.

The New Zealand horse was Phar Lap, a great 'stayer' perfect for running long-distance races like the Melbourne Cup. Phar Lap's staying power was attributable in large part to what subsequent post-mortem examinations proved to be an unusually large heart. With it, Phar Lap ran to a big victory in the 1930 Melbourne Cup as the clear favourite, and cash-strapped punters across the nation rejoiced. Unfortunately for trainer Harry Telford and the punters, Phar Lap died in the US less than 18 months later after winning the Agua Caliente Handicap in Mexico. Many Australians at the time believed that the horse had been poisoned — a theory that has since been disproved — and the mourning in Australia was intense. Australians love to bet, and since very early in the colonial period had loved and needed horses. In the middle of a period of economic and social trauma, they'd particularly loved and needed this horse.

The questionable cricket tactic involved what's known as 'bodyline'. Bodyline was used by the touring English cricket team in 1932–33 in a successful attempt to curtail the exploits of the young Don Bradman, statistically the greatest cricketer to have played the game. Bodyline involved bowling directly at the batsman's body, with fielders clustered around the batsman ready to take a catch. In the days before protective helmets and proper chest and arm guards, this tactic was dangerous, especially when bowled with the velocity and accuracy of coalminer Harold Larwood, England's gun fast bowler.

Australia had always been fanatical about proving itself against Britain on the cricket field (who needs a republic when you can beat the Poms at cricket?). In the period where the issue of debt repayment added a fraught layer to British–Australian relations, the sight of representatives of the mother country using a tactic that went against the spirit of the game was enough to rouse crowds to screams of abuse and threats of violence. The Australian Board of Control for International Cricket made a formal protest to the cricket authorities in England, and the two nations even discussed the issue at a governmental level.

England won the series, and the rules got changed to ensure it didn't happen again, but for many the bodyline controversy seemed to symbolise some of the darker anxieties produced by Australia's relationship with Britain.

IN THIS CHAPTER

» Trying to avoid war in the 1930s

» Standing alongside Britain and facing up to embedded problems

» Heading off to fight on the other side of the world (again)

» Linking up with America as war comes to the Pacific

» Reorganising Australia's wartime economy

Chapter **16**

World War II Battles

ustralians in the 1920s and 1930s, like much of the rest of the world, wanted to do anything rather than think about the prospect of war. Hard to blame them — the 'Great War' of 1914 to 1918 was enough to cure just about anyone of an appetite for war. Australia put its hopes in an ongoing security alliance with Britain (and the British construction of a strategic port in Singapore), and in appeasement, as Japan, Italy and Germany all showed increasing signs of military aggression in the 1930s.

When World War II began in 1939, Australia did as it had in World War I, by declaring itself at war and on the side of Britain, and sending troops off to the Middle East. Things took a different turn, however, in 1941 when Japan attacked US, Australian and British territories in the Asia-Pacific region. For the first time in Australia's modern history, invasion looked to be not just possible but also inevitable as Japan swept dramatically southward, conquering as it went. In the light of this threat, pragmatism forced a new alliance to be forged — with America — and the Australian economy was for the first time shifted to a complete war footing.

In this chapter, I look at how World War II dramatically focused everyone's thinking about who and what could be relied on to defend the country in a time of crisis.

Building Up to War

Throughout the 1930s, while the international scene looked increasingly grim, plenty of politicians and ordinary people were willing to do just about anything to avoid getting embroiled in another disastrous world war — the memory of the first one was still burned vividly on everyone's memory.

Australia's military forces, still being run by men who had commanded the forces in World War I (1914 to 1918), stagnated and declined. Simultaneously, defence spending was slashed because of the Great Depression.

The chief defence policy centred on the British garrison and naval base at Singapore, which had been promised and built (in fairly stop-start fashion) since the early 1920s. Singapore was a naval base without a fleet: Britain had promised to send ships in the event of war in the Pacific. Worried Australian politicians and representatives kept prodding the British for estimates of exactly how many ships would be sent, but no specific answers were forthcoming.

By 1938, Australia had belatedly begun building up its war resources — although politicians continued to argue about the best way to do it. Events of 1941 showed the politicians were right to be worried about Singapore — but also showed that perhaps they should have worked harder in the 1930s to ensure that Australia was more war-ready in a highly unstable international environment.

Defences through the Great Depression

Even though Labor had been one of the main players in setting up a citizen's militia before World War I, the experience of the conscription controversies in 1916 and 1917 had permanently soured them towards it. (Refer to Chapter 13 for the incredibly divisive impact conscription had on the Labor Party and Australian society in general.) When Labor took power under Jim Scullin in 1929, one of the first things it did was stop compulsory military training for the civilian militia.

Then the economic trauma of the Great Depression hit, and government spending on all non-essentials was slashed. Defence fell into this category and, as a consequence, the amount of funding directed to armaments, training and the military dropped drastically in the early 1930s.

At the same time as defence expenditure was being slashed, attempts were made to ensure that the potential (at this stage, anyway) aggressors — Germany, Italy and Japan — were placated. 'Appeasement' (which nowadays is often met with derision but in the 1930s was simply the name of a strategy) became the popular slogan.

After another Labor Party split (refer to Chapter 15), Joe Lyons's new United Australia Party took power from Scullin's Labor Party in 1931. Lyons was an 'arch-appeaser' who was horrified by war. Active in the Labor Party in World War I, he was a strong campaigner against conscription and now wanted to make sure that war was avoided at all cost.

Lyons had long phone conversations with British Prime Minister Neville Chamberlain (who was also pro-appeasement), and met with the Italian dictator Benito Mussolini in an attempt to secure an Anglo-Italian agreement. Even after Chamberlain abandoned attempts to placate German dictator Adolf Hitler early in 1939, Lyons didn't give up hope that some sort of settlement could be reached. Like most appeasers, Lyons thought just about anything was worth agreeing to if it meant avoiding war.

Lyons, along with his deputy Robert Menzies, was also active in trying to stop war in eastern Asia, where Japan had invaded and occupied large parts of China in the 1930s. The Australian Government pushed for a settlement with the Japanese but the British — who had profitable business interests in China — weren't so keen.

HISTORICAL ROOTS

Lyons was prime minister from 1931 till his death in April 1939, and focused on appeasement of the potential aggressors for most of this time. When appeasement didn't work and war finally broke out, however, Australia, like many Allied nations, wasn't as prepared for conflict as they could (or should) have been.

Embracing the Singapore Strategy

The fear of invasion from nearby Asia had been a dominating factor in the original movement to Federation. This obsession meant that in the years following Federation, Australians continued to be preoccupied with the question of what sort of defence could be mounted against potential threats from the immediate north. A nation small in population on a large land mass was felt to be particularly vulnerable and ill-equipped to defend itself.

Britain, however, was still one of the biggest and most powerful nations in the world in the 1920s, and Australia's security and prosperity was in its interests. As well as involving itself in settlement schemes and development projects (refer to Chapter 14), Britain might also want to make sure that Australia's defence was taken care of. Singapore was the result of this thinking.

HISTORICAL ROOTS

What became known as the Singapore Strategy was a strategy built around the navy and oceanic defence. The British Royal Navy had maintained global dominance at sea for more than a century, and the port of Singapore straddled sea lanes between the Pacific and the British colony of India. Singapore was also close to Australia, which, as an island continent, was thought to be a good candidate for a navy-based defence.

In the 1920s, under an agreement reached with Australia, the British set about turning Singapore into a serious naval base to defend and control the surrounding waters. The base, which was completed in the late 1930s, could comfortably hold and outfit a navy in the case of war — but no navy was provided. Britain gave assurances that in the time of real emergency, ships would be sent, but Australian politicians weren't assured.

As early as 1933, ex-Australian prime minister Stanley Bruce warned Lyons from London that if war began in the Asian-Pacific region while Britain was already caught up in a European war, the chances of effective British navy reinforcements being sent to Singapore were minimal.

New Labor Party leader John Curtin (who replaced Scullin in 1935) said that Singapore was close to useless in the defence of Australia, but didn't have much more to offer the national conversation, not offering any realistic alternatives until the late 1930s.

HISTORICAL ROOTS

Bruce and Curtin both turned out to be right on Singapore. When war came to the Pacific in 1941, Britain was already up to its neck trying to fight off Nazi Germany. They had little to spare for Singapore, which fell in February 1942 (see the section 'Britain can't do everything: The fall of Singapore', later in this chapter). But Curtin, who was by then Australia's prime minister, had changed his tune. Rather than stick to Curtin's original line about Singapore being useless as a defence outpost, Curtin's foreign minister, Doc Evatt, told Churchill (Britain's prime minister at the time) that any abandonment of it would be seen by Australia as an 'inexcusable betrayal'. So Churchill reinforced Singapore, and when it fell many thousands of British, Indian and Australian soldiers became prisoners of war.

Belatedly prodded into action

Towards the end of the 1930s, the liberal/conservative parties under Joe Lyons concentrated their efforts at getting guarantees that the British naval base at Singapore would be adequately garrisoned. When no guarantees were forthcoming and as war became more inevitable, new policy measures were adopted to try to rectify Australia's inadequate defence. For his part, Lyons tried to create a 'Pacific Pact' with President Roosevelt in America, but was rebuffed.

The Labor Party, meanwhile, was criticised for being 'isolationist' — opponents claimed Labor politicians had their heads in the sand, hoping that keeping out of all overseas conflict would mean no Australians would get caught up in war. Their new leader, John Curtin, had his work cut out coaxing his party to come up with a more viable defence policy.

Curtin was in touch with people in the army who hated the Singapore Strategy (see preceding section) for two reasons:

>> They were annoyed that the strategy meant most defence funding was going to the navy to support the sea defence idea that was at the heart of the strategy.

>> They didn't think the strategy would work. Britain, they thought, wouldn't send enough ships in enough time to make any difference.

Curtin gleaned ideas from his friends in the army and began converting Labor's defence policy into a more active, self-reliant one. Curtin proposed using planes to solve the defence dilemma, arguing that an air force could be built up in Australia and used purely for local defence purposes, thereby precluding the need to rely on Britain's Singapore Strategy or other overseas ventures.

In 1937, an election took place that was dominated by the question of defence. Lyons ran a campaign saying the most important thing was to maintain a strong defence relationship with Britain. Labor campaigned on more planes and fewer ships, self-reliance and some links with the US, but lost because they were seen as still too isolationist.

Ironically, after the election win, Lyons became concerned enough about the situation to try to establish American links. And he introduced a significant expansion of the defence budget. In December 1938, a new three-year defence program began to bring Australia to war readiness. As part of the program, £63,000,000 was allocated for training and equipping new troops, building two destroyers, fortifying Port Moresby in Papua (under Australian protectorate control since the defeat of Germany in World War I) and building an air force station in Townsville.

Before the 1937 election, Lyons had signed a statutory declaration promising never to bring in conscription, but in 1938 he recruited Billy Hughes, ex-World War I prime minister and still serving in Lyons's government, to run a huge publicity campaign to encourage volunteers for militia training.

In July 1939, the government, now led by Bob Menzies (who replaced Lyons as prime minister when Lyons died in early 1939), began a national register of all men aged between 18 and 65. The Labor Party and unions opposed it, saying it wouldn't be anything other than a kind of conscription database, but the measure went ahead.

Dealing with Early War Problems

In September 1939, war finally began when Germany invaded Poland, which Britain had pledged to protect. Britain declared war and so, as a consequence, Prime Minister Bob Menzies told radio listeners, Australia was now also at war. Although most of the pre-war anxiety had related to threats of war from Japan in the Asian Pacific, Australia found itself again sending troops to the Middle East to fight in a European war.

In the early years of the war, however, Australian troops had their work cut out for them in more ways than one, because, along with the horrors of war, they also had to deal with numerous tactical, organisational and logistical problems.

Problems with tactics and technology

While Britain and other countries were completely overhauling their outmoded World War I tactical theory in the late 1930s, Australia was stuck using old methods and theories. Battle preparation wasn't brilliant, and tactics tended to the foolhardy. Experience would gradually alter this, as would the removal of the 'dead wood' of old commanding officers who were no longer effective in modern battle (see following section).

When it came to technology, the Australian forces weren't well provided for in this area, either. A good example? The Australian 6th Division began the war still using horse transport rather than trucks and vans! Even the biggest traditionalist could recognise that it was time to move on. And communications technology, increasingly important in modern warfare, was woeful. The 6th Division wasn't issued with wireless sets until after the campaign in Greece in April and May 1941. And the 9th Division — who fought at Tobruk in northern Africa — also had hardly any wireless equipment.

Problems with officer training and promotions

Before the start of the war, officers in the Australian forces were given promotions according to seniority and according to whether they'd served in World War I. This might have worked all right in peace time, when the vast bulk of the armed service was part-time militia, but it couldn't be sustained in wartime combat.

By the time of the Greece campaign (see the section 'War in the Mediterranean', later in this chapter), most of the battalions had new commanding officers, all promoted on merit rather than seniority. On top of that, most of the new officers coming through received the benefit of British training. While Australian officer training in tactics and technology had stagnated in the 1920s and 1930s, the British Army had brought in new officer training material. Fighting with the British in northern Africa and the Mediterranean meant the Australian officers benefitted from this — they were sent to British officer training classes.

By 1941, Australian officers were younger, more up to date with training and tactics, and displaying an ability to adapt to new terrain, situations and circumstances.

Problems with weapons

If you're in a war and you have a problem with weapons, then you really have a problem; this was Australia's at the start of 1941. There weren't enough heavy-calibre weapons to support infantry soldiers — which meant Australian soldiers eagerly captured automatic weapons from enemy battalions whenever they could. Neither did Australian troops have any decent anti-tank guns, nor any 'bunker-busters'. Resolving this dilemma took a while and hampered operations in both northern Africa and in Greece and Crete.

Overseas Again

In September 1939, Menzies declared war along with Britain, but he wasn't keen on the idea of sending Australian forces overseas to fight in places like the Middle East and Europe when Japan remained such a threat locally. But his minister in London — Richard Casey — made some rash promises to match the offer of a division made by New Zealand, which Menzies reluctantly agreed to. In 1940, Menzies and Australia said goodbye to Australian divisions of the second AIF (Australian Imperial Force) to be sent overseas with volunteer soldiers. (The first AIF was the Anzac diggers who went to Gallipoli and the Western Front of France in World War I.)

War in northern Africa

The second AIF was being trained in Egypt with the expectation that, like in World War I, they would be sent to a western front in France. From the middle of 1940, however, battles began in northern Africa. From early January 1941 at the Battle of Bardia, AIF divisions were involved in the victorious campaign against the Italian Army, then in the more ignominious (yet still fighting) retreat against the Germans, and held out at the siege of Tobruk until December 1941. From July to November 1942, Australian forces were involved in the battle of El Alamein.

In the process, the second AIF made the transition from stodgy pre-war military hierarchy to professional fighting outfit. A lot of the problems in the initial organisation became quickly apparent once in combat (especially against the formidable German Army). The divisions in the Middle East were lucky, however — unlike the 8th Division in Singapore in 1942 (which you can find out more about in the section 'Britain can't do everything: The fall of Singapore' later on), they had the luck of some easy early battles, and were able to make their mistakes and learn from them. By 1942 and the battle of El Alamein, the AIF was a far more adaptive and battle-hardened force.

Capturing Bardia and Tobruk

Bardia was the site of the first Australian battle in the war, and in early January 1941, Australian forces took the town, forcing 40,000 Italians to surrender.

A couple of weeks later, Australian forces won Tobruk from the Italians, taking 100,000 prisoners. No doubt the Australian troops were starting to think, *Mate, this is too easy.*

With the arrival of Field Marshal Rommel and his formidable German Afrika Korps, things got difficult. Rommel was soon pushing Allied forces back across northern Africa, and placing the city of Tobruk under siege. The Australian 6th Division was withdrawn to fight another losing battle (see the section 'War in the Mediterranean', later in this chapter) while the 9th Division stayed to fight in Tobruk.

Enduring the siege of Tobruk

Tobruk remained as the last Allied outpost left in northern Africa after all the other territory initially won from the Italians had been seized back by Rommel. For eight months, troops held out with supplies being run in by sea and on 7 December 1941 Tobruk was finally relieved. During the siege, 800 Australians had been killed during the incessant perimeter battles with Rommel's Afrika Korps forces.

Winning at El Alamein

The battle for El Alamein in 1942 was one of the epic battles of World War II, where victory swung momentum decisively to the Allies. The 9th Division took part in the main phases of this conflict as part of a British Army that was commanded by General Montgomery.

By this time most of the early problems that the AIF had encountered (refer to the section 'Dealing with Early War Problems') had been dealt with. Most of the 9th Division's battalion commanders were officers who had proved themselves in the 1941 operations. Just as importantly, they finally had enough wireless communications, better heavy weaponry (with plenty captured from the enemy) and even an anti-tank platoon. Amateur hour was over. (For more on Australia's war effort in northern Africa, see *Australia's Military History For Dummies*, Wiley Publishing Australia.)

War in the Mediterranean

At the beginning of 1941, Greece was Britain's only ally still fighting in Europe. Although the Greek Army had managed to repel the Italian Army, it would have no chance against the Germans.

The campaign to save Greece from German invasion couldn't even be placed in the 'really good idea at the time' category. The campaign looked like a bad idea from the start — one of those doomed hopeless fights that you couldn't hope to win. Given the various strategic, firepower and manpower advantages the Germans had as their blitzkrieg swung into Greece, the chances of stopping them was effectively zero. But British Prime Minister Winston Churchill convinced his war cabinet (which visiting Australian Prime Minister Bob Menzies was also sitting in) that it was a worthwhile thing to do. Britain had promised Greece that it would do so, and Churchill thought it might impress the Americans, who at this stage were still on the sidelines of the war but watching with interest. Even if it was a doomed campaign, Churchill figured, defending the birthplace of democracy (ancient Athens in Greece) was bound to play well with the Americans — who loved that kind of thing.

Defending Greece may have made some sense within the scope of grand strategy, but down in the battlefield it meant doomed endeavours for the largely Australian and New Zealand troops who were being sent in to do the defending. Allied forces lost Greece to Germany and in the process 320 Australians died and 2,000 became prisoners of war (POWs). Australia was learning the hard way (again) about the pitfalls of being a junior partner to large powerful nations caught up in a life and death global struggle.

After getting kicked out of Greece, Allied forces also lost Crete to the downward sweep of German forces. By 1 June 1941, some 15,000 British and Anzac troops had been withdrawn from Crete. The island had been overrun by an army of 30,000 German paratroopers and, even though about 7,000 had been shot as they parachuted down or just after landing, the German assault was too much to withstand.

This Time It's Personal: War in the Pacific

In many ways the first two years of World War II — September 1939 to December 1941 — went according to expectation for Australia. An Australian volunteer force was raised and sent overseas to fight on the side of the British Allies in far-off places — Africa, Europe, the Middle East — just as had happened in World War I. But on 7 December 1941, things changed dramatically. Japan attacked US, Dutch and British territories throughout South-East Asia, and began a territorial conquest that took more land and sea area at greater speed than any other military campaign in history — better than the Huns, the Romans, the Brits themselves, Napoleon, you name it.

For the first time, Australia itself was threatened with invasion, lost its overseas territories and suffered attack on its towns and cities. With northern Australian towns being bombed, Prime Minister Curtin insisted that Australian troops be sent home and, famously, turned to America for help. America, luckily, decided Australia was an ideal place from which to launch a counterattack.

American and Australian forces managed to turn the tide against Japan, with the Australian military, now a far cry from the amateurish outfit of the late 1930s, proving to be one of the best jungle-fighting forces in the world.

But just as they reached peak efficiency, Australian forces were relegated to a strategic backwater. In the second half of 1944 and in 1945, the man in charge of the American effort in the Pacific, General MacArthur, made sure that only American troops would have the prestige of the final conflicts with Japan. Australian forces were restricted to mopping up operations, many of them of no strategic use whatsoever, but the result of political imperatives — General Blamey from the Australian Army and Prime Minister Curtin needed to keep Australian forces fighting in order to improve Australia's bargaining power after the end of conflict.

Britain can't do everything: The fall of Singapore

Ever since the beginnings of white settlement in 1788, Australian security had been predicated on the protection given the country by the British Empire. For practically the entire 19th century, Britain had been the undisputed global superpower. This situation had changed during and immediately after World War I, but in Australia it took a while to sink in.

The strategic linchpin of Britain's defence of Asia, India and Australia was the sea port of Singapore on the Malay Peninsula. Since the port was established in the early 1920s, Australia had been assured that no enemy could harm it while Singapore was held by the British. Consequently, Singapore's fall sent shockwaves through Australian society.

On 8 December 1941, a massive Japanese air force began its assault on British Malaya. A large Japanese landing force also began to make its way with lightning speed down the Malay Peninsula towards Singapore, which lay at the very tip. The Australian 8th Division was sent in to reinforce the defence.

Previous to the Japanese invasion of Singapore, the assumption had been that the only threats to Singapore would come from the sea, because the land to its north was seemingly impenetrable jungle and heavy scrub. The Japanese soon proved the terrain to be quite penetrable indeed, especially when utilising their *driving charge* tactic — taking calculated risks to keep forward-moving momentum constant and keep the enemy (in this case, Indian, British and Australian troops) on the back foot.

Japanese forces used a high-tempo, fluid form of fighting and the Australian 8th Division was completely unable to combat it. The Australians also had the following factors against them:

>> They were given practically zero sea or air support.

>> The Singapore guns were set in concrete and pointed out to sea (invasion from land seeming that inconceivable to the boffins who'd planned the defence originally).

>> They hadn't had the chance to develop into a formidable fighting force as had the other AIF divisions serving in northern Africa (refer to the section 'War in northern Africa', earlier in this chapter).

The last factor in the preceding list was probably the biggest issue. At the start of the war, Australian forces had faced chronic problems (refer to the section 'Dealing with Early War Problems'). Whereas other divisions had been able to get over these problems during months of more low-level skirmishing and battles against often substandard enemies, the 8th Division got hit by a ruthless and tactically brilliant fighting force almost as soon as it stepped off the boat.

Singapore fell on 15 February 1942 and 13,000 Australian soldiers from the 8th Division became Japanese prisoners of war.

Attacks on Australia

Australian towns on the northern coast were especially vulnerable to Japanese attack because the Japanese were intent on eliminating any potential airfields that might threaten their occupation of Java, Borneo and Timor. In early 1942, Japanese forces launched attacks on the Australian mainland.

In Darwin, 243 people were killed on 19 February 1942. Two weeks later, the Battle of the Java Sea took place and HMAS *Perth* was sunk, with half the crew of 680 being killed. Dutch, British, Australian and American warships all attempted to halt the Japanese advance but were comprehensively beaten. On 3 March 1942, 70 people died in Broome from Japanese bombing, and casualties were also suffered at Wyndham. Invasion and occupation by the Japanese became a real threat.

Over 21 months, Darwin was attacked 64 times by Japanese bombers, the final raid occurring on 13 November 1943. Overall, 97 attacks took place on northern Australia in 1942 and 1943, on Darwin, Broome, Wyndham, Derby, Katherine, Horn Island, Townsville, Mossman, Port Headland, Noonamah, Exmouth Gulf, Onslow, Drysdale River Mission and Coomalie Creek. All of a sudden Australia felt very much alone — and northern Australian especially so.

PRIME MINISTER CURTIN: RELUCTANT HERO

John Curtin was leader of the ALP for ten years from 1935 to 1945, and prime minister for four years from 1941 to 1945. He led the Labor Party to a momentous electoral victory in 1943, running with the campaign pledge of 'Victory in war, victory in peace', which proved to be spot on. Curtin was the one political leader who proved capable of bringing Australians together in the war, and he also developed plans for reconstruction that were implemented after the war.

When Curtin became party leader, Labor began to build up a more substantial defence and external affairs policy. In 1935 and 1936, Curtin also oversaw 'unity conferences', whereby the party split was healed with old supporters of ex-NSW premier Lang (refer to Chapter 15) being welcomed back into the party. Labor once again began to be seen as a viable alternative to govern.

Curtin took government in October 1941, and two months later had a series of local disasters and calamities to deal with as Japan swept south. Curtin announced, 'Australia looks to America, free of any pangs as to our traditional links or kinship with the United Kingdom'. Churchill was furious, Roosevelt thought it a bit panicky and Australians were divided — but at least the prime minister was showing clear leadership.

At the time of the Japanese attacks, two Australian divisions were being brought back from the Middle East for the far east Asian theatre. Britain's Churchill and America's Roosevelt decided these divisions were most needed to defend the strategically vital Burma. Curtin, backed by his top military advisers, disagreed. Churchill ignored him. Curtin got angry, and eventually had his way.

The events all took a heavy toll on Curtin. Waiting for the troop ship to arrive back in Australia, knowing the troops were travelling defenceless through hostile sea, was torment for him. He didn't sleep for nights on end, just paced around in the garden of the Lodge in Canberra, smoking himself to an early grave. This image of Curtin — the reformed alcoholic who had doubts about his ability to lead a nation at war and took power only reluctantly, and then worried himself sick over the lives of his troops — has endured in Australian memory, making him one of the most loved of Australia's prime ministers.

Um, America — can we be friends?

Luckily for Australia, America was drawn into the war against Japan when Japan launched its initial attacks in 1941, which included bombing Pearl Harbor in Hawaii and attacking American territories in the Philippines. Even more luckily for Australia, America decided that Australia would be an ideal place in which to build up its own forces and from which to launch a counterattack across the Pacific. President Roosevelt ordered American General Douglas MacArthur to take up a command post over the South-West Pacific Area, with headquarters in Australia, and soon after American forces and equipment began to arrive in Australia.

In March 1942, General MacArthur arrived in Australia, establishing headquarters in Melbourne, before moving it to Brisbane for the launching of offensives. People breathed a big sigh of relief: 'Thank God for the Yanks' was the general sentiment. By this stage, the general feeling was that the Japanese forces were at Australia's door — see Figure 16-1 for just how much area was under Japanese control by 1942. Even though MacArthur and the Americans had had their own bungles and defeats — such as Pearl Harbor and surrender in the Philippines — the overriding sensation when MacArthur arrived was that things would now turn out all right.

By June 1943, close to 178,000 American servicemen were based in Australia. Overall about 1 million Americans passed through Australia during the war, most of them arriving during 1942. This passage made them the greatest temporary influx of foreigners in Australian history, barring the gold rushes of the 1850s, and their impact on Australian life, and women's lives particularly, were profound and far-reaching (see the sidebar 'Here come the Americans: "Overpaid, oversexed and over here"' for more on this).

Turning the tide in the Coral Sea and on the Kokoda Trail

Through 1941 and the start of 1942, the Japanese Army swept through Asia and the Pacific with unbelievable force and speed. But in May 1942, the tide of the war started to turn in the Allies' favour, with the first real defeat of Japanese naval forces in the war — at the Battle of the Coral Sea.

The Japanese were intent on capturing the strategically vital Port Moresby: If Port Moresby was taken, their control of the surrounding sea lanes would have been close to total. In early May, ships from the US and Australian navies moved to stop the Japanese.

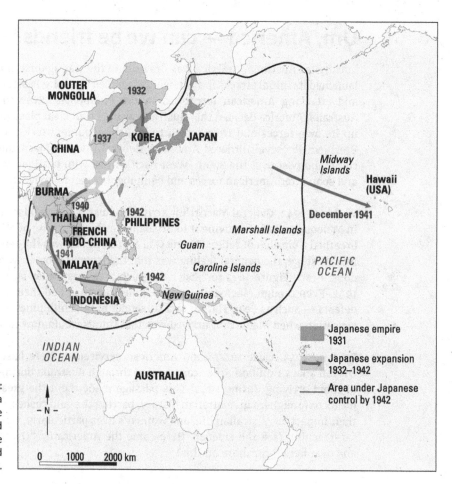

FIGURE 16-1:
By 1942, the area
under Japanese
control included
parts of the
Pacific and
South-East Asia.

The two fleets (Allied and Japanese) never sighted each other because this more modern naval battle involved aircraft carriers launching planes on long-range bombing raids on the enemy's ships. Both sides suffered loss of lives and ships, and although Japan won the battle on points (numerically more ships were sunk on the Allied side), the forward momentum of the most rapid territorial invasion in history was for the first time blocked.

On 21 July 1942, the fighting moved onto land, as some 13,000 Japanese troops landed on the north coast of New Guinea and begin a rapid advance up the Kokoda Trail towards Port Moresby. The Australian civilian militia (who by law were only allowed to fight on Australia's mainland or its territories), heavily outnumbered, fought a rearguard battle.

HERE COME THE AMERICANS: 'OVERPAID, OVERSEXED AND OVER HERE'

When US troops 'invaded' Australia, young women of all classes started going out and having good times with the visiting servicemen. This drew rebukes not just from Australian soldiers (who, wearing as they were the same sort of uniform that the diggers had worn in World War I, were looking — let's face it — a little daggy and outdated) but from the older generation of Australian women as well. These women could be found issuing disapproving sermons from such bodies as the National Council of Women, the Women's Christian Temperance Union and the United Association of Women. In Australia and in Britain, the phrase 'overpaid, oversexed and over here' was used to sum up the outrage many people felt over the influx.

Because of the arrival of cinema and Hollywood movies in Australia in the 1920s and 1930s, a generation of young Australian women were far more primed than their mothers to be swept off their feet by American strangers. But the American strangers themselves sure made the task a lot easier — some women reported with astonishment that they actually seemed to enjoy women's company. American troops provided gifts and compliments, and the new cultural phenomenon of men being at ease with women. This experience was a new thing for plenty of Australian women in the 1940s.

Australian men in the early 20th century may have had many qualities, but ease with women usually wasn't one of them. Men and women's social lives were far more separate than they are nowadays — for example, when women went to the pub they couldn't drink with men, and had to go to a separate 'ladies lounge'. For much of the 19th century men had outnumbered women disproportionately — first as convicts then as gold-seekers — which meant that individual women often had the advantage of being highly sought after and appreciated, but the disadvantage of being in a highly masculine culture. And plenty of men just didn't know how to be comfortable with women because they weren't used to being so. Experience as soldiers on the Western Front in World War I did little to change that. Plenty of women figured that the Americans had arrived just in time — and not necessarily to save Australia from Japanese invasion.

Reinforcements arrived in the form of AIF divisions fresh from the Middle East and, for the first time, civilian militia and volunteer soldiers fought together on the Kokoda Trail. By September 1942, Australian forces had turned the Japanese back. This (and Timor) was the closest to Australia that Japanese forces ever advanced.

PRISONERS OF WAR: AN EXTENDED SUFFERING

Being captured and becoming prisoners of war (POWs) was a new experience for Australian troops — as was coming to terms with it for the people left back home. In World War I not many prisoners had been taken — the fighting was mostly contained within static trench lines. But in World War II, swift seizures of large territories were common, especially in the first two to three years of the war while the Allies were losing.

POWs captured by Italy and Germany were, on the whole, treated according to the basically humane protocols of war (although Russian prisoners were treated brutally). But, as the figure shows, POWs of Japan suffered terribly. Malnutrition and disease, water torture, cigarette burns, beatings and floggings were common. POWs were used for live bayonet practice or medical dissections, and many women in the camps were routinely mutilated. All this was organised and approved from the top officers down.

Australian War Memorial Negative No 019199

Between January and March 1942, 22,000 Australian POWs were taken in Malaya, Singapore, New Guinea and the Dutch East Indies (modern-day Indonesia).

Of these, 13,000 were sent to the Burma–Thailand Railway, built by the Japanese to begin moving supplies in for an attack on India. The Japanese used POWs as forced labourers, working in thick jungle, clearing land, felling trees, drilling into rock and building bridges to construct the railway line. Of the 13,000 Australian POWs sent to the railway, 2,800 died.

Sickness and malnutrition wiped out many more. In total, some 8,000 Australians died as POWs of the Japanese. This represents close to half of all Australian deaths in the conflict with Japan.

Yet, these worst of conditions again revealed something distinctive about Australian national character. After the war, various observers reported that the differences in the behaviour of POWs of certain nationalities were striking. British POWs tended to fall back on class hierarchies in dealing with each other and maintaining order. Many American POWs adopted a more freebooting approach — creating a climate of 'every man for himself', with rations being sold off to the highest bidders as extortionists secured much of the scarce food and supplies. In most cases, Australian soldiers fell back on their mateship ethos. The egalitarian rhetoric of mateship turned out to have some real basis in Australian behaviour.

Jungle victories

In 1942, the fighting against Japan had been a combination of pure desperation and scrambling defence. In 1943, the initiative began to swing. Victories on the Kokoda Trail (refer to the preceding section) and at Milne Bay on the east coast of Papua helped soldiers realise how to fight best in jungle terrain. Australian troops now saw that, after a long period of seemingly invincible progress, Japan could be beaten in jungle warfare.

In New Guinea in 1943, Australian forces had the task of capturing Japanese bases on the Papuan coast, and so enabling the seizure of crucial nearby waters — the Vitiaz Strait, Dampier Strait and the Bismarck Sea.

The 1942 experience of fighting in jungle in the earlier campaigns in New Guinea had been a shock for troops in the AIF who had mostly trained in Egypt and fought in the deserts of northern Africa. However, by the time of the New Guinea campaigns of 1943 and 1944 — at Salamaua, Wau, Lae and Sattelberg — the Australian military was coming to grips with the tropical terrain, whether in hill country, mountains, river estuaries or grasslands.

LIFE DOWN UNDER

After learning the tactics of successful Japanese attacks, Australian troops began adapting and using the same tactics: '*Bush-bashing*' (beating a path through the thick jungle) round the enemy flanks was used effectively, as was continual infiltration and penetration of enemy lines. Junior commanders began exercising increased responsibility as units operating in the field became more dispersed in their operations. Commanding officers became better at delegating autonomous roles to these junior commanders, and better at taking feedback from immediate subordinates. The mentality underlying Australian operations became more fluid and flexible, as the Australian divisions began to establish tactical dominance over Japanese forces.

At the same time, Australia began to enjoy material dominance as well. By the time of the New Guinea offensives of 1943 and 1944, Australian troops were better supplied than the enemy (using innovations such as dropping supplies in with parachutes), and had superior numbers as well. In early 1943, six infantry divisions — three AIF and three militia — were restructured as 'jungle' divisions. The amount of artillery and vehicles was reduced (not many roads in the jungle) and everything not essential for general operations in jungle conditions was eliminated.

Petering into significance

The upside of having America on Australia's side was clear, but the downsides were notable as well. Any alliance with an emerging superpower was always going to be a highly unequal partnership. General MacArthur proved a great wartime leader to have onside for as long as his ambitions, America's wishes and Australia's needs were all in sync — which they were for most of 1942 and 1943. But from 1944, as the advance on Japan picked up pace, MacArthur made sure that only American forces were used — and would get the credit — for the frontline re-conquests. Unlike its dealings with Britain, where the War Cabinet often accepted Australian input, Australia was largely shut out of the real planning and decision-making that was taking place at the apex of power.

From April 1944, Australian troops no longer had any great importance to MacArthur. Whereas initially he'd had to rely almost entirely on Australian troops, plenty of American divisions were now at his disposal. He began landing American troops well in advance of Australian troops and sending Australian troops on mopping-up operations against Japanese forces that had been effectively knocked out of the active theatre of war.

In 1945, Australians were part of the campaign to take Java and Borneo. They were also involved in clearing the Japanese from Australian-mandated territory — Bougainville, New Britain and the Aitape–Wewak region of New Guinea. By this time, the Australian Military Forces (or AMF — the combined forces of the AIF and the Australian militia) had emerged as one of the most capable and effective jungle fighting armies in the world. The Japanese had been defeated by them in every campaign since 1943, and the British Army were eager to get AMF expertise for jungle warfare at any opportunity.

Bob Menzies (who was leader of the federal opposition at the time, after losing power in 1941) said the 1945 campaigns had 'no relation to any first-class strategic objective in this war'. He was right. But Australian Prime Minister John Curtin wanted to make sure that Australia had some say in how the postwar Pacific was to be dealt with — and fighting was the chief way of ensuring this, even if the fighting was strategically useless. Curtin claimed, 'Australians wish to have a say in how the Pacific area is to be managed, and we realise that the extent of our say will be in proportion, not to the amount of wheat, meat or clothes we produce to support the forces of other nations [like, for instance, America], but the amount of fighting we do'.

Curtin's claims made perfect sense on a geo-political level, but for the troops on the ground it was hard fighting battles that were ultimately pointless. It was also not great for morale for battlefield commanders to receive — as actual battle directions — instructions from army leaders such as, 'Take your time. There's no hurry'.

Tackling Issues on the Home Front

The biggest changes for most Australians during World War II were on the home front. For the first time, the whole economy was converted to production for war needs. Heavy industry was developed for the production of weapons, and leading businessmen and industrial bigwigs were brought in to oversee centrally planned industry. Rationing and control was built up under new government bureaucracies, women flooded the workplace and a new tax system was brought in.

Industrialisation and business expansion

In the late 1930s, heavy manufacturing started to become more important to the Australian economy. During World War II, this sort of manufacturing became the new kingpin, as Australian factories started producing automobiles, chemicals, electrical products, iron and steel.

War was the pivot in Australia's economic transition to manufacturing. A combination of new military requirements and needing to fill the gap left by overseas imports (which during the war were no longer reaching the country) meant new industries were developed or boosted. Great improvements were made in output, technical capacity and management of all different levels of production (from the factory floor to investment management divisions).

INDUSTRIALISTS IN POLITICAL POWER

A highly creative blend of business industrialists and politicians were in government planning during the war period. General Motors-Holden's managing director Larry Hartnett was appointed Director of Ordinance in the Department of Munitions, and BHP heavyweight Essington Lewis became Director-General of the same department.

These 'new industrialists' were determined to transform the whole Australian economy and ensure that it had the sort of heavy industrial base that other modern countries had. Clearly an element of self-interest motivated their arguments, yet a strongly nationalist theme was also apparent in their ideas and rhetoric, and they found themselves gravitating to the nationalist Labor Party instead of what you might consider their 'natural' political allies, the liberals and conservatives. These industrialists wanted a home-grown aircraft industry and less reliance on the British navy as much as they sought a breaking down of Australia's dependence on British imports.

HISTORICAL ROOTS

The new focus on manufacturing would put Australia in good stead for the post-war years, as skills were acquired, big plants established and multinationals moved in with big investments of capital to help expansion. For the first time, manufacturing productivity per worker was greater than that on farms. (See Chapter 18 for more on the long boom conditions that began in the 1950s, and manufacturing's role in the prosperity.)

Rationing and control

As the whole nation applied itself to the fighting of war, a shift from meeting peacetime needs to meeting wartime needs took place in the Australian economy. This shift involved government intervention to cut back production for consumer demands — in a word, *rationing*. Aside from the governmental mechanisms to make this happen, ordinary people had to be persuaded that rationing was a good thing. The federal government swung its publicity machine into action, creating propaganda to encourage people to embrace these new restrictions with enthusiasm.

In October 1940, petrol rationing was introduced. In June 1941, Menzies got back from a few months in Britain, convinced that things were serious and that Australians weren't worried enough about the threat posed by global war. He declared Australia to be on a total war footing and announced new measures to

>> Control shipping, road and rail

>> Further restrict petrol use for civilian purposes

>> Increase defence measures

>> Increase the workforce with women and others who weren't enlisted

In 1941, the new Labor Government inherited these measures to create a thorough system of rationing to control what was made and built, but the implementation of these measures was quite shambolic. The scheme was overseen by the Tariff Board, with heads of different government departments unaware of what it was designed to achieve let alone how it would be implemented.

Prime Minister Curtin appointed a new Director of Rationing (Herbert 'Nugget' Coombs; see Chapter 17 for more on Coombs) who got in touch with economic planners in Britain who had been tackling the same problems, and grabbed as many available thinkers and bureaucrats as he could to get things moving.

The policies produced by Coombs and his team worked. Coupons for food and other commodities were introduced as the production of many items, including beer, was limited. Company profits were restricted to 4 per cent per annum, with prices controlled to ensure this happened. In February 1942, the Prohibition of Non-Essential Production Order was introduced, which listed the articles now forbidden to be produced. In September 1942, the Curtin Government launched the first of a series of 'austerity' campaigns, linking the idea of austerity at home with helping the war effort abroad.

Coombs and his team did such a good job of developing wartime policies — and then selling those policies to Australians — that Prime Minister Curtin took the stopgap team of publicists, academics and bureaucrats and made them the core of what would become the most significant governmental shaper of subsequent decades of Australian life: The Department of Post-War Reconstruction (see Chapter 17).

Women in war times

During the war, as men were leaving for fighting overseas, many women entered newly opened positions, both in the armed forces and at home.

In April 1941, the Minister for the Navy (Billy Hughes, who had been Australian prime minister in World War I) decided to let women be employed as telegraphists in the Royal Australian Navy. Soon after this, a Women's Royal Australian Naval Service was formed. In August 1941, the Australian Women's Army Service was created, and by 1945 it numbered some 25,000.

Women also stepped in to fill the gap left by men in industries at home. Women tram conductors began working in August 1941 and other industries followed.

In 1942, Labor Prime Minister John Curtin established the Women's Employment Board to regulate wages and conditions for women doing 'men's work' for the duration of the war.

For the first time in many industries, women during World War II were getting paid at equal rates to men — which meant that women's pay effectively doubled.

Taxing everyone and building a welfare system

As well as introducing rationing and implementing more control of everyday life (refer to the earlier section 'Rationing and control'), Curtin also introduced new tax and welfare measures during the war that would have far-reaching effects on the lives of all Australians for years to come.

In April 1943, a new federal income tax system was introduced, with 'pay as you go' instalments deducted from each wage payment. This tax was in addition to the extra Wartime Tax that all companies were already paying. The tax system was new in two ways. Firstly, it was a move made by the Commonwealth to take away the state's power to raise income tax. Secondly, income tax was now applied not just to the middle class, but to workers as well — and this from the party of the workers, Labor!

Because it was wartime, and because the Commonwealth promised big revenue returns to the states, the states were in a position where they couldn't really persist with their income taxes. Little fuss was made, but the designers of the Constitution and the Federation-era politicians would have been shocked if they were still around to see it (not many were). Raising income tax had always been assumed as a basic plank of the states' rights, and now it was gone. This was the decisive moment in state–Commonwealth relations for the entire 20th century. After this, there could be no mistaking who wore the big boots in the Federation house.

The main reason for this new taxation approach was economic — income had been shooting up in the boom conditions of full employment during the war, and the government wanted to soak up a lot of this excess spending power. If it didn't, too much would have been spent on beer and the trots! Inflation was proving a problem, and all resources that could be redirected to serve the war economy should be made to do so. However, the new taxation approach also meant Labor could implement a system based on another of its core goals — building a welfare safety net for all citizens.

Previous to World War II, Labor's policy on introducing welfare was simple — 'the rich should pay'. A welfare scheme put forward by ex-Labor prime minister Joe

Lyons in 1938 had been knocked back by Labor because it proposed to tax everyone — workers, the middle class and the rich. In 1943, however, the Labor Government under Prime Minister John Curtin and Treasurer Ben Chifley did just that.

IN THEIR WORDS

In February 1943, Chifley announced plans for the new tax and for a new welfare state in order to build 'a better future for the world . . . [to secure] for all . . . improved labour standards, economic advancement and social security'. Chifley's announcement was immediately denounced by one of Labor's own senators, Don Cameron, who called it 'a confidence trick . . . which won't mean any increased purchasing power for the working masses', and the Melbourne Trades Hall Council debated whether to support or attack this new change in Labor policy. Chifley's response was to deny the accusation that he was selling out the working class by taxing them. 'If there is to be a universal right to all the benefits, then there should be a universal contribution, and I have no doubt that in time this form and system . . . will be applied in most countries of the world.'

Chifley, and Curtin's Labor Government, was right. Under pressures of inflation and the demands of a wartime economy that was straining at the leash, the welfare state was born. In the decades following, similar measures were applied throughout the western world.

IN THIS CHAPTER

» **Focusing again on innovative legislation**

» **Remaking Australia in a postwar world**

» **Ending the old 'Brits-only' migration policy**

» **Finding a new voice on the world stage**

» **Going too far down the nationalisation path**

Chapter **17**

Making Australia New Again

After World War II came the reconstructing. For Australia, this was more than simply reverting from a wartime society to the previous world of peace. Under new Labor Prime Minister Ben Chifley, reconstruction aimed for an ambitious remodelling of Australian society — one that would fix the problems that had led to economic depression and social disaster in the years previous to war. The massively increased powers given to the federal government during the war made sweeping change possible.

The first Minister for Immigration, Arthur Calwell, set about fast-tracking Australia's social, economic and demographic changes with a radical new migration program which — for the first time — encouraged non-British migrants to move to Australia in large numbers. In foreign affairs, a new engagement with world politics developed; Australia's Minister for External Affairs, 'Doc' Evatt, played a pivotal role in the formation of the United Nations, and leaders continued to question who to be 'besties' with (with Britain again coming out the winner).

This chapter looks at the rapidly changing world of postwar Australia. Not every change worked out as planned, but the postwar period had a huge impact on the Australia we know today.

Restarting the Social Laboratory Under Chifley

After World War II, the vision of Australia as a social laboratory in which society could be radically changed for the better — a vision that had been put on hold during the previous three decades of war, social division, economic depression and more war — became a real possibility again. The man chiefly responsible for seeing the vision become reality was Ben Chifley.

Chifley was born in the 1880s and could remember the great bank crash and economic depression of the 1890s (refer to Chapter 11). Growing up in NSW, he'd worked on the railways and eventually become a member of the 'labour aristocracy' — a train driver.

IN THEIR WORDS

Chifley remembered his time as a train driver fondly, saying, 'I used to get a lot of pleasure at night with 14 carriages behind me. There was always something fascinating about the eyes of 14 carriages looking at you round the bends. . . . I feel I have kept so close to engine-driving that I could go back to it tomorrow. You know, when you're driving an engine you've got a lot of power. They may question your decision afterwards, but, while you're in charge of that engine, nobody can!'

In government and as prime minister, Chifley proved himself to be a master when it came to driving the country's biggest engine. John Curtin made him treasurer and also Minister for Post-War Reconstruction during World War II, and Chifley soon became something more than the right-hand man. While Curtin argued with Churchill and worried himself sick about returning soldiers and the problems of fighting a war, Chifley had the task of keeping the country running. He did it so well that after Curtin died in 1945, Chifley was voted in by the Labor Caucus as prime minister, despite not being formally Curtin's deputy.

Most of Chifley's best work was done behind the scenes — before meetings, in meetings, after meetings, smoking his pipe and yarning with other members. He soon showed his capacity for real presence on the prime ministerial stage as well, overseeing a greater number of serious legislation in the parliamentary term of 1946–49 than had occurred in any parliamentary session since Federation.

The Chifley Government was elected in the 1946 election with a strong majority in both the House of Representatives and the Senate. Many of Chifley's plans had been in the works for years before that.

IN THEIR WORDS

Labor in the 1940s saw themselves as architects of a new society, as trailblazers in the making and unmaking of social conditions. As Chifley put it, 'I try to think of the Labor movement [as] bringing something better to the people, better standards of living, greater happiness to the mass of the people. We have a great objective — the light on the hill — which we aim to reach by working for the betterment of mankind not only here but anywhere we may give a helping hand'.

Labor's greatest achievements — and their biggest blunders — during this period stem from this one ambition.

Chifley's Postwar Reconstruction

Chifley got his start planning the 'new' Australia when Curtin set up the Department for Post-War Reconstruction in 1942 and appointed Chifley department minister. Chifley brought in the young maverick bureaucrat Herbert 'Nugget' Coombs from the Department of Rationing for the job of drawing up blueprints for Australia's future.

After Chifley became prime minister in 1945, the plans that had been developed by the Department of Post-War Reconstruction over the previous three years began to be put into action. The expanded powers of the Commonwealth Government didn't go down well with everyone, however, and Chifley soon found himself facing challenges in the High Court.

Focusing on public works and welfare

The postwar Zeitgeist was to use government planning to make society a fairer and more prosperous place for all. Prime Minister Chifley was determined to make Australia a new place, with more opportunities and better protection for everyone in it, to ensure that the various calamities of the past 50 years — economic depressions, world wars, bank failures — were eliminated entirely. Chifley embarked on a project to remake Australia and, overall, he was remarkably successful.

Some of the postwar plans that were implemented include

>> A set of public works to be initiated at the first sign of a fall-off in full employment conditions

>> A housing program to deal with the construction backlog from the 1930s Depression and World War II

- >> A policy designed to protect low-income workers and their families from the expected postwar leap in rents and prices

- >> An offer to ex-servicemen to upgrade education qualifications, attend university and improve technical skills

- >> The 40-hour week

- >> New dental and medical schemes, new hospitals and increased medical research

- >> The founding of the Australian National University

- >> A reorganisation and expansion of CSIRO

- >> The establishment of a national shipping line

- >> The establishment of a compulsory wheat stockpile

- >> The agreement with General Motors to begin manufacturing the first all-Australian built car, the Holden

Developing the public service

As Chifley's government ramped up its postwar reconstruction, so too was Commonwealth bureaucracy transformed and rapidly expanded, opening up new opportunities in the public service. This meant that plenty of young intellectual talent entered the public service and went straight into elevated positions of authority, representing an influx of new ideas and energy that hasn't been seen in government departments before or since. More than any other department, these new recruits gravitated to Chifley's Department of Post-War Reconstruction, forming the 'Chifley brains trust' (what Chifley liked to call his 'long-haired men and short-skirted women') and shaking up government planning.

HISTORICAL ROOTS

By and large, this new group in the public service had been educated in the 1930s. During the chronic unemployment and destitution experienced in the Depression, their thinking had been sharpened into a determination to radically alter society, focusing on social equality and economic fairness. None of these people had been government bureaucrats before the war, and all lacked the traditional conservatism that public servants tended to have.

The most well-known and influential of these young people who were rethinking society was Herbert 'Nugget' Coombs (see the sidebar 'Coombs: Nugget dynamo').

Although in staff numbers the Department of Post-War Reconstruction was one of the smallest of all government departments, it had the most wide-ranging sphere of influence. Within it, the 'brains trust' dealt in research, planning and publicity — they came up with the new plans and ideas for the postwar period and then used marketing and publicity to sell them to the Australian people.

COOMBS: NUGGET DYNAMO

Herbert 'Nugget' Coombs was chief economic adviser to Chifley and afterwards Menzies, was increasingly interested in Indigenous rights, the arts and the environment, and was involved in the creation of the Australian National University as a premier research institution. As such, Coombs has claims to being, if not the most powerful, at least the most influential Australian of the years between the 1940s and the 1970s. He was as much an activist as an adviser or bureaucrat, and proposed many radical and offbeat ideas while at the same time ensuring consensus was reached and good practical decisions were made. (As a small man with a pushy and assertive nature, Coombs quickly acquired the nickname 'Nugget'.)

Like so many of his generation who would play a crucial role in postwar reconstruction, Coombs's intellectual training in the 1930s was deeply affected by the Great Depression. Beginning working life as a schoolteacher in country Western Australia, Coombs went to university, studied the economy and wrote a thesis on central banking. The seemingly dull choice of doctorate thesis was a direct result of his ambition to work out ways to permanently change the way governments, economies and societies work, and to put in place mechanisms that would guarantee economic cataclysms didn't happen again. In the Department of Post-War Reconstruction, he was able to put these new ideas into practice.

As Director-General of Post-War Reconstruction, Coombs's task was to oversee the drawing up and implementation of big plans to remake and reconstruct Australia after the war — all this despite his only previous experience of wielding executive authority being, as he put it, as a primary school teacher. This done, he busied himself in Australia's involvement at various postwar international conferences to redesign the global monetary order. The General Agreement on Trade and Tariffs (GATT) and the International Monetary Fund were created in the late 1940s, and Coombs played a part in the creation of each.

Coombs became governor of the Commonwealth Bank in 1949, which later became the Reserve Bank in 1960. He kept tight monetary control of Australia's economy for most of the 1950s, and then began loosening policy in the 1960s. In 1968, Coombs was elected chancellor of the Australian National University — which he had helped begin in the 1940s — was made chairman of the newly established Council for Aboriginal Affairs, and chairman of the (also newly established) Council for the Arts. In the 1970s, he became a strong advocate for Indigenous rights and autonomy. The old policy of assimilation had failed, he argued, and Aboriginal communities must be given 'unquestioned authority' in their own society. He died in 1997, described as 'a mobile sacred site'.

Increasing legislative interventions

Chifley's government brought in a great deal of legislation that aimed to increase the power of the federal government to intervene in the daily life of Australian society.

Legislation introduced by the Chifley Government includes the following:

>> Aluminium Industry Act, establishing a joint Commonwealth–state authority to smelt aluminium

>> Australian National Airlines Act, setting up an aviation monopoly under one government-controlled airline, Trans Australian Airlines (TAA)

>> Commonwealth and State Housing Agreement Act, setting up a commission to oversee the construction of public housing for rental not purchase

>> Commonwealth Bank Bill, giving the Commonwealth power to centrally direct banking and control monetary policy

>> Commonwealth Conciliation and Arbitration Act, entrenching arbitration as the essential mode of resolving industrial disputes, against militant (and communist-controlled) unions such as the waterfront and coalminers unions

>> Education Act, establishing a Commonwealth Office of Education and a Universities Commission

>> Pharmaceutical Benefits Act, giving people access to cheap medicine

Coming up against High Court troubles

After World War II, and at the same time as Chifley was trying to expand Commonwealth powers (refer to preceding section), High Court judges began to reverse an earlier precedent set down in 1920 in the Engineers Case (which you can read about in Chapter 14).

The earlier 1920 ruling essentially gave the Commonwealth permission to push the scope of its power to the very limits originally set down in the Constitution. From 1946 on, High Court judges began to set aside this ruling, and go back to an earlier interpretation. Known as 'inter-governmental immunity', this earlier interpretation largely meant that state governments had their own sphere of powers, and the Commonwealth should do everything to stay out of this sphere.

This meant that Chifley's Labor Government, which after the 1946 election enjoyed unparalleled dominance in both houses of parliament, began to find that its greatest obstacle was not in the House of Representatives or Senate, but among the group of judges whose job it was to interpret the Constitution.

Some of the major pieces of legislation passed by the Chifley Government but knocked back by the High Court include

» Pharmaceuticals Benefits Act (although the Pharmaceutical Benefit Scheme survived)

» Australian National Airlines Act (although TAA survived)

» Banking Act (which also helped knock Chifley out of government — see the section 'Treading on an Ants' Nest — of Angry Banks', later in this chapter)

Calwell and the Postwar Migration Revolution

In the 1940s, Australia experienced a conversion on the issue of migration that would change the basic nature of its society. In a 'Brits-only' nation with an anti-immigration stance against non-Brits that fitted with the fortress mentality of a small Australia, a new policy took hold, one that embraced large-scale growth and European migration. The new policy was supported by both sides of politics but it became the personal project of Labor's Arthur Calwell, the first immigration minister. Under his guidance, the migration project was used to not only fast-track Australia's development but also break the mould of old 'establishment' Australia.

HISTORICAL ROOTS

The one big migration scheme the Australian Government had been involved with in the first 40 years since Federation had been an unmitigated disaster (refer to Chapter 14). However, World War II had quickened everyone's thinking about the need to expand the nation's population. A paper prepared by the Menzies Government in 1941 gave high priority to postwar immigration: 'We must build up our population to the extent that we shall be able to defend ourselves, and also have a balanced economy'. This policy had been continued by the Curtin Labor Government, even when most were expecting and fearing an economic downturn at the end of the war, with heavy unemployment.

After World War II, two completely new factors emerged: The realisation that the required increase to Australia's population couldn't be met by Britain and a growing desire to create a (slightly) more mixed society.

Looking beyond Britain to meet migration needs

Before 1914, Australia had one of the highest rates of natural population increase in the western world — some 17 births per year per 1,000. This collapsed dramatically over the next 20 years to be 7 per 1,000 by the 1930s. Although population growth had picked up again in World War II (reaching 11.5 per 1,000), it was expected to drop away again afterwards.

Meanwhile, thanks to war and the real threat of invasion, politicians of all stripes were announcing that Australia needed to quadruple its population within 15 to 20 years, to get to about 20 million by the early 1960s. This was hyperbole (representing an increase of some 11 million migrants, more than double the existing Australian population), but it set the tone of the debate. Whereas all previous discussion of migration had been hemmed in by fears that too many new arrivals would mean fewer jobs to go round, now the vision of sustained growth and rapid development took hold.

Just one problem existed. The inter-departmental committees who were researching and reporting on this matter soon realised that there was no way in the world that all those migrants could be supplied by Britain, as all government-planned migration had been previously. If large-scale migration was to go ahead, it would require not just British but also European immigrants, who were quaintly titled 'white alien immigrants'. (It didn't even begin to occur to policy-makers to think about letting in non-Europeans.) Politicians feared this would be a hard sell to a populace that prided itself on its 98 per cent British stock and its almost entirely British cultural patterns and public institutions.

The solution? Don't tell the public! A public relations smokescreen was put in place, whereby new immigration minister Calwell could assure the public that while some immigrants would be needed from the European continent, for every one European ten British migrants would arrive, thereby ensuring the previous ethnic ratio would be maintained. This, however, was never remotely possible, and in the years that immediately followed the ratio was often the reverse.

Breaking the mould of mainstream Australia

Calwell, Labor member for the parliamentary seat of Melbourne, had strong incentive to become Minister for Immigration, and strong incentive for a heavily non-British level of migration. He wanted to do more than fast-track Australia's development — he wanted to junk the English Protestant culture that had become such a dominant factor in mainstream Australia.

HISTORICAL ROOTS

The 'social laboratory' experiment that Australia had embarked on after Federation had been built on a successful multiethnic consensus — that of 'Britishness'. Colonial Australia had been made up of traditional ethnic antagonists — English, Irish, Scots and Welsh — who had been thrown together higgledy-piggledy. Surprisingly, wonderfully, they had managed to get along. This had come apart during World War I, thanks to overseas events (rebellion in Ireland) and local ones (the conscription controversy), when Irish Catholics were accused of being anti-Britain and anti-war. The Labor Party split, lost just about all of its Protestant British parliamentary members, and became dominated by the ethnic and religious minority Irish Catholics (refer to Chapter 13 for more on this). Calwell, although himself — and like most Australians — a composite product of Irish and Welsh, Catholic, Anglican and Protestant, identified strongly with the Irish Catholic strand and became hostile to mainstream and establishment Protestant Australia. He came of age during this massive change in Australian life, and was deeply marked by it.

In 1944, Prime Minister Curtin went to England, where he declared Australia as 'trustees for the British way of life', and stepped up plans to recruit British orphans and ex-servicemen with assisted passage to Australia after the war. But Calwell (at the time Curtin's Minister of Information) was developing a very different idea of how to manage immigration. He wrote to then-Treasurer Chifley, telling him he thought Australia needed a Department of Immigration, and he was just the man to run it.

IN THEIR WORDS

Calwell wanted a 'polyglot Australia', more like the American melting pot society than the homogenous Australo-British. He told Chifley of his 'determination to develop a heterogeneous society: A society where Irishness and Roman Catholicism would be as acceptable as Englishness and Protestantism; where an Italian background would be as acceptable as a Greek, a Dutch or any other'. This, in Australia in 1944, was little short of a revolution in social attitudes.

Within a year, Calwell was immigration minister and implementing his changes. He established new Immigration Department offices in New York, Ottawa, New Delhi and San Francisco. He set off on a whirlwind overseas trip, visiting 23 countries (most of them in Europe) in just over 12 weeks, working out deals with governments and migration bureaus and getting the great postwar migration experiment rolling. (See Figure 17-1 for an example of an emigration poster from this period.)

TECHNICAL STUFF

Between 1947 and 1949, the numbers of new immigrants in Australia increased more than fivefold, from 31,765 to 167,727, and between 1947 and 1951, Australia received more than 170,000 postwar refugees from Europe.

Australia

land of tomorrow

FIGURE 17-1:
An emigration
poster from 1948.

Most of these immigrants and refugees were immediately christened 'Balts' by Australians — because many of the nations they came from surrounded the Baltic Sea — or just 'Refos'. Calwell, however, came up with a new name to use instead of the derogatory terms being invented: 'New Australians'.

LIFE DOWN UNDER

The radical new direction in Australia's immigration and development was never put to Labor Caucus, let alone the Australian people at an election or referendum. Even the 'Displaced Persons' program to accept postwar European refugees was agreed to only by Calwell and Chifley, and never taken to cabinet. A very good reason existed for this lack of openness and transparency — if asked their opinion in these cases, the Australian people, the Labor Caucus and cabinet would most likely have all said a resounding No to the idea. Yet despite this, the postwar migration experiment proved to be a big success, as most Australians showed a capacity for tolerance to these new arrivals (helped by a booming economy and full employment).

Within a generation, Australia had undergone the greatest ethnic, linguistic, cultural and demographic transformation of any nation in modern history, aside from the post-1948 state of Israel. And the dominance of British Protestant Australia was buried forever.

Shifting Balances with Foreign Policy

Britain's central role in Australia's foreign policy shifted fundamentally in the 1940s. Not only did the US ensure Australia's security in the Pacific theatre during World War II (refer to Chapter 16), but in the postwar environment, Australia's Attorney-General Doc Evatt also played a key role in the formation of the United Nations. Here, he advocated a greater say for 'small nations' such as Australia, keeping some distance from larger powers such as Britain, America and Russia.

But Australia was far from ready to leave the British embrace. Chifley made the economic and strategic support of Britain a priority in the late 1940s, at the expense of Australia's economy and his own popularity.

Giving a voice to all nations in the UN

Herbert Vere 'Doc' Evatt was Attorney-General and Minister for External Affairs between 1941 and 1949. Before that, he had been part of NSW Premier Jack Lang's Labor Government from 1925 to 1927 and then a High Court judge in the 1930s. In the 1950s, he would be Labor's opposition leader (after Chifley died in 1951), but it was his work as Minister for External Affairs in the 1940s that was the highest achievement of his career.

In 1945, Evatt went with deputy leader Frank Forde to San Francisco as delegate to the United Nations conference and, once there, showed Australia was capable of speaking with a voice quite distinct from Britain's. Evatt advocated that small- and middle-ranked nations should have much greater say in the new organisation than had been originally conceived by the major powers of Britain, Russia and the US. He managed to get greater powers for smaller nations written into the UN Charter, and was able to ensure a strong commitment to full employment was also included.

Choosing between America and Britain

Even though Curtin had made his famous 'look to America' statement in 1942, and American armed forces rather than British forces used Australia as a base from which to launch a counterattack against Japan in World War II (refer to Chapter 16), loyalty to Britain still loomed large in Australia in the 1940s.

LIFE DOWN UNDER

Before Chifley brought in Australian citizenship in 1949, the majority of Australians surveyed — 65 per cent — said that they would prefer to be classed as British rather than Australian in nationality. People stood up to sing 'God Save the King' before films began in cinemas, and at concerts, plays and sports events. Maps in school classrooms showed all the parts of the world (including Australia) that were part of the British Empire coloured in pink. The oath of loyalty at state schools ran 'I love my country, the British Empire; I salute her flag, the Union Jack'. The sense of British kinship in postwar Australia still ran incredibly strong.

However, after World War II, Britain was destroyed as an economic powerhouse and Australia was no longer able to depend on Britain for defence or trade. America, meanwhile, was beginning to expand its economic interests and investments, and its reach into overseas markets.

Which way would Chifley choose to go? Surprisingly, the fiercely Labor man with a streak of Irish Catholic belligerence chose loyalty to Britain.

Like most Australians, Chifley instinctively saw Australia as part of an alliance of British peoples who were stationed in different parts of the world. In fact, he managed to shock British cabinet ministers in London in 1947 when he declared that only the United Kingdom, New Zealand and Australia 'fully represent the British tradition and outlook'. At the time, the British Labour Government were trying to engineer a new vision for the Commonwealth, one that included non-white, non-Anglo subjects of the old Empire as equal citizens in the new Commonwealth, and Chifley's cheerful statement was about as politically incorrect as you could get. But most Australians would have nodded their heads in automatic agreement.

IN THEIR WORDS

Chifley's sense of loyalty to Britain was shown to be stronger than the attraction of a closer alliance with America when he asked, 'Are we to ignore the plight of the United Kingdom because some temporary customer [that would be the US] requires these goods and is prepared to pay dollars for them? Are we to deprive our greatest customer, friend, and ally of these goods?'

While Australians may have agreed with the sentiments behind Chifley's actions, they didn't always agree with the actual actions. Chifley's insistence on supporting

Britain involved maintaining petrol and food rationing in Australia long after they'd ceased to be necessary. Chifley argued that the more Australia restricted consumption of butter, sugar, meat, clothes and building materials, the more that could be sent to Britain. This proved increasingly unpopular and, ultimately, was one of the policies that brought about the downfall of the Labor Government in 1949.

HISTORICAL ROOTS

A big irony can be found in the perception of Labor versus Liberal governments in the postwar era. Chifley's successor as prime minister, Liberal Bob Menzies, was both renowned and notorious (depending on your point of view) for being 'British to the bootstraps'. At the same time, the Labor Party was renowned and notorious for being, if not anti-Britain, at least more independent in its policy. Yet it was Labor's most beloved leader, Ben Chifley, who wounded his own Labor Government by insisting that helping Britain came before meeting Australian needs.

Treading On an Ants' Nest — of Angry Banks

Labor had always dreamed of *nationalising* the banks (putting them under government ownership). This dream had gathered strength during the financial crises of the Great Depression, when many in the labour movement blamed banks for obstructing Labor Government attempts to improve conditions and provide work for the unemployed, through refusing to extend any more credit and insisting existing debts be paid back.

In 1945, a reasonably mild piece of legislation on banking introduced by the Chifley Government contained one inflammatory element — making it compulsory for all levels of government to do their banking with the government's bank, the Commonwealth. This legislation was challenged in the High Court and overturned. Chifley then decided to be done with half measures and set out to nationalise the banks. More than any other single issue, this move cost Labor power.

Taking a tentative step

The Banking Bill and Commonwealth Bank Bill, from 1945, resulted in some five months of debate in parliament before they were both passed into law. The Acts were meant to give the Commonwealth Bank more power as a central and reserve bank.

The Banking Act was challenged in the High Court by the City of Melbourne. The brilliant young lawyer Garfield Barwick made a case against Section 48 of the legislation, which prohibited private banks accepting any business from a state or local government authority. Surely, Barwick argued, that interfered with the states' 'implied immunities' doctrine, which outlined the states' spheres of powers and which the High Court used in interpreting the Constitution. The judges agreed with him.

Going full-steam down the nationalisation road

The Saturday after the High Court ruled against the 1945 Banking Act, Chifley met with his cabinet to decide what to do next. The High Court seemed to be saying the Commonwealth couldn't insist on what banking was done where, unless the government took over the whole field of banking for themselves. 'All right then', said Chifley (or something like it), 'how about we nationalise the blighters?'

IN THEIR WORDS

Chifley went round the table getting everyone else's opinion. Everyone agreed with nationalising the banks. Then they got to Chifley, and someone jokingly asked where Chifley stood. Chifley replied, 'With you and the boys. To the last ditch'. And to the last ditch it turned out to be.

In October 1947, Chifley brought the Bank Nationalisation Bill before the House of Representatives. This Bill proposed to make government acquisition of the business, assets and shares of private banks compulsory. When introducing the Bill, Chifley spoke powerfully, summing up the Labor philosophy for socialising key structures in the economy (which had, after all, been part of their party platform for decades). Chifley said the banks had been to blame for the unsustainable 1920s boom and the 1930s bust. Since 'the money power' was so great, he said, the entire monetary and banking system should be controlled by public authorities 'to meet the needs of the people', just as with the supply of gas, water and electricity. Private banks would be eliminated entirely.

HISTORICAL ROOTS

As leader of the opposition, Robert Menzies was in a bit of a bind. After all — who likes banks? Plenty of ordinary people had feelings towards banks ranging from the mildly negative to the vengefully angry after the Depression era. Menzies figured that a 'save your great friends, the banks' campaign wouldn't get very far, so he broadened the argument. Menzies declared that this was the thin end of the wedge — the banks might be brought under government control today, but tomorrow all the neighbourhood milk bars, farms or fishing boats might be taken over. No business would be safe. The banks were happy to pour money into this campaign as well, and promptly did so. But people didn't need much encouragement to be afraid — it seemed like bad old Labor was re-emerging with plans to make Australia socialist.

Ultimately, the argument was settled again in the High Court. Barwick, arguing against Attorney-General Doc Evatt, said that the crucial aspect was Section 92 of the Constitution. Put in place to protect the right to trade across states, Barwick said this was 'a constitutional guarantee to the people of a right of immunity to the individual against sweeping government action. It is an individual freedom to move from place to place and the section protects the right to conduct business across state lines'. He won the day. Labor appealed to the Privy Council in London, but they refused to overturn the High Court's ruling.

This final judgment was given at the end of October 1949, just days before the federal election. In the election campaign, free enterprise versus state control became a big issue. Menzies didn't exactly romp it in, but he won enough parliamentary seats to form government.

5

1950 to 2000: Prosperity and Social Turmoil

Discover how the second half of the 20th century dealt a completely unexpected hand that many in government had tried to engineer but which no-one was really prepared for as they staggered out from 30 years of war and economic depression — widespread prosperity.

Understand how prosperity led to social change and Australia was forced to change some outdated policies, with the White Australia Policy being discarded — eventually — and Indigenous Australians recognised as full Australian citizens with equal rights.

Examine the ways prosperity's end in the 1970s brought economic challenges, as the old mechanisms used to maintain economic welfare and progress stopped working and the 'fortress mentality' that had sustained Australian settlement was wound back.

Chapter **18**

Ambushed — by Prosperity!

By the middle of the 20th century, Australia hadn't experienced a period of sustained growth since before all but the oldest old-timers had been born — in the long boom of the 1850s to the late 1880s. The 50 years from the 1890s onwards had featured two cataclysmic economic depressions (1890s and 1930s), two global wars (1914–18 and 1939–45), and one decade of unrealistically high (indeed, 'unlimited') expectations fuelled by insanely high levels of government borrowing (1920s).

People emerged from World War II wondering where the next knockout punch was coming from, and Chifley's Labor Government spent the first few years after the war trying to prepare the country for it (refer to Chapter 17). Instead, Australians were dealt the last thing they were expecting: Sustained and sustainable economic growth.

One politician more than any other proved adaptable enough to respond creatively to the new phenomenon of material prosperity and suburban expansion. This was Robert (Bob) Menzies, founder of the modern Liberal Party. Menzies managed Australia's postwar surge so well that the electorate rewarded him handsomely — with 16 years of political ascendancy and power.

Menzies captured the heartland of middle Australia, the expanding suburbia, with policies and talk perfectly pitched to encourage and support young families busily establishing themselves in new areas. The suburbs themselves now included working as well as middle-class families, made up of European immigrants as well as traditional British-Australian families.

While things looked pretty rosy, the threat of communism continued to rumble beneath the surface. Menzies was able to use fear of this threat to his political advantage, and it caused another split in the Labor Party.

Economics of the Postwar Dreamtime

Australia in the 19th century had its long boom — from the 1850s to the late 1880s — and now Australia in the 20th century would have its long boom, too. This one had its origins and seedtime in the war and postwar period of the 1940s, and really took off in the 1950s and 1960s.

For the first time in its history, Australia was avowedly pursuing a heavy manufacturing industry, most of which was based in the urban centres of Adelaide, Melbourne and Sydney. For the first time also, a large-scale migration program was underway that concentrated on bringing in new migrants not for the purpose of populating the 'empty' rural interior, but to work in the heavy industries being developed. The bold new migration program begun under Calwell in the 1940s (refer to Chapter 17) was maintained and extended by the Menzies Government, ensuring that all the new jobs were being filled as fast as they could be created.

Developing industry and manufacturing

After World War II, heavy manufacturing became the new kingpin of the Australian economy. Automobiles, chemicals, electrical products, electronics, and iron and steel production all took off in a big way. The expanding manufacturing sector meant new factories opening up and new jobs being created. Full employment was maintained and unions and arbitration agreements made sure that wages were high. Many Australians who had come back from World War II and the continued surge of immigrants from war-devastated Europe took advantage of these favourable conditions.

TECHNICAL STUFF

In the five years from 1945 to 1950, the number of jobs in the manufacturing sector went from 751,000 to 917,000. By the early 1960s, about 400 new plastics factories (employing some 10,600 people) existed, along with 500 chemicals factories (employing 22,000) making more than 1,300 different kinds of chemicals. BHP alone expanded its employment from 16,300 in 1952 to 43,000 in 1962.

LIFE DOWN UNDER

HOLDENS — FROM FUNCTIONAL TO FANCY

Holden began in Australia as part of a project to establish manufacturing industries that could be converted to military and defence purposes in the event of war, which in the mid- to late 1940s was largely expected to be once again imminent.

Launching the Holden car in 1949, Prime Minister Ben Chifley said that establishing 'this gigantic new industry' was important not only economically, but also 'from a national defence point of view', World War II having 'warned Australia of the vital need for producing here the vehicles needed for transport in a time of crisis'.

Fittingly for a car that began as a kind of 'national interest' project, the early Holden models emphasised practicality. The exterior appearance had a simple, if clunky, no-frills line, while the fittings inside were plain. But the Australian buyers soon wanted something more. Despite the postwar rhetoric from government and manufacturer alike about these cars filling a utilitarian and practical need for the national interest, what Australian buyers really wanted to drive were big American-style cars.

Throughout the 1950s, as the initial war fears waned, the now attainable dream of widespread prosperity was reflected in the changing style of Holden models being released. The public wanted more equipment in their cars, such as heaters and radios, and more colour and style, and this is what they got. Out went postwar austerity and preoccupation with efficiency and functionality; in came an explosion of new tailfins and trimmings.

In May 1953, the 100,000th Holden came off the production line at the Fishermans Bend plant in Melbourne. By the end of June 1955, more than 2 million motor vehicles were registered in Australia. In a population of not yet 10 million, this meant that nearly half the families in Australia were driving cars.

While heavy industry, automotives and steel saw a surge in growth, the more traditional areas of manufacturing — tobacco, textiles, food and clothing, all of which required less technology, capital and accumulated skills — dwindled.

Accepting 'new' Australian workers

Australia's manufacturing surge wasn't the only boom going on. The population was booming, too. A high birth rate (see Chapter 19 for more on the baby boom) and large-scale immigration made for a population expanding more rapidly than most other comparable nations.

After Menzies took over government from Chifley in 1949, he left the immigration taps on. In 1951, Australia moved further away from a British-only focus for immigrants when it was a co-founder of the Intergovernmental Committee for European Migration. Soon after, new agreements were struck with Holland, Germany and Italy. In 1954, a General Assisted Passage Scheme was put in place to enable more European immigrants to arrive.

The Greek population in Australia grew from 12,300 to 77,300 in the 14 years from 1947 to 1961. Also expanding their inflow were Italians (who grew from 33,600 to 228,000), the Dutch (from 2,200 to 102,100), and Germans (14,600 to 109,300). And in 1955, the one millionth 'New Australian' — 21-year-old newlywed Barbara Porritt from Yorkshire — was officially welcomed to Australia as part of the post-war migration scheme.

Most immigrants to Australia arrived willing to work — and they found it. Immigrants could often be working in a new factory in one of the major Australian cities a week after getting off the boat. In contrast to their attitude in the first 50 years following Federation, unions were also keen to have new immigrants, because they'd been assured that immigrants would be paid at award rates and wages, so wouldn't undermine the established pay rate. On top of that, the newly arriving immigrants generally became part of workplace unions automatically (even if a lot of them weren't told that when they started), which meant more funds for union coffers. The Australian Workers Union controlled the entire workforce involved in the massive Snowy Mountains Scheme (see the sidebar 'Building the Snowies'), with union fees compulsorily deducted from everyone's pay packets.

Indigenous Australians push back against new policies

In the 1940s and 1950s, official government policy for Australia's Indigenous population shifted from the 'protection' policies established in the early 1900s to 'assimilation'. In some ways a significant step up from the quasi-apartheid of previous decades, assimilation would too become notorious.

The 1930s saw the first wave of Indigenous activism, as many campaigned against the policies of racial separation and racial discrimination conducted by state-based Aboriginal Protection Boards. (Refer to Chapter 15 for more.) By the 1940s these campaigns were starting to change reality on the ground. A mass walk-off from Cummeragunja Station in NSW in 1937 led to a parliamentary inquiry into the activities of the Protection Board. In 1940 it was closed down for good, and replaced by the NSW Aboriginal Welfare Board. The Welfare Board dropped 'protection', and racial separation, and adopted 'assimilation', with other states soon following.

BUILDING THE SNOWIES

The Snowy Mountains Hydro-Electric Scheme was the ultimate big-picture postwar reconstruction scheme, begun by Chifley's Government then continued by Menzies's. The scheme was built in the Australian Alps to provide electricity for NSW, Victoria and the Australian Capital Territory (which contains Canberra), and was the biggest and most complex engineering project ever undertaken in Australia, involving 100,000 workers drawn from 33 different countries. Enormous tunnels were bored through the mountains to divert the melting snow in the Upper Snowy River through a series of 16 dams and 7 power stations to the Murray and Murrumbidgee Rivers. As it descended, the water flow provided hydro-electric power and could then be used for irrigation purposes.

The full project took 24 years to complete, but the initial stages were opened through the 1950s, with the first major power station of the Scheme, 'Tumut 1', becoming operational in May 1959.

The leader of the scheme was New Zealand–born engineer William Hudson, who ran the project for 17 years from 1949, and personally toured European refugee camps selling the scheme and the work opportunities it offered to prospective migrants. The project was finally completed in 1974.

Then, in the late 2010s, the Scheme unexpectedly gained itself a new chapter, when the Turnbull Liberal–National coalition government initiated a new 'Snowy 2.0' project. The plan is to create a new underground power station, connected to two of the older Snowy Hydro dams through a 27-kilometre network of tunnels. By the end of 2021, it was the largest renewable energy project being developed in Australia.

In 1950, a newly elected member of federal parliament, WA Liberal Paul Hasluck, began to make blistering critiques of the brutish negligence of the state Protection Boards. He argued that, given how badly the states had mucked it up, Aboriginal Affairs should become a Commonwealth responsibility. He also advocated the new policy of assimilation, saying that all Australians, black and white, had the right to participate fully in Australian society, and certainly not to be excluded because of their race. In 1951 he became Minister for the Territories and took control of Aboriginal policy in the Northern Territory. Over the next decade, he drove a broad policy of assimilation, trying to ensure Aboriginal Australians could enter into Australian life fully.

In Hasluck's eyes assimilation was 'a policy of opportunity. It gives to the Aboriginal and to the person of mixed blood a chance to shape his own life'. This was an admirable change from the policy of separation that had preceded it, and it at least took as its bedrock starting assumption the fundamental equality of all human beings. But, on the ground, many of the local administrators and bureaucrats who operated the special Aboriginal Acts didn't operate with this bedrock assumption. The policy of assimilation became just another way of trying to push Indigenous people around, and trying to force them into changing their behaviour, who they associated with, and how they saw themselves.

In the 1940s, state Protection Boards had also started to issue certificates of citizenship to Aboriginal people. On the surface of it, this looked at least to be a good step in the right direction, ensuring that Indigenous Australians could now enjoy legal and political equality with other Australians. But in order to 'qualify' for this status and certificate, an Indigenous Australian had to 'prove' his or her good character in all sorts of ways which other Australians didn't. They not only had to prove they were of good character, industrious and sober, but also had to have 'dissolved tribal and native associations' outside of your own immediate family.

LIFE DOWN
UNDER

What this meant Aboriginal Australians had to do or prove to ensure they deserved to be Australian citizens is worth thinking about. Being fine and upstanding and sober and law abiding were yardsticks a significant number of non-Indigenous Australians probably couldn't brag about living up to. More than that, they had to actually deny, or terminate, connections with cousins, with uncles and aunts, with friends, and with neighbours.

As you might expect, most Indigenous Australians point-blank refused to do this. They didn't become citizens in a genuine sense until after it ceased to be 'conditional', in the 1960s.

Meanwhile, many Aboriginal people throughout regional and remote Australia continued to live outside of government reservations. In the Northern Territory, and in large parts of Western Australia and Queensland, they still formed the bulk of the rural workforce, as stockriders, housekeepers and workers on cattle stations and other holdings. They were systematically paid less in wages than white workers, but they largely retained contact with their traditional lifeways and practices. Crucially, their relationship to Country continued unbroken, even as they participated in the non-traditional, non-Indigenous economy. While these strong connections continued to provide the durable parameters of daily life in Australia's Top End, crime rates and incarceration levels were low, and alcohol abuse was also low.

Suburbia! The Final Frontier

Expansion from the inner city had happened previously — suburbs had sprouted in the 1880s and then again in the 1920s — but in the period following World War II suburban growth took on a momentum beyond anything seen before. Cultural commentator Robin Boyd said that people moving into the new suburbs were a new batch of pioneers, following on from the 19th-century pioneers. He was being a little sarcastic — it was Boyd who described postwar architecture as the 'great Australian ugliness' — but at the same time Boyd had a valid point. A new generation of young Australian couples and families were moving into areas that had previously been farmland, orchards and paddocks, and building houses and turning them into homes.

TECHNICAL STUFF

Home ownership in Sydney went from 40 to 60 per cent in the period 1947 to 1954, and was 71 per cent by 1961. In Melbourne, some 178,000 houses were built between 1945 and 1960. Practically all of the new houses were built in the suburbs of the major cities, and then occupied by families who owned them, rather than being owned by landlords and rented out.

LIFE DOWN UNDER

Owner-occupiers got to make their own decisions about what style the house should be built in, what to do with the backyard, what extensions to add as children got older and what things to knock down. Inside the house, the postwar manufacturing boom provided a plethora of white goods to purchase and fill the home with. If any enthusiasm was lacking, people only had to switch on their new television sets — advertising took off in a major way in the 1950s, with most of it geared towards the new suburban families, and it came through the box on legs that began to dominate life in the living room and after dinner.

Many families found suburban life, and the new communities it created, suited them perfectly. Others, particularly women, found suburban life unstimulating and isolated.

White goods make good friends

After World War II, life on the quarter-acre block became the dominant Australian pursuit. With the rapid expansion of suburban living came a concomitant expansion of money spent on white goods, domestic appliances, and suburban gadgets and tools. Refrigerators, washing machines, television sets and a family car all became well within reach of the majority of Australians. The world we now largely take for granted — of instant conveniences and household appliances — first took hold during the 1950s, as Australian production of household appliances increased enormously.

The raw figures detailing this 1950s growth in production are telling. Between 1950 and 1960 annual Australian production of

>> Washing machines went from 31,000 to 201,000

>> Refrigerators went from 150,000 to 237,000

>> Petrol lawn mowers went from 1,070 to an astonishing 246,000

These figures made for a revolution in day-to-day life. They were mirrored, or indeed caused by, an explosion in advertising. After a long hiatus in the 1940s, when the war period had curtailed advertisements' scope, advertising budgets increased through the 1950s to encourage the steeply rising consumption levels.

In 1952, £40 million was spent on advertising. By 1956, the figure had more than doubled to £100 million. Newspapers and radio, both long-standing sustainers of advertising campaigns, continued to run ads, but were both now outshone by what *The Broadcasting and Television Year Book 1958* excitedly labelled 'the greatest selling force ever discovered' — television.

LIFE DOWN UNDER

Waves of advertising took advantage of the demographic phenomenon of the 1950s — newly prosperous Australians determined to luxuriate in and enjoy their prosperity, predominantly urban and suburban in make-up, and increasingly preoccupied with their 'quality of life' rather than simple survival.

New neighbourhoods and isolation

The rapidly expanding suburbs were often raw and without basic infrastructure — paved roads and deep drainage for sewerage sometimes lagged behind for years. But most people's experience of this new frontier of expanding suburbia was broadly positive. Moving out of the older suburbs, families met as neighbours in need of each other, and many made friends locally to help get over the initial hardships.

Without established communities or government to do things for them, people formed neighbourhood groups and new communities to do it themselves. Young, nuclear families spent much of their weekends organising and working on committees at local school halls, churches, Scouts and Girl Guides, and at football, netball and cricket teams.

LIFE DOWN UNDER

The 1950s and early 1960s saw a greater division of labour between men and women than has been seen in Australia before or since. For most of the week during the day, the new suburbs were populated largely by young mothers, because most men travelled into the city and to jobs that paid well enough to support the family. Many of the women had been in work during and immediately after the war, but were now involved fully in the life of the family home.

For some women, having many other young women on the same street all working in the domestic sphere was a source of reassurance. For others, it was deeply depressing. New suburban houses on large blocks away from old, established neighbourhoods bred new pockets of isolation and loneliness. More than one housewife would have thought there must be more to life than this as she bent over at the sink doing yet another round of dishes.

LIFE DOWN
UNDER

The effect of this isolation in new suburban life was clearly shown in the problematic use of Bex — a strong compound analgesic made up of aspirin, phenacetin and caffeine. Bex was marketed as a suburban 'pick-me-up', aimed chiefly at wives and mothers who might be feeling run-down. But 'mother's helper' proved highly addictive. By the late 1950s, the excessive use of Bex and other medicines like it was becoming a significant social problem. The Bex phenomenon offers a window into the underside of what at the time was proclaimed to be an era of sunshine and progress, and of happy homes and families.

The Rise and Rise of Bob Menzies

Bob Menzies was the political colossus of the postwar period. After being unceremoniously dumped from power by his own party in 1941, he began a long slow road of political rehabilitation that culminated eight years later when he was voted in as prime minister. On the way he'd formed the modern Liberal Party — still the major non-Labor party in Australian politics today — and devised an effective form of political appeal to the middling classes of mainstream Australia that would hold him in good stead for the 16 years of power that would follow.

Menzies's political enemies and detractors put his political success down to a cunning capacity for encouraging paranoia about the communist threat. However, you don't put together the longest period of one-government rule in Australia's history by virtue of tricks and cunning alone. Many of his policies were geared towards families who were establishing themselves in the new suburbs, and a lot of his best achievements were underpinned by governmental qualities that don't sound overly sexy — competence, stability and basic good sense — but were exactly the qualities needed for economic prosperity to flourish. Menzies also cemented his popularity through appealing to women, and left a lasting legacy for every Liberal prime minister who followed.

Appealing to 'the forgotten people'

After losing office in 1941, Bob Menzies spent a while licking his wounds — 'I think I'll lie down and bleed awhile', he was reported as saying — but in the following year, he began a series of radio broadcasts that outlined a new vision of central political values that would underpin his immense dominance in the years after the war. Menzies made his appeal to what he called 'the forgotten people' — the middle class. He said they were forgotten because they lacked the organised protection that the unions gave to the working classes, or the power and clout that great wealth gave the privileged and rich.

These 'forgotten people' were, Menzies said, the 'salary-earners, shopkeepers, skilled artisans, professional men and women, farmers and so on . . . they are the backbone of the nation . . . what really happens to us will depend on how many people we have who are of the great and sober and dynamic middle-class — the strivers, the planners, the ambitious ones'.

A large part of Menzies's success had to do with speaking a new kind of political language. Radio and television meant that, for the first time, politicians could give speeches that people could hear not only at the town hall or a local political rally, but in the kitchen or the lounge room as they sat around with the family or did dishes after dinner. Menzies adjusted more quickly than any other politician to radio and television, and his speeches and policies were perfectly attuned to this new listening environment, emphasising families and homes over workers and bosses.

Like Joe Lyons in the 1930s, Menzies made the values of thrift, independence and providing for oneself the main attributes of his political persuasion, and made his message connect perfectly with the rapidly expanding phenomenon of home ownership. The home, composed of independent individuals in warm, human relationships, was pitched against the dull, mindless regimentation of socialism and bureaucracy.

Appealing to women

Another reason for Menzies's success was his inclusion of women in both his political organisation and his policies. The Australian Women's National League — which, with 40,000 members, was the biggest non-Labor organisation in the country — was crucial to the formation of the Liberal Party in 1944, and pushed strongly for family-friendly policies.

On the condition that members were given guaranteed positions in the Liberal Party, the Australian Women's National League disbanded once the Liberal Party was formed. The alliance between the two groups meant the new Liberal Party gained all the League's organisational power, and its branch memberships and resources, while the League's main interest — advocacy for wives and mothers — became one of the core features of Liberal Party policy when it took power in 1949.

Menzies introduced big deductions for taxpayers with dependent spouses and children — a perfect policy for the suburban family where the husband was sole breadwinner and the wife the 'dependent spouse' — and extended child endowments to cover all children. These policies benefitted more than one million families, and were brought in (in the words of the Minister for Social Services) to help 'parents of families of young, stalwart Australians'.

Appealing to everyday freedoms

The Menzies Government took on the responsibility of maintaining full employment and providing all the basics of social welfare. In this way, it continued the pattern established by the Curtin and Chifley Labor Governments of the 1940s.

But the real departure for Menzies was in the strategies for expanding opportunities and freedom for as many people as possible to enjoy. The Chifley Government had been intent on promoting social and economic security, and looked towards the power of the central state to achieve this. This 'social democracy' approach was very popular at the time globally, and was adopted throughout Europe and Britain in the postwar years.

For Menzies and the rejuvenated Liberal movement, though, the key words were opportunity, prosperity and freedom.

The word 'Liberal' is itself based on the word 'liberty', which means 'freedom', so you can appreciate why Menzies and the rest of his party made a big thing out of it. But their commitment went further than name tags. Menzies, speaking at his campaign launch in 1949, talked about free choice, individual savings and hard work as being the bedrock of the Australian way of life. And he argued that the more control government had over people's daily lives, the worse off everyone becomes.

IN THEIR WORDS

Menzies argued, 'Every extension of Government power and control means less freedom of choice for the citizen'. Government activities such as the state control or ownership of finance, banking and other key industries meant a state-controlled economy. And controlling the economy meant 'controlling human beings', by prohibiting their ordinary exercise of free choice in saving, investing and buying things. 'The abolition of choice is the death of freedom', he concluded.

Menzies and his government were perfectly happy to use all the various established state authorities and institutions in carrying out policies — including the arbitration system and tariff protection (both described in Chapter 12). But unlike the Chifley Government, and the other social democracies around the world, Menzies and co deployed the different levers of government at their disposal to encourage private ownership and success. They did everything they could to ensure that people could buy their own suburban blocks of land and become home-owners, and give their children much more advanced education than their parents' generation had attained. Their focus was putting as much freedom of choice in the hands of ordinary people generally. Rather than social democracy, this was 'liberal democracy' — in other words, an approach that emphasised aspiration, striving, opportunity and the chance of achieving individual prosperity for oneself, one's family and one's children.

Since Menzies's time, Australia has seen other Liberal Governments, and eight Liberal prime ministers. Just about every single policy approach that Menzies adopted or followed has been changed, altered or completely abandoned. But the emphasis on ordinary freedom of choice for all Australians, on equality of opportunity in life and before the law, has endured all the way through.

GENERATION NEXT

With the victory of Menzies and the Liberal Party in 1949, a new generation entered parliament. Most of these newly elected members had recently returned from fighting in World War II. They were fired up by the possibilities of the postwar world, and they were attracted overwhelmingly to the Liberal and Country Party coalition rather than Labor. Once in government, they encountered the idealistic generation that had preceded them — the Depression-era thinkers, planners and bureaucrats who had been drawn to Labor's program of postwar reconstruction, and were now entrenched in the public service. These two different generations faced each other — and co-operated.

While the bright sparks attracted to Canberra in World War II saw the future Australia as best created by a Commonwealth Government with strong centralised powers, the new generation of politicians spoke about freedom of choice and individual rights and liberties. On the face of it, these two groups having to work together would seem to be a disaster.

And yet they worked together remarkably well. Beneath the political noise and bluster of the time, far more was shared between these two groups than separated them. Most of the main policies begun under Curtin and Chifley were continued and maintained by Menzies with little alteration, including

- The expanded immigration scheme

- Economic policies that promoted high growth and full employment

- High tariffs to encourage local industry and manufacturers

- Big nation-building schemes (such as the Snowy Mountains Hydro-Electric Scheme)

Tackling the Communist Threat

The fear of communism that continued in Australia through the 1950s was nothing new — it had existed since the early 1920s. But in the 1950s this fear began to take on a more all-encompassing, global tone. The world, most agreed, was now divided neatly in two: The democratic, capitalist west against the Soviet Union and China. An undeclared 'cold war' smouldered away throughout the late 1940s into the 1960s and beyond, breaking out into occasional spot fires such as the Korean and Vietnam Wars, which Australia was involved in during the 1950s, 1960s and 1970s. (See Chapter 19 for more on Australia's involvement in the Vietnam War and the divisive effect this had.) Suspicions were everywhere, with people on the lookout for disloyal Australians who might be on the side of the enemy.

For Menzies, the fear of communism chimed perfectly with his strong belief in the need to encourage individual freedom and opportunity against an interfering state — because communist ideology tended to produce the ultimate interfering state. Menzies even went so far as to try to ban the Communist Party.

For Labor, the fear of communism, and the way Menzies used this fear, wasn't good. It hampered Chifley who, while Labor Prime Minister and after, tried his best to counter communism inside the unions and within his own party. The communist bogey destroyed Chifley's successor, Doc Evatt, who lurched into paranoid conspiracy theories during and after the Royal Commission into the Petrov Affair, which investigated information about a Soviet spy ring in Australia. And the fear surrounding communism, ultimately, brought on another Labor split, which would be as damaging in its electoral effects as the first one had been in 1916.

Menzies tries to ban the Communist Party

Menzies succeeded Chifley's Labor Party at the end of 1949 with a policy of banning the Communist Party. Then, in 1950, the outbreak of the Korean War pitted Australian forces against the communist regimes of first North Korea and then China (see the sidebar 'Fighting communists overseas: The Korean War'). This naturally intensified anti-communist feeling in Australia. In 1951, the Liberal–Country coalition took control of both houses of parliament with another election win, after a campaign that heavily emphasised anti-communism. Once he had control of both houses, Menzies passed his bill to outlaw the Communist Party of Australia.

However, the road block of the High Court appeared, just as it had against Chifley's bank nationalisation legislation in 1948 (refer to Chapter 17), ruling against the Communist Party Dissolution Act. So Menzies took his anti-communist crusade to a referendum in September 1951, essentially asking voters to allow the Constitution to be changed so the Act could be allowed.

After his performance during the forming of the United Nations in the late 1940s (also covered in Chapter 17), arguing for a No vote in this referendum was to be Labor leader Doc Evatt's finest political moment. Evatt argued that voting Yes in the referendum would give too much power to the state. The new legislation would mean people could be accused and convicted of being communists without even knowing who their accusers were, and would take away centuries-old rights of law. Menzies said the threat of imminent war against hostile communist powers made the legislation necessary — 'to protect the nation against treacherous agents acting for a foreign power'.

FIGHTING COMMUNISTS OVERSEAS: THE KOREAN WAR

On 25 June 1950, armed forces from communist North Korea crossed the border with South Korea. The United Nations Security Council put out a request for help and the United States decided to send in troops to help their South Korean allies. Within a week, Australian forces were committed as well. The decision to send Australian troops was made by Percy Spender, the Liberal Foreign Minister, without any prior permission given by Prime Minister Menzies, who at the time was in a ship crossing to America for a defence conference.

Spender found out that Britain was planning to send troops to help America, and knew that after that any announcement of Australian troops would be hardly noticed. So he hassled the acting Prime Minister, Country Party leader Arthur 'Artie' Fadden, into announcing the troop commitment early, before Menzies could be contacted. Spender then took on the onerous task of calling Menzies to give him the news. Menzies didn't say much, but his furious silence would have spoken volumes.

Fadden's announcement was the first time Australia had committed to a conflict without waiting for Britain to move first, and helped underscore to America the value of an Australian alliance. The ANZUS Treaty (between Australia, New Zealand and the US) was signed the next year.

The UN forces initially did well in Korea, with a surprise landing near Seoul under General MacArthur. They pushed North Korean forces back into their own country and seemed intent on even possibly entering China. China had become a communist state the year previously and felt itself threatened. The Chinese threw their vast army into the war on the side of North Korea. Thereafter, it became a protracted war of attrition similar in many ways to the trench warfare of World War I, with neither side able to gain a significant advantage. Australian forces suffered more than 1,500 casualties, 339 of whom were killed by the time a truce was called. The war unofficially ended in July 1953.

When the results from the referendum were in, the nation was split almost exactly down the middle:

>> Yes: 2,317,927

>> No: 2,370,927

Three states supported it, and three states were against. The difference in votes was equal to about half the crowd at that year's Australian Rules Football grand final at the MCG.

A man called Petrov and another Labor split

Just as World War I had led directly to the first major split in the Labor Party, so too did the Cold War produce another major Labor split. And this split again meant the Labor Party was consigned to opposition for the best part of a generation.

LIFE DOWN UNDER

On 13 April 1954, Menzies told parliament and a listening Australia that the Australian Security Intelligence Organisation (ASIO) had been contacted by Vladimir Petrov, a Russian diplomat based in Canberra. Petrov wanted to defect to Australia and promised to provide information to prove communist spy rings operated in Australia. Menzies announced he would set up a Royal Commission into the matter.

The Royal Commission began its hearings into what became known as the Petrov Affair just 12 days before the next federal election. Clearly, the scandal of a Russian spy in Canberra now defecting would help Menzies rather than Evatt, who had already been criticised for being too friendly with communists after he'd campaigned against the banning of the Communist Party a few years previously (refer to the preceding section). Despite the Petrov factor, Labor actually managed to secure more votes than the coalition at the 1954 election, but failed to win enough seats to take office.

IN THEIR WORDS

Evatt now chose to appear as counsel for two of his own staff at the Royal Commission. His style of questioning and general approach was weird to the extreme as he hunted about for proof of a Liberal/ASIO/Catholic conspiracy regarding Petrov's alleged spy rings. Finally, the Commission lost patience and he was removed from the hearing. Evatt was furious, but others were beginning to wonder if he'd lost the plot completely.

A month later Evatt turned on the right wing of the Victorian State Executive of the Labor Party. They were mostly Catholic, and fiercely anti-communist.

Evatt released a press statement attacking 'a small minority group of members' in Victoria who had become progressively disloyal to Labor's leadership. 'Adopting methods which strikingly resemble both communist and fascist infiltration of larger groups', Evatt said they were intent on deflecting 'the Labor Movement from the pursuit of established Labor objectives and ideals'.

Some truth to what Evatt said existed — the 'Catholic Movement' had organised itself into cells to infiltrate trade unions to combat the Communist Party's cells. The Catholic right was making it increasingly difficult for Labor to manage its affairs, proving wilfully independent and hard to deal with. But by attacking them so directly, and basing his attack to some large part on his own paranoia about Liberal plots and conspiracy theories, Evatt was leading his own party into political wilderness.

In April 1955, at the next sitting of parliament in Canberra, seven MPs in the House of Representatives declared themselves no longer Labor Party but 'Labor Party (anti-communist)'. By the time of the next election, they were running as the Democratic Labor Party, or DLP.

While the immediate effects weren't as bad as the first major Labor split in 1916 (when Labor Prime Minister Hughes left the party and took 25 members with him, a large slab of Labor's parliamentary presence), here the main damage would be done at elections, and in the passing on of preferences.

TECHNICAL
STUFF

Candidates who were running as part of the DLP almost never had enough votes to get into the House of Representatives, so their voters' second preferences became crucial. The DLP directed their voters to give their second preferences to the Liberal rather than the Labor Party. This meant that a large chunk of previously solid Labor voters — most of whom had voted Labor their whole lives — departed en masse for the Liberals.

In September 1955, the report of the Royal Commission on Espionage was delivered. After 18 months of inquiry, the commission had produced information that proved important to overseas anti-espionage operations, but no hard evidence for Australia. No spies were announced and denounced, and no prosecutions were recommended.

The next month, Evatt told parliament that he had established beyond doubt that there was no Soviet espionage and infiltration into Australia because he had written to the Soviet Foreign Minister, Mr Molotov, and asked him so himself! This, in the ears of most Australians at the time, was bizarre — writing a letter to the foreign minister of the nation that was generally accepted to be the big enemy to ask him if he'd been spying on us lately seemed, quite frankly, nuts.

IN THEIR WORDS

Menzies, no fool, got up after Evatt's announcement and said that 'the right honourable gentleman, suffering from persecution delusions, is introducing us into a world of sheer fantasy', and called an election almost immediately to see if most Australians agreed with him.

Many Australians did agree. The Labor Party lost ten seats in the December 1955 election. Evatt clung to the Labor leadership for a few more years but his chances of becoming prime minister were effectively over. His health had been declining throughout the events described here — and both allies and enemies speculated that this affected his judgement. Regardless, his health certainly contributed to his difficulties. And Labor's problems continued for more than a decade after Evatt left the political scene. They wouldn't see power again until 1972.

IN THIS CHAPTER

» Letting go of Britain as economic and strategic security blanket — reluctantly!

» Watching as the baby boomer tidal wave hits

» Bringing in sweeping changes with Whitlam

Chapter **19**

Taking Things Apart in the 1960s and 1970s

The long boom and widespread prosperity in Australia during the 1950s and 1960s brought a whole new series of challenges. Throughout this period, it became increasingly clear that Australia's traditional protector and economic partner of the previous 170 years, Britain, was no longer willing or able to play the same roles. New economic growth and trade with previous mortal war enemy Japan and with ally America became the new focus.

The other big drama of the 1960s and 1970s was essentially the conflict between the old guard and the young challengers. On the side of the established power were Prime Minister Menzies, Labor opposition leader, Arthur Calwell, and even the entrenched members of the public service. On the side of the challengers were the baby boomers.

This new generation was predominantly middle-class and better educated than their parents' generation. They were the first generation to watch television, to go to university, and to begin their careers in a period of full employment and continued rapid economic expansion. They pursued a libertarian lifestyle that rejected many of the social models and mores of their parents. They protested against conscription and marched to end Australian involvement in the Vietnam War. While the earlier problems of ensuring prosperity and stability seemed to be resolved, new issues of social justice for Indigenous Australians and women came to the fore.

The first prime minister to harness some this mood for change was Harold Holt, who took over after Menzies retired in 1966; unfortunately, Holt drowned the following year. The next was Gough Whitlam. He led the Labor Party back into power after 23 long years in the political wilderness, and then devoted much of his brief period in government to implementing a generation's worth of change. Unsurprisingly, many people found this to be too much too soon. Simultaneously, the economic goal posts were shifting. The long boom had been going for so long that politicians, voters and social planners all tended to take it for granted. Under Whitlam's rule (and due to various global factors largely beyond his control) the music stopped, but Gough kept dancing — until the Governor-General turned out the lights.

In this chapter, I look at how postwar Australia grappled with the big question of how to proceed in the world when two of the overarching certainties and influences on life in the first half of the 20th century — British economic and military power, and the vicissitudes of world war and depression — had been demolished.

Moving On from Empire

LIFE DOWN UNDER

In the 1950s and 1960s, Australians still predominantly thought of themselves as British. Part of what they thought made Australia so good was its continuance and improvement of the 'British way of life', with its institutions, legal code, language and cultural practices that had arrived in Australia through the previous 150 years.

Yet, as the two countries changed, people began to question whether their relationship should change as well. Britain made the decision for Australia and ended the close association when it chose to enter the European trading market in the 1960s. Australia felt abandoned, and had no choice but to turn to other arrangements with other nations. Oddly, one of the most important new relationships was with Japan, the nation Australia had recently been locked in a terrible war with. Another nation was less odd — America, the country that had been called on for help during the invasion crisis of 1942. And when America asked for help in South-East Asia, Australia moved quickly to comply.

Still loving Britain

Britain was embedded in the political, social and cultural fabric of postwar Australia even as the two countries were drifting apart economically. This led to a desire to maintain the deep political roots that connected Britain with Australian democracy.

War hero Field Marshal Sir William Slim was appointed the new Governor-General in 1953, and was a wildly popular choice, chiefly because he was British.

Having Slim around reminded people of Britain's 'finest hour' of the modern age, when Britain had stood alone against the might of Nazi Germany in the early years of World War II.

In the 1950s, the British House of Commons presented the Australian House of Representatives with the gift of a new mace. The mace was a close copy of the original held in Westminster, and was, said the presenting British MP, 'the symbol of the Crown which unites our two parliaments and our two peoples'. At the same time, the National Library of Canberra purchased and put on permanent display one of the original surviving copies of the Magna Carta, the 13th-century agreement between King John and the English nobles guaranteeing rights and liberties, and considered one of the foundation documents of parliamentary democracy.

Queen Elizabeth II toured Australia in 1954, the first reigning monarch to do so, and everyone went nuts in a paroxysm of imperial loyalty. As part of her six-month Coronation Tour of 12 Commonwealth countries, the Queen spent eight weeks touring Australia, visiting every capital city except Darwin and taking in some 70 country towns at a hectic rate of five engagements per day.

LIFE DOWN UNDER

The Queen's visit was the last major public event in Australia before the arrival of television (in 1956, just in time for the Melbourne Olympics), and so people who wanted to see her had to line the streets as she went by. Practically the entire nation wanted to see her — a staggering 75 per cent of Australia's then population (between 6 and 7 million from a total of 9 million people) came out in person to wave hello to the Queen.

Losing Britain all the same

At the same time as Australia was declaring its love for Britain politically and culturally, Britain was becoming less important as a trading partner. Although the Imperial Preference system was renegotiated in Australia's favour in 1956, in 1961 British Prime Minister Harold Macmillan announced that Britain would be seeking full membership of the European Economic Community (EEC, a precursor to the European Union).

IN THEIR WORDS

For Britain, this move was a no-brainer — trade with the rest of the Commonwealth was declining, and Europe was expanding rapidly into an economic powerhouse — but in Australia, the reaction was deep shock. The Country Party leader, John McEwen, was one of the most shocked, because Britain entering the EEC would mean Britain accepting barriers against Australia's primary produce — wheat, wool and dried fruits. 'We were left without a friend in the world', McEwen said. The *Australian Financial Review* thought differently, arguing, 'We may have to stop thinking about Britain as "Home" and start thinking urgently about getting to know very much more of our Asian neighbours' needs'. This was a novel idea, especially for a country that still maintained an anti-Asian immigration policy.

Yet, the times were undeniably changing. In 1967, for the first time in its history, Australia decided not to follow Britain's devaluation of the pound, and Britain slipped to seventh on the ladder of Australian export markets. In February 1973, the UK–Australia trade pact came to an end as Britain entered the EEC. All previous preferential trade agreements between the two countries were now off.

Looking to Japan and America

With economic ties to Britain lessening, Australia had to look elsewhere. In a great irony, the enemy of less than 20 years earlier, Japan, was now one of the strongest options economically.

LIFE DOWN UNDER

In 1957, an Australian–Japanese Commerce Agreement was struck. For the Australian public, who still had images of POWs and World War II uppermost in their minds when they thought about Japan, this agreement proved a hard sell. But after Britain went after membership of the European community in 1961 (refer to the preceding section), public opinion changed significantly. The 1957 Agreement with Japan was renewed in 1963, and this time everyone greeted it warmly.

In 1966, Japan overtook Britain as a leading export market for Australia, and by 1970, more than 50 per cent of Australia's exports went to Asia. Japan replaced Europe as Australia's major market for wheat and wool in 1972.

Trading with America proved to be an easier sell to the Australian people. Rather than being the chief enemy, America was the nation that had, in most people's eyes, helped save Australia in World War II. Australia and the US also shared similar origins. Both had begun as British settlements and colonies, and America provided a template for what a viable alternative to Britain might look like for Australia. On top of that, with the Korean War from 1950 to 1953, the signing of the ANZUS Treaty in 1951 and the Vietnam War from 1962 to 1972, Australia's defence interests were intimately bound up with America. (See the following section for more on Australia's involvement in the Vietnam War.)

Throughout the 1950s and 1960s, America was a significant trading partner for Australia. By the late 1950s, the US had replaced Britain as the chief recipient of Australia's beef exports. When Cuba went communist under Fidel Castro in the late 1950s, America placed a trade embargo on the country, opening up a big market for Australian sugar.

Most of all, however, America was valuable to Australian economic life because of its large-scale investment. Australian postwar manufacturing and industry couldn't have expanded at the rate that it did without massive amounts of American capital being invested. By 1965, American interests controlled more than 90 of Australia's top 300 companies.

Defending Australia . . . with America

In 1962, Bob Menzies declared 'no country in the world more than ours needs great and powerful friends'. Ardent British imperialist that he was, Menzies didn't actually mean just Britain but also America. Britain, less powerful with every passing year, was withdrawing from the Asia–Pacific region just as America, engaged in a global strategic struggle with Russia and China, was seeking to fill the post-colonial vacuum. Bases to assist US communications and equipped with nuclear missile-carrying submarines were established on Australia's North-West Cape, and later a highly classified satellite ground station was set up at Pine Gap near Alice Springs. The alliance met with the strong approval of the Australian people — at elections it was a consistent vote-winner for successive Liberal governments in the 1950s and 1960s.

REMEMBER

The reality of being in an alliance with a 'great and powerful friend' can, however, involve following the powerful ally into regional conflicts and wars — if you're dependent on a global superpower for your security, you're going to find yourself popping up in all sorts of unlikely places. In the 1960s, this meant taking sides in a civil war in Vietnam, where communist and non-communist forces were clashing.

In 1962, Australia sent 30 military advisers to help train the South Vietnamese Army, signalling the quiet beginnings of a long-term involvement. In July 1964, the first Australian battle casualty occurred and in November of the same year, Menzies reintroduced compulsory military service: Men aged 20 were liable for two years' service if selected by a lottery of birthdates.

In April 1965, Menzies decided to send a battalion of combat troops to Vietnam. Although Menzies said this was based on a request from the government of South Vietnam, the real decision had been made in cabinet three weeks prior to his announcement and three weeks prior to a request from South Vietnam being made (and, even then, the request was only made after some behind-the-scenes prompting). It was agreed in cabinet that the US would appreciate a material display of support, especially as other large powers such as Britain and France seemed to be dragging their feet.

IN THEIR
WORDS

Arthur Calwell was the Labor opposition leader at the time, and fiercely against conscription — he had denounced his own leader, John Curtin, for introducing a limited version of it in World War II. Calwell made a prescient speech against Menzies's decision to send the first combat battalion to Vietnam: 'We do not think it is a wise decision. We do not think it is a timely decision. We do not think it is a right decision. We do not think it will help the fight against communism . . . Our men will be fighting the largely indigenous Viet Cong in their own home territory . . . They will be fighting . . . in support . . . of an unstable, inefficient, partially corrupt military regime . . . our present policy will, if not changed, surely and inexorably lead to American humiliation in Asia'.

Ultimately, Calwell's prediction proved to be spot-on. At the time, however, the threat of communism's spread further south and downward into Australia's immediate neighbourhood, and the desire to aid America proved powerful inducements to get involved and stay involved. In 1966, Australia's new Prime Minister, Harold Holt, trebled troop involvement to 4,500, which included for the first time National Service conscripts. By 1969, Australia had deployed more than a third of its available combat strength in Vietnam (more than 8,500 troops). Overall, some 60,000 Australians participated in the war, and 521 Australians were killed by the time Saigon fell and the South Vietnamese were defeated in 1975.

LIFE DOWN UNDER

FROM ROCK AND ROLL TO MERSEYBEAT

American influence on Australian popular culture was clearly seen in the late 1950s as the popularity of rock and roll music took off. In 1958, the first Australian top-40 chart of popular music was released. Australian Johnny O'Keefe released a string of hits — including 'Shout', 'She's My Baby' and 'Move Baby Move' — and in 1959 began hosting the show *Six O'Clock Rock*.

British influence on Australian popular culture wasn't completely done for, however, as the Beatlemania phenomenon showed. The Beatles toured in 1964, and the response to the English group was so rapturous it approached mass hysteria. In Adelaide, the band was greeted by the biggest crowd they'd ever seen — an estimated 300,000 people (about one-third of the city's total population) lined the 15-kilometre route from the airport.

For teenagers in the mid-1960s, the defining question of allegiance became whether you were a fan of the British 'Merseybeat' (and so a Mod) or the American rock and roll (a rocker).

The new Merseybeat sound had immediate influence on Australian music. By 1966, the Easybeats were making it big, and their song 'Friday on My Mind' reached number six on the charts in Britain, followed with other hits such as 'She's So Fine' and 'Wedding Ring'. Normie Rowe proved another hit with local Australian audiences, and his first three singles all made the top 40.

Was it worth it? Considering that after the fall of South Vietnam to the communist Viet Cong no other nearby nations collapsed into communist dictatorship, you'd have to say a resounding No. But there's no way of measuring what might have happened if there had been no holding operation in Vietnam, which delayed communist success by more than a decade. Then there was the Realpolitik — sometimes you just have to go in to bat for the superpower that happens to be underwriting your security.

Attack of the Baby Boomers!

The baby boom of the late 1940s and 1950s created a generation growing up in a new environment of prosperity. Whereas the varying fortunes and hardships of world war and economic depression had largely shaped their parents' outlook on life, baby boomers were the beneficiaries of improved standards of living and education. The 1960s and 1970s will be forever marked with the imprint left on it by this generation.

For the baby boomers, gaining a university education began to approach the norm rather than being the reward of an elite. The emergence of highly educated baby boomers in Australian society had a profound impact on entrenched attitudes in Australian culture, administration and government. Long-standing policies such as the White Australia Policy came to be seen as untenable in the modern era. Music, tastes, fashions and philosophies took distinctly new directions, and a new air of rebellion became manifest.

Ending White Australia

The greatest occasion of mass crowd hysteria previous to the Beatles tour (see the sidebar 'From rock and roll to Merseybeat') had been in 1919 when then Australian Prime Minister Billy Hughes had returned to Australia from the Versailles Peace Conference, boasting that he'd secured Australia's White Australia Immigration Restriction Policy. Crowds were spontaneously rapturous then, but 45 years later, White Australia's keenest enthusiasts weren't given to outbursts of spectacular emotion.

LIFE DOWN UNDER

Increasingly, the divide between those for and those against the continuation of the White Australia Policy became generational. People from all parts of the political spectrum who had reached maturity in Australia before World War II couldn't help but think that abandoning the policy was akin to national suicide. For the generation coming of age in the 1960s, the policy was a national embarrassment that needlessly offended most of Australia's immediate neighbours — not to mention the vast majority of newly independent nations in the Commonwealth (the new association that had emerged from the old British Empire).

Getting White Australia policies removed proved to be a long, drawn-out process that only succeeded as the 'new guard' began to assert their influence in both the Liberal and Labor Parties and in the public service.

In the red corner — the Labor Party

Arthur Calwell was the Labor Minister who engineered the great migration revolution in the late 1940s when he abandoned the established Brits-only migration policy, and opened the migration door to people from all over Europe (refer to Chapter 17). However, while Calwell was for a 'melting pot', he wanted the pot to only contain European ingredients. He saw the White Australia Policy as a vital plank protecting workers from too many (low-paid) non-European workers entering the country, and Calwell proved to be one of the fiercest guardians of White Australia, both in power and out.

IN THEIR WORDS

In the early 1960s, while the party was still in opposition, the younger generation within the Labor Party — including Don Dunstan, Gough Whitlam and Lance Barnard — tried to have a commitment to the White Australia Policy removed from the party platform. Calwell led a rearguard action against this move. 'Only cranks, long-hairs, academics and do-gooders' wanted to get rid of the policy, he said — Australian workers would never accept its removal.

After repeated attempts at successive annual Labor Party conferences, the White Australia Policy commitment was finally removed from party policy in 1965. And even then most of the old guard — such as Calwell and the immigration spokesman, Fred Daly — only agreed because they assumed that the change was cosmetic, and that the bipartisan agreement for Australia to maintain complete 'social homogeneity' would mean the White Australia Policy would continue to be applied in practice.

On the blue side — the Liberal Party

In the Liberal–Country Party coalition government, a similar phenomenon to the Labor Party experience took place.

The top bureaucrat in the immigration department was Peter Heydon, who had taken over in 1961. Having represented Australia in India in the 1950s, he was acutely aware of how offensive newly independent non-white nations found the policy, and he was determined to do something about it.

Figuring that a large-scale public debate and its attendant controversies would be counterproductive, Heydon, along with many of the younger generation of career bureaucrats, set about effecting a quiet revolution. By loosening the administrative restrictions to the point of non-existence, Heydon and his supporters dismantled the policy from within, even while denying in public that there was any intention of removing it as official policy.

When ex–world champion cyclist Hubert Oppenheimer became Immigration Minister in 1963, he worked with Heydon. In 1964, Oppenheimer took to cabinet a proposal to review the non-European elements of Australia's migration policy. The changes being requested were relatively small, Oppenheimer said, and would resolve administrative inconsistencies that would have to be dealt with eventually. Oppenheimer argued it was better to make these changes now, rather than being forced to make them later, unwillingly, with controversy and the opprobrium of world opinion. The idea of a policy review was supported by most of the younger generation in the cabinet but ran into a road-block — Prime Minister Menzies.

IN THEIR WORDS

Like Calwell, Menzies had been pivotal in ensuring Australia had made the great demographic leap postwar to allow substantial inflows of non-British migrants. However, again like Calwell, he was now very much of the old guard. To the objection that the White Australia Policy was discriminatory, he had previously retorted that it was 'a good thing, too', adding that it was 'the right sort of discrimination'.

Ending the policy finally . . . sort of

Despite the wishes of many, the White Australia Policy couldn't be abandoned until after Menzies retired at the start of 1966 and his long-time understudy, Harold Holt, took over as prime minister.

INSISTING ON THE RIGHT TO SAY NO — TO WAR

One of the most remarkable changes to the national psyche that baby boomers left for future Australian generations was the simple idea of refusing to fight in a war. For the first time in Australian history, a significantly large minority of the younger generation refused to involve themselves in a war Australia's leaders had committed to.

While pro-American feeling had helped the Liberal–Country coalition secure a massive election victory in 1966 and then a narrow victory in 1969 (on the back of ongoing support for American forces in Vietnam), from 1970 the tide of resistance rose rapidly. Opposition to the war crystallised when Menzies and then Holt introduced forms of conscription.

(continued)

(continued)

Conscription had a track record of fostering animosity in Australian life. The greatest social division the nation ever experienced had been during the conscription referendums of World War I, which led to a split in the Labor Party (refer to Chapter 13). In the 1960s and early 1970s, the opposition to conscription became far more generational. In 1970, marches were held across Australia to protest against Australia's involvement in Vietnam, with a large part of the opposition stemming from Australian males being forced to fight. Across the country, an estimated 200,000 people marched, with 100,000 of these joining the one Melbourne protest (see figure), making these protests the largest street demonstrations in Australian history. In 1971, Liberal Prime Minister McMahon announced that just about all Australian troops would be home by Christmas, and the new Labor Government in 1972 abolished conscription completely.

At his first parliamentary appearance after becoming prime minister, Holt announced policy changes that removed restrictions on non-Europeans, citing the changed international environment in which 1960s Australia found itself. (At the time, 12,000 Asian students were entering Australia annually to study, trade with Asia was expanding rapidly, military and diplomatic involvement with the region was becoming ever-more intricate, and tourism within the region was also growing.)

However, the bipartisan commitment to what Holt described as the 'maintenance of the essential homogeneity of its people' continued. In short, Australia was reserving the right to maintain controls and restrictions on migration flows, but was now recognising the need to do so with a little more nuance and deftness of touch than its previous preference for the ultimate in blunt instruments, the White Australia Policy.

No serious alteration in the proportion of non-white immigrants in Australia took place until the late 1970s, when a new social policy — multiculturalism — was established in place of social homogeneity (see Chapter 20 for more on this development).

Gaining rights for Indigenous Australians

The new mood in national affairs meant that the 1960s and 1970s witnessed two significant shifts in the way Indigenous Australians were treated. Success at a referendum in 1967 meant that Aboriginal people would finally receive equal treatment under the Constitution and under Commonwealth law. Simultaneously, a movement for land rights began to flourish, asserting that Indigenous Australians had special rights to parts of Australian land that all Australians should acknowledge and respect.

Riding for Indigenous rights

In 1965, Charles Perkins, an Indigenous soccer star who became Australia's first Indigenous university graduate, began a series of 'Freedom Rides'. Inspired by footage of American civil rights campaigners then being broadcast on television, Perkins initiated a series of bus rides to various parts of rural NSW, bringing public attention to towns where racism was entrenched in local practices. In one town, Indigenous ex-soldiers were refused drinks at the local RSL. At another, Indigenous children weren't allowed to swim in the town pool.

The Freedom Rides took place as a popular campaign to remove discriminatory provisions from the Australian Constitution was reaching its peak. Mass petitions were raised and public meetings held until May 1967, when a referendum was held on the question. On 27 May, an overwhelming 90.8 per cent of Australian voters said Yes to the question of finally including Aboriginal people in the national census and giving the federal government the power to make laws for Indigenous people (taking it away from the states). The referendum marked an epoch.

LIFE DOWN UNDER

Australia didn't change entirely just because of one referendum. The following year, Charles Perkins and 'Pastor Doug' Nicholls, two generations of Aboriginal activists, were refused drinks at a Cairns pub because of their skin colour. Charles Perkins came to the conclusion that while civil rights campaigns were essential, they weren't enough on their own.

'If we're not in Canberra, we're history', Perkins bluntly told other Aboriginal activists. What he meant by this was Indigenous Australians had to be involved in actual policy-making and government if real fundamental change was going to occur. Four years after leading the Freedom Rides, he began work in Canberra as Chief Research Officer in the newly established Office of Aboriginal Affairs (created after the 1967 referendum). In this role, Perkins began extended tours across Australia, talking and listening to different Indigenous communities.

At the same time another Indigenous man, Neville Bonner, had concluded the same thing as Perkins — Canberra was where the main game was if you really wanted to change how things were done. He'd grown up poor in northern NSW and regional Queensland, and what education he received came chiefly from himself and the books that he could find. He became a labourer and carpenter working for some 20 years on the Indigenous Settlement on Palm Island in Queensland, also becoming president of the One People of Australia League. He became the first Indigenous Australian to enter parliament when he became a Liberal Senator for Queensland in 1972. In parliament, he spent a decade arguing forcefully for Indigenous rights, land rights and environmental causes.

Pushing for land rights

In 1966, Gurindji Aboriginals in the Northern Territory walked off the cattle stations where they'd been working. The walk-off, which began as a protest against intolerable working conditions but soon became a nine-year struggle to gain title over their land, marks the beginning of the modern Aboriginal land rights movement.

The distinctive Aboriginal flag was designed and used for the first time in 1971 as part of a campaign to win recognition for Indigenous land rights. In December of the following year, protesters pitched an Aboriginal 'Tent Embassy' on the lawn outside Parliament House in Canberra. In the same month, the new Labor Government set up a Department of Aboriginal Affairs, and established a judicial inquiry into Aboriginal land rights. The inquiry reported in 1974 that, where traditional land ownership rights could be proved as enduring in Aboriginal reserves and unalienated Crown lands, Indigenous Australians should be given title.

In 1975, Labor Prime Minister Gough Whitlam flew to the Northern Territory and in a ceremony loosely based on the one used by John Batman and the Wurundjeri people in 1835 (refer to Chapter 7) poured earth and sand through Gurindji clan leader Vincent Lingiari's hands, symbolising the return of land to local Indigenous ownership.

In December 1976, the Fraser Liberal–Coalition Government passed the Aboriginal Land Rights Bill.

Fighting for women's rights

Women gained rights over their lives in crucial new ways as the baby boomers came of age. At the beginning of the 1960s, a new form of contraception for women — the contraceptive pill, or just 'the pill' — became widely available. In the 1970s, 'fault-free divorce' was introduced. Both measures gave women considerably more freedom in deciding what they wanted to do in their lives. Simultaneously, entrenched inequalities — in such things as pay and treatment — were being vigorously opposed.

The pill was a form of birth control that meant that women had close-to-complete control over their own reproduction. Now they could be sexually active without the constant risk of unwanted pregnancy, and could choose much more effectively when they did have children. This had clear flow-on social effects. Clearly, many women valued such a freedom, because by 1970 a third of all Australian women between the ages of 15 and 49 were taking the contraceptive.

In 1975, the Family Law Act was passed. Coming into force from January 1976, the Act established that divorce could be granted after 12 months' separation and 'irretrievable breakdown' in the marriage. (Previous to this, *fault*, such as adultery, had to be proven before a divorce could be granted.) A new Family Court was established, to apply principles of fairness and justice to people 'undergoing the misfortune of a broken marriage', and to resolve all related disputes around marriage, divorce and child custody.

LIFE DOWN UNDER

The long-term effect of the 'fault-free' divorce in Australia has been mixed. On the definite plus side is the simple fact that it is now easier for married couples who have since come to dislike each other intensely to get away from each other — or, indeed, for women trapped with violent or controlling husbands to leave. On the minus side is the acute grief that is often caused by protracted custody battles, as well as the loss of marriage as an enduring social institution, something stronger than the often passing whims of infatuation and personal attraction.

For women, the combined effects of the contraceptive pill and the fault-free divorce were enormous. Instead of marriage and raising a family being the only real option for women, possibilities started to open up.

Crashing — or Crashing Through — With Gough

In 1972, Gough Whitlam led the Australian Labor Party to victory after 23 years in the political wilderness. While Menzies had retired in 1966 (after 17 years as prime minister) and many substantial alterations had taken place in the years since, it was Whitlam's ascension in 1972 that broadcast — in loudspeaker, at full volume — that a break with the immediate past of Australia's history was being inaugurated. Whitlam described his approach as 'crash-through or crash' and his three years of prime ministership, like his six years leading the opposition preceding it, proved him right on both counts.

It's (finally Labor's) Time!

Gough Whitlam replaced Calwell as leader of the Labor Party in 1966, and spent much of the next six years seriously renovating the political platform of the party — getting agreement on finally eliminating Communist Party alliances and shared union ticket agreements, removing a stated and explicit commitment to the White Australia Policy, and dropping Labor Party opposition to state aid to independent (read Catholic) schools.

Whitlam himself was very much of the 'new guard' — unlike previous leaders and heroes such as Chifley, Curtin and Calwell, Whitlam was no working-class hero. Instead, he was profoundly middle class in origin, which made him closer to Menzies than Chifley in background. He concentrated on appealing to Australians who had largely left the class allegiances of traditional neighbourhoods behind when they moved into new suburbs after the war, and were more concerned about 'quality of life' issues such as health, education, urban infrastructure, regional development, social justice and equity.

In 1969, Whitlam recorded the largest pro-Labor swing since Federation — 7.1 per cent of the national vote swung to Labor as the Coalition majority was sliced from 40 to 7 seats. The Coalition only held onto power through preferences given by the DLP (refer to Chapter 18 for the 1955 Labor split and the DLP).

In the following two years, Whitlam managed to rub many on his own side the wrong way — Gil Duthie, the parliamentary whip, described him as 'tactless, arrogant, domineering' — but he had certainly cut through with the public. Opinion polls showed Labor was more popular than all other parties combined. Labor's 1972 election policy launch was attended by sports stars and celebrities, and Whitlam launched the most famous political slogan in Australian history — 'It's Time' (for a change).

On election day, the swing to Labor was 2.5 per cent, which was the smallest of any swing either way in the previous five elections. It was, however, enough for Whitlam to get over the line and win.

THE WHITLAM ATTITUDE: SOCIAL DEMOCRACY

The liberal democratic vision of equality developed by Menzies and the Liberals was a kind of 'fair field for all and no favour', where everyone could pursue their opportunities in life equally, and with no-one enjoying special legal or political privileges. (Refer to Chapter 18 for more on this.) When the same Liberal and Country Party coalition government, now led by William McMahon, entered a contest against Gough Whitlam's Labor Party 23 years later, Whitlam articulated a very different vision of equality.

McMahon said the Liberal Party approach was built on encouraging the 'freedom, the talents, and the dignity of the individual' to succeed on their own terms in society. Whitlam responded a few days later, at his electoral campaign launch, with what would become famous as his 'It's Time' speech.

Whitlam argued for a social democratic equality instead. He said it wasn't enough to simply remove legal and political inequalities. Instead, all Australians had to make a 'massive attack' on material and social inequalities too. It was time for 'a new drive for equality of opportunities . . . opportunities that this nation should offer in abundance for all its people'.

To realise this, Whitlam outlined a raft of new proposals for a more extensive federal government intervention into many more parts of people's lives — including in schools, hospitals, public transport, sewerage, pensions, universal health insurance and national compensation schemes.

At the 1972 election, a majority of Australian voters agreed with this vision of equality. Since then the pendulum has continued shifting, back and forth, as new generations and individuals embrace different views of what real equality means and what it should look life in Australian society.

The Whitlam typhoon

Once in government, Whitlam didn't waste time. Even before the government was officially sworn in, he formed what was nicknamed 'The Duumvirate' (meaning a government of two) with his deputy, Lance Barnard. They divvied up most of the large ministerial portfolios between them and got to work.

In the space of two weeks, 40 decisions were made and acted on. The actions included the following:

>> Conscription was ended.

>> All previously arrested draft-resisters were released.

>> Australia's previous votes on anti-apartheid resolutions in the UN were reversed.

>> The first steps to granting Aboriginal land rights were taken.

>> The Australian Arbitration Commission was asked to reopen its hearing on equal pay for women.

IN THEIR WORDS

Turning up for Labor's inauguration, old hand Fred Daly looked around and was struck by how different Labor parliament members looked — 'What a change from our predecessors: trendy dressers, bearded long hairs, short back and sides — you name it, we had it. "It's Time" had done the trick.'

After the government was fully sworn in, the pace was maintained. In 1973, Whitlam introduced 118 bills to parliament in the first autumn period of sitting (between February and April), and 103 were passed (the average from 1950 to 1972 had been 53). Parliament had its greatest number of sitting hours in 50 years. The number of Commonwealth departments increased from 27 to 37, and 39 new international treaties were struck.

Over the course of Whitlam's term:

>> All tuition fees at Australian universities were abolished.

>> Maternity leave was granted for the first time for working mothers in the public service.

>> A set of national awards — the Order of Australia — replaced the traditional imperial honours list.

>> A new Racial Discrimination Act was introduced.

>> A new scheme of medical and hospital benefits came into operation, giving Australians free health care.

>> The old Tariff Board was abolished and protective tariffs for Australian industries were cut by 25 per cent.

When it came to introducing reforms, Whitlam wasn't going to die wondering.

When the wheels fall off . . .

Under Whitlam, big changes were made in a short period of time. Even on Whitlam's side of politics, some thought too much was being done too soon. The amount of time that members of parliament had to spend in parliament debating and passing bills reduced the amount of time they could spend in their electorates explaining all the changes that were being made. In such a drastically transforming environment, where so many previously presumed certainties were being upended, this was risky. Combined with a rapidly deteriorating global economic situation, it proved to be fatal.

In October 1973, the Israeli–Arab conflict in the Middle East led to international oil embargoes. Oil quadrupled in price by the end of 1973, and the 'oil shock' effects were felt around the world.

In Australia, inflation was soon 'galloping like a Randwick runner' (in the words of old Labor diehard Fred Daly) and production was stagnant, making for a new phenomenon of 'stagflation'. Whitlam ignored Treasury advice and continued with massive high-cost projects — over three years, public expenditure doubled. While this was going on, some of Whitlam's other reforms were having a negative impact on the economy. The effect of significant tariff cuts and women being granted equal pay were felt across major industries — particularly textiles. Unemployment surged past 250,000 in 1975. After decades of the unemployment rate generally remaining below 3 per cent, in 1975 the unemployment rate climbed to 4.9 per cent.

Meanwhile, the Minister for Resources, Minerals and Energy, Rex Connor (known affectionately as 'the strangler' for his not entirely subtle methods of persuading political friends and enemies around to his viewpoint) had been negotiating for a $4 billion overseas loan to develop Australian resources — oil, gas and uranium. However, the difficult economic environment made raising this level of funds difficult.

Connor dealt with shadier and shadier characters in his attempt to meet the elusive (and, ultimately, disastrous) dream of securing Australian control over its own resources. Indeed, Connor's London-based broker and intermediary with Middle Eastern funds, Tirath Khemlani, looked like a caricature of a shady dealer. By this stage, Connor had lied to Whitlam — who had consequentially unwittingly lied to parliament — saying that he was no longer seeking such funds. When the truth came out, all hell broke loose.

The loans affair wasn't the only scandal and stuff-up that dogged the end of Whitlam's Government, but it was the biggest. After it came to light, the opposition leader, Liberal Malcolm Fraser, forced a constitutional crisis in parliament.

The opposition had the majority in the Senate, which meant it could *block supply* — or deny the government the funds it needed to govern. Although usually the opposition would not interfere in the government's mandate to govern, Fraser jumped at the chance to do so, wanting to force Whitlam to call an election — which a clearly unpopular Labor Government would lose. Whitlam refused and stood his ground. The nation stopped, and watched.

In the end, the impasse was resolved by the Queen's representative, the Governor-General Sir John Kerr. On 11 November 1975, Kerr sacked Whitlam and appointed Fraser the interim prime minister until elections could be held. Having already declared 'Well may we say God save the Queen, because nothing will save the Governor General!', Whitlam urged supporters to 'maintain the rage', and added for good measure, 'shame, Fraser, shame'. However, the election held soon after swung things decisively in the favour of the Liberal–Country Party coalition. Fraser came to power with a large margin.

If you're keen on finding out some more on politics in Australia during the 1960s and 1970s (and the machinations and underlying systems that led to Whitlam's dismissal), see *Australian Politics For Dummies*, 2e, by Nick Economou and Zareh Ghazarian, Wiley Australia Publishing.

Chapter **20**

When Old Australia Dies . . . Is New Australia Ready?

U p until the mid-1970s, an 'old Australia' still existed — a nation in many ways unchanged since the first decades after Federation. Even with the baby boomers and social libertarians of the 1960s, not to mention the Whitlam typhoon of the early 1970s (refer to Chapter 19), where everyone was loudly talking about change, a basic continuity with the previous decades still prevailed.

Economic policies were still geared to a 'Fortress Australia' mentality, wages were still centrally fixed, and capital inflows to the country were heavily regulated. At the same time, the old White Australia Policy was still maintained in deed, if not in word — despite prime ministers Holt and Whitlam both proclaiming the end of the old restrictions on non-European migrants (as covered in Chapter 19), the ethnic make-up of Australia's migrants was almost 100 per cent European.

Within 20 years, all that was gone. Migrants were now arriving from all over the world, labour and financial markets had been deregulated, and tariffs had been massively scaled back. Australia was an open and robust economy playing to its strengths in world trade. Simultaneously, fierce arguments were taking place about which elements of past Australian social and cultural values and practices should be maintained and which should be junked.

Ultimately, in a sink or swim world, Australia was learning how to float. In this chapter, I chart the way these changes were made, the dramatic and panicked responses they produced, and the ultimate effects they had.

The Coming of Malcolm Fraser

After demolishing Labor Prime Minister Gough Whitlam in the 1975 election, Liberal leader Malcolm Fraser dominated the political scene until 1983. Like Whitlam, Fraser was committed to making sure Australia played its part as a 'good global citizen'; however, his vision of what this actually meant differed markedly from his predecessor's.

For Fraser, Australia's global role included a strong commitment to the alliance with the US and to anti-communism. He repeatedly warned against the Soviet naval presence in the Indian Ocean and pushed for expanded American communication stations in Australia. Australia's role also involved creating a more multicultural society and a willingness to countenance large-scale influxes of Indochinese refugees from the Vietnam War — something Whitlam had made clear his distaste for.

ISSUING THE FRASER CHALLENGE

IN THEIR WORDS

In a public address made in 1971 (while he was languishing on the back bench after denouncing the Liberal leadership), Fraser summed up his view of the world, arguing, 'Through history, nations are confronted by a series of challenges, and whether they survive or fall by the wayside depends on the manner and character of their response'. The challenge for Australia, he said, was to continue to 'advance the egalitarian society, [to] promote equality of opportunity, [to] seek to relieve hardship, [and] plan to maximise opportunity'. The Australian response to the fall of Vietnam and its subsequent refugee crisis, and Fraser's establishment of multiculturalism as official national policy, would be an illustration of this. Fraser's ambition was to not just continue the bold social experiment of Australian life but also extend it to include not just white Britons, nor simply continental Europeans, but people of all races and all cultures.

Launching the good ship Multi-Culti

One of Fraser's greatest achievements was the active launch of a serious new social policy — multiculturalism — which managed to widen most Australians' circle of mutual tolerance beyond that of Europeans to include practically all ethnic groups in the world.

HISTORICAL ROOTS

In August 1973, Whitlam's Immigration Minister, the flamboyant Al Grassby, had made a speech entitled 'A multi-cultural society for the future', the first time 'multicultural' had featured in the department's rhetoric. *Multiculturalism* was a profoundly new idea — of finding 'greater strength in diversity' — and Grassby was loudly proclaiming to Asian nations that the old discredited White Australia Policy was 'dead and buried'. But the actual effect on policy and immigration was slight, as Singapore's Prime Minister Lee Kuan Yew tartly pointed out in the same month: Australia, he said, would take *skilled* Asians but 'not our hewers of wood or our drawers of water'.

Taking in Vietnamese refugees

Fraser was the first prime minister in Australian history to insist on and oversee a large-scale intake of non-European migrants. In real terms rather than rhetorical terms, the old White Australia Policy ends here.

TECHNICAL STUFF

By the time Fraser took over in 1975, the migrant intake had been slashed from 140,000 (in 1971) to 50,000, largely as a response to the economic problems of inflation and unemployment (refer to Chapter 19). Of this intake, only 1,000 were refugees. Of the top seven nations supplying migrants to Australia, not one was a nation from the three continents closest to Australia — Asia, Africa and South America.

Fraser restored the Immigration Department (after Whitlam abolished it) and returned to high migration levels, as new migrants from the Asian region began arriving. The first Vietnamese 'boat people' began arriving in April 1976, and the public barely noticed. In 1977, boat numbers grew and by 1979 the government realised it had a crisis on its hands. Fraser's solution was to stop the numbers at their source — joining with other nations to pressure the Vietnamese Government to change its approach, and agreeing to take substantial numbers of refugees from South-East Asian refugee camps.

By the end of 1982, Australia had accepted some 70,000 Indochinese refugees (only 2,059 of whom were unauthorised boat arrivals), the biggest number of refugees per head of population accepted by any nation in the world. In 1971, only 717 people in Australia were of Vietnamese birth. By 1981, this number had increased tenfold; Vietnam was Australia's biggest regional migrant source, with 29 per cent of migrants coming from there. By 1991, 124,800 people in Australia were of Vietnamese birth.

Fraser told his immigration minister that accepting Vietnamese refugees was an ethical obligation, arguing 'we were fighting alongside these people' (in the Vietnam War).

Implementing multiculturalism

Fraser also implemented the findings of the 1978 Review of Migrant Services (known as the 'Galbally Report'), which concluded that 'further steps to multiculturalism are needed'. For Fraser, the further steps included establishing an Australian Institute of Multicultural Affairs, a new special broadcasting service channel (SBS) that aimed to cater for a more multicultural audience (see the sidebar 'Introducing multicultural television for all Australians' for more details), and a government commitment to responding more actively to the needs of migrant communities of different ethnic backgrounds. This was a policy direction that the Hawke Government (which replaced the Fraser Government in 1983) would also adopt and pursue.

With the passing of 40 years, the introduction of a more multicultural form of Australian citizenship can be seen to have been remarkably successful. Since 1947, Australia has absorbed some 7 million new arrivals — the highest per capita absorption of any nation in the world except Israel. Today, one in four Australians was born overseas — compared to, say, the US, the classic 'melting pot' society, where one in ten people was born overseas. And while between 1947 and 1975 practically all new arrivals were from Europe, from 1976 the top nations of origin have included Vietnam, the Philippines, Hong Kong, Malaysia, India and China. Census figures show that by the early 2000s, the main countries of birth aside from Australia were an extraordinarily rich bag — Britain, New Zealand, Italy, China, Vietnam, Greece, India, the Philippines, Germany and South Africa. Given all this, the most remarkable thing about the diverse backgrounds of modern-day Australians is not the occasional flashpoint of antagonism (such as the ugly race riots at Cronulla in 2005) but just how little ethnic tension there is.

Fraser foiled! By shifting economic sands

Fraser provided a sense of stability after the tumult of the Whitlam years, but the same economic problems that fatally handicapped Whitlam also brought Fraser down. The long boom of prosperity that lasted in Australia from the late 1940s to the early 1970s was over, and the basic policy settings that had guided Australian economic life in this period were no longer producing the same results. Fraser's economic traditionalism, and his inability to fix the financial and trade problems that beset Australia in the late 1970s and early 1980s, ultimately doomed his prime ministership.

INTRODUCING MULTICULTURAL TELEVISION FOR ALL AUSTRALIANS

As part of the new policy of multiculturalism, Fraser launched the Special Broadcasting Service (SBS) television channel in 1980. At its launch he said, 'These programmes are not going to be designed for one particular cultural group at one moment, and for another particular cultural group at another moment, [but] designed to appeal to a very wide cross-section of people within Australia, designed in such a way that all Australians would want to see the programmes that are conducted on multicultural television . . . In that sense, multicultural television is not something that divides, that sets apart, as just a foreign language broadcast would tend to do, rather it is something that tends to unify and have people understand better what this Australia is all about'.

Fraser's economic policies seemed to imply that he thought the only reason economic bad times had hit was because Whitlam had messed things up. This was partly true — Whitlam and all except his last treasurer (Bill Hayden) set a new benchmark for fiscal irresponsibility — but it ignored the dramatic global collapse in areas that had supported Australia's long boom. Fraser governed with the expectation that the economy would soon return to normal with zero policy change away from the old orthodoxies — plenty of industry protection and corporate tax breaks, and no changes at all to central wage fixing.

Fraser tried cutting government expenditure and managed to push inflation down a little but in 1978 unemployment surged past 400,000, with the unemployment rate hitting 6.3 per cent in 1978 and 1979. Whitlam had made a dramatic start to dismantling Australia's trade barriers in 1973 when he cut tariffs by 25 per cent. In a bid to lower unemployment, Fraser increased tariffs again for the automotive, textile, clothing and footwear industries. In the long run this was a blind alley — it was left to the Hawke Labor Government to again wind back the protective barriers.

Life, Fraser had said in another context, wasn't meant to be easy. When it came to the economy in the 1970s, it seemed especially not meant to be easy, particularly when those in power and influence were steadfastly ignoring the writing on the wall.

Deregulation Nation

Beginning in 1983 with the newly elected Labor Government of Bob Hawke, a new period of substantial economic reform began in Australia. These reforms managed to produce short-term excess, medium-term crisis and unemployment, and long-term prosperity and success. The main changes were:

>> Financial deregulation between 1983 and 1985

>> Cut-backs to tariff protection between 1988 and 1991

>> Moves to a more flexible enterprise-based wages system between 1992 and 2007

Deregulating the financial and labour markets as well as dismantling the old protectionist tariff barriers that underpinned the heavy subsidies of 'Fortress Australia' radically reshaped Australia's trajectory in the world. These reforms took place thanks to the stewardship of three very different prime ministers from the two major political parties: Hawke and Paul Keating from Labor, and John Howard from the Liberals.

All three had to face down significant opposition from economic traditionalists within their own parties. All three produced compromises that ultimately helped to free up Australia's economic growth in a balanced way — making Australia far more open and dynamic than, say, the social welfare states of many European nations, while avoiding the harsher extremes reached by committed free traders Thatcher in Britain and Reagan in the US.

Welcoming in 'Hawke's World'

Bob Hawke was a larrikin — fond of drinking, womanising and hanging out with his mates. He was also an incredibly sharp mind and good advocate, winning a Rhodes scholarship and becoming firstly the Australian Council of Trade Union's legal advocate and then its president. One of the most popular people in public affairs in the late 1970s, Hawke decided to mend his ways and take a shot at the country's highest office. He gave up the grog and swore off the women (well, mostly), and in September 1980 retired as president of the ACTU to become a member of parliament for the Labor Party.

In February 1983, Prime Minister Malcolm Fraser called a snap election. Bob Hawke immediately replaced Bill Hayden as leader of the Labor Party, and Labor went on to a convincing win in the national election on 5 March. Hawke was prime minister for the rest of the decade, eventually being replaced by the ex-treasurer Paul Keating.

A gregarious egalitarian, in his time as prime minister Hawke built an enviable reputation for overseeing dramatic change without alienating too many people. Although by the end of his time in office he would be open to the accusation of trying to please and appease everyone ('old jellyback', Keating called him derisively), for the first few years Hawke built up a remarkable record of introducing massive changes through agreement and consensus rather than confrontation.

At a meeting of Labor's Federal Executive just before Hawke became leader, he wrote down on the back of an envelope three words — Reconciliation, Recovery and Reconstruction — and told everyone 'this is what we should go into the election with'. They did, and it worked.

Other key words in Hawke's platform included:

>> Consensus

>> Consultation

>> Relocation

>> Retraining

Striking an Accord

In April 1983, just a month after being elected, Hawke held a National Economic Summit in Canberra, aiming to reach agreement between unions, employers and government on the best way to proceed in fixing the economy. At the summit, Hawke reached an agreement with the unions to keep wage-claims down — the Prices and Income Accord.

The new Accord meant that the Labor Government and the unions now owned the domain of arbitration and centralised wage fixing. They used it to drastically bring down the number of days lost to strikes, produce more jobs and grow productivity.

In exchange for union restraint, the government pledged to bring inflation down to manageable levels, make room for more jobs and higher levels of productivity, and provide better services. The Accord worked — about 1.5 million jobs were created through the rest of the 1980s, and unemployment dropped from its 1983 peak of 10 per cent to 6 per cent in 1989. Periodically renewed, the Accord lasted for the next 13 years, and covered wages, taxes and superannuation.

Floating the dollar

In 1983, Australia's exchange rate, which had always been tightly regulated, was beginning to founder badly, unable to cope with the vast new amounts of speculative and investment capital that were washing round the globe. Speculators took advantage of Australia's fixed rate of exchange, pumping large amounts of short-term capital into Australia, forcing the dollar upward in value and taking the profits. Both Hawke and Treasurer Keating became convinced that it was no longer feasible to defend an unsustainable exchange rate against the market. As Keating succinctly put it: 'There's too much money out there'. The idea was to let the value of the Australian dollar float freely. This way, speculators would no longer be betting against the government, but against each other.

To the head bureaucrat at the Treasury — John Stone, the most respected Treasury chief in living memory — this seemed like pure madness. Stone argued Australia was a small nation that shouldn't be left completely vulnerable to the whims of global capital. Meanwhile, the chief of the Reserve Bank, Bob Johnston, argued the opposite. Between these two divergent views, another uncomfortable fact for Hawke and Keating was that their Labor Party had always been strongly against any deregulation of the fixed exchange rate.

Events came to a head at the beginning of December 1983. International funds poured into Australia to exploit another revaluation of the Australian dollar. The authorities couldn't keep the momentum in check, and looked in danger of being completely overwhelmed. In the week leading up to Friday 9 December, international financiers had targeted Australia with a total of $8 billion. The Reserve Bank's attempts to control monetary flow to contain inflation were falling apart, and the bank was forced to buy almost $1.5 billion in just a few days. The bank and the government could no longer maintain reasonable and sustainable monetary management.

On Thursday 8 December, in an argument that went all Thursday night and into Friday morning, Hawke, Keating, their advisers, and (on the phone) Johnston, all pitted themselves against the established economic orthodoxy of Stone. In the early hours of Friday morning, the decision was finally made. At 5 pm Friday, Keating and Johnston appeared together at a press conference to announce that the Australian dollar was to be floated and allowed to find its own value on the international market.

IN THEIR WORDS

It's difficult to overestimate the significance of this act, not only for the real and immediate practical effect it had but for the tidal shift in Australia's governing psychology. Johnston later unhesitatingly declared it 'The decision of the decade . . . It was the overt breaking of our isolationism. Without it, there is the mentality of living behind the moat. The float linked the Australian economy, for better or worse, with the rest of the world. It would teach us some very severe lessons but we [had] to learn those lessons'.

Breaking the protection racket

The Australian nation came into being in 1901 as a kind of fortress — psychological, economic and social. A key plank of this fortress was a wall of protective tariffs that meant that local industries, particularly manufacturers, could survive without being threatened by cheaper competitors from around the world.

HISTORICAL ROOTS

The cost of keeping other, cheaper goods and capital investment out of Australia became increasingly apparent in the late 1960s and early 1970s. When from 1966 the Tariff Board began to publicise the level of tariff assistance received by each industry, people slowly became aware of just how astronomically high the costs of subsidising industries were, and public debate began.

Although Gough Whitlam made a dramatic across-the-board 25 per cent tariff rate cut to all industries, it was with Hawke that the real and intricate work of long-term structural adjustments and winding-back of tariffs began.

Feeling the effects of short-term excess

In 1986, the number of Australian millionaires passed 30,000 for the first time. In the same year, Australia's gross foreign debt passed $100 billion. In the new era of deregulated finance, plenty of easy credit was available, and ordinary households eagerly took advantage of it — as did a brash new generation of entrepreneurs.

A pinch of 1980s excess . . .

After financial deregulation, an explosion of credit lending occurred. For the five years prior to 1983, annual credit growth had been 16 per cent. For the five years after 1983, it jumped to 21 per cent. Business debt increased massively and many households took out big loans to buy assets and houses. Two decades of high inflation made people decide that the best thing to do was gear up on debt and buy assets that would (they assumed) rapidly increase in value.

LIFE DOWN UNDER

Throughout the 1980s, larrikin, buccaneering individualist types took over the companies previously run by the financial 'establishment' and stripped them of assets. These people were brash; they were crass; they were — for a brief span of time in the 1980s —Australian heroes. Hawke and Keating loved them, declaring them to be the new spirit of daring Australians who were roughing up the old protected environment of the banking establishment. Australian people started to like them, particularly after one of them — Alan Bond — bankrolled a successful bid to beat the US and win the America's Cup yachting race. Others, such as

Christopher Skase of Qintex, and John Elliott of Fosters Corporation, became well known as well.

Between 1983 and 1987

➤➤ Banks kept lending

➤➤ Credit kept expanding

➤➤ Lenders were competing wildly

Add to that fast population growth and the larrikin 'buccaneer' mentality, and you have a recipe for a wildly inflating bubble.

. . . Followed by the worst and most protracted recession in 60 years

During the second half of the 1980s, manic excess took over. The shift from the closed economic shop of the 1970s had been partially successful, but the Labor Government had created an imbalance. Freeing up the financial market while leaving heavy centralised labour regulations and distortions in the real economy meant that, even with the increased credit, it was difficult to increase real productivity. But the government had lost any appetite for continued reforms. After the 1987 election victory, complacency had set in, and the boom went into unsustainable overdrive. Inflation started spiralling upwards.

The government's Accord agreement with the unions was underwritten by the commitment to be always pushing for growth: Real wage cuts in exchange for more jobs. This made it very difficult to slow things down when the economy was going too fast. Instead, the government tried an interest rate crunch. Between autumn 1987 and January 1990, interest rates were pushed up and up until they hit an incredible 20 per cent.

In October 1987, share prices on Australian stock exchanges took a record fall. In 1989, several large corporations — Equiticorp, Qintex, Hooker Corporation and Spedley Securities — collapsed, to be followed by others. The brash stars of the 1980s, such as Skase, Bond and Elliott, began to crash and burn.

The hopes for a soft mild landing proved impossible. Instead, an acute contraction set in — in other words, a recession. Both Hawke and Keating had boasted that with their brave new dawn of a new economic era, recessions were no longer necessary. Now they were humiliated, although Keating tried to brush it off as 'the recession we had to have' (which didn't go down too well with the electorate).

IN THEIR WORDS

A TREASURER EXPLAINS HIMSELF

Paul Keating was treasurer in the 1980s before becoming prime minister in 1991. Even his enemies (of which he had plenty) acknowledged that, in the area of selling the ideas of how Australia should approach the new challenges of the late 20th century, he was beyond comparison.

Keating's reflections on the effects of these big changes (made during an interview with Paul Kelly) are a prime example of his renowned wit and sharp tongue: 'What was Labor, in economic terms, before 1983? As a party, it believed in regulation . . . It believed in tariffs. We had abysmal rates of productivity . . . We had low profits, therefore low investment. We had high unemployment. What did we abandon? [as a nation] . . .

'Yes, we are less sovereign in some respects. We had the sovereign right to make the wrong exchange rate. We had the sovereign right to build a tariff wall, which made us poor. But are these sovereignties we really enjoyed? I don't think so . . . Would we wish today to be as we used to be, a monoculture, closed in by tariffs, essentially limited to producing raw materials or semi-finished goods for the world? Whereas, today, we are part and parcel of the age of services or information, of elaborately transformed goods. All this has come by being domestically and internationally competitive'.

TECHNICAL STUFF

In 1990, the OECD declared Australia fourth on the list of nations in debt (behind Brazil, Mexico and the USSR). The Victorian state government alone was $32 billion in debt as Australia's foreign debt hit $95 billion. Farm returns fell by 8.1 per cent. Telstra, the major (state-owned) telecommunications company, slashed jobs by 2,500. In the four months to September 1990, the jobless rate jumped by 60,000.

Although ultimately salutary for the Australian economy, the recession meant tough times for a lot of people. The road back would be hard and protracted.

Deregulating the labour market

The old system of arbitration in Australia that had been functioning for most of the 20th century centred on Justice Higgins's landmark 1907 Harvester Judgement, which insisted that a 'fair and reasonable wage' was the basic and inalienable right of Australian workers (refer to Chapter 12).

The *deregulation* of the Australian labour market — deregulating centralised wage fixation, and shifting to enterprise bargaining between bosses and workers — was begun by Labor Prime Minister Keating in the early 1990s. But it was Liberal Prime

Minister John Howard (who beat Keating in the 1996 election) who really ran with the idea. As far back as August 1983, John Howard announced: 'The time has come when we have to turn Mr Justice Higgins on his head'.

In 1993, Keating called for a new model of industrial relations based on enterprise bargaining between bosses and workers. Under Keating, arbitrated wage rises would be kept as a simple safety net for the minimum payable wage, rather than an overarching structure determining what everyone got paid.

The 1996 Coalition election policy was to keep the award system but also introduce individual agreements, establishing a 'no losers' pledge, which meant no worker would lose pay in deregulated reforms. This was crucial for most Australians — the 'no disadvantage' test would be incorporated after the Liberal 1996 election win in the new Australian Workplace Agreements (AWAs).

LIFE DOWN UNDER

John Howard would learn just how important Australians felt this 'no disadvantage' test was when, after his 2004 election win, he brought in Work Choices, the next phase in workplace deregulation and individual bargaining, which didn't include such a test. Work Choices helped create 500,000 jobs over 18 months, but many workers in the electorate saw it as a policy that provided unfair advantages to businesses. The new jobs didn't stop the electorate throwing Howard out at the next election, after a campaign run entirely on the pros and cons of Work Choices.

Fighting the Culture Wars

Paul Keating and John Howard danced around each other for over 15 years. Between 1977 and 1991, the Department of Treasury was the domain of first Howard then Keating. Between 1991 and 2007, the office of prime minister was occupied by first Keating then Howard. Both of them were converts to the idea of making Australia a more open and competitive, wealth-producing economy. But each strove to connect these changes with different strands of the Australian character, with one (Howard) being socially conservative and mainstream and the other (Keating) being a global progressive more sympathetic to cultural elites. Howard and Keating became lightning rods for two very different brands of Australian cultural identity.

Keating's Government put more and more resources into its Arts and Aboriginal programs, and its cultural policies. In 1993, in the midst of the recession, the Arts received a 10 per cent funding increase. Keating followed this with a 'Creative Nation' announcement in 1994, which promised the Arts an extra $200 million, and put an extra $100 million per year aside for Aboriginal programs.

Howard saw himself as mainstream rather than establishment, and on the side of ordinary Australian families against the generation of intellectuals who had come of age during the Whitlam Government and who now were in ascendancy in the policy-making institutions. By the time Howard's Government left office, he was funnelling an incredible $29.7 billion into family support for low- and middle-income families — bigger than annual spending for defence!

Both Keating and Howard were 'cultural warriors', fighting hard to defend their ideas of what Australia should stand for. Both played favourites, endeavouring to reward those in the cultural sphere who mirrored their own views, while seeking to marginalise their cultural enemies. Popularly referred to as 'the culture wars', Keating and Howard were the two principle antagonists in this argument, but both had armies of more than willing foot soldiers.

Keating fires the starting gun

Keating was a strange and intriguing combination for an Australian politician. Cutthroat and ambitious, he was from the legendary (and notorious) right faction of NSW Labor, the members of which were known for their merciless attitude. As Hawke's treasurer from 1983, Keating had been largely responsible (along with Finance Minister Peter Walsh) for introducing many of the economic reforms that changed Australia beyond recognition. When he began a campaign to unseat Hawke as prime minister, he made it clear that he wasn't content with completely overhauling Australia's economic mechanics — he wanted to do the same with Australia's self-image.

At the annual Press Gallery dinner in December 1990, Keating let rip on Australia's need for leadership at a critical time, when it was 'teetering on the brink' of becoming a great nation. And he was just the chap to take us there. Once he became prime minister in 1991, Keating didn't lose much time.

IN THEIR WORDS

Keating hated the dominant cultural tradition that emphasised Australia's connection with Britain, seeing it as provincial and colonial. He taunted the Liberal Party in parliament for kowtowing to the British, saying 'even as it walked out on you and joined the Common Market, you were looking for your MBEs and your knighthoods and all the rest of the regalia that comes with it . . . You can go back to the fifties, to your nostalgia, your Menzies . . . and the whole lot. They were not aggressively Australian, they were not aggressively proud of our culture and we will have no bar of you and your sterile ideology'. One observer described the roar of approval from Labor's backbench as unlike anything heard in the parliament for years. The speaker of the House, meanwhile, told Howard that he was going to have a heart attack if his face went any redder.

Keating was the first radical nationalist of either major party to be prime minister, and certainly the first to actively repudiate Australia's past security, trade and cultural alliances with Britain. Instead, Keating tried to completely integrate Australian culture into the Asian region, and even went on to declare that the flag would probably have to go — arguing Australia shouldn't have 'the flag of another country [the Union Jack] in the corner of it'.

Keating was declaring that Australia had to chart a radical new path away from its Australo-Briton past, saying that just as the economic realities had been turned on their head in the 1980s, so too should the cultural assumptions. Keating wanted a new kind of national patriotism, and many urban progressives and cultural elites were wildly enthusiastic at the idea.

What he and his supporters didn't count on was Howard also coming up with a new and reworked idea of national image, which would entwine certain traditional elements of Australian culture with its new economic and military presence on the world stage.

Bumps on the multi-culti road

While the Review of Migrant Services in 1978 (see the section 'Launching the good ship Multi-Culti' earlier in this chapter) had established multiculturalism as the new social policy to encourage tolerance and diversity in Australian life, the change was not entirely smooth. By the late 1980s, the multicultural and migration programs were attracting criticism on economic and cultural grounds, as follows:

IN THEIR WORDS

>> **Economic:** The high migration program was creating short-term economic problems in 'social infrastructure', inflating house prices and increasing pressures in the big cities. Some of those selected as migrants were not proving to be particularly beneficial to Australia's economic life — family reunion was now becoming a dominant factor in selecting potential migrants rather than the economic or skill-set contribution they could make to Australia. The unemployment rate for non–English speaking recent immigrants in Australia ('recent' means living in the country for fewer than 12 months) was 42 per cent. In some ethnic communities, this rate was as high as 87 per cent. This was completely different to the immigration program's situation in the postwar decades up to the 1980s.

>> **Cultural:** For some people, the government didn't seem to place enough emphasis on making new migrants commit to perceived Australian values and loyalty. By the late 1980s, the new multiculturalism didn't seem to allow any room for an avowal of Australia's distinctive characteristics and values. Ex-Labor minister Peter Walsh described the prevailing mentality in the social

progressive left and multicultural lobby as 'all other cultures are superior to the liberal democratic, mostly Anglo-Celtic culture, which has been pervasive in Australia for a hundred years or more'.

Walsh went on to ask, with feeling, 'what psychotic disorder, what deep-seated self-loathing, causes people who are the beneficiaries of that [Australian liberal democratic] heritage to constantly vilify and denigrate it?' The language here is extreme, and gives some idea of the sense of outraged besiegement that many mainstream Australians were feeling at the loudly broadcast and radically new ideal of Australian identity.

In 1988, Hawke set up a Committee to Advise on Australia's Immigration Policies, chaired by Dr Stephen FitzGerald. Subsequently known as the FitzGerald Report, the committee's findings surprised and annoyed Hawke by making criticisms of the current migration and multicultural model, reporting a widespread collapse in approval of both high immigration and multiculturalism. People were suspicious, concluded the report, about 'special deals' and 'professional ethnics' — favours being doled out to ethnic lobby groups both inside and outside the government.

The next year a public document was produced: The National Agenda for a Multi-cultural Australia. The document argued that the best thing for Australia to do was to strike a balance — guaranteeing cultural rights and social justice to all Australians (whether Aboriginal, British-Australian or non-English speaking background), but maintaining also 'an overriding and unifying commitment to Australia'. Citizenship and equality should be made big enough and strong enough to encompass ethnic and linguistic diversity.

This document was an attempt to swing the pendulum back to the centre, but was an early victim of the culture wars. Keating attacked his political opponents (mainly Howard) for not embracing the new multicultural Australia, and made moves to abandon all previous ties of British loyalty and integrate entirely into the Asian region. Howard in turn attacked Keating for selling out the core values of mainstream Australians. The pendulum was swinging wildly back and forth from one extreme to another.

Howard versus the 'brain class'

John Howard established himself as treasurer in the Fraser Government in 1977 and by the 1980s he was the Liberals' foremost parliamentary debater and one of its leading thinkers. While an economic radical, he was a cultural conservative, and was badly out of step with the new 'embrace diversity' direction being pushed by the Hawke Government in the 1980s. After a gaffe about slowing Asian migration, he was dumped as opposition leader and was thereafter constantly taunted and humiliated by Hawke and Keating for being a relic of the Menzies past.

When Howard finally came to power in 1996, he was determined to change the nature of cultural debate in the country, and to relax the tight strictures that had been applied by the Hawke Government, the multicultural lobby groups and the generally left-leaning intelligentsia (more crudely dubbed 'the chattering classes'). These groups had, in Howard's opinion, ensured any voices of questioning or dissent were consistently marginalised or vilified. He famously (or notoriously) declared that he wanted a 'relaxed and comfortable' Australia — relaxed with itself and its past, and comfortable about its place in the world, without needing to apologise or ingratiate.

Howard's alienation from the 'brain class' — the university-educated professionals, academics, 'creatives' (from areas such as film and television), and multicultural and Indigenous lobby groups and leaders — encouraged him to forge a bond with the 'ordinaries'. Howard focused on everyday mainstream Australians with typical Australian aspirations (such as home ownership, prosperity and good education for their children) and values (such as fairness, tolerance, having a go, showing initiative, and not seeking or providing special treatment or deals).

Although Howard didn't like multiculturalism — he dropped the department devoted to multicultural affairs — he was fine with different cultures and people arriving in Australia. Over the course of his prime ministership, Howard raised migration levels to historically high levels. But rather than the multicultural emphasis on diversity, he insisted on a greater emphasis on loyalty to what he saw as Australia's universal values of egalitarianism, freedom and tolerance.

LIFE DOWN UNDER

Howard so liked his version of old Australian values that when setting up a referendum vote for a new preamble to the constitution he even tried to have 'mateship' inserted (his efforts didn't last long).

Howard's relations with Aboriginal leaders and Aboriginal groups started badly and got worse. He was publicly humiliated at a Reconciliation Convention in May 1997, when the audience stood up and turned their backs on him. He lost his temper and started berating them from the platform, banging the lectern angrily. Howard's actions weren't a good look for a prime minister, and it was an ugly incident that ended badly for both prime minister and his audience. Aboriginals refused to negotiate with Howard's side of politics — the side that happened to be in power for the next 11 years — relegating them to the margins of influence. Howard's incapacity to reach out and bring Aboriginals into his national conversation is ultimately a mark against him, and a sign of his own limitations as a leader.

Pauline Hanson enters the debate (and turns Howard's head)

Pauline Hanson was a Liberal candidate in the Queensland seat of Oxley in the 1996 election campaign when she made a series of race-based comments that the Liberal Party thought offensive (and politically disastrous) enough to disendorse her. She ran instead as an independent, commenting freely on the problems of Australia, including special deals for 'the Aboriginal industry' and 'too many Asians'. She won her seat with a landslide of votes.

In April 1997, Hanson launched the One Nation Party at Ipswich Civic Hall. Her policy aims were to

>> Restrict foreign ownership

>> Restore tariffs

>> Cut or halt immigration

>> Restore equality between Australian citizens

>> Reject the 'Aboriginal industry'

>> Reject multiculturalism

HISTORICAL ROOTS

Hansonism, as it became known, was a reaction against both the cultural and economic revolutions of the 1970s, 1980s and 1990s. Hanson attracted strong support from those who felt they'd been left behind and left out of the new national direction. The opening up of the economy and removal of tariff supports and subsidies had been enormously beneficial for some industries but had spelt the death knell for others. Many felt that culturally established notions of Australian nationhood were being up-ended. The deepness and severity of the early 1990s recession had meant large-scale job losses, at the same time as older notions of nationhood were being disavowed in preference for Aboriginal rights and multicultural diversity.

At the Queensland state election in June 1998, regional Queensland deserted the National Party (traditionally the party for regional voters) for Pauline Hanson's One Nation party. Urban Liberals, angry at Howard's failure to denounce Hanson's attitudes, went to the Labor Party. In the final count, One Nation won 11 seats.

The effect of One Nation's success was immediate. In response, Howard went populist. He cut immigration (it went from 82,560 in 1996 to 68,000 in 1998) and froze tariff cuts. For a long while, Howard also held back from criticising Hanson's views and policy proposals, partly because he said he liked the fact that people now felt free to air their views, and partly because he didn't want to lose the votes of all the people who liked what Hanson was saying. (Howard did eventually publicly condemn Hanson.)

Even with Howard's changes, One Nation still received over 1 million votes (or 8 per cent of the primary vote) in the 1998 federal election, nearly costing the Liberal Party their win.

In the end, Hanson was brought down not by electoral defeat but by what looked like the shonky work of her own political party. Investigation revealed that the party had been set up to run not as a political organisation but as a business. Hanson spent time in jail, but her convictions were overturned by Queensland's Court of Appeal. Subsequently, she became perhaps less divisive in the eyes of many, as repeat appearances on various reality TV shows increased her human appeal in the lounge rooms of Australia. The culture wars had raged on without her.

A decade later, Hanson returned to the political arena, rejoining One Nation, becoming its leader again in 2014, and winning a seat in the Senate at the 2016 election with three other members of her party. And in case anyone wondered exactly whose party it is, it's been renamed the Pauline Hanson One Nation Party (just so we're quite clear).

Battling Over Native Title

Caught up in the culture wars, but also playing along beside them, was the fight for Aboriginal land rights. In 1992 and 1996, the High Court made two legal rulings that transformed the status of Indigenous land ownership and land right claims.

The doctrine of *terra nullius* (in Latin meaning 'land belonging to no-one') had been the legally defined state of Australian land when Cook arrived in 1770 and laid claim to the east coast of Australia. The British argument at the time was that even though people were obviously living on Australian soil, because they weren't involved in heavily cultivating or ostensibly 'improving' the land, but were living nomadically, they did not have any legitimate legal title to the land. (Yep — it sounded a bit dodgy at the time as well.)

When the High Court overturned the doctrine of terra nullius in the 1990s, the consequences were dramatic.

Acting on the Mabo judgement

In the Mabo judgement of June 1992, the High Court found that, having demonstrated unbroken ongoing cultural connection with the land, the Meriam people (from some of the Torres Strait Islands) had a common law right to native title.

Once the judgement was announced, Prime Minister Keating was keen to ensure it would have more wide-reaching ramifications, using the judgement not only as a beginning of a new series of land management and access laws, but also as a tool for initiating reconciliation between Indigenous and non-Indigenous Australians. His feeling, strongly felt by many others, was that all of Australian society's achievements and prosperity had been built on an original act of dispossession of Australia's first owners, and that Australia as a nation would never be able to rest easy with itself until some serious recognition had been made of this.

IN THEIR WORDS

In 1992, in what became known as the Redfern Speech, Keating said that the problems that continued between black and white Australians were some of the central challenges that Australians still had to resolve. He suggested that this resolution might begin 'with an act of recognition. Recognition that it was we who did the dispossessing. We took the traditional lands and smashed the traditional way of life. We brought the diseases. The alcohol. We committed the murders. We took the children from their mothers. We practised discrimination and exclusion. It was our ignorance and prejudice. And our failure to imagine these things being done to us . . . We failed to ask, how would I feel if this were done to me? As a consequence, we failed to see that what we were doing degraded all of us'.

Aboriginal leaders and the Labor Government were involved in intense negotiations to draw up native title legislation after the Mabo judgement. This legislation was passed through parliament before Christmas 1993.

The Liberal–National coalition were bitterly opposed to the legislation, and felt that mainstream Australia had been shut out of the conversation and the negotiations. Three years later, the Coalition would return to power, and it would be Howard, not Keating, who would be in the driving seat when the next High Court decision on native title — the Wik judgement — was made.

Panicking after the Wik judgement

The Wik judgement of December 1996 found that native title to the Wik people's traditional lands on the Cape York Peninsula had continued simultaneously with the operation of pastoral leases in the area. This was an enormous change to the Mabo ruling (itself an enormous reversal of the established 'empty land' doctrine), which had seemingly established that native title existed only when continuous possession could be proven — not when freehold rights or leases had been granted for the land in question. Wik now stated unequivocally that native title wasn't necessarily extinguished but could coexist simultaneously with the pastoral leases in the area.

The High Court found (by a narrow 4–3 majority) that pastoral leases were not necessarily exclusive. The Court found that previous communications by the Secretary of State, Earl Grey, to the Governor of New South Wales in 1847 and 1848 made it clear that Aboriginals were not to be excluded from land under pastoral occupation, stating 'these Leases are not intended to deprive the Natives of their former right to hunt over these Districts, or to wander over them in search of subsistence, in the manner to which they have been heretofore accustomed, from the spontaneous produce'. (Refer to Chapter 7 for more on Earl Grey and his arguments with the colonials.)

The president of the Native Title Tribunal (set up in 1993 to assist with native title claims) said that native title claims on pastoral leases would have to be determined on a case-by-case basis. Negotiation would need to commence between pastoralists, miners and others and local Aboriginal people about gates, fences, vehicles and camping rights. With 40 per cent of Australia covered by pastoral leases, this was big news.

As prime minister, Howard's job was to pass a new set of laws to deal with the Wik finding. Pastoralists, farmers, miners, Australian populists and conservatives went into meltdown, insisting that laws be made to extinguish any native title that threatened leases. Howard couldn't do this — in all likelihood it would just be overturned by the High Court. He had to strike a balance, shifting the weight of rights strongly in favour of existing lease-holders without abrogating the entire High Court finding. The Nationals leader, Tim Fischer, promised his constituents that there would be 'bucketfuls of extinguishment'.

But Howard and Fischer had another problem besides the High Court and furious constituents — the Senate, where they didn't have the numbers required to pass a bill. The Labor Party, supported by a strong allegiance from Aboriginal leaders, was hostile towards the legislation, and was willing to force an election on the issue.

If Labor had forced an election centred on native title, the outcome would have in all likelihood been disastrous for both Labor and Aboriginal leaders. One Nation's populist anti-Indigenous rights members would have flooded in on a tide of fear-mongering sentiment. For Howard, the outcome would have been disastrous, too. He may have got some kind of legislation through, but any legitimacy as a prime minister who could claim to be leader of the entire nation would have been destroyed. Independent Senator Brian Harradine said a 'race election' 'would have torn the fabric of our society and set race relations back 40 or 50 years'.

Senator Harradine, who held the balance of power in the Senate, was moved to strike a compromise with Howard to give the Coalition enough numbers to get the legislation through — with some additional amendments. Howard got his laws through, which had enough 'extinguishment' in them to placate the farmers and populists, and Australia was saved a race election with the dire consequences that Harradine had predicted for it.

LIFE DOWN UNDER

The success of Howard's negotiated resolution can be seen in that, not much more than two decades later, hardly anyone remembers Wik and its outcome. Mention 'Wik' to people and you'll largely get blank looks. If it had gone to election, the word would be seared into the national consciousness, like 'Vietnam' or 'Great Depression' or 'Gallipoli'.

While neither side in the argument got everything they wanted, neither *could* get everything they wanted without causing greater anger, division and nastiness.

At the same time, though, an intractable problem in remote and regional Australia has been getting, if anything, worse. It's what sociologists describe as a 'wicked problem' — namely, the intractable sort about which no easy, simple or immediately direct solution is available. The problem is one of domestic and sexual violence, caused in significant part by drug and alcohol abuse, in some remote Indigenous communities.

INDIGENOUS AUSTRALIANS IN REMOTE REGIONS AND CITIES

In the middle of Indigenous land rights contests, a terrible tragedy has been unfolding in remote regions of Australia. The collapse of Indigenous employment in the cattle and other industries since the 1960s, along with the arrival of modern social epidemics of alcohol and substance abuse, have resulted in systemic breakdown of traditional Indigenous communities. Indigenous incarceration rates have skyrocketed since the 1960s, and probably worst of all is the levels of domestic violence and often systematic sexual abuse of women and young children in some remote Indigenous communities. These issues are often in striking contrast to the success of Indigenous Australians in the cities and more closely settled regions of Australian. You can make a strong argument that, for our modern day well-meaning talk about equality, justice and reconciliation, the gap between Indigenous and non-Indigenous Australians on a range of social indicators is the great national failure posterity will judge us extremely harshly for.

In 1965, the Commonwealth Conciliation and Arbitration Commission brought down an equal wage decision for Indigenous labour in the rural economy. This was a great achievement; however, many employers simply sacked their Aboriginal workers once they were entitled to higher wages. The changes also came just as large pastoral stations were shifting away from horseman and stockriders for their cattle across their huge properties.

Farms the size of English counties now turned to machines such as helicopters to help with annual musters and other work. Whereas in the early 20th century some

(continued)

(continued)

90 per cent of cattle station workers in the Northern Territory were Aboriginal people, unemployment in Indigenous communities became wide-spread. Simultaneously, the sale of alcohol to Aboriginal people in the regions became unrestricted. And all of this happened at the same time as land rights were being won, with legislation passed by the Whitlam and Fraser governments.

The changes in Aboriginal communities meant that the 'homelands movement' of the 1970s, whereby Indigenous Australians strove to establish their own stations on traditional Country in remote parts of Australia, had to grapple with powerful agents that worked to dissolve the traditional structures and authorities of Elders in Indigenous life. The accumulated consequences of these factors all coming together simultaneously have been devastating.

Indigenous levels of incarceration have shot up exponentially since the 1960s. Aboriginal deaths in custody required a Royal Commission in the late 1980s. The impact on women and children has been worst of all. Domestic violence and sexual abuse against Indigenous women and children led to an inquiry into the Protection of Aboriginal Children from Sexual Abuse. One of the chairs was Indigenous human rights advocate Pat Anderson, and when the inquiry's final report was released in 2007 it caused a furore. The report, *Little Children are Sacred*, outlined a truly terrible degree of human harm and damage to children and young women.

Since the 1960s and 1970s, an enormous gap has opened up between the quality of life enjoyed by Indigenous people who live in urban areas and more closely settled regions of Australia and their compatriots in the remote regions. For the first group of Aboriginal Australians — those living in cities — education levels, income levels, health and affluence are comparable to non-Indigenous Australians. For Aboriginal Australians living in remote regions, though — often plagued with staggeringly high unemployment, lack of industries, dysfunctional health and education, and struggling with domestic violence, and alcohol and substance abuse — the situation is entirely different. In the 1990s, it was reported that about one third of Aboriginal Australian women in the Northern Territory were being assaulted, including sexual as well as other physical abuse, each year. More than 20 years later, the situation doesn't seem to be changing in any fundamental way.

This is, on its most basic and human level, a terrible and tragic thing that Australians — Indigenous and non-Indigenous alike — are still working on trying to solve. If I had to point to the one thing in the Australia I live in that causes me deep shame and anguish, it's this.

For a much more in-depth discussion of these issues, and the ways Indigenous people are looking to lead the identification of the priorities in their communities — and the development of policies, delivery of services and design of programs — see *Indigenous Australia For Dummies*, 2e, by Larissa Behrendt, Wiley Australia Publishing.

6

2000 and Beyond: Seeking Solutions to Global and Local Problems

Discover how Australia has entered the new millennium still dealing with issues from the outside world — including protecting our borders, dealing with the China question, and meeting the challenges of COVID, Big Tech and climate change.

Examine the ways Australia has also faced challenges and issues at home, such as apologising to the Stolen Generation, changing prime ministers and calling out misogyny in parliament.

Understand the two Australias emerging today, and the big questions this creates for politics and culture.

Chapter **21**

Into the New Millennium

A ustralia finished the old millennium with the Sydney Olympics in 2000, when the whole world got to watch a two-week party in Sydney (apparently there were some athletic contests as well). The events seemed a good omen, with the opening ceremony viewed by millions throughout the world (exactly what they made of the hundreds of Ned Kelly helmeted figures jumping around is anyone's guess). At the ceremony, the Olympic Flame was lit by Cathy Freeman (see Figure 21-1), the Indigenous athlete who would go on to win gold in the 400 metres. And thousands of Australians happily enlisted as volunteers and guides to help the games go off without a hitch.

The beginning of the new millennium in 2001, however, contained darker portents and divisions. During a dispute in August over boat people on the *Tampa*, the issue of border protection revealed a deeply divided nation. And the terrorist attack in the US on 11 September (which became known as '9/11') brought shock and a subsequent 'War on Terror', which Australia would join, sending military forces to Afghanistan and Iraq. By the end of the first decade of the 21st century, Australia had still to resolve the problems implicit in border protection, and still had forces serving in Afghanistan.

Meanwhile, a social movement gathered momentum, demanding a national apology to Indigenous Australians who had been forcibly removed from their families in childhood — the Stolen Generations. Australia was benefitting from the economic reforms introduced in the 1980s and 1990s — the economy was going 'gangbusters' — but the nation still had problems to resolve.

In this chapter, I chart some of the key events and watershed moments in Australia's first decade of the new millennium.

Still Dealing with the Outside World

Australian challenges in the new millennium included unresolved problems from previous decades as well new and unexpected threats. The question of how best to deal with unauthorised arrivals on Australian shores (often referred to as 'boat people') continued to vex opinion, as it had in the late 1980s and throughout the 1990s. The worldwide clash between the west and Islamic extremists after 9/11 drew Australian troops into Afghanistan and Iraq, and lay behind the Bali Bombings of 2002, where many Australians died.

Protecting the borders

The first boat arrivals of people claiming refugee status in Australia occurred in the late 1970s after the Vietnam War (refer to Chapter 20 for more on this). Indochinese refugees were received then but, crucially, the vast majority of them were processed offshore in other countries first. From the late 1980s, new waves of people claiming refugee status began to arrive in boats on the Australian coast — and the government was far less friendly. The Keating Government introduced mandatory detention of all unauthorised arrivals, a policy which John Howard strengthened when he became prime minister. Border protection policies were pivotal in the 2001 election held shortly after the 9/11 attacks on the World Trade Center in New York.

HISTORICAL ROOTS

Many observers have noted the contradiction at the heart of modern Australian society. The nation that has arguably the most successful migration program of the last 60 years, which has proved remarkably tolerant of practically all new arrivals of migrant groups in government-controlled migration programs, is largely hostile to the arrival of any unauthorised refugees in boats. Exactly who is in the boats — Cambodians, Chinese, Iraqis, Sri Lankans, Somalis — doesn't seem to matter. It's the fact of them arriving without proper processing that does. This goes back to the unofficial compact struck between the government and the people in 1947, when Labor's Chifley Government began bringing in large numbers of non-British migrants without first asking the Australian people (who would have probably said No — refer to Chapter 17). The compact runs something like this — Government: 'Okay, we may not let you decide who is allowed to migrate to Australia, but we promise that migration will be highly regulated and tightly controlled'; People: 'Oh, all right then. But you mind those borders!'

During the 1980s, the Immigration Department held unauthorised arrivals in a very loose sort of custody. Old migrant hostels in major cities were used as the officials made a quick decision on whether the refugee applicant could stay or go. But a 1989 High Court decision (and a dramatic increase in the number of people arriving in boats) changed the situation. The High Court found that an official's decision in processing one of these applications was 'an improper exercise of the power to determine refugee status'. This increased the incentive for people to appeal any adverse decisions on a refugee's status made by immigration department officials. The number of refugee advocates and lawyers lodging appeals grew exponentially: By 2007, 72 per cent of all appeals in the Federal Court related to migration.

In 1992, Keating tried to swing the balance away from the courts and back in favour of the government. Mandatory detention was introduced and tribunals established to try to re-assert executive control over the judiciary. The High Court upheld mandatory detention, but only on functional grounds — if people were being held for long periods of time purely as a deterrent against other would-be refugees, this was in contravention of basic human rights.

BOB IS DEFINITELY NOT YOUR UNCLE

In 1990, Prime Minister Bob Hawke summed up Australian attitudes to refugees when taking a hard line against then-arriving Cambodian boat people, saying: 'We're not here with an open-door policy saying anyone who wants to come to Australia can come . . . People are saying they don't like a particular regime or they don't like their economic circumstances; therefore, they're going to pull up stumps, get in a boat and lob in Australia. Well, that's not on. We have an orderly migration program. We're not going to allow people just to jump that queue . . . lob here and Bob's your uncle. Bob is not your uncle on this issue'.

Flashpoint Tampa

After the introduction of mandatory detention in the 1990s, the next flashpoint in Australian border protection occurred in 2001 under the Howard Government. More than 8,000 boat arrivals had turned up in the three years previous, and sources indicated the numbers would only increase. Australia lacked the kind of well-thought-out treaty agreement with nearby nations (such as Indonesia) that had served Fraser well in the 1970s. The detention centres were full.

Then, in August 2001, a Norwegian boat, the MV *Tampa*, picked up refugees whose boat was sinking in Indonesian waters. (The refugees were trying to reach the Australian territory of Christmas Island.) The *Tampa* skipper began plotting course for nearby Indonesia when there was a kind of mutiny. The refugees demanded the captain take them to Christmas Island, Australia or another western country.

The *Tampa* reached Christmas Island but Howard refused to let them land. The SAS (elite Australian Army forces) boarded the *Tampa* from rubber dinghies and took control of the ship. Howard then had to find countries that would be willing to take and process the refugees, because he swore they wouldn't be landed in Australia. Eventually, the Pacific Island nations of Nauru, Manus and New Zealand agreed to take most of the people. Later, a proper detention and processing centre was set up on Nauru, and the system was dubbed the 'Pacific Solution'.

Howard went on to comprehensively win the 2001 election, partly due to the strong stand he'd taken on the *Tampa*.

Critics said Howard had exploited the *Tampa* crisis for electoral purposes. The government's refrain 'We decide who comes to this country and the circumstances in which they come' was repeating nothing more than what had been said by both Labor and Liberal prime ministers since Federation, but with the background of *Tampa*, it took on a new resonance.

By 2010, under a Labor Government, government decisions on boat people were still leading to long-term incarceration of unauthorised arrivals, a violation of human rights. The basic conundrum — how to maintain effective control over Australia's borders while maintaining universal human rights — was again a major issue in the 2010 election.

Dealing with the Bali bombings

On 12 October 2002, a terrorist attack was carried out by Islamic militant extremists in Kuta, the tourist district of Bali — an island in the Indonesian archipelago. Bali had long been regarded by Australians as a holiday haven, and the nightspots were targeted because they were seen as a site of 'western decadence' — men and women out drinking, dancing and having a good time. (One person's western decadence is another's good night out, it would seem.)

An initial bomb went off inside 'Paddy's Pub', driving people in the bar outside onto the street, where a car bomb went off. The damage and casualties from this second bomb were considerable because the blast was massive — it left a one-metre deep crater in the street.

FIGHTING OVERSEAS

In 2001, the 9/11 terrorist attacks on the World Trade Center and other targets in the US signalled the beginning of what would become known as the 'War on Terror'. Australia, under John Howard's prime ministership, became one of the key players in the US's subsequent 'Coalition of the Willing', agreeing to send troops to Afghanistan in October 2001 and Iraq in 2003 and 2005.

Australia provided 1,550 troops to Afghanistan in October 2001 for Operation Slipper, the conflict that ousted the Taliban Government. Despite this removal, Australian forces and support personnel would still be in Afghanistan at the end of the decade.

In Operation Falconer in 2003, Australia provided one of the four main combat force contingents for the invasion of Iraq. Navy ships, 500 Special Forces soldiers and various patrol aircraft, transport aircraft and F/A-18 Hornet fighters were deployed.

In 2005, combat troops were redeployed in Operation Catalyst, and supported Iraqi security forces in Iraq's southern provinces. They were finally withdrawn between June 2008 and July 2009 under the new Rudd Labor Government.

Overall, 202 people were killed, of whom 88 were Australian, the highest number of any nationality. Many burns victims were kept submerged in local hotel swimming pools, and then flown to special burns units in Perth and Darwin.

Six years later, on 9 November 2008, three men convicted of organising and carrying out the bombings — Amrozi Nurhasyim, Imam Samudra and Ali 'Mukhlas' Ghufron — were executed by firing squad in Indonesia.

Facing Up to Challenges at Home

Australia's economic life in the 2000s went from strength to strength. The hard and often painful decisions taken in the 1980s and 1990s to scale back industry subsidies and deregulate the financial and labour markets (refer to Chapter 20) were paying off. The Asian financial crisis of 1997 and the global financial crisis of 2008 were both weathered by a robust and open economy. China's development boom boosted demand for key Australian commodities as the ratio of export to import prices hit 60-year highs.

Yet, the nation still clearly felt it had unfinished business on the domestic front in relation to the treatment of Indigenous Australians, many of whom had in previous generations been unwillingly removed from their families as children. After a landmark report in the late 1990s, this broad group of people became known as the 'Stolen Generations'. A national apology seemed in order, but Liberal Prime Minister Howard refused. After a Labor Government was elected in 2007, the new prime minister, Kevin Rudd, issued a national apology in parliament.

In tandem with this was a feeling that, despite the creation of more wealth for more Australians and a greater access to more products and services, people weren't necessarily happier.

Apologising to the Stolen Generations

The term *Stolen Generations* refers to Aboriginal Australians and Torres Strait Islanders who were removed from families by federal and state governments in the years 1869 to 1969. For much of the period, Indigenous Australians didn't have full rights as Australian citizens. Aboriginal Protection Acts, Aboriginal Protection Boards and 'Protectors of Natives' could remove Aboriginal children from parents and families without needing to establish the neglect or maltreatment of the children.

In 1997, the Human Rights and Equal Opportunities Commission published their *Bringing Them Home* report, condemning past government policy of forcibly removing Aboriginal children from their parents. Public support grew for the idea of an official apology, and an annual 'Sorry Day' began to be held. The Howard Government disputed the validity of the term 'Stolen Generations' and rejected any government apology. The Rudd Government took power in December 2007 and declared an apology would be one of the first orders of business in the new parliament.

IN THEIR WORDS

The Federal Parliament's apology was given by Prime Minister Kevin Rudd at 9.30 am on 13 February 2008: 'Today we honour the Indigenous peoples of this land, the oldest continuing culture in human history. We reflect on their past mistreatment. We reflect in particular on the mistreatment of those who were Stolen Generations — this blemished chapter in our nation's history. We apologise for the laws and policies of successive parliaments and governments that have inflicted profound grief, suffering and loss on these our fellow Australians. We apologise especially for the removal of Aboriginal and Torres Strait Islander children from their families, their communities and their country. For the pain, suffering and hurt of these Stolen Generations, their descendants and for their families left behind, we say sorry. To the mothers and the fathers, the brothers and the sisters, for the breaking up of families and communities, we say sorry. And for the indignity and degradation thus inflicted on a proud people and a proud culture, we say sorry.'

Creating more wealth for more people

Australia's survival of both the 1997 Asian financial crisis and the 2008 global financial crisis illustrated the twofold causes of its economic success. To begin with, Australia had done a good job getting its economic house in order in the 1980s and 1990s, and so was less susceptible to crisis as other previously booming nations proved to be in 1997. Secondly, China's economic development took off in the early 2000s, and carried Australia happily in its slipstream. For as long as China's demand for Australia's commodities remained at its current level (that is, voracious), an extended period of economic boom seemed secure, for the first time in some 40 years.

In the light of Australia's economic security, the main questions were

>> Will the windfall be wasted?

>> How come we're not satisfied and happy?

In the 1980s and 1990s, Australia adopted international ideas and implemented them according to Australian values. A core Australian value had always been egalitarianism. In the new approach, this translated as 'equity': Fairness of opportunity and reward for people willing to work hard and apply themselves.

In the modern era, the main way in which successive Australian governments have sought to apply this equity is via the tax system. In the early 2000s, this system was made highly redistributive for middle- to lower-income brackets. This meant that while less than the OECD average was spent on social security benefits, more effective wealth redistribution took place in Australia than under some of the more 'welfare-state' European nations. This was due to

>> Welfare payments being means-tested and not simply given out to everyone regardless of their wealth

>> Very low taxes paid by the poor

>> Very high family subsidy payments provided

TECHNICAL STUFF

In the early 2000s, the poorest 20 per cent in Australia received more in government support than any other OECD country. The proportion of children who didn't have either parent in employment dropped from 18 per cent in the late 1990s to 13 per cent in 2007–08. Suicide — a classic indicator of breakdown in social cohesion — fell in the same period, with the rate of suicide for men aged between 20 and 24 (a traditional high-risk category) halved. A definite positive indicator of strong social networks — the rate of volunteering in the community — jumped from 24 to 35 per cent in the 11 years from 1995 to 2006.

At the same time, the open economy was proving highly effective at producing more wealth. Between 1992 and 2007, real income per head rose more than 40 per cent, while real wealth per head doubled. This was helped by what Reserve Bank governor Glenn Stevens described as 'the largest mineral and energy boom since the late 19th century', a direct product of Chinese demand. But the strength of the economy was already in evidence during the Asian financial crisis of 1997. Australia's open markets, strong institutions, competition, balanced budget and independent central bank became a model for others to follow. A technology boom, a property boom, a financial services boom and a resources boom were all built on these strengths.

But, increasing prosperity didn't necessarily make us more satisfied as a nation. Issues such as the vulnerability of the world's environment and (closer to home) decreased housing affordability caused (and continue to cause) anxiety. Australians in the early 2000s had a similar experience to those living at other moments of high-boom prosperity — the 1880s and the 1950s are two good examples — that wealth doesn't make your problems go away.

IN THEIR WORDS

Social commentator and demographer Bernard Salt commented on the Australian Bureau of Statistics' *Measures of Australia's Progress 2010* by saying that the prosperity and wealth delivered throughout Australian society hasn't made us more satisfied. 'We're rich beyond our wildest dreams compared to 20 years ago and yet it's still not enough. It's very different to the Depression generation or the war generation, who were very satisfied with their lot and didn't expect much. We can have plasma TVs, we can have holidays in Bali, we can have mobile phones, we can go to restaurants every night of the week . . . and yet the national sport is despair.' Or, in other words: Sometimes the real challenge is realising that you've never had it so good!

LIFE DOWN UNDER

Part of the strength of Australian society in the early 2000s, though, didn't have to do with the levels of prosperity and material abundance that many people enjoyed (as worthwhile as these things were). The strength had more to do with the continued power of associational life — the people-powered, grassroots person-to-person organising with which any free society sustains itself. In the 1990s and 2000s, membership of the major political parties and trade unions plummeted, which didn't spell great news for long-term political engagement or stability. But Australians remained great 'joiners' — in neighbourhood associations and various community groups, in Scout and Neighbourhood Watch groups, and in football and netball teams, weekend cycling groups and book clubs. You name it, and we were in it. The mutual cooperation and the day-to-day, face-to-face organising this required made for a strong society, with high levels of social trust. These would prove to be one the most important reservoirs of what social scientists call 'social capital' in times of crisis ahead.

HISTORICAL ROOTS

In the 20th century, Australia had become renowned from early on as a 'strong state' society — a place where people had no problem with government playing a strong or dominant part in taking care of social welfare or other problems. But this was built off the back of strong local community life, and of 'citizens doing it for themselves'. They formed their own associations, with boards made up of community and church leaders, to not only try to persuade government to help out where they thought it was needed, but also organise local welfare, charity, education and social life.

New political directions

In December 2007, John Howard's Liberal–National Party coalition was defeated after 11 years of power by the Labor Party, led by Kevin Rudd. Kevin Rudd ended John Howard's long tenure as prime minister by assuring the electorate that he was an economic conservative (like Howard) but a social and political progressive (very unlike Howard).

After taking government, Rudd immediately signed the Kyoto Protocol (an international treaty on cutting greenhouse gas emissions) and delivered an apology to Indigenous Australians who had been taken from their families by the state (refer to the section 'Apologising to the Stolen Generations' earlier in this chapter), both things the Howard Government had refused to do. Then the global financial crisis hit, which moved Rudd to declare that 'the great neo-liberal experiment of the past 30 years has failed', and his government oversaw an economic stimulus package that was largely credited (along with a continued resources boom) with helping Australia avoid the economic trough many north Atlantic countries fell into.

TWO CHALLENGES FOR A STRONG SOCIETY IN A NEW CENTURY

One of the great challenges of Australian life in the early 21st century was (and continues to be) how you balance a strong society, and a strong and effective state. A free, open and equal society needs both of these things.

The second half of the 20th century saw a significant increase of government activity in taking care of challenges that had previously been met by community groups and cooperative societies organising for themselves. Australians used to participate in a broad range of institutions that were hugely diverse — ranging from political parties to churches and community groups such as Rotary. Whether in church on Sunday, in a community group meeting during the week, at the kids' local footy club training session, or in any of the other serial social interaction moments (walking the dog, going to the pub, fetching some of the neighbour's lemons from across the street), they learned to span diverse organisations, and to meet and mix and work things out with all different sets of people. They learned to get on with each other, and how to rub along okay despite differences. To be 'a good mixer' was for many decades almost the highest Australian accolade! A second challenge is in some ways quite related. It's the increasing prevalence of the internet and social media in people's daily lives and interactions, and how this affects the way we all get along with each other. Social media didn't exist at the start of the 2000s, and the internet only barely so. In the second half of this decade, it suddenly became a newly dominating factor in how people communicated and how people consumed news about what people in the rest of Australia and the rest of the world were up to. The 2007 federal election and the victory of Kevin Rudd's Labor Party (described in more detail in the section 'New political directions') became known as the first ever 'social media election'. 'Kevin07' became the first well-known social media slogan that migrated onto T-shirts and into everyday talk, accompanying Kevin Rudd onto breakfast talk shows and FM radio. Overseas a young, eloquent member of the United States Senate called Barack Obama was transforming the race for the White House, by in part tapping the new communities and enthusiasm that existed online for his own presidential candidacy.

An extraordinarily potent new technology and means of communication was fundamentally reshaping national conversations around the world. The degree to which it could add new layers of associational life, interaction and engagement onto old ones, or the amount it risked actually eroding face-to-face contact and community engagement? That's a question, and a challenge, which we're still wrestling with in the 2020s. But the 2000s was the decade when it first emerged as real, and urgent.

Oddly, the strongest parts of the Rudd Government's initial success — a commitment to the environment and state-financed economic stimulus — also became key areas of criticism that helped bring about Rudd's demise as prime minister. A government rebate scheme for domestic ceiling insulation was meant to both be environmentally innovative and provide instant employment. The reality often proved to be shonky installations by unqualified tradespeople with little oversight or regulation, with the result, tragically, being deaths from house fires and electrocution. After the new leader of the opposition, Tony Abbott, refused to support the Carbon Pollution Reduction Scheme, a key election policy, Rudd decided to delay the scheme until 2011, and his support in the community (previously very high) began to plummet. This was exacerbated by the announcement of a new 'Super Profits' tax on resource and mining companies, Australia's highest-performing sector, which was a public relations disaster.

At the same time, critics of Rudd inside his own party were growing increasingly restive, as he was criticised for not including government ministers in anything beyond the most cursory discussions about policy, preferring to do most of the planning within his own office with his own staff. On 23 June 2010, his deputy leader, Julia Gillard, confronted him. The next day, Rudd decided not to recontest in the party ballot on leadership when it became obvious that he'd get very few votes. Gillard became Australia's first female prime minister.

HISTORICAL ROOTS

From 2001, Gillard had played increasingly important roles in opposition as spokeswoman on population and immigration, Indigenous affairs, health and industrial relations. As shadow minister for industrial relations, Gillard was instrumental in the campaign against the Coalition's 'Work Choices' laws. This, backed by massive support from the head union organisation (the ACTU), was pivotal in the fall of the Howard Government. From December 2007, Gillard was deputy prime minister in the Labor Government, as well as Minister for Education, Employment and Workplace Relations.

Shortly after becoming prime minister in June 2010, Gillard called an election. The election campaign was tight, and the election result narrower than any other in 50 years. The Labor Party lost support in Queensland, Kevin Rudd's home state, and in Western Australia (where the mining tax had been particularly unpopular). In affluent, inner-city areas, some support went to the Greens (a party with policies that focus on the environment and social justice). Despite all this, after the election Gillard was able to secure a deal with rural independents, a Green-affiliated independent and the first Greens member of the House of Representatives (Adam Bandt) to ensure that Labor retained government.

After being one of the first nations to grant women the vote in 1902, Australia's first female prime minister was sworn in a bit more than 100 years later. At the same time, the office of Governor-General had its first woman occupant — Queenslander Dame Quentin Bryce swore Julia Gillard in as prime minister. These were great achievements, but shouldn't be taken to assume that gender equality had been totally achieved, in politics as anywhere else. (See the following chapter for more.)

WREAKING DEVASTATION ON BLACK SATURDAY

In late January and early February 2009, an intense heatwave hit south-eastern Victoria, with temperatures consistently registering in the low, mid and high 40s (degrees Celsius). These high temperatures, combined with dry, blustery winds, came on the back of a ten-year drought that had rendered the bushland of rural Victoria a tinderbox. On Saturday 7 February, the spark ignited and for a while it looked like the whole state might light up.

Winds of above 100 km per hour gave fires the velocity of firestorms in several parts of the state. The Marysville and Kinglake area, a popular weekend retreat just north-east of Melbourne, was one of the worst hit. In the early evening a cool change began finally blowing in from the south-west but this also proved devastating. Long flanks of slow-burning fire were suddenly swung round and became blazing fronts. Towns and areas that had been previously bypassed by the fires were now in the direct line.

Overall, 173 people died and 414 were injured. In addition to this, the fire destroyed over 2,000 houses (see figure), displaced more than 7,500 people, and blackened 1.1 million acres of land. The Black Saturday fires were the eighth deadliest bushfire event in recorded world history.

Chapter **22**

Facing Off Between Two Australias

I n some ways, telling history becomes harder the closer to the present day you get. Everything's so fresh and current, not to say chaotic and jumbled, that it can be difficult to get any sense of distance from the events that shape the era, and determine their underlying meaning.

For that reason, in this chapter I concentrate on answering two big questions:

» What the hell just happened?

» What on earth does it actually mean?

A big chunk of it is the result of seismic shifts in global realities — in geopolitics, in technology, in the behaviour of states towards each other and towards their own citizens. But a lot of it, too, comes down to a widening divide opening up between two different Australias. These two Australias, which I've tagged 'Cosmopolis Australia' and 'Heartland Australia', have very different attitudes, priorities and assumptions about who we are and what the world is like. Thanks to the changes in technology, the growth of social media and changes in the way people use traditional media, these two Australias often spend their time in conversation with themselves rather than with each other. (This, if nothing else, explains some of the mutual bafflement, not to say sporadic hostility.) The way this has happened is also one of the main stories of this chapter.

By the end of this chapter, I'm also hoping you'll be better placed to start dealing with the most important question for every person, and every nation, to answer.

Where are we heading next? And what do we need to do in order to get there safely?

A Dozen Years with a Changing Beat

Some time periods feel a whole lot more extreme than others. History in that sense has been described as *arrhythmic*. It doesn't tick along at the same steady beat the whole way through. A nation's history — and the world's history, and every individual human life story — will include long periods of time where everything is fairly regular and normal. Things may be easy, may be hard, but they're at least familiar. Then other periods of life and history are better filed under 'kablam'.

The dozen odd years dating from roughly speaking the 2008 global financial crisis up until and including the global pandemic that resulted from the outbreak of the novel coronavirus in 2020–2021 unarguably goes into that second category. This chapter goes into the history between these two major, world-changing events. Or, in other words, the history between two major 21st century kablams.

Between these two events, Australia witnessed the paralysis of global financial markets (and its resultant cure), and took part in an experiment in massive public debt never before tried (at least not in peacetime), creating a legacy that now extends off on future projections into the distant never-never. At the same time, geostrategic tensions and conflict between major world powers have re-emerged.

Completely new forms of technology and communication proliferated in the 20 years since the new millennium. These helped Australians generate new forms of community, and new communities, but also made us vulnerable, as individuals and as a society, to new dangers and types of threat previous generations would have found it difficult to conceive of.

Radical divisions in world view have become more and more constant. Different parts of Australia see the world in totally different terms, and often blame each other for things going wrong or problems remaining unresolved. The 'if you don't agree with me and everyone I know you should be cast into outer darkness' approach has become more and more the norm of public debate and disagreement. For a national community trying to arrive at the best possible decisions about where we head to next, this approach is obviously pretty unhelpful, and stands as one of the major challenges for us to work through in the 2020s.

SOME SEISMIC GLOBAL EVENTS

Remember the 2010s? Probably you do, given that they were practically last week. They had their share of seismic events and momentous scene shifts. Here's a reminder of some of the biggies:

- December 2010–2011, Arab Spring

- March 2011, Fukushima nuclear disaster

- May 2011, Osama bin Laden killed

- November 2012, Barack Obama's second term a second term of office with Joe Biden as his Vice-President.

- November 2012, Xi Jinping becomes Chinese leader

- June 2014, Islamic State emerges in the Middle East

- July 2014, Flight MH17 shot down over Ukraine

- August–October 2014, Black Lives Matter movement begins

- January 2015, *Charlie Hebdo* Islamist terror attacks in Paris

- April 2016, Paris Agreement climate talks reach agreement but remain non-binding

- June 2016, Brexit referendum, UK votes to leave the European Union

- November 2016, Trump becomes US President

- April–May 2017, Macron becomes President of France

- October 2017, #MeToo movement begins, protesting against sexual harassment and abuse

- August 2018, Australia excludes Chinese telecommunications company Huawei from its 5G network

- March 2019, Christchurch mosque shootings by Australian white supremacist

- December 2019, UK election, Boris Johnson wins, Brexit is on

- December 2019, virus in Wuhan

- May 2020, Black Live (still) Matter as massive protests follow George Floyd's murder in the US

- January 2021, Trump supporters assault on Congress, Washington

LIFE DOWN UNDER

In Australia the office of national leadership — that of the prime minister — at times looked like it would have to be refitted with a revolving door, as one 'palace coup' followed another, and ordinary people reacted with confusion, then cynicism and even contempt. Not once in the period from 2007 to 2021 have the Australian people been able to pass their verdict on a government and its leader that they installed at a previous election — none of the prime ministers in that time lasted long enough to contest the next election. In the middle of this chaos the two major parties — Labor and Liberal — were able to jump from one leader to the next and build relatively stable administrations. Labor held power from 2008 to 2013, and the Liberal–National coalition formed government in 2013 and were still in power at the beginning of 2022.

So does that mean that the constant changes in prime minister were a surface-level phenomenon? No. They point to the increasing brittleness of political support on either side, with more policy swerves and leaps as consequence. This goes deeper than politics, of course. This brittleness is also seen in the changing nature of public conversation and personal lives, as a new 'information revolution' transforms how people talk, think and act towards each other. In Australia, this trend has exacerbated previous patterns and tendencies, and generated two different Australias: Heartland Australia and Cosmopolis Australia. (See the section 'Leaders, Politics, Culture and Two Australias', later in this chapter, for more.)

The Australian Cavalcade of Events

In the first three years from 2010, Australia saw three changes of prime minister. This isn't by any means a foolproof indicator of political instability, but given that Australia's previous three prime ministers had clocked up nearly 25 years between them, it at least indicated a dramatically shifting political leadership rhythm.

The switch to Malcolm Turnbull in 2015 seemed to promise more stability, but in the end the opinion polls came for him too. And then in 2019 the Liberal–National collation pulled out a 'miracle' election win — moving Scott Morrison into the prime minister's chair.

Revolving the door for prime ministers

In 2010, Prime Minister Julia Gillard led the Labor Party to a narrow election win over a Tony Abbot-led Liberal–National coalition (refer to Chapter 21 for more). Although not commanding an absolute majority in the lower house of parliament (which is how you normally secure government in parliamentary democracy), Gillard struck agreements for the support of the Australian Greens (led at the time by Bob Brown), and regional independents. With this support, she was able to form government.

There was a political price-tag attached to gaining this support though. It was built on a commitment from Gillard to introduce a price on carbon. This, though, was easier said than done. Labor had been trying to get an emissions trading scheme into legislation since 2009. A major reason they hadn't been able to pass any legislation was the hostility of the Greens to their proposals. The Greens denounced Labor's carbon emissions scheme (as developed and then reworked by Labor Minister Penny Wong and Prime Minister Rudd). They argued that it didn't go far enough, quickly enough. Wong, for her part, said she figured getting a scheme up and running with broad support from key stakeholders and Australians was challenge enough. Hindsight seems to prove Wong right on that score.

Back in 2009, though, the Greens assumed that the legislation would be passed regardless, because it had support from the coalition. But then Tony Abbott replaced Turnbull as Liberal leader and quite spectacularly withdrew Liberal support — and all bets were off. The public mood was shifting too, and what had been a lay down vote-winner in 2007 (carbon emissions restriction schemes) was now being seen more and more as a threat to Australian jobs, industries, and the prices of ordinary goods and services — 'a great big tax on everything', as Abbott never tired of describing it. Rudd could have taken the issue to the polls again, and made the election an unofficial referendum on climate change policy, but instead shelved it.

Gillard took over from Rudd in 2010 and began to deal with climate change policy by saying that the first and most important thing was 'to establish a community consensus', to slow down a bit, and certainly not rush it. She said that if elected prime minister she would 'make the case for a carbon price at home and abroad'. During the election campaign itself, however, she reversed this, and assured the public that 'there will be no carbon tax under a government I lead'. The price of a subsequent deal with the Greens to secure government after the 2010 election, however, was a price on carbon emissions. So in some ways we'd come full circle. But the mood of the public had turned sour. Many felt that this agreement was a breach of Gillard's promise to the voters during the election campaign. The crash in public support was immediate and, as it turned out, unrecoverable.

In 2013, Kevin Rudd challenged Gillard for the leadership of the Labor Party. He won that battle and took the party to the next election — where he lost the war (or at least the prime ministership) to Abbott.

Abbott promised to end the price on carbon, stop asylum-seeker arrivals on boats, and restore the nation's finances. He succeeded dramatically well in the first two of these challenges. On the third point though he struck out. Abbott's attempt to enforce financial prudence in his government's first budget in 2014 led to his own crash in public support. Like the two prime ministers before him, Abbott's time in the sun would not last long (see the following section).

Here's some of the key events in these three prime ministerships:

>> **2010, disaster on Christmas Island:** Christmas Island is a tiny dot very far away in the Indian Ocean, and it happens to be Australian territory. Asylum seekers or, more pertinently, the people smugglers who took money to conduct them to Australia to claim refugee status and permanent residence, pinpointed this territory as a destination. An increasing number of dilapidated boats made the extremely dangerous journey. In December 2010 tragedy occurred — 48 people drowned after a boat carrying 90 asylum seekers sunk off the island's coast. The tragedy further underscored the human crisis that the traffic was encouraging, and seemed to highlight the Labor Party's inability to tackle the problem.

>> **2012, NDIS:** Gillard's Government introduced landmark National Disability Support Scheme (NDIS) legislation into parliament in November 2012. The project of ensuring all people with disability and their carers would receive the support they needed had originally been suggested at the 2020 Summit held shortly after Kevin Rudd's Government came to power. The Summit — which was held in April 2008 and brought together 1000 leading Australians to discuss ten major areas of policy innovation — became notorious as not much more than a gabfest, but this idea had legs. The NDIS was legislated in 2013 and has continued with bipartisan support by successive governments as well — in itself a bit of a win for such a politically fractious and divided decade.

>> **2013, end of people smuggling of asylum seekers:** Operation Sovereign Borders — introduced by the new Abbott Government in 2013 — re-established the integrity of Australia's maritime border. The traffic in thousands of asylum seekers — some 50,000 between 2009 and 2013 — arriving in Australia abruptly halted. This also put an end to the tragedy of over 1000 deaths of asylum seekers attempting the journey during this time.

>> **2014, two planes down:** In March 2014, a Malaysian Airlines flight took off from Kuala Lumpur airport en route to Beijing, carrying 239 people, including six Australians. Soon after take-off, the plane just plain vanished. Searches across continents and ocean floors were conducted for years afterwards but, as yet, the plane remains unaccounted for. Then in July another Malaysia Airlines Flight took off, this time from Amsterdam, and also failed to reach its final destination.

>> **2014, Joe smokes a big cigar, and a budget takes people by surprise:** Treasurer Joe Hockey handed down the Abbott Government's first budget in May 2014, asking Australians to collectively tighten their belts after Labor's spending during and after the global financial crisis. This was one of the Abbott Government's big agenda items on taking power. Things went badly off-script, however. Funding cuts to services that some of the most vulnerable people in the community (including pensioners, low income workers and

students) were relying on, and which hadn't been spoken of pre-election, caused immediate public backlash. Photographs of Treasurer Hockey and Finance Minister Mathias Cormann laughing while smoking expensive-looking cigars right before announcing the budget only reinforced the 'friends of big business fat cats' stereotype. The Abbott Government's popularity, already a touch on the grim side, turned dramatically south, and kept heading down.

>> **2015, Abbott makes a 'captain's call' and knights a prince:** So, how do you feel about reintroducing knighthoods into Australian life? This wasn't a question most people thought about — indeed, most hadn't really thought about it for decades since the practice had been abandoned in the 1970s. Then Abbott surprised pretty much everyone, including colleagues, by reintroducing knighthoods early in his time as prime minister. As it turned out, the vast majority of Australians found their answer near to hand, and it generally sounded something like, 'Are you nuts?' For a country that had always prided itself on its lack of social distinctions, this seemed a backward step, and one that confirmed many people's view of Abbott as a politician with social values out of step with ordinary mainstream Australia. On Australia Day in January 2015, Abbott knighted the UK's Prince Phillip. This 'captain's call' decision was for many Liberal MPs the last straw, and he was replaced by Malcolm Turnbull several months later.

Turnbull's time

In 2015, Malcolm Turnbull challenged Abbott for leadership of the Liberal Party and won — becoming Australia's new Prime Minister in the process. The reason Turnbull said Abbott had to go because he wasn't providing economic leadership — oh, and because he'd lost 30 straight fortnightly opinion polls so his chances of regaining public support were pretty much gone . . . (See the next section for more on how this reasoning played out for Turnbull.)

Representing the 'small L liberal', progressive wing of the Liberal Party, and attuned to the ideals and causes that preoccupied the university-educated, inner-city situated, cosmopolitan and globally focused part of Australia, Turnbull ditched knighthoods within roughly 28 seconds of becoming prime minister, and focused energy much more strongly on issues such as climate change, same-sex marriage and economics. Stronger economic growth, more trade, more innovation and higher productivity was the new signature tune. And Turnbull could point to his own successes prior to politics — in business and as an entrepreneur he'd amassed a significant fortune — to show that, as he put it, 'I wasn't just another professional politician mouthing talking-point platitudes'.

'IT DOESN'T EXPLAIN EVERYTHING, IT DOESN'T EXPLAIN NOTHING': WOMEN AND MISOGYNY IN POLITICAL LIFE

Women have been active participants in Australian political life since at least the 1880s and 1890s, when they campaigned for the right to vote and to stand for Parliament at elections. (Refer to Chapters 11 and 12 for this story). They were successful, achieving these combined rights before anywhere else in the world. By the 1940s, the middle class women and suburban housewives of the Australian National Women's League had become one of the most formidable grassroots campaigning organisations in the country. Their commitment to Robert Menzies's newly formed Liberal Party was a key element in its success (refer to Chapter 18.)

By the 1990s, however, women were severely unrepresented in parliament on both sides. To help deal with this, Labor brought in gender quotas to ensure more women became MPs. (And the quotas succeeded. By 2020, Labor women had achieved near 50/50 parity in parliament (well. . . 41 per cent). The Liberal side was still badly lagging behind though, with only 20 per cent of Liberal MPs women.)

When Gillard became prime minister she at first played down the significance of her being Australia's first woman in the job, preferring to be treated solely on the merits of her contribution as political leader. The extremely divisive nature of political debate in the aftermath of Rudd's fall, however, was only heightened by arguments over Labor's proposed mining profits tax and tax on carbon. Gillard being a woman featured prominently in the pejorative statements, slogans, pictures and comments being made about her.

The fact that her performance as prime minister was coming in for extremely negative criticism wasn't the problem — there's never been an Australian prime minister who hasn't come in for extremely negative criticism. It's part of the rough and tumble of open democratic life. But heavily misogynist attitudes were directed at her as well. Banners at protests read 'Bitch', and 'Ditch the Witch', making clear that, well, this isn't just rough and tumble; this is a gender thing.

By October 2012 Julia Gillard had had enough, and let rip in parliament.

'I will not be lectured about sexism and misogyny by this man. I will not . . . not now, not ever', she said in response to opposition leader Tony Abbott's arguments that the government should be ashamed of its parliamentary Speaker's sexist test messages that had just come to light. Speaking without prepared notes (beyond a selection of Abbott's own comments in years previous), she let loose on entrenched stereotypes of 'abortions being the easy way out', on housewives doing the ironing, and all the implications that women shouldn't be considered equals participating on equal terms in public life. She finished with the suggestion that Abbott 'should think seriously about the role of women in public life and in Australian society because we are entitled to a better standard than this'.

Gillard's words struck a deep chord of recognition across Australia, and beyond. Initially not much noticed by the press gallery in parliament, within days her speech was trending globally, and for the rest of the 2010s clips of the speech continued to be watched and rewatched. (By the end of the decade, it had been watched more than 3 million times, making it by a comfortable margin the most watched parliamentary speech in Australian history.)

Part of the reason it continues to be watched is because it's just great viewing — fiery, impassioned, intense. Another reason is because the issues Gillard highlighted remain — and don't look to be going away any time soon. Tellingly, while in government Tony Abbott, Gillard's great political enemy, made a similar argument about gender bias against Peta Credlin, his chief of staff. Credlin was heavily criticised for her abrasive approach towards colleagues, MPs and ministers. Abbott made the point that her behaviour was essentially standard practice for chiefs of staff. In a television interview, he wondered whether these same criticisms would be made if 'Peta' were 'Peter'.

Social media though, and the sort of public conversations which occur on them, is a key part of this story. On platforms like Twitter and other social networks the toxic virulence aimed at women who are participants in the public arena — female journalists and politicians especially — has to be seen to be believed.

In February 2021, an ex-political staffer, Brittany Higgins, alleged that she'd been sexually assaulted inside Parliament House late one night in the weeks before the 2019 election. The allegations have led to a trial for rape (in progress at the time of writing). More widely than that, they triggered a national outpouring of grief, rage and mortification. The alleged assault in the 'People's House' at the top of the big hill in Canberra served as a lightning rod for wider experiences and traumas that different women have experienced and dealt with in workplaces all over Australia. Enormous rallies and public demonstrations followed.

At the end of November 2021, Sex Discrimination Commissioner Kate Jenkins filed a wide-ranging review into parliamentary workplaces. Her report found that some 50 per cent of people working in parliament had experienced bullying, sexual harassment or sexual assault — a fairly shocking number for any workplace in the 2020s, and especially so for the symbolic centre of the Australian national community.

The Jenkins Report submitted 28 recommendations to set about changing the workplace culture at Parliament House. These included restrictions on alcohol, new codes of conduct for MPs and staff, new oversight bodies to review complaints, and gender equality targets and diversity targets, as well as the elimination of sexist and discriminatory language from parliamentary debate. They indicate how much that the firsts that Australian women such as Julia Gillard and Quentin Bryce (Australia's first female Governor-General) have achieved are by no means the end of the equality story in Australian life.

Under Turnbull's government two really significant changes were enacted:

>> Same-sex marriage became legal, after a public plebiscite on the question in 2017 gave everyone a sense that the question had been put to the people, and commanded a majority.

>> New foreign interference, espionage and cybersecurity laws were put in place to grapple with a whole new order of threat to Australian interests, society and sovereignty. These threats came from multiple sources, but dominantly from China.

The public plebiscite on same-sex marriage was held as a mail-in vote — after parliament had reached an impasse on whether to legislate for marriage equality or not. (A total of 13 unsuccessful attempts to pass legislation in parliament in 13 previous years had provided reasonable evidence of that.) In a democracy with a Bill of Rights, the matter could have been settled in court rather than via public plebiscite, and opinion was divided about whether this was a good or bad thing. Surely, argued some, basic inalienable rights, such as the right to marry, shouldn't require the majority of fellow citizens voting 'Yes'.

Others argued differently. They thought that a significant shift in one of Australia's most basic and elemental institutions was exactly the sort of thing which should be debated, and put to democratic vote. If nothing else, a vote would help secure 'buy-in' — that is, if the issue achieved majority support, most people would then accept it, even those who voted against it. And this proved to be the case. More than 60 per cent of people who responded to the mail-out plebiscite gave same-sex marriage the big tick.

LIFE DOWN UNDER

In the three years following same-sex marriage becoming legal in Australia, some 14,000 same-sex couples got married, with 59 per cent women marrying women, and 41 per cent men marrying men. And so far the sky hasn't fallen in. The change may not have happened in the way everyone reckoned it should, but same-sex marriage has been embraced by most, and become part of the ordinary fabric of life. It's hard to argue against the merits of these outcomes.

Turnbull was initially very popular. However, he struggled to keep support in the conservative echelon of his party, and with the regional and outer suburban demographics who were more inclined to view his sunny ebullient optimism with suspicion.

ISSUING AN ULURU STATEMENT FROM THE HEART

By 2015, the need to recognise Indigenous Australians in the Constitution had been agreed on both sides of politics, and a Referendum Council had been established with equal numbers of Indigenous and non-Indigenous Australians to advise on the best route to ensuring this. A series of community consultations culminated in a conference at Uluru, in the physical centre of Australia, in May 2017. This conference then issued its final recommendation to government (actually, addressed directly to the Australian people) at the end of June. Called the Uluru Statement from the Heart, this statement suggested establishing in the Constitution a national advisory assembly, made up of and elected by Aboriginal and Torres Strait Islander peoples. Parliament would be required to consult with this body on any legislation touching Indigenous matters. It was to be a 'Voice to Parliament'.

The Voice to Parliament proposal has attracted strong support. It's seen as a way of giving Indigenous Australians an explicit channel of input on both legislation and the ongoing national conversation. But it has attracted strong criticism as well. Establishing a national assembly that is explicitly available to only one group of Australians — is that enhancing or debilitating Australian democracy?

This is the crux of the argument. It's not so much a case of the head versus the heart, as one of two genuinely different expressions of the 'heart of the nation'. This is a fiendishly difficult public problem which, as yet at least, defies any clear consensus.

Turnbull undone

What brought Turnbull undone was 31 straight bad opinion poll results, and an inability to manage the very different views within one of Australia's greatest current challenges — namely, energy policy and (very much related to that) climate change.

IN THEIR WORDS

Turnbull had justified his challenge to Abbott in significant part on the fact that Abbott had become, like Julia Gillard previously, crushingly unpopular. 'We have lost 30 Newspolls in a row. It is clear that the people have made up their mind about Mr Abbott's leadership,' he said. This sounded nice and crisp and cut-through at the time, but wilted significantly afterwards — particularly when the Turnbull Government also passed this marker of a fortnightly opinion poll survey in April 2018.

The trigger for Turnbull's downfall came in a heated disagreement within the Liberal Party over a national energy policy that included targets to reduce carbon emissions while simultaneously trying to ensure that energy prices would be kept low.

HISTORICAL
ROOTS

The irony for Turnbull would certainly not have been lost on him, given that he had been leader of the Liberal Party when in opposition in 2009 — and had lost the leadership to Tony Abbott over his response to the Labor Government's proposed carbon emission scheme. After negotiations with then Prime Minister Rudd, Turnbull had agreed to a deal on amendments to Labor's Carbon Pollution Reduction Scheme, and had urged Coalition MPs to support the revised scheme. However, Abbott was persuaded by arguments made by Liberal Senator Nick Minchin, and strong feedback from grassroots supporters and regional communities, that this was a disastrous direction to take, for both the Liberal Party and the nation generally. Turnbull was replaced as leader of the Opposition over climate change policy in 2009 — and was again replaced in 2018, this time as prime minister. If nothing else, it demonstrated the old proverbial line that whilst history may not ever repeat itself exactly, it sure can *rhyme*.

Believing in election miracles

Turnbull's replacement — this time as prime minister — was Scott Morrison, who came in with an election due in several months. He was given next to no chance of leading the government to victory — not by opinion polls nor by political pundits. Even his close collaborator, Treasurer Josh Frydenberg, later admitted he hadn't expected the government to be returned.

However, Morrison ran an extremely disciplined campaign. He concentrated on doing two things:

» Attack Labor's extensive election platform, focusing especially on the recent Labor track record of increasing taxes

» Talk up the ordinary values of what Morrison later called the 'Quiet Australians' — the ideals of personal freedom and the chance to prosper on your own terms in life

And it worked. (See the sidebar 'Election 2019: Flashbulb moment on the two Australias' for more on this election win, and what it said about where Australia was at.)

IN THEIR
WORDS

On the night of the election win, a jubilant Morrison told his crowd of supporters, 'I've always believed in miracles!' It was the most unexpected federal election result since the ALP's Paul Keating delivered 'One for the True Believers' in 1993. After this, though, the miracles pretty much dried up for Morrison. In the first year of his prime ministership, an extremely dry summer created conditions that led to the most extensive bushfires in Australian history. While the number of lives lost didn't compare to previous, more localised tragedies (such as the Black Saturday bushfires in 2009, or Ash Wednesday in 1983), these fires extended across three states, and burnt for months, destroying homes and properties, and devastating rural communities.

LIFE DOWN UNDER

Prime Minister Morrison was heavily criticised for the Commonwealth Government's lack of response for the Black Summer bushfires in December 2019 and January 2020. (Nor did it help when word leaked out that he'd gone on holiday to Hawaii with his family in the middle of it.) The Australian public, as frequently the case when confronted with a crisis, weren't that interested in the niceties of state and Commonwealth jurisdictions, even if fire-fighting services were almost entirely conducted in states. They just wanted the problem fixed.

Tackling Three Seriously Significant Issues

As 2020 rolled around, Australia and Australians had no shortage of big issues to wrestle with. Three monumental ones standout, though — our relationship with China, 'Big Tech' and how to respond to the COVID-19 pandemic.

That big China question

In July 2020, the Australian government released an innocuously titled 'Strategic Defence Update', which signalled one of the biggest challenges Australia has faced in its history.

The challenge, essentially, is this: how does Australia deal with a nearby geostrategic leviathan nation, which has become our greatest economic trading partner and helped power our own economic boom for 15-odd years, but has also become the most aggressive threat to our national security as a self-governing, open society?

Plot-spoiler: This question has no easy answer.

The Strategic Defence Update effectively tore up the old rule book, which had been articulated as recently as the Defence White Paper in 2016. This had assured everyone that the chance of military conflict in our region was 'remote'. The new Update pointed out that we could no longer assume that if a country became hostile to Australia, we would have a 10-year window to prepare and counter the threat. Instead, the Update emphasised the need to quickly acquire new long-range weapons. (It didn't mention nuclear-powered subs, but they do fit that description nicely).

At the same time, both sides of parliament had been involved in joint committees on intelligence and security. These committees identified China as the biggest threat to Australian sovereignty by a considerable margin. Evidence pointing to this conclusion included:

>> Systematic state-operated espionage and cyber attacks on Australian Parliament and other key institutions

>> dangerous moves to secure sovereignty over internationally contested, strategically important, parts of the oceans

>> economic coercion (such as tariffs specifically targeting Australia)

>> the complete severance of all official dialogue coupled with a dramatic increase of threatening language from 'Wolf Warrior' Chinese diplomats and officials.

HISTORICAL ROOTS

The 'great war', cyber hostility, economic coercion and public browbeating of Australia by China didn't exactly come out of nowhere though. In the ten years to 2022 a dramatic shift in China's behaviour towards other nations has manifested itself. Some of the key moments for Australia in this decade include moments such as:

>> 2012: Xi Jinping became General Secretary of the Chinese Communist Party, and in 2013 President of the People's Republic of China. China is ruled as an authoritarian dictatorship by the Communist Party, so if you control these organisations you control its government and state. Since taking these posts, Xi has consolidated more state power in his hands since any Chinese leader in the past 40 years. At the same time, Chinese Government actions internationally have become dramatically more aggressive. This has caused a rise in tensions with almost all of its nearby regional neighbours, and with the United States, Canada, Britain, Australia and other nations.

>> 2018: Australia passed foreign interference laws, and banned Chinese telco Huawei from any involvement in developing Australia's 5G networks, due to fears it would compromise national security and sovereignty. (It was a lead that would be followed by other nations globally.)

>> 2020: Australia called for an independent investigation into the origins of the coronavirus outbreak (which spread from Wuhan in China from December 2019).

Both the telco ban and the call for an independent investigation into the origins of COVID-19 were given prominence in the instantly notorious '14 Grievances' released by the Chinese embassy in Canberra in November 2020. These Grievances explicitly spelt out the things Australia had done wrong in the eyes of the Chinese government — and what it would have to fix before better treatment could be expected. This list of 'behave — or else' non-negotiables implied the dilution or curtailment of Australia's sovereignty as a self-governing nation, and so raised some fairly basic problems. Insisting, for example, that the government in Australia needed to control free media and press in order to stop 'unfriendly or antagonistic media reports' about China, or prohibit members of parliament from voicing opinions and views similarly critical, would mean that whatever you called 'Australia' subsequently, 'independent free nation' wasn't really it.

Simultaneously, this public dispute was paralleled by what intelligence experts described as 'grey-zone tactics'. These were methods of hostile aggression, generally cyber and online, against government entities and critical infrastructure providers. The aim of these tactics is to compromise or fundamentally weaken a nation's capacity to govern itself, and defend itself from outside aggressors.

The big questions in the here and now for Australians to debate are these:

>> How to maintain national sovereignty?

>> How to maintain one's independence as a self-governing independent nation?

>> How does a small nation protect itself in a periodically malign world?

>> And what should it do when the threat comes from its largest and most important trading partner?

The first three are not new questions for Australia. But they have gotten an awful lot sharper and more pertinent as we enter the 2020s. The fourth question though is completely new. We've never had the 'great threat is also your great economic trading partner' combo before. Like some of the other issues outlined in this chapter, this issue makes for another fiendishly difficult problem for 2020s Australia to wrestle with.

The People versus Big Tech

Social media, search engines and the internet generally have now become almost totally embedded in people's daily lives. This is now basic infrastructure that most people can't live their life without — similar to running water, roads and functioning sewerage.

The Australian Competition and Consumer Commission (ACCC) is one of those seemingly extremely boring parts of Australian life, but which periodically do some extremely interesting and influential things. The ACCC is an administrative outfit (which Australian parliaments and governments love inventing, often to deal with tricky questions and controversial issues), and it carries serious heft — it can initiate enforcement action in the courts, and is able to impose some of the largest penalties on companies anywhere in the world. (Try 10 per cent of your company's annual turnover as penalty — that's enough to seriously hurt).

In 2019, the ACCC picked a fight with the biggest and most powerful corporations on the planet: Google and Facebook. A year later, just for fun, it took on Apple too.

The ACCC found that Google especially had acquired a position of almost total dominance as an online provider, operating as both publisher and advertiser simultaneously. Google and Facebook's influence over the public consumption of news also looked fundamentally problematic for a free society.

The ACCC argued Facebook and Google's continued dominance was harming the interests of Australian consumers. Consumers generate the vast rivers of human data that are harvested online daily and then sold to the highest bidders at auction, and, the ACCC argued, they effectively have very little choice about or control over this.

HISTORICAL ROOTS

Anonymous trolling on social media, too, has altered the nature of public debate. Barring actual court orders, tech giants have been intensely reluctant to hand over identifying information, even when accounts have engaged in criminal conduct, such as stalking and defamation.

In the wake of the ACCC's findings, new laws were put forward, looking to change the scope and power of global media platforms. At the time of writing, a new Federal Court order is being planned to require social media companies to disclose identifying details of trolls to police or victims, without consent, which could enable a defamation trial.

The scope and power the ACCC has compared to other regulatory bodies in other parts of the world means that what happens here is being followed closely by regulators and people in Europe, Britain, Canada, the United States and other parts of the world as well. File it under 'watch this space. . .'

The People versus COVID

The global pandemic was one of the 'once in a century' events that altered practically every component of people's lives. In fact, this one occurred almost exactly 100 years after the so-called Spanish Flu epidemic that hit Australia in 1919 and 1920. (How do you like *that* for timing?) The Australian response makes it another flashbulb moment of Australian culture, casting light on what we value and what we're willing to sacrifice — and for how long, and for what.

By late 2021, Australia was the third most successful country in the world at minimising deaths per head of population due to COVID-19. After initial 'vaccine hesitancy' and lack of vaccine availability, well over 90 per cent of people over 16 had been fully vaccinated, putting Australia near the top of the 'league table' of nations globally. Neither of these successes would have been possible without:

» Strong state action

» Widespread community support

» High levels of trust in government and the state.

The COVID-19 novel coronavirus began in Wuhan, China, late in 2019, and quickly spread across the entire world. Australia was one of the first countries to shut its borders to flights from China, and then to all international flights, which helped limit how rapidly the virus spread. Different Australian states then closed their borders to each other as virus outbreaks occurred in different cities and population centres. Some of the most extensive and long-lasting lockdowns anywhere in the world were imposed by different state governments in Australia in 2020 and 2021. (That's right Victoria, we're talking about you here.)

Large parts of the Australian population, at times a majority of its 26 million people, found itself under essentially house arrest for weeks and months. It was a total suppression of daily movement and freedoms unlike anything seen in Australian history, even in wartime. It fundamentally, if temporarily, stripped away practically every basic freedom in democratic society:

>> Of movement

>> Of work and business

>> Of religious practice

>> Of any public gatherings at all

You could no longer go to your friend's house. You couldn't go get your hair cut. You could walk along a beach, maybe, for an hour, as long as you were wearing a face mask (even if no-one else was within a mile of you). The amazing thing here is just how willing people were to give up these freedoms for what proved to be inordinately long and indefinite periods of time. They did this for their own perceived safety, and those of their loved ones. They also accepted the restrictions for the common good — for strangers they'd never met, and never would meet: fellow citizens who were vulnerable to infection because of age or already compromised effort. Given how much talk there is nowadays about the decline of public trust this was a significant achievement.

The longer that COVID lockdowns continued though, and the more they recurred, the more sceptical, cynical and just plain fed up people got. This could be seen especially in Melbourne, which set the world record for number of days in hard lockdown across 2020–2021. A significant minority pushed back, ignored the rules, protested, and argued that the government was guilty of significantly authoritarian overreach. That great reservoir of trust which authorities, governments and their medical advisers had been able to draw on initially was now close to emptied.

A strict authoritarian government response, it turns out, is permitted in an open democratic society. But it has to be temporary, and only for as long as the emergency lasts. Beyond that . . . you're pushing it.

CATCHING UP ON THE CLIMATE WARS

If public debate is anything to go by (and most of the time that's pretty much all we've got), then Australian opinion about how to deal with anthropogenic (or human-caused) climate change has been hugely divided in the first decades of the 21st century. At any given moment, it's been subject to sudden reversals as well as long drawn-out pendulum swings. At different elections from 2007, Australians have:

- Decisively embraced immediate and transformative climate action
- Just as decisively, rejected this approach completely

In 2019, at the most recent election at the time of writing, a climate change policy was the primary cause of Independent Zali Steggall's defeat of Tony Abbott in the inner-city Sydney electorate of Warringah. Simultaneously, climate change was also the chief reason Labor's Joel Fitzgibbon (with similar policies to Steggall's on climate change) went within a whisker of losing his seat in the Hunter Valley coal-mining region of NSW — a seat held by himself and his father before him for decades.

So what's going on?

The split over climate change has run strongly between the regions and outer suburbs on the one side, and cosmopolitan urban city Australia on the other. Also, though, it's a split that has emerged from ordinary Australian voters themselves. Time and again, people have told pollsters that climate change is an overriding priority that exceeds practically all other major public questions and absolutely must be dealt with immediately. And, time and again, it has remained a priority right up until the costs of dramatic reductions in carbon emissions have become apparent to voters.

The prosperity and cost of living questions bound up in climate change policies are, if anything, more acute in Australia than most comparable developed nations. Unlike countries such as the United Kingdom, New Zealand, Japan, South Korea and Europe (although more like the United States and Canada) Australia is a sort of fossil fuel superpower. An enormous proportion of its economic dynamism and growth has come from the industries that have boomed in recent decades to meet the voracious global appetite for primary fuels and raw minerals extracted from or beneath Australian soil. Gas, coal, iron ore and the like have supercharged (or, at other moments, simply sustained) economic growth. They've been our largest exports, and helped provide cheap energy for various industries and for households.

Punishing or damaging these industries would have been a significantly larger act of economic self-harm in Australia than elsewhere. The passionately put argument against this view, of course, has been that a destroyed and broken planet offers no long-term prosperity. Neither, though, is future generations impoverished by self-incurred economic degradation. Most other developed nations, too, have low-emission nuclear industries to help realise cheap, reliable low-carbon energy in the short term.

Other nations have made bigger and bolder pledges of cutting carbon emissions, but often failed to realise them. Global climate agreements struck at high-profile meetings of the world's nations date from the Kyoto Protocol of 1997 through to the Bali Climate Change Conference of 2007, Copenhagen in 2009, Paris in 2016 and Glasgow in 2021. These have almost entirely failed to ensure binding targets for individual nations, with debate ongoing as to how much of the emissions cutting burden should be shouldered by the developing nations, which are currently the biggest source of rising emissions.

Australia is per capita one of the highest emitters of carbon gases in the world. In reputation, economic size and general influence, Australia also tends to punch above its weight on the global stage. In the eyes of some, this puts an ethical imperative on us to lead from the front, to set an example. At the same time, though, Australia's actual contribution to emissions is miniscule — somewhere in the region of 1 per cent. Australia could reduce its carbon emissions to completely zero tomorrow, and not make barely a dent on solving human-induced global warming.

So what to do?

Again, we've stumbled across another of our ongoing 'wicked problems' — the fiendishly difficult issues which defy a simple, clear solution.

At the beginning of the 2020s, however, some signs are emerging that the political and public opinion tectonic plates are shifting. At the time of writing, the two major political parties — the Labor Party, led by Anthony Albanese, and the Liberals, still led by Scott Morrison — have converged on similar moderate policy ground. Both are looking to technology developments as much as anything else to ensure that future carbon emission cuts are realised. Both are going out of their way to ensure that key stakeholders — the general public, mining industries and blue collar workers, and the business community — are all on the same page.

Crucially, the world situation is signalling significant change. Not so much in the commitments of the major nations to cut carbon emissions (which may or may not come to fruition), but in the shift in global capital and investment markets, and other main economic players. These markets and players are indicating that those who find a way to reduce their carbon footprint will be rewarded, and those who don't will be effectively handicapped accordingly. This is the great potential game-changer. The economic costs of not making significant changes begin to outweigh the economic benefits of keeping on going. No other policy area in contemporary Australian life, though, is more prone to those already mentioned sudden reversals and changes — so watch this space!

Leaders, Politics, Culture and Two Australias

Australian prime ministers aren't like American presidents — they're not directly elected into power by the people. To get to be prime minister, you need to first be a member of parliament, and then leading the political party that has control of parliament through holding a majority of seats in its lower house. (If you want a more in-depth explanation of this process, *Australian Politics for Dummies*, 2e, by Nick Economou and Zareh Ghazarian, Wiley Australia Publishing, is a great place to start). And if a political party decides it wants to change its leader — and so remove a sitting prime minister — well, it can change its leader. This is how Australian democratic politics works. All the same, when it happens voters can feel like they've been jumped. The Prime Minister is the nation's leader — the decider-in-chief. There is a certain aura that accrues around the office. Knocking off a PM outside of elections is no small thing.

As leaders, the recent prime ministers — Rudd, Gillard, Abbott and Turnbull — all made bad decisions. They also made good decisions. Often, though, they failed to sell them to the public, to their own party members, or their own parliamentary colleagues. Were they the first prime ministers to fail in this way? Of course not. New leaders often fail in getting things right, especially as they're starting out. But in this modern era, failing meant either electoral wipe-out or political death by colleagues. No time to learn on the job. No period of grace. Get it wrong, or do some things people don't like, and that's it — your support in the polls collapses. Your job's on the line.

On top of this, the two major parties have lost a lot of the intense, almost tribal support which voters in previous generations displayed towards the Red (ALP) or Blue (Liberal) Teams. Nowadays voters shop around more, and are much more likely to change who they vote for from one election to another. This means the government could fall quite easily, at the next election, no matter how big their current majority is. The number of people who will vote either way at an election is now nearly half the public (or around 40 per cent), whereas it used to be closer to a fifth or even a tenth (10 to 20 per cent).

IN THEIR WORDS

The consequences of this modern era if you are a government or a leader were described by journalist George Megalogenis in the following way: 'It means when you go to work, even the day after you get elected, you only have about a third of the electorate committed to you and two thirds ready to dump you almost immediately'.

From tribe to brand

The major Australian political parties have become less tribal and more retail. Up until the 1980s and 1990s, in ex-Prime Minister John Howard's estimation, about 80 per cent of the population could be classified as 'rusted on' supporters of either Labor or the Liberal–National coalition. The two main parties were mass membership organisations, with grassroots and community-based support. Labor's organisation was connected to a trade union movement that a majority of Australian workers were members of. The Liberal side utilised street-by-street community presence, through social occasions, BBQs and other assorted engagement activities managed by their state-based organisations.

The activities of both parties were all very close to the face of ordinary people in their daily lives. That is no longer the case. The two major political groupings still gain the vast proportion of parliamentary seats at each election, but they are less and less people's first choice, and instead have to rely on secondary preferences.

These days people are less affiliated with one of the political sides, or 'tribes', and are more likely to pick and choose. They may vote for one party at one election, but six weeks into the next government have decided that party is actually a pack of heartless idiots, and so turfs them out next time round. At the same time, political parties have begun exhaustively conducting their own private polling and research among ordinary voters. When support for a political leader begins to plummet, things tend to end badly for the political leader in question. And this has been the bottom line, really, if you want to explain the musical chairs routine in the prime minister's office for the 2010s.

Politicians no longer receive unquestioning support and trust. This connects to broader societal trends, where offices, and authority in various forms, are just that much less respected now than previously. In a long-term which began in the 1960s, Australians (in line with people worldwide) have become increasingly good at questioning authority. They call out abuses of power in institutions that were previously venerated — in the defence force, in schools and orphanages, in relations between men and women, in the workplace, on the sports field. This calling out hasn't eradicated the abuses themselves, of course — that remains an ongoing, perhaps unending story in human relations.

LIFE DOWN UNDER

Australians have always had a bit of a larrikin, anti-authority side. But we've now taken this even further. We no longer defer to any authority — our bosses, our elders, the police, the Church bishop, the soldiers in uniform — in nearly the same way we used to. And people who want to be leaders have to be phenomenally good at talking up inclusivity every step of the way. Authority has lost a lot of its gloss, a lot if its, well . . . authority. Even a country renowned for its aggressively egalitarian enforcement of 'tall poppy syndrome' has historically held deep respect for the role of national leader. Nowadays, increasingly less so.

Politics? Downstream of culture

Politics is connected to ordinary life. It's 'downstream of culture', as the saying has it. Moving from distant past to recent past to just-last-week past brings politics more dominantly into focus, because in an open society such as Australia's, politics and political debate, conducted in public and in front of everyone, offer some of the most immediate reflections of what people are preoccupied by. Considering current Australian politics is an excellent way to cut to the chase of what people are worried about, afraid of, passionate about, enraged by, greedy for, energised by and idealistically yearning for.

Every election is a snapshot in time, where everyone gets to step forward and give some indication of what they think is the right and wrong direction for the national community to be travelling in. This is especially the case in Australia where, unlike practically every other comparable nation in the world, voting is compulsory for everyone.

The ongoing saga of recent politics is a good reflection of what's going on in wider society for another reason. For pretty much all of modern Australian history, and modern global history too, we've seen an increasingly larger and more pervasive *state* (all levels of government) at work in the lives of its citizens. The state has taken on roles that previous generations would never have dreamt likely or practicable — including regulating and funding health and hospitals, overseeing education curricula and schools and monitoring internet use.

This means people are running into the state, or tripping across it, every day of their lives, and seeing it play out in the lives of their families. Politicians — the people who run the state, or who are charged with responsibility for it — are front and centre of people's minds in a way that wasn't the case even 50 years ago, and definitely not 100 tor 200 years ago. This became vastly more pronounced during the 2020–21 COVID epidemic, where the Prime Minister, the state Premiers, their ministerial cabinets, and their health experts, became constant presences on our news feeds, as people devoured hours' worth of press conferences trying to find out whether they were allowed to resume their daily lives and businesses, and why or why not.

Culture? Downwind of politics

In *cultural* terms (as in, people's basic preoccupations, ways of doing things, and values and preoccupations), Australia seems to be becoming an increasingly divided place, with two distinct halves of the nation opening up.

These two halves could be tagged 'Cosmopolis' and 'Heartland' Australia. They have split on almost all the big debates occurring in the national conversation since 2010. These include:

>> Climate change

>> Coal mining (especially the India-supported Adani mine in Queensland)

>> Euthanasia

>> Gay and transgender rights and identity

>> Indigenous treaty and a First Nations Voice to Parliament

>> Religious freedom

>> Same-sex marriage

>> Teaching practices, cultural values and history curricula in schools

>> Commemorating Australia Day

The digital revolution of the past 20 years has meant people get their news and views from narrower fields, and from places more specific to their own particular preoccupations, biases and interests. Which is fine, great even — we're all about personal choice in life, right? But even so . . . this trend has served to isolate us into separate groups more than previously.

Even as the amount of information we daily consume has rocketed almost exponentially, so too has the lens we filter it through — the lens of values, issues and preoccupation — become narrower. And one consequence of this has been an increasing divide between two halves of Australia, where people more and more occupy mutually exclusive conversations. This divide means that in any great public debate the two Australias don't talk to each other; instead, they talk about each other to themselves. Or, in social medial especially, they prefer belligerent shouting at the perceived other camp.

Australians used to participate in a wider range of groups that met face to face and organised their activities together. This might have been through churches, sports clubs, community groups, political party branches and hobbies. Being involved in this span of different groups meant people learned to get along with each other. Nowadays, though, these kinds of organisations are minority pursuits. Even fewer people engage in multiple membership groups. As these groups have shrunk, so too it seems has our ability to coexist and tolerate each other.

Where you sit on the Cosmopolis–Heartland divide will give a general indication of what side of each of the listed debates you tend to come down on. Your position will also tend to indicate where you get your news and views from.

Rather than the older 'mainstream' Australia, now two main streams exist, which could become their own rivers.

Cosmopolis Australia

In this camp is densely urban and inner suburban Australia — younger, university and tertiary educated Australia. These are global-thinking citizens of the world, who are more likely to find work and travel across the planet from one job to another than into Australia's regional hinterland.

Cosmopolis-dwellers are educated, wealthy, cosmopolitan, most likely to vote Greens and Labor, with strongholds in media, publicity, academia, advertising, financial services, law and various personal services. They will likely have voted yes to same-sex marriage and support euthanasia, back LGBTQI rights against religious freedom, support an Indigenous treaty and a Voice to Parliament, and condemn government failure to legislate more dramatic change to eliminate carbon emissions and ban coal mining.

And on the other side of the divide . . .

Heartland Australia

This is self-identifying 'ordinary', outer suburban and regional Australia. Heartland Australia is less likely to have university degrees, more likely to be a tradie or manual worker, and also more likely to be part of a recently arrived migrant community and be more religiously conservative. They are more preoccupied with families and intergenerational familial relationships. They believe strongly in tolerance and the fair go, but also in having the freedom to get on with their lives without intrusion from others. They think kids at school should be taught how to read and write and about the nation's history before they should focus on progressive causes. They are what Scott Morrison described, after his 2019 election win, as 'the quiet Australians'.

Heartland Australia was on the whole happy enough to support same-sex marriage — a 'fair go' means believing in equality, after all, and 'marriage equality' resonated. (Although the areas of highest religious conservatism and recent migration, such as the suburbs of western Sydney, weren't convinced.) Heartland Australia also stands by the mutual tolerance that made multiculturalism and mass-migration one of the great Australian success stories from the 1950s onward.

Exhibit A for the Heartland–Cosmopolis disconnect? Look no further than the 2019 election.

ELECTION 2019: FLASHBULB MOMENT ON THE TWO AUSTRALIAS

Scott Morrison's Liberal Party election victory in May 2019 reads like a snapshot in time. It was not a landslide, but was unexpected, and remarkably 'against trend' of expectation and public conversation. What had happened? Research conducted in its aftermath showed the result came down to the battle between Heartland and Cosmopolis Australia.

Labor's proposed tax policies divided the electorate. So too did talk of the ongoing 'climate change emergency', and debate about the proposed Adani coalmine in Queensland.

At the election, Labor attracted strong support among middle class, university educated voters — or Cosmopolis central. These voters didn't abandon the Labor Party, which actually gained votes in white-collar, high-income, highly educated areas. But a significant number of blue-collar, low-income workers, ALP's traditional supporters, did.

Meanwhile, people in outer metropolitan seats, including young families, and recent migrant, religiously conservative communities, rejected cosmopolitan, globalist values, and moved away from Labor. In Queensland, in outer suburbs and in regional areas especially, people switched their votes. (Often these votes went from Labor to United Australia Party and One Nation, but second or third preferences indicated on the ballot papers meant the votes eventually ended in the Liberal-National coalition corner.)

Morrison meanwhile, campaigned big on the classic 'ordinary freedoms' and values that have been central to Australian life since pretty much the whole of our history as a self-governing nation. He appealed to tradies and families, who often enough hadn't been to university, but were earning decent livings. He identified strongly as an ordinary, rugby-loving, suburban Dad. On the night of the election, he said it was the 'quiet Australians' who had won the victory:

> *It has been those Australians who have worked hard every day, they have their dreams, they have their aspirations; to get a job, to get an apprenticeship, to start a business, to meet someone amazing. To start a family, to buy a home, to work hard and provide the best you can for your kids. To save your retirement and to ensure that when you're in your retirement, that you can enjoy it because you've worked hard for it.*

At the beginning of 2022 it was still impossible to say with any certainty which side of politics would win the next election and form government. One thing though continued to be quite certain — whichever side was more successful in appealing to *both* Heartland and Cosmopolis Australia would come up trumps.

Is that possible, though? To genuinely appeal to both, with the divide seemingly getting bigger and bigger? Maybe. Maybe not. This isn't the first seemingly intractable problem that's faced the nation though, and Australia's journey has consistently surprised. In the 2020s it's still doing so. We can look forward to what the next bend in the road will show.

7
The Part of Tens

Discover how to impress people with some quirky piece of knowledge about what has been invented in Australia or by Australians who have gone on to take off in the world.

Gain a quick idea about what the real 'game-changing' moments or events in Australian history were — the sorts of things after which nothing is ever quite the same again.

Chapter **23**

Ten Things Australia Gave the World

Think of Australia as an accidental social experiment that began when a bunch of unwanted convicts were sent out to plant a settlement on the east coast of a continent entirely occupied by Indigenous Australians. It wasn't planned as a bold new venture in nation-building, but that's what it became. Along the way, it produced more than a few new innovations that the rest of the world soon adopted.

The Boomerang

It's a weapon, it's a toy, it's a battle club, it's a fire-starter and hole-digger, it's a musical instrument, and it's also a twin-airfoil rotating wing that uses gyroscopic precession to return to the hand of its thrower. It's the boomerang, and it's hard to imagine a more popular Australian symbol, except perhaps the koala. International boomerang competitions are held every year with events such as Accuracy, Endurance, Trick Catch, Long Distance, Maximal Time Aloft and the Aussie Round. The boomerang also holds the record for an object thrown the furthest, outdistancing the space-age Aerobie.

The Ticket of Leave System

Perhaps befitting a nation that began as a convict dump, one of Australia's first innovations was in punishment. The ticket of leave system was the first experiment in the operation of prison parole anywhere in the world.

Initiated by Governor King in the early 1800s as a cost-cutting measure, the ticket of leave was a licence for convicts to be free and support themselves. It was conditional: Until the time to be served had been completed, the ticket could be withdrawn on grounds of misbehaviour (or a Governor's hangover). King used them for any convicts who arrived and had a trade or enough money to look after themselves. This way the Governor didn't have to fork out to find food, lodging and clothes for the convict.

The system also gave the world a valuable lesson: If you truly wanted to reform a convicted criminal, giving some incentive to behave like a decent law-abiding member of society was generally a better bet than floggings and brutality.

The Secret Ballot

Being able to vote for your choice of candidate is essential to a democratic society, but once upon a time votes were publicly displayed, and voter intimidation was commonplace. It wasn't until 1856 that voters were permitted to vote in private, so that no-one could intimidate or bribe the voter, or link the vote to the voter — and it started in the colony of Victoria. The secret ballot system took off and was adopted in New Zealand, the UK, Canada, and finally in the US, where it was called the 'Australian Ballot' (not to be confused, of course, with the Australian Ballet).

The Eight-Hour Day

Fancy working 12 hours a day as a basic minimum? That's what most labourers had to do before 1856. The Eight-Hour Movement — 'eight hours work, eight hours recreation, eight hours relaxation' — began in industrial Britain in the early 19th century, and was incorporated into the working-class Chartist movement. It didn't meet with much success in Britain or Europe, however, and workers had to wait for stonemasons in Melbourne in 1856 to finally secure the right to an eight-hour day (refer to Chapter 8).

Feature Films

Short movies had been around for some ten years before anyone got the idea to string a bunch of short films together into a single long one. This film was *The Story of the Kelly Gang*, filmed in Melbourne in 1906, which ran for 70 minutes. The bad news: Only 17 minutes of the world's first full-length movie survive. The good news: Kelly's last stand is still in there.

The Artificial Pacemaker

Many people with heart conditions are grateful for the invention of the artificial pacemaker, a device that uses electrical impulses to regulate the heartbeat. In 1928 this invention — the brainchild of a doctor, Mark Lidwill, and a physicist, Edgar Booth, both Sydneysiders — was used for the first time to revive a stillborn infant. The modern pacemaker is a tiny device, but Lidwill and Booth's invention required the patient be plugged into a light socket!

The Practical Application of Penicillin

Penicillin was the first antibiotic that was effective against serious diseases and infections. Although the drug had been known about for some time, penicillin came into real usage during World War II, mostly due to the work of Australian scientist Howard Florey, who figured out a way to mass-produce it. The drug was so valuable during the war that penicillin was actually extracted from the urine of treated patients and reused (yuck factor times ten).

Florey should hold a record for the greatest number of lives saved by his invention — an estimated 80 million — but as the modest guy himself said, 'Developing penicillin was a team effort, as these things tend to be'.

Airline Safety Devices

In 1956, two passenger airliners collided over the Grand Canyon in Arizona, becoming the deadliest aviation disaster so far recorded. What had gone wrong was just about impossible for investigators to work out afterwards— everyone involved in flying the planes was dead. As a result of this tragedy, 'black boxes' — devices that record the information on the cockpit instruments as well as the voices of the crew — were required to be installed on all commercial airplanes. These flight recorders, which were instrumental in improving air safety, were the invention of the Australian engineer Dr David Warren.

While we're on the subject of airline safety, you know those inflatable slides you read about in the safety information provided on a plane? The ones that, after everyone is safely off the plane, turn into life rafts? They're standard equipment on most passenger planes the world over, and they're another Aussie invention — this time by Jack Grant, who worked for Qantas back in 1965.

Permaculture

These days, as our human population continues to increase, most people agree that environmental sustainability is a very big deal. *Permaculture*, from 'permanent agriculture', is an approach to designing ecologically sound, self-sufficient human settlements and farms, developed by Australians Bill Mollison and David Holmgren in the 1970s. Permaculture is particularly aimed towards restoring depleted land: Today permaculture experiments are in progress everywhere from the Dead Sea in Jordan to the Ometepe volcano in Nicaragua.

Spray-on Skin

Spray-on skin sounds bizarre (how on earth do you *spray* skin tissue?) but has proved to be a lifesaver for people suffering severe burns. The process is a form of growing and then applying skin tissue that is dramatically less traumatising — with much less physical pain and practically zero scarring. The process also means the number of days needed to grow the skin culture before application is dramatically cut — rather than the 21 days required for traditional skin grafts, tissue can be sprayed onto the wound after only five. This difference in time is the game-changer that saves lives.

Spray-on skin was developed in Perth during the 1990s by English-born Australian plastic surgeon Fiona Wood and others, but had never been used en masse until the terrible 2002 Bali bombings. Most of the survivors were flown to the Royal Perth Hospital, where Wood and others used the spray-on skin technique. They saved 28 patients suffering from severe burns to portions of their bodies that ranged from 2 to 92 percent.

Chapter **24**

Ten Game-Changing Moments

A ustralian history, like any history, has many 'fork in the road' moments: Pivotal turning points that change the direction in which things are going. Don't believe me? Here's ten of 'em!

Cook Claims the East Coast of Australia

Previous to Lieutenant James Cook sailing up the eastern coast of Australia in 1770, nearly 200 years of discovery and contact between the nations of western Europe and Indigenous Australia had had little effect. Most of the first Europeans had been traders, and the locals (that is, the Aboriginal Australians) had nothing particularly exciting to trade — no cinnamon, coffee, nutmeg, cloves or gold. And the land itself, which Dutch traders and some Spanish and Portuguese explorers had seen along the northern, western and southern coasts, seemed the last word in dull, barren and uninteresting.

Cook arrived on the *Endeavour*, and sailed up a coast that he found so luxuriant and inviting that when he got to the top he decided to claim the lot on behalf of King George III of England. Without Cook, and this trip, things would have been very much different. We probably wouldn't even get to periodically belt the Poms at cricket.

Henry Kable Claims a Suitcase — and Rights for Convicts

Like a good soap opera, the story of Henry Kable and Susannah Holmes appealed to everyone. They were young and good-looking, and met in jail while serving time and waiting to get transported. They took a shine to each other and . . . well, soon enough there was a baby. Then, horror, the authorities stepped in and separated them. After some public hue and cry, they were all reunited and happily bound for Botany Bay as part of the First Fleet, with a concerned public having kicked in donations to give them a good start in the new colony.

Getting off the boat in NSW in 1788, it became apparent that the ship's captain had somehow managed to lose the expensive luggage they'd bought with the public donations. Kable sued the ship's captain, won the case and got fully compensated.

Here lies our game-changer. In England, convicted criminals lost all their legal rights: They couldn't hold property or give evidence in court, and certainly couldn't sue a ship's captain. In the very first days of arrival in NSW, however, that got turned upside down, and the Kable case shaped the basic nature of colonial (and eventually Australian) society more than any governor, bushranger or prime minister.

The precedent set by the Kable case was that, despite the population being chiefly made up of convicted felons, this would be no slave-style society with two distinct legal and economic castes. Soon enough, convicts occupied every economic niche available in the new society, owned more than half the property and wealth, and were acting altogether cocky.

Gold Discovered

After the discovery of gold in NSW and Victoria in 1851, Australia provided one third of the world's gold for the next decade. In Australia, the population trebled over the same decade, and colonial society was transformed. Australia stopped being the place mothers could use to scare their children into behaving (with something along the lines of, 'If you don't behave, you'll end up bound for Botany Bay'). Now every shipping line in the world was running most of its vessels to the ports of Melbourne and Sydney, as thousands of gold-seekers descended on the colonies. So much for terrible convict exile.

Aside from losing the stigma and shame traditionally associated with the convict colonies, Australia now jumped to the forefront of modern life. Railways, cities, commerce, leisure, sports — by the end of the 1850s, Australia was no longer some marginal backwater that produced wool and not much else; it was at the vanguard of social change and political development.

Women Get the Vote in South Australia and Federally

Australia led the way in granting full votes for most men in most colonies in the 1850s — a good 70 years before Britain — but this was more an accident of inflation rather than the result of a committed campaign (refer to Chapter 8 for more on this quite bizarre turn of events). With women it was different — no-one was going to automatically hand them the vote. It took intelligent organisation, agitation and campaigning.

Women gained the vote (or suffrage) in South Australia in 1894 and in 1899 in Western Australia. (In South Australia, this was granted to all women, including Aboriginal women.) These changes meant that the vote was also granted to most women nationally after 1901, as the Constitution was designed to accept the most radical colonial legislation as the standard — although the same Act excluded Indigenous Australians and people of Asian, African or Pacific nationality.

Women gaining the vote in Australia was two decades before women in Britain and America, and four decades before women in France. The Australian experiment (along with New Zealand's version, in 1893), was able to reassure the bigger countries. Women's suffrage proved to be a game-changer not just in Australia but the whole world, by showing that — surprise, surprise — life as we know it wouldn't end if women got the vote.

Building a Fortress out of Australia — the White Australia Policy

After Federation in 1901, one of the first things Australia did was pass a draconian, racially exclusive immigration act. Commonly known as the White Australia Policy, the act was designed to keep out any prospective migrants who weren't from Europe. The act proved so successful that pretty soon it was being used to keep out most people who weren't British.

Weirdly, a key motivator of this (let's face it) downright distasteful piece of legislation was the desire to create an egalitarian and progressive society. A 'fair and reasonable wage' became law, and old-age pensions were brought in along with 'New Protection' legislation to protect local jobs (refer to Chapter 12 for more on all this). The White Australia Policy was brought in to try to protect this — the logic being that foreign workers would happily work for a pittance, thus driving everyone's wages down. Australia's success as a social laboratory eliminating the poverty, inequalities and bad wages endemic to most societies of the time was seen to be underwritten by legislation keeping everyone else out.

Unfortunately, the act also made for an increasingly parochial and insular mindset. Australia became increasingly suspicious of outside influences and ideas. Australia was revamped in the last decades of the 20th century — economically and socially — and the White Australia Policy, deeply embedded in the national psyche, proved to be one of the hardest elements to remove even after the legislation had been repealed.

Australia splits over Conscription

It's not often that you get to split a nation with a referendum. That's what happened in 1916 and 1917 when the government twice put to the people the question of compulsory military service for the armed forces then fighting in World War I.

Originally, both sides of politics had been keen about Australia's military involvement in the war, but years went by and casualty lists grew more horrific. Then in 1916 Ireland exploded into insurrection against the English.

In the years since British settlement in colonial Australia, a difficult consensus and unity had been forged, which helped meld traditional ethnic antagonists together — Irish, English, Welsh and Scots, who had hated each other for centuries, had found themselves having to live and work side by side in Australia. For the most part it was extraordinarily successful, with no real ghettoes or ethnic underclasses, but the Irish rebellion fired up old tensions.

Then along came the conscription controversy. The issue split the Labor Party, and it split the country — and Australia took about 50 years to recover fully (refer to Chapter 13 for more detail on this game-changer).

Australia on the Western Front

Everyone thinks 'Gallipoli' when you talk about Australia and World War I. But for all its instant-myth drama, Gallipoli was, strategically speaking, a sideshow. The main game in the war was the Western Front in France — whoever won there, would win the war. In 1918 the Australia Corps played a pivotal role as one of the main spearhead thrusts that broke the German lines, shattered their morale and ultimately won victory.

More than any other time before or since in Australia's history, Australians helped decisively swing the momentum in the main theatre of a global war against the chief enemy. For a country not even 5 million strong, that's punching above your weight. The success on the Western Front was the decisive event in World War I for Australia, giving the country a new confidence as a nation that could meet all others as equals on the world stage.

The Post–World War II Migration Program

If Australia finished World War I with a new sense of confidence in the world (refer to the preceding section), it finished World War II with a new sense of vulnerability. Brought face to face with the risk of invasion, Australia decided it had to 'populate or perish' — and so develop Australia's economy and industries as rapidly as possible to be better able to handle any other threat of invasion.

This meant throwing the doors open to more than the Brits. For the first time since the gold rush 100 years earlier, people began to converge on Australia from places beyond just Britain. For the very first time, a government was arranging and organising the migration. For the next 30 years, Europeans — including Latvians, Greeks, Germans, Italians and Poles — would make up a significant bulk of the population program. The rigid 'Brits-only' restrictions, which had been applied more and more after the White Australia Act was introduced, began to loosen — and Australians finally got to enjoy some decent espresso coffee.

Lake Mungo Woman

In 1969 an archaeological dig in Lake Mungo in NSW uncovered a woman buried about 26,000 years ago. The woman's body had been cremated then methodically smashed to pieces, presumably in a funeral rite. Five years later in the same area a man's body was discovered. He was about 30,000 years old, his body a complete skeleton and, even after the thousands of years, it was still clear the body had been heavily marked with red ochre before burial in a grave. (Further archaeological finds at Lake Mungo suggest that human occupation of the area dates as far back as 50,000 years ago.)

These findings confirmed two things. Firstly, the age of the findings was remarkable — the 1960s was the first decade when such findings forced people to think of Aboriginal occupation of Australian as extending for not just hundreds, or thousands, but for tens of thousands of years. This, by any calendar, is long. Really long. Secondly, the findings gave clear evidence of cultural activity (funeral rites) and trading — the red ochre that the man was painted with didn't come from nearby but from a great distance away. It was some of the earliest evidence of humans behaving in a recognisably modern human way anywhere in the world.

Mabo

When Cook first claimed the eastern coast of Australia in 1770 he did so ignoring the original inhabitants' ownership of the land. The logic was that as the Aboriginals weren't living in houses, ploughing ground, constructing fences, raising livestock, growing crops (and what-not), they weren't proper owners of the land — they lived on it too lightly. The country was, therefore, *terra nullius* — Latin for 'land belonging to nobody'. Cook didn't actually use the term himself, but its assumption was pretty plain when he claimed the country for the Crown, just as if no one else was living there.

This changed in 1992. The High Court overturned the doctrine of terra nullius, recognising that native title to the land had been in existence when Cook and the British settlers first arrived. The High Court declared that while native title had been eliminated where the Crown had sold land, Aboriginals in those parts of Australia where they continued to live in unbroken connection with the land (such as, in this case, Eddie Mabo's people on the Meriam Islands in the Torres Strait) continued to have native title.

Index

bounty payment, 117
Bourke, Governor, 112, 113, 122
boxing, 237
Bradman, Don, 275, 309
Brady, E. J., 265
Brady, Matthew, 102, 103
bribery, 96
Brisbane, 106, 177, 185–186, 202
Brisbane, Thomas, 94
Britain
  conflicts of, 39, 40
  cricket and, 183
  crime within, 37–39
  distancing from, 373–374
  economic connections with, 304–305
  economy within, 84, 117
  France and, 42
  industrial revolution within, 92
  influence of, 138, 246
  loyalty to, 346–347, 372–373
  maritime dominance of, 33
  military of, 313–314
  prisoners of war (POWs) from, 327
  social turmoil within, 84
  wars of, 52
  within World War II, 315–316, 320–321
British East India Company, 42, 52
British-European settler society, 28
Broken Hill miners' strike, 205
Bruce, Stanley, 264, 266–272, 283–286, 305
building industry, 10–11, 181, 199, 200, 291
Bullecourt battle, 249–250
The Bulletin (magazine), 210–211, 235
Burke, Robert O'Hara, 161–163
Burns, Tommy, 237
bush-bashing, 327–328
bushranging/bushrangers, 64, 101–104, 167–171
Buxton, Thomas Foxwell, 128
'Buy Australian' campaign, 268
Byrne, Joe, 171, 172, 173

C

California, 134, 276
Callister, Cyril, 271
Calwell, Arthur, 335, 341–345, 375–376, 378
cameleers, 164
Campbell, Eric, 302–303
Campbell, William, 135
Canberra, 106, 267
Canowindra, 168
carbon emissions, 429, 443
Carriers' Union, 235–236
Carstensz, Jan, 32
Casey, Richard, 317
Catholic Church, 196
Cayley, George, 77
Chartist movement, 143, 146, 151, 187, 188
Chief Protector, 129
Chifley, Ben, 280, 333, 336–337, 346–348
child labour, 196
China, 20–21, 30, 42, 419, 437–439
Chinese immigrants, 153, 238–239
Chisholm, Caroline, 138, 139
Christmas Island, 430
Churchill, Winston, 314, 319
civil rights campaign, 237
Clarke, Marcus, 186
Clarke brothers, 168, 170
climate change, 429, 442–443
Cohen, Edward, 194
Collins, David, 57, 64
Colonial Liberalism, 187–189, 190–191, 192–194
Commercial Bank of Australia, 117, 201
common-law partnerships, 9, 80
Commonwealth Bank Bill, 347–348
Commonwealth Franchise Act, 230
Commonwealth Government, 272–273
Commonwealth Parliament, 225–228
Commonwealth Shipping Line, 254
communism, 300–301
Communist Party of Australia, 300–303, 365–369

I

immigration
 of asylum seekers, 430
 to Australia, 117
 economic collapse and, 119
 employment within, 355–356, 402
 following World War II, 341–345, 461
 growth of, 20
 Muslim, 164
 nationalities within, 153
 of refugees, 391–392, 414–415, 416–417
 restrictions on, 15
Immigration Act, 280
Immigration Restriction Act, 225, 234–242, 280, 377–381, 459–460
income tax, 332–333
Indigenous Australians. *See* Aboriginals
Indonesia, 32
Industrial Workers of the World (IWW or 'Wobblies'), 282–283
industry
 blackbirding within, 241
 development of, 354–355
 eight-hour workday within, 147–148, 454
 growth of, 63–64
 non-White participation in, 240
 strikes within, 14, 203–205, 229, 259
 turmoil within, 203–205
 women within, 331–332
 during World War II, 329–330
infanticide, 27
inflation, 60, 63, 395, 398
infrastructure, 10–11, 195, 270–271, 303, 357, 360
internal trade, 209
inventions, 157, 453–456
Ireland, 16
Irish Catholics, 256
Irish ethnic group, 15, 254–257
Isaacs, Isaac, 226, 283
Italian immigrants, 153

J

Jandamarra, 131
Japan, 305, 319, 321–322, 323–325, 374–375
Jenkins, Kate, 433
Jerilderie, 172–173
Johnson, Jack, 237
Johnson, Reverend, 49, 58
Johnston, George, 69, 70

K

Kable, Henry and Susannah, 43, 61, 458
Kalgoorlie, 208
Kangaroo Island, 112
Keating, Paul, 120, 399, 400–406, 407, 415
Kelly, Dan, 171, 173
Kelly, Ned, 171–174
Kerr, John, 387–388
Kerr Hundredweight gold nugget, 135
King, John, 163
King, Philip Gidley, 62–65, 77
Kokoda Trail, 323–325
Korean War, 365, 366

L

La Trobe, Charles, 127, 136, 137, 140
Labor Electoral League, 206
Labor Party
 conflict within, 16, 17
 control by, 233–234
 decline of, 258
 Irish Catholics and, 257
 migration viewpoint of, 378
 origin of, 14
 overview of, 205–207
 rise of, 384–385
 socialism and, 281–282
 split of, 260–261, 293–299
 in state governments, 282
 values of, 445

About the Author

Alex McDermott is an historian and author who's taught, written, researched and produced history across different fields and platforms for twenty years now. He edited and introduced Ned Kelly's *Jerilderie Letter* (Text Media, 2001), worked on the Making History Initiative's ten history documentaries for Screen Australia and the ABC (2007-2009) and multiple SBS documentaries with different production companies (2009-2019). Since 2014 he has been a consultant historian, curator and creative producer at the Museum of Australian Democracy at Old Parliament House in Canberra, focusing particularly on the 'Democracy DNA' Exhibitions (launching in 2022), for which he has been history curator. He is currently writing a book about Alfred Deakin.

Dedication

This edition is dedicated to four people who set my passion for history going, and kept it going, 'like a fat gold watch'.

In my childhood my two grandmothers, who lived on two different sides of the world, enthralled and fascinated me with stories of the past. Listening to and talking with both Elizabeth Bennett (d. 1980) and Kathleen McDermott (d. 2014), remain memories of sheer delight.

As an adult I was again spectacularly lucky. I became good friends with John Hirst (d. 2016), my teacher and mentor in Australian history. Simultaneously, the conversations with my father, Shane McDermott (d.2019), were punctuated by never-ending chatter about history and politics.

I feel an enormous debt of gratitude and love towards all four of these wonderful people. I am glad to have known them. May they rest in peace.

Author's Acknowledgements

The team at Wiley, as always, magnificent. For this second edition my points of contact have been patient and stimulating, understanding and demanding in all the right measures! To Lucy Raymond, Charlotte Duff, Ingrid Bond and Leigh McLennon – great work, and huge thank yous.

On the history side, the number of acknowledgements could easily balloon this section out to the size of the rest of the book. Of all these though, and for this project in particular, special mention has to go to John Hirst, who read and responded to the first edition, and discussed over copious morning coffees as the book was first being written in 2010. This time round Henry Ergas has stepped into the fray. He read and responded to some early drafts of the additional material for the second edition and showed great generosity in letting me draw on some of that prodigious degree of historical knowledge and all round erudition of his. To them both I feel a great debt of gratitude for their feedback and thoughts.

Finally, and yes, most importantly really, I want to acknowledge people who love history, and want to read about it. In the past 20-odd years I've had the good fortune to teach history to students at university, to write it for popular and specialised audiences in books and articles, to research and produce it for people watching documentaries on television, and for people visiting State Libraries and Museums. This has allowed me to follow my passion of reading, writing and producing history pretty much every day. I can't really imagine a more enjoyable thing to be doing in life, and without people being interested in asking questions and trying to find out more about how we all came to be as we are today . . . well, I'd be out of the best job in the world. So, to everyone who enjoys history, a big, huge unmitigated thank you. It's a privilege being part of this great ongoing conversation with you.

Publisher's Acknowledgements

Some of the people who helped bring this book to market include the following:

Acquisitions, Editorial and Media Development

Project Editor: Tamilmani Varadharaj

Acquisitions Editor: Lucy Raymond

Technical Reviewer: John Hirst

Editorial Manager: Ingrid Bond

Copy Editor: Charlotte Duff

Production

Proofreader: Susan Hobbs

Indexer: Estalita M. Slivoskey

The authors and publisher would like to thank the following copyright holders, organisations and individuals for their permission to reproduce copyright material in this book.

- Page 25: © State Library of NSW. Map is from: Transactions of the Royal Society of S.A. Vol. 64, 1940 Map II.Information transferred from the Mitchell Library shelflist catalogue as part of the eRecords Project 2009-2010.Mitchell Library copy at: M3 804eca/ 1788/ 1A.
- Page 147: © State Library of Victoria
- Page 255: Max Dupain. A Barmaid at Work in Wartime Sydney. Pettys Hotel, Sydney, 6pm, 1941.
- Page 258: Australian War Memorial Neg number ARTV05167
- Page 270: © State Government of Victoria
- Page 326: Australian War Memorial Negative No 019199
- Page 344: © Joe Greenberg/Museum Victoria
- Page 380: © Newspix
- Page 414: © Romeo Gacad / Getty Images
- Page 424: © Shutterstock